Bl

D0909785

IMPERIAL STUDIES NO. XXII

General Editor: GERALD S. GRAHAM
Rhodes Professor of Imperial History in the University of London

The Colonial Office
in the Early
Nineteenth Century

IMPERIAL STUDIES SERIES

1927–1954

I   *Political Unrest in Upper Canada, 1816–1836,* by AILEEN DUNHAM.

II   *The British West African Settlements, 1750–1821,* by EVELINE C. MARTIN.

III   *British Colonial Policy and the South African Republics, 1848–1872,* by C. W. DE KIEWIET.

IV   *British Policy and Canada, 1774–1791: A Study in 18th Century Trade Policy,* by GERALD S. GRAHAM.

V   *Colonial Admiralty Jurisdiction in the Seventeenth Century,* by HELEN J. CRUMP.

[VI   *Education for Empire Settlement,* by ALEC G. SCHOLES.

VII   *The Provincial System of Government in New Zealand, 1852–76,* by W. P. MORRELL.

VIII   *Railway and Customs Policies in South Africa, 1885–1910,* by JEAN VAN DER POEL.

IX   *The 1820 Settlers in South Africa: A Study in British Colonial Policy,* by ISOBEL EIRLYS EDWARDS.

X   *Governor Arthur's Convict System: Van Diemen's Land, 1824–36,* by W. D. FORSYTH.

XI   *Canada and the British Army, 1846–1871,* by C. P. STACEY.

XII   *The Earth Goddess,* by G. HOWARD JONES.

XIII   *The Colonial Office, a History,* by HENRY L. HALL.

XIV   *European Beginnings in West Africa, 1454–1578* by J. W. BLAKE.

XV   *The Crucial Problem of Imperial Development.* A Record of the Conference on Imperial Development convened by The Royal Empire Society in November 1937, edited by Professor A. P. NEWTON.

XVI   *The Struggle for Imperial Unity, 1868–1895,* by J. E. TYLER.

XVII   *The Establishment of Constitutional Government in Newfoundland, 1783–1832,* by A. H. McLINTOCK.

XVIII   *European Powers and South East Africa, 1796–1856,* by MABEL V. JACKSON-HAIGHT.

XIX   *The Berlin West African Conference, 1884–1885,* by S. E. CROWE.

XX   *The Free Port System in the British West Indies: A Study in Commercial Policy 1766–1822,* by FRANCES ARMYTAGE.

XXI   *Forerunners of Drake: A Study of English trade with Spain in the early Tudor Period,* by GORDON CONNELL-SMITH.

The Colonial Office in the Early Nineteenth Century

D. M. YOUNG
Associate Professor of History, University of New Brunswick

PUBLISHED FOR
THE ROYAL COMMONWEALTH SOCIETY
BY
LONGMANS
1961

LONGMANS, GREEN AND CO LTD
48 GROSVENOR STREET, LONDON WI
RAILWAY CRESCENT, CROYDON, VICTORIA, AUSTRALIA
443 LOCKHART ROAD, HONG KONG
PRIVATE MAIL BAG 1036, IKEJA (LAGOS)
44 JALAN AMPANG, KUALA LUMPUR
ACCRA, AUCKLAND, IBADAN, KINGSTON (JAMAICA)
NAIROBI, SALISBURY (RHODESIA)

LONGMANS SOUTHERN AFRICA (PTY) LTD
THIBAULT HOUSE, THIBAULT SQUARE, CAPE TOWN

LONGMANS, GREEN AND CO INC
119 WEST 40TH STREET, NEW YORK 18

LONGMANS, GREEN AND CO
137 BOND STREET, TORONTO 2

ORIENT LONGMANS PRIVATE LTD
CALCUTTA, BOMBAY, MADRAS
DELHI, HYDERABAD, DACCA

FIRST PUBLISHED 1961

PRINTED IN GREAT BRITAIN BY
THE BOWERING PRESS, PLYMOUTH

CONTENTS

Foreword   vii

Preface   ix

1 The Origin and Practice of the Colonial Office,
    1794–1821   1

2 The Office Remodelled, December 1821–July
    1825   47

3 The New Office at Work, 1825–30   84

4 'The Office'   124

5 The Financial System of the Office   147

6 Interdepartmental Relations   169

7 The Colonial Office and the Treasury   202

8 The Colonial Office and the Civil Service   241

APPENDIX I   A List of Secretaries of State and Under-
Secretaries in the Office of the Third Secretary of State,
1794–1830.   263

APPENDIX II   A List of Private Secretaries to the Third
Secretary of State, 1794–1830, with a Note on the Role of
the Private Secretary.   264

APPENDIX III   A Table Summarizing the Official Careers of
the Clerks in the Office of the Third Secretary of State,
1795–1830.   266

APPENDIX IV   A Report on the Establishment of the Colonial
Office in 1814.   274

APPENDIX V   A Comparative Statement Illustrating the
Changes made in the Establishment of the Colonial Office
in January 1822.   277

APPENDIX VI   The Establishment of the Colonial Office in 1831.   278

APPENDIX VII   An Interview with a Prospective Clerk, 1824.   280

APPENDIX VIII   Comparative Statement of the Increase of Business in the Secretary of State's Office, War and Colonial Department, for the Years 1806, 1816, and 1824.   282

APPENDIX IX   Regulations for Numbering and Docketing Despatches and Papers Sent to the Colonial Office.   285

APPENDIX X   The Government and Joseph Hume.   287

Bibliography   288

Index   305

FOREWORD

The Imperial Studies Series owes its origins to the initiative of Professor A. P. Newton, and to the imaginative support of the then Royal Empire Society who took responsibility for launching the first volume in 1927. Since that date, apart from the interruptions of war and its aftermath, monographs dealing with various phases of imperial or commonwealth history continued to appear annually until vastly higher publication costs, beyond the capacity of a strained Society's treasury, brought the project to a halt. This year, thanks largely to the efforts of devoted chairmen like Sir Charles Ponsonby, additional endowment has enabled the Series to come back to life after a seven years' coma.

The fundamental principle of publication remains the same. As my predecessor, the late M. J. Rendall, emphasized in earlier forewords, the Series is designed 'not so much for writers of established reputation as for those who are mature in mind but young in years'. In other words, it aimed to help the young scholar over the hurdle of his or her first book. But a good Ph.D. dissertation is not always a good book; the writing of a thesis is essentially an exercise in research to satisfy examiners that the candidate knows how to find and weigh source materials and to make sensible judgments on them. Normally, it is a long and arduous struggle from thesis to book, involving the reduction of many hard-won paragraphs and the sacrifice of many precious but irrelevant discoveries for the sake of unity, clarity and economy.

Although this study concerns the complicated and detailed growth of the modern Colonial Office from a 'hole in the corner' with a few clerks to a stable and enterprising department, Dr. Young has not let the necessary minutiae of his narrative submerge the main threads of an important administrative evolution. In an age that still possessed considerable faith in state action, the belated and extraordinarily cautious develop-

vii

ment of a civil service is not the least remarkable aspect of a problem which Dr. Young handles with judicial care and imagination.

GERALD S. GRAHAM
Chairman of the Academic Committee

Royal Commonwealth Society,
London, W.C.2.

PREFACE

Writers on British administration are, by and large, theorists or practitioners of the administrative craft. Many are retired civil servants or senior statesmen able to recall, perhaps, the pungency of Lord Curzon's official minutes, and always conscious of the interplay of personalities at the higher levels of government. Others are specialists in constitutional history or in political science with an ingrained talent for seeking out institutional relationships. It is with some diffidence that I attach myself to this company. When I began serious historical research, I was concerned with a problem on the periphery of Empire, the development of New Brunswick in the 1820s. My inability to find a satisfactory explanation for the colonial secretary's policies in that one colony led me to contemplate the feasibility of a comparative study of several colonies. As a preliminary step, I began the preparation of an outline of colonial administration in general, and of the Colonial Office in particular. My enquiry into the structure of administration proved so much more fruitful than I had anticipated that I undertook the preparation of this book. Although it began as an enquiry into colonial policy, and has been influenced by these origins, it became a study of a British government department, and it is as a chapter in the history of the British civil service that it should be judged.

One reader of the manuscript has suggested that I should have continued beyond 1830. There were two very good reasons for not doing so. First, the book has a unity as it stands and, secondly, the sheer volume of correspondence after 1830 presents a forbidding task of reading and analysis. Moreover, at the time of writing, it seemed probable that the late Dr. Eveline Martin would complete the study of the administrative career of Sir James Stephen that she was so eminently qualified to write, and for which she had long been gathering materials.

The learned help of many people has made this book possible. For several years I have had the advice and encouragment of Professor Gerald S. Graham. He supervised my research, and as editor of the Imperial Studies Series has shown great patience in seeing the book through to publication. I am also under great obligation to Dr. Eveline Martin, whose close questioning enabled me to get my subject into perspective; and to Mr. R. B. Pugh, who carefully 'vetted' the thesis in the light of his specialized knowledge. The members of the various seminars that I attended at the Institute of Historical Research offered useful criticism; and not infrequently provided important items of information.

I shall not attempt to give the names of the many archivists and librarians who have aided me. They are the unseen but indispensable assistants of every writer of history. The number of institutions at which most of my research was carried out—the Public Record Office, the British Museum Reading Room, the British Museum Manuscript Room, the Institute of Historical Research, the Royal Commonwealth Society Library, the Public Archives of Canada, the National Library of Scotland, and the Goldsmith's Library of the University of London—makes a far shorter list than that of the individual officials to whom I am indebted.

My studies in England were made possible through the award of a Lord Beaverbrook Overseas Scholarship in 1951, and its renewal in 1952 and 1953. It has also been my good fortune to receive the benefit of the personal interest that Lord Beaverbrook takes in the work of his scholars. A grant from the Canadian Humanities Research Council helped me to complete my researches in London during the summer of 1954, and one from the Memorial University of Newfoundland enabled me to spend several weeks in Ottawa in the summer of 1956.

I wish to express my thanks to the Royal Commonwealth Society for sponsoring, and, with the generous assistance of the Social Science Research Council of Canada, for financing the publication of this book. At all times my wife's assistance and encouragement have been indispensable.

D. M. YOUNG

The University of New Brunswick,
Fredericton.
February 28th, 1961.

1

THE ORIGIN AND PRACTICE OF THE COLONIAL OFFICE 1794–1821

The most striking feature of British administration in the first quarter of the nineteenth century was the extent to which the work of government departments was performed by the ministers themselves. The younger Pitt, at the beginning of the century, personally studied and decided on all important questions at the Treasury.[1] Lord Liverpool's standing with his colleagues in his twenty-five years as Secretary of State and Prime Minister rested primarily on his assiduity as a man of business. Castlereagh and Canning wrote almost all of their despatches themselves[2] and Peel and Palmerston, who served their apprenticeships during this era, continued throughout their careers to keep authority firmly in their own hands and did not believe that even permanent under-secretaries should have any significant part in the making of decisions.[3] Practice largely coincided with the constitutional convention that decreed that the policy for which ministers assumed responsibility should be entirely their own, though it might be modified in response to the criticism of colleagues in the Cabinet.

In theory and largely in fact there was a clear division of function between the political men and the permanent officials[4] in the offices that Sir Charles Trevelyan later described as 'par excellence *Government* offices'—the offices of the Secretaries of State, the Treasury, and the Board of Trade. The policy-making duties were performed by the politicians, whose tenure was dependent on their retaining the favour of their colleagues and of the House of Commons. With few exceptions the permanent

---

[1] Pares, R., *King George III and the Politicians*, p. 161.

[2] Webster, Sir C., *The Foreign Policy of Castlereagh 1815–1822*, p. 35 and Temperley, H., *The Foreign Policy of Canning*, p. 263.

[3] Pugh, R. B., 'The Colonial Office', *Cambridge History of the British Empire*, III, p. 720.

[4] The permanent officials were more prominent in colonial affairs at the beginning of George III's reign than they were at the end of it. See Spector, M. M., *The American Department of the British Government 1768–1782*.

members of the staffs were employed almost entirely in the performance of routine or mechanical tasks. The senior permanent officials supervised the offices, looked after accounts, and prepared formal documents. Most clerks spent the greater part of their working lives in the routine of copying. This at least had the advantage of making them extremely familiar with the official papers, for their memories must have served in place of filing systems; papers could never have been produced on demand had reliance been placed on the indexes of the period.

Scholars have examined the records of several of the central departments of government in considerable detail,[1] the outstanding exception being the Treasury. The volume of business was not great and the prevailing philosophy of government, at least in the first two decades of the century, did not encourage policies of change that were likely to add excessively to the number of administrative decisions. Long tenure in office during a period of political stability made ministers familiar with the administrative machinery in all its aspects; they themselves, and not the permanent officials, were the chief repositories of the knowledge and experience of the affairs of their departments. The tradition established by the younger Pitt of choosing able young men and associating them closely with the affairs of government produced a select body of experienced men of business who, by the eighteen-twenties, were the active ministers in the government. When they began to undertake basic reforms of institutions and laws they looked outside their own departments for expert advice and assistance. Huskisson did so in his reform of the trade laws of the Empire in 1825[2] and so did Peel in his reform of the criminal law.[3] The Treasury made use of royal commissions[4] in its reform of the revenue departments (1818–24) and in its consolidation of the Irish with the English exchequer (1821).

[1] Sir Charles Webster and Harold Temperley, the Foreign Office; Mrs. Helen T. Manning, the Colonial Office; Grace Cockroft and Anna L. Lingelbach, The Board of Trade; F. O. Darvall and J. A. Gulland, the Home Office. See bibliography.

[2] See Chapter VII.

[3] Gulland, J. A., 'The history of the criminal law reforms of the period of Peel's home secretaryship, 1822–1827'. Summary of thesis, *Bull. Inst. Hist. Res.*, VIII, pp. 182–4.

[4] See Fay, C. R., *Huskisson and His Age*, pp. 113–14 and 286–90.

Government business increased significantly over the first quarter of the century. Most departments were able to handle a share of the additional work without changing their procedures. In fact, the overall administrative structure was very flexible, and it was possible for the Board of Trade to be transformed into an almost exclusively executive department dealing with economic affairs; it had been established originally as a consultative body to supply expert opinion on trade and colonial matters. While domestic business was increasing only moderately, what appeared at the time to be an enormous increase in the volume of business took place in connection with the affairs of the overseas territories. The absence of British-style local institutions of government in India and the conquered colonies retained at the end of the Napoleonic Wars made necessary a great number of authorizations and instructions that had not been required under the traditional system of governing the overseas colonies. India was not a problem, for responsibility for Indian affairs was shared by the Government with the directors of the East India Company, which created its own private administrative structure, the India Office,[1] and remodelled it as occasion demanded in response to the pressures of increasing business. Under this arrangement the Board of Control,[2] the government office responsible for India, did not have a heavy administrative load.

It was in the Colonial Office that the political heads first openly admitted their inability to handle personally the volume of regular business.[3] To the burden of supervising the government of conquered colonies was added the work arising from the efforts of the anti-slavery group to force the introduction of measures for the improvement of the condition of the slaves throughout the Empire, the countless tasks associated with the supervision of a convict settlement half-way around the world in New South Wales, the supervision of emigration to the British possessions, and the financial questions that arose in several colonies as a result of the financial stringency in the United Kingdom. Logic would suggest that the department should have been divided or some arrangement made to devolve responsi-

---

[1] See Foster, Sir William, *The East India House its History and Associations.*
[2] Foster, Sir William, 'The Board of Control'. *Trans. Roy. Hist. Soc.*, 1916.
[3] See Chapter II.

bilities on statutory boards. Apart, however, from the establishment of the Slave Registry Office under an Act of Parliament of 1819 and the setting up of a Board of Ecclesiastical Commissioners, in 1824,[1] to supervise the affairs of the Church of England in the colonies, nothing of this sort was done until later in the century, though Huskisson planned a land board in 1828.[2] A suggestion,[3] in 1823, that the Board of Trade be divided and the small amount of specifically colonial business in its hands to be placed under a separate minister may conceivably have been associated with the realization that the Colonial Office, as constituted, could not handle the work assigned to it. More likely, since the suggestion came from the Board of Trade, it was inspired by the desire of that department to give honourable office to a member of the Board and to rid itself of unwelcome duties. In 1829 the Duke of Wellington suggested to his Lord Privy Seal that he help out in the Colonial Office.[4] Though he certainly disapproved of the extent to which his Colonial Secretary left matters in the hands of his underlings, Wellington's immediate concern was to find employment for an able minister who had no departmental responsibilities.

When the Colonial Secretary found it impossible to handle the business of his department in the approved manner, he met the situation by devolving more responsibility on permanent officials in his office and took steps to improve their individual efficiency. The political head continued to leave his imprint on all significant decisions but the place of the civil servant in decision-making was clearly recognized. It was impossible, of course, to create immediately the *esprit de corps* that would make able men willing to labour in obscurity for the good of the state. Sir James Stephen, who became Permanent Under-Secretary in the Colonial Office in 1836, was the outstanding figure of the transitional period. His great importance was recognized by his contemporaries but his reaction to the bitter attacks made on him indicates that the system had not evolved sufficiently by the time of his retirement in 1848 for him to feel that his role was accepted as a normal one.

[1] See below pp. 76–7.   [2] See p. 107.
[3] Arbuthnot, Charles, *The Correspondence of Charles Arbuthnot*, ed. A. Aspinall, p. 44.
[4] Aspinall, A., 'The Cabinet Council, 1785–1835'. *Proc. Br. Acad.*, XXXVIII, p. 154.

By mid-century, however, it was increasingly recognized by officials, if not by the public, that clerks did, as Stephen said in his comments on the Northcote-Trevelyan Report in 1854, 'most essentially contribute' to the measures of government.[1] A proposal in that report that civil servants be divided into 'mechanical' and 'intellectual' classes was itself a recognition that clerks had assumed a new role. Twenty years earlier the idea that clerks should be expected to perform intellectual duties was not even accepted by the clerks who were performing them.

'From the first year that I was in this Office' wrote Henry Taylor, senior clerk in the West Indian department of the Colonial Office, in 1833,

> I have been employed, not in the business of a clerk, but in that of a statesman. So far as the West Indian Colonies have been concerned, I have at all times since that period done more for the Secretary and Under Secretary of State for the time being, of their peculiar and appropriate business, than they have done for themselves. I have been accustomed to relieve them from the trouble of taking decisions, of giving directions, of reading despatches, and of writing them. In ninety-nine cases out of a hundred the consideration which has been given to a subject by the Secretary of State has consisted in reading a draft submitted to him, and his decision has consisted in adopting it; and the more important the question has been, the more have I found my judgement to be leant upon.[2]

The assigning of more responsible duties to clerks in the central offices of government was but one of many changes made in the organization of the public service between the end of the American Revolution and the year 1855, by which date the modern Civil Service may be said to have come definitely into existence. In 1779 the Whigs began an attack on the sinecures and inefficient offices at the disposal of the Crown which, they alleged, gave George III undue influence over Parliament. In 1780 Parliament authorized the appointment of a non-parliamentary commission to enquire into the public service, the first such enquiry since the Hanoverian succession. The reports of that commission in the following years led to the abolition of

---

[1] H.C. 1854–5 XX (1870) 77–8.
[2] Taylor, H., *Autobiography*, I, pp. 139–140.

many ancient offices and the consolidation of others.[1] Offices
that no longer performed a useful function were to be abolished
whenever possible, others were to be consolidated to avoid
duplication and to increase efficiency and they were to be held
by persons who carried out the duties. 'Institutions directly
repugnant to good management' were to be eliminated. 'All
parsimony is of a quality approaching to unkindness', said
Burke and, since his chief goal was the elimination of the royal
power to corrupt Parliament, officeholders were treated generously. When an office was marked for abolition provision was
made for generous compensation or provision was made for it
to continue in existence during the lifetime of the holder. Even
reversionary rights to office, that is the promise of the succession
to offices whenever they should become vacant by retirement or
death, were honoured. Since some offices had been granted in
reversion to very small children, it was many years before all
the grantees succeeded to their places. In addition, there was
some backsliding, particularly in the colonies; many appointments were made to offices intended to be exercised by deputy
until a parliamentary Act of 1814 definitely put an end to this
abuse.[2]

The Whig campaign effectively reduced the influence of the
Crown.[3] Though some sinecures and pensions were left in
existence to enable the Crown to reward worthy servants, the
reforms definitely made the government service more efficient.
Even more, it made the House of Commons very conscious of
the possibility of reducing expenditure on salaries and pensions.
Gradually the emphasis on the elimination of corruption was
transformed into a dogmatic insistence on economy and efficiency in government that owed more to Adam Smith and
Jeremy Bentham than it did to Edmund Burke. Among the
notable reforms effected was the gradual introduction of the
paying of fixed salaries in all government offices in place of the
fees that had hitherto formed the largest part of the incomes of
many officials.

[1] Keir, D. L., 'Economical Reform 1779–1787', *Law Quarterly Review*,
July, 1934, pp. 368–385.
[2] See Parry, J. H., 'The Patent Offices in the British West Indies', *E.H.R.*,
LXIX (1954).
[3] See Foord, A. S., 'The Waning of "The Influence of the Crown" ',
E.H.R., LXII (1947).

During the war years, although a few notable enquiries were conducted by committees of the House of Commons, there was no systematic and sustained pressure for economy in the administration. In the years of depression, low wages and low prices after the war, 'economy' became a persistent cry. The payment of the interest on the national debt took more than sixty per cent of the Government's annual income. The military and naval forces were greatly reduced from wartime but were, of necessity, larger than they had been at the beginning of the wars because of new commitments in Europe, the possession of additional colonies, and the country's interest in the suppression of the slave trade. Of all the expenditures of government only the relatively small portion devoted to the administrative costs of government seemed open to reduction.[1] Every department was larger and was paying much higher salaries than in pre-war years.[2] The economists, demanding a reduction in expenditure on abstract principles, found themselves supported by the country gentlemen who were demanding a reduction in taxation. Driven to desperation by low prices, poor crops and high poor rates, some backbenchers not only supported every move designed to force the Government to economize but, in 1821 and 1822, openly agitated for a capital levy or a repudiation of the national debt. Every situation produces its representative figure. In 1820, Joseph 'Economy' Hume,[3] the radical M.P. for Aberdeen, began a close questioning of government accounts and received the blessing of the country gentlemen for his niggling and futile economies. His needling attacks were to keep officials alert for many years. The depression was followed by prosperity in the mid-twenties and then by another, but milder, recession in the late twenties. By 1828 the utilitarian approach to economy and efficiency in government was officially accepted. In that year the House of Commons committee on finance examined the expense accounts of ambassadors, condemned the paying of pensions to those in the lowest ranks of the Civil Service, and maintained that the pay in government offices should be

[1] The fourth report of the House of Commons 1828 Committee on Finance gives details of income, expenditure, borrowing, etc., for each year from 1792 to 1827. See H.C. 1828 V (519) 543–665.

[2] H.C. 1830–31 VII (92) 299–415, 'Returns of the Number and Pay or Salaries of all Persons Employed in Public Departments: 1797–1827'.

[3] See Appendix X.

the same as that prevailing in private houses of business for similar work.

One result of Parliament's interest in the administrative departments was an effort beginning after 1800 to introduce common standards of pay, conditions of service and superannuation throughout the government service. Since the main emphasis was financial, the Treasury took the lead. The term 'Civil Service', applied to the permanent employees of government in the United Kingdom, came into use sometime before 1820 but it seems to have been used at first only by Treasury officials.[1] Traditionally each office had its own separate and independent service and the ministers of the Crown, in defence of their traditional powers, openly obstructed the Treasury in its attempts to introduce and supervise an integrated public service.

The department of government that administered the colonies after 1801 was erected in 1794 as a division of the office of secretary of state. This office, a single one descended directly from the thirteenth-century office of King's secretary, was first divided in Henry VIII's reign. Since the Restoration it had been shared by two secretaries, sometimes with a third, for Scotland at times between 1707 and 1745, and for America 1768 to 1782. The Secretaries of State were equal in authority but in practice an arrangement was always made between them, with the consent of the monarch, by which each assumed responsibility for specific business. In the absence of one Secretary of State another could perform his duties. The offices shared a common repository for old records, the State Paper Office, a common estimate was submitted to Parliament for contingencies and, beginning in 1795, fees were shared. Relics of the original connection of the secretary's office with the royal household were preserved in the provision of messengers' services by the Treasurer of the Palace Chamber and the provision of furniture by the Lord Chamberlain's office. The Secretaries of State also shared equally the responsibility for ancient instruments of government. They were the keepers of the sign manual, under which the King's formal instructions were issued, and of the signet, in origin the most personal to the monarch of the three

[1] For an early example of its use see C.O. 323/185 Lushington to Bathurst, Aug. 3, 1816, f. 243. The quotation is given in Chapter VI below, p. 163.

seals in the realm; the great seal and the privy seal were used on instructions issued under the signet, the use of which was in turn authorized by an instruction issued under the sign manual.

In 1782, after the abolition of the American department, the office was divided into 'Foreign 'and 'Home' departments, with war and the colonies as well as the internal affairs of the British Isles falling within the Home Secretary's jurisdiction. That division of business existed until July 1794 when, in order to facilitate the entry of the Whigs into Pitt's government, the work of the Home Secretary was divided and an additional secretary of state appointed. Henry Dundas, who had been Home Secretary since 1791, agreed to give up the Home Office and home affairs and to establish a new office for war and the colonies. Dundas, in addition to being Home Secretary, had for several years been the minister responsible for the affairs of India and, since his interests were primarily imperial, he had no objection to giving up home affairs and Ireland so long as the affairs of all the overseas dependencies were to be under his direction.[1] The suggested arrangement was not very clearly explained to the Whig leader, the Duke of Portland, who agreed to accept the Home Office under the impression that he was to have the whole department. Pitt certainly had no intention of placing the execution of war policy in the hands of Portland and, with the support of the King, he prevailed on Dundas to make an agreement with Portland possible by surrendering to him the colonies and their patronage.[2] Dundas had to be content with the King's assurance that he did not 'quite approve of the West Indies being added to the Home Department.'[3]

An interesting sidelight on the creation of the War Office was provided by references to it in the House of Commons in 1795 and 1797.[4] On both occasions the opposition asserted that Dundas had, by accepting the new office, rendered himself incapable of sitting in the House of Commons. The reply of the

[1] Matheson, Cyril, *The Life of Henry Dundas, First Viscount Melville* 1742–1811, p. 202. Later proposals to place India and the colonies under a single minister were made by Canning in 1809 (Hist. Mss. Comm. *Bathurst Papers*, pp. 93 and 97) and in 1816 and 1817 by Tierney (See Manning, Helen T., *British Colonial Government after the American Revolution*, p. 478). Lord Liverpool feared a similar proposal in 1824 (See below p. 79).
[2] Matheson, C., *Henry Dundas*, pp. 202–5.
[3] *Ibid.*, p. 204.
[4] *Ibid.*, pp. 212 and 243.

Government was to the effect that it was the Duke of Portland who had accepted the new office, that Dundas had, in fact, merely been relieved of some of the duties that he had held.

Dundas continued as war minister until the Pitt government resigned in 1801. On several occasions, by his own account, he asked Pitt's permission to resign but Pitt refused to allow him to do so.[1] In December 1799 he actually sent a letter of resignation to George III[2] which the King stated he would not consider 'unless Mr. Secretary Dundas has obtained the full acquiescence of Mr. Pitt to such an idea, which I do not at present expect.'[3] Dundas had maintained from the beginning that since war policy was largely decided by the Cabinet and the Prime Minister, there was no need for a war minister.[4] However, constitutional practice required that a Secretary of State transmit the Government's decisions to the commanders in the field and on the seas and since Pitt obviously did not wish to entrust this duty to his Home Secretary, the War Office remained in existence. As an earlier writer had phrased it:

> . . . all warlike preparations, every military operation, and every naval equipment must be directed by a Secretary of State. Neither the Admiralty, Treasury, Ordnance, nor Victualling Boards can move a step without the King's commands so signified.[5]

When the loss of the King's favour forced the dissolution of Pitt's ministry in 1801, the question of the division of responsibilities between the offices of the Secretaries of State was again discussed. Dundas had a scheme[6] for restoring the responsibility for the conduct of the war to the Home Office and placing the colonies under a Secretary of State who would also be the President of the Board of Trade. The Cape of Good Hope and Ceylon would, under this scheme, have been included with India under the Board of Control. In the government of Henry Adding-

---

[1] Matheson, Cyril, *Henry Dundas*, p. 276.
[2] *Ibid.*, pp. 276–7.
[3] *Ibid.*, p. 277.
[4] Dundas to Pitt, July 9, 1794, published in Costin W. C., and J. S. Watson, *The Law and Working of the Constitution: Documents 1660–1914*, vol. II, pp. 346–7.
[5] Quoted in Spector, M. M., *The American Department of the British Government, 1768–1783*, p. 79.
[6] Feiling, K. G., *The Second Tory Party 1714–1832*, p. 399.

ton that replaced the Pitt administration, the War Office was held by Lord Hobart (17 March 1801–14 May 1804). The Duke of Portland was a member of this ministry, continuing at the Home Office until June when he was persuaded to accept the honourable post of President of the Council. On his resignation, the King authorized Lord Hobart and the incoming Home Secretary, Lord Pelham, to divide the business as they saw fit.[1] On August 12 the colonies were officially transferred to the Secretary of State for War, the transfer of responsibility being effected by a formal letter from Lord Pelham to Lord Hobart:

> I have the King's commands to signify to your Lordship His Majesty's pleasure, that all the correspondence with the Governors of His Colonies, should, for the future, be carried on by your Lordship, instead of the Secretary of State for the Home Department.
>
> In consequence of this arrangement, I shall immediately take the necessary measures for preparing all the Books and Papers connected with that Correspondence which I find in this Office, and will transfer them to your Lordship with as little delay as possible. I have already directed a List of the Governors to be transmitted to your Lordship, in order that you may communicate to each of them His Majesty's pleasure on this occasion.
>
> I take this opportunity of informing your Lordship, that the Duke of Portland, previous to his resigning the seals of the Home Department, received the King's commands in regard to the Successions to the vacant Governments in the Colonies.[2]

In 1816 and 1817 Tierney, the chief Whig spokesman in the House of Commons, in moving resolutions for the abolition of the office of the third Secretary of State, declared that the transfer of the colonies, 'the fairest flower in the garland of the home department', was a political job that had been dictated by considerations of patronage.[3] It was an effective debating point in the old Whig tradition of attacking the Crown under the guise of 'economical' reform. If he could have shown that the abolition of the War Office in 1801 was seriously considered as an alternative to the transfer, then his argument might have

[1] Pellew, G. P., *The Life and Correspondence of the Right Honble Henry Addington, First Viscount Sidmouth,* I, pp. 400–1 and 411–12.

[2] C.O. 323/176, f. 7.

[3] *Parl. Deb.* XXXIII, 892–921 and XXXVI, 51–82: referred to in Manning, H.T., *British Colonial Government,* p. 478.

had some validity. But if the war was to be ended, as it was intended that it should be, while the office was to be continued, then transferring the colonies was a common-sense measure. This was especially so since the incorporation of Ireland into the United Kingdom, which had recently been effected, had added considerably to the duties of the Home Secretary.

The colonies can seldom have suffered such neglect as was to be their lot in the next decade. Some colonies received only two or three despatches a year, and for a colony to receive more than twenty a year was virtually unknown, unless it happened to be of military concern at the moment.[1] Only the most urgent matters received attention,

> Colonial despatches went unanswered, colonial governors reported crises, complained of their wrongs, and even died, without the minister seeming to be aware of the fact.[2]

The organization available to the Colonial Secretary within his own department can be inferred from the fact that not a single person moved from the Home Office to the War Office when colonial business was transferred from the one to the other. A memorandum prepared twenty years later records the event with brief simplicity:

> In the course of this year the Colonial Business was transferred from the Home Department and one clerk was added to the Establishment, together with an Extra Chief Clerk.[3]

The transfer was merely one of records and responsibility, arranged by agreement between the secretaries and requiring only the labour of a few porters to carry the volumes of documents from one building to another. In the War Office, clerks, accustomed to 'the habits of official business', could immediately undertake the routine chores of preparing formal documents. If they had any personal knowledge of colonial affairs, it had been gleaned during service in the Home Office or Board of Trade before 1795 or in their contact with the eastern colonies while serving under Henry Dundas. The complete absence of ready information on which to draw when a decision was to be made,

---

[1] See Appendix VIII.
[2] Manning, H. T., *British Colonial Government*, p. 475.
[3] C.O. 323/194 December, 1821, f. 179.

the lack of an extensive personal experience in dealing with colonial governments, and the reliance on meagre official records go far towards explaining the wooden replies to some colonial queries by such able men of business as Windham, Castlereagh, and Liverpool, the Secretaries of State from 1805 to 1812. The records of the department certainly did not provide much enlightenment on colonial problems. The Duke of Portland had handled colonial affairs for almost seven years, from 1794 to 1801, and, as a scholar who examined the records for that period has remarked, he 'was really remarkable for the mediocrity of his intellect.'[1] Portland's successors had to give their primary attention to the conduct of the war against Napoleon, which had broken out again in May 1803. Parliament took a great deal of time and energy, particularly of those ministers who were in the House of Commons. Windham complained of being

> . . . called upon to read and to write, to consider and to decide, when . . . exhausted and worn down with . . . duty in Parliament.[2]

Some significant decisions were made in these years, particularly with regard to the establishment of government in the conquered colonies, but ministers were unable to give systematic attention to colonial problems.

Until 1800 the vestigial remnants of the administrative structure that had been created for the government of the old empire set the pattern for the government of the colonies which remained. After the abolition in 1782 of the Board of Trade and of the American Department, their functions were continued by men who had had experience in those offices. The person most intimately concerned in the years immediately after 1782 was Grey Elliott, who became head of the plantations section of the Home Office and transferred to the office of the new Committee of the Privy Council for Trade and Plantations when that body was placed on a permanent footing in 1786.[3] The Home Secretary carried on the official correspondence with colonial governors, but the Privy Council committee, which soon adopted

[1] Manning, H. T., *British Colonial Government*, p. 90.

[2] Br. Mus. Add. Mss. 37906 Windham Papers, Windham to Amyot, Sept. 16, 1809, f. 344.

[3] See Lingelbach, Anna L., 'The Inception of the British Board of Trade', *American Historical Review*, XXX, 701–728.

the name of its illustrious predecessor and became known as the Board of Trade, was the main repository of detailed knowledge of the colonies. All acts of the colonial legislatures were referred to it by the Secretary of State, and it took a leading part in drawing up governors' instructions.[1] Its moving spirit was its president, Charles Jenkinson, first Earl of Liverpool, and so long as he remained active his office collected and assimilated information and was able to give advice on many colonial subjects. Unfortunately, the active imperial interest of the Board of Trade was much reduced about the same time as colonial business was transferred to the new department.[2] The vision of empire had survived in Jenkinson despite defeat, but he left no active successor, so Secretaries of State busy with war could look neither to their own department nor to that of a well-informed colleague when information was required. Several years were to elapse before a new preoccupation with the colonies resulted in the creation of that adequate body of information which is the *sine qua non* of effective administration.

The official establishment of the new office, fixed by an order in council passed on 27 February 1795, consisted of a secretary of state, his private secretary, one under-secretary, six clerks, a housekeeper, and two office-keepers. In addition to this authorized establishment the Secretary of State could hire on his own authority extra personnel to be paid from the funds available to his office for contingencies.[3] From the very beginning two porters were hired to supplement the regular establishment. In 1798 a number of extra clerks were hired for copying, and from that time until 1816 there were always extra clerks on hand; two of those hired in 1798 were employed full time until 1816 and appeared in the office at times after that date.[4] The extra chief clerk, already mentioned as having been hired at the time of the transfer of the colonies to the office, was an extra clerk

[1] Beaglehole, J. C., 'The Royal Instructions to Colonial Governors: 1783–1854: a Study in British Colonial Policy', unpublished Ph.D. thesis, London, 1929, pp. 49–52.

[2] Cockroft, G., *The Public Life of George Chalmers Chief Clerk to the Board of Trade 1786–1825*, p. 107.

[3] C.O. 701/1 is the account book showing the payments for contingencies in the early years.

[4] Most of the information on extra clerks has been gleaned from the contingent accounts C.O. 701/1 and 2.

appointed by the Secretary of State. He drew a salary of £1,000, which was somewhat less than that of the regular chief clerk. The number of persons in the office was also increased from time to time by additions to the official establishment; in 1799 a précis writer was authorized, and in 1801 an additional clerk.[1]

The position of Granville Penn, the extra chief clerk appointed in 1801, was somewhat anomalous. William Windham (Secretary of State, February 1806–March 1807), whose own deep interest in the disposal of patronage made him somewhat of an expert on the subject, contended that

> He has been made to stand in the way of a second Under-Secretary which the state in the office required, and yet to keep the name of a clerk, so as to deprive the person coming to the head of the Office, if this contrivance were yielded to, of his rights of nomination.[2]

Penn, the grandson of the founder of Pennsylvania, inherited considerable family property. He was obviously a man of some attainments, for he later published a number of theological and semi-scientific works and a biography of his great-grandfather, Admiral William Penn.[3] He was Lord Hobart's private secretary at the time of his appointment and it is quite likely that Hobart felt the need for a highly placed clerk to carry out confidential duties, since the regular clerks that he had inherited had all been appointed by Henry Dundas. Whatever the reason for Penn's appointment, Windham certainly regarded him as protected by the traditional immunity of clerks from dismissal on a change of ministry. Windham was able, however, to persuade him to retire on a pension of £550 a year, paid from the contingency fund, and to gain the consent of the Prime Minister to the appointment of a second under-secretary for the office.[4] The second under-secretary was placed on the establishment on 26 November 1806. The appointment was intended to be a political one and Windham's nominee resigned with his patron in March 1807.

[1] The orders in council passed for this purpose up to 1807 are listed in C.O. 701/14, p. 10 (+71). The pagination of this volume is defective; the numeration is repeated after page 71. The plus sign denotes the second section.

[2] Hist. Mss. Comm., *Dropmore Papers*, Windham to Lord Grenville, Feb. 1806, VIII, p. 33.

[3] D.N.B. XV, 748–9.

[4] *Dropmore Papers*, VIII, pp. 103 and 209–10.

Windham's successor, who had also been his predecessor, as Secretary of State, Lord Castlereagh (July 1805–February 1806; March 1807–October 1809), appointed two Under-Secretaries on his return to the office. Since one of these, his half-brother, the Honourable Charles Stewart (March 1807–April 1809), found time to command a hussar brigade under Sir John Moore in 1808,[1] the addition of an under-secretary was largely nominal. Castlereagh's chief helper was Edward Cooke (May 1804–February 1806; March 1806–October 1809), an able administrator with long experience in Irish affairs who had been Under-Secretary to Castlereagh's uncle, Lord Camden (May 1804–July 1805), and who later served with distinction at the Foreign Office when his friend appointed him Under-Secretary in that department in 1812.[2] In his handling of the war Castlereagh distinguished himself—'the best War Minister that we have ever had' according to Sir John Fortescue[3]—but the conduct of the war took much of his and Cooke's time; so that although he wrote some able colonial despatches and made some important decisions, the infinite care and patient attention to detail, which alone would create an understanding of the individual problems of every colony, could not be bestowed on colonial affairs. Castlereagh's failure to develop effectively the administrative framework that Windham had set up indicates what Webster points out as a weakness in his later career; he 'trusted too much to his own powers of work and too little to the assistance of a well-organized department.'[4]

Lord Liverpool (October 1809–June 1812), who followed Castlereagh, placed more reliance on his under-secretaries. He was still under forty, and of his coevals not even Canning had had such extensive experience in high office, for already he had been a Secretary of State for more than seven years: at the Foreign Office (1801–4) and at the Home Office (1804–6; 1807–9). Later he was to be Prime Minister for fifteen years (1812–27). Doomed in popular history by Disraeli's flippant tongue as the 'arch-mediocrity', he received little sympathetic appreciation during all his strenuous years in office; even a

[1] D.N.B., XVIII, 1165.
[2] Webster, Sir Charles, *The Foreign Policy of Castlereagh 1815–1822*, p. 37.
[3] Fortescue, Sir John, *British Statesmen of the Great War*, p. 228.
[4] Webster, Sir Charles, *The Foreign Policy of Castlereagh 1815–1822*, p. 35.

supporter within his ministry could only describe him after his collapse as 'a man who had fewer personal friends and less quality for conciliating men's affections than perhaps any Minister that ever lived'.[1] He certainly had a lack of social grace—'Pray arrange this prettily and not à la Liverpool', wrote the Margravine of Anspach to Lord Bathurst on 4 November 1814.[2] But he also had a subtle understanding of his friends and a gift for inspired gossip that could charm a restless colleague—'Miss Austen . . . in male attire', C. R. Fay has aptly dubbed this side of his character.[3] His powers were 'courage, conciliation and industry'[4] and he used them to lead the country to victory in war, to survive the difficult early years of the peace, and to institute significant reforms at home and a liberal foreign policy abroad in the last years of his administration.

There was no observable improvement in administrative techniques in the handling of colonial business under Lord Liverpool, but replies to colonial queries became more comprehensive and more frequent than hitherto. From short notes written on letters received it is obvious that this improvement must be credited chiefly to the youthful Robert Peel (10 June 1810–4 August 1812) who, as Under-Secretary in charge of the colonial department, was in his first political office.[5] In fairness to Peel's predecessors it must be remarked that he was the first under-secretary in the office able to devote his entire attention to colonial affairs for more than a few months (see Appendix I), and it must also be noted that under his successor, Henry Goulburn (4 August 1812–11 December 1821), there was an immediate further improvement in the handling of colonial affairs. But then, Goulburn already had had experience as Under-Secretary at the Home Office (February 1810–August 1812), he had the assistance of clerks who had undoubtedly gained in experience under Peel, and he was serving with a Secretary of State who was able to devote considerable attention to colonial affairs.

Henry, third Earl Bathurst (10 June 1812–30 April 1827),

---

[1] *The Diary of Henry Hobhouse* (1820–1827), ed. A. Aspinall, p. 136. Hobhouse was under-secretary at the Home Office.

[2] *Bathurst Papers*, p. 304.

[3] Fay, C. R., *Huskisson and His Age*, p. 174. See also p. 81.

[4] Feiling, K., *The Second Tory Party*, p. 255.

[5] Robert Peel (1788–1850): Henry Goulburn (1784–1856).

Lord Liverpool's successor as Secretary of State, was the real
founder of the Colonial Office. Self-effacing to a fault, he made
so little impression on the early nineteenth-century writers of
memoirs that the early histories of the period scarcely mention
him. Even Charles Greville, who was his official private secretary for nine years,[1] seldom referred to him in his diary and
admitted at the time of Lord Bathurst's death in 1834 that he
did not feel that he had really known him.[2] The general impression of Lord Bathurst was that he was a man who took
neither his official duties nor the affairs of the world very
seriously, a man of considerable ability but lacking in industry
and ambition. His conversation, according to Greville, was very
humorous but it was never serious, consisting mainly of a series
of anecdotes.[3] He wrote rapidly and with great assurance, seldom finding it necessary to make a correction in his drafts.
Discretion, loyalty, an excellent memory, a well-informed mind,
an ability to express himself clearly, and an aptitude for compromise made him a valued man in the cabinet. At heart he
was a sceptic with little faith in the possibility of improvement
either in men themselves or in the conditions in which they
lived; he gave his full support to the principles, ideas, and institutions of the old order. But his support of the old was neither
blind nor stupid. He admired men of purpose and goodwill
both among his colleagues and his subordinates and though, in
his later years especially, he leaned heavily towards the Duke
of Wellington and the Archbishop of Canterbury, he was sympathetic to Wilberforce and the evangelicals, and worked good-
naturedly with the liberal economists in the Tory party without
in any way sharing their ideas.

He came from a family that had been almost continuously
associated with the government service since the time of the
Restoration. His father was for a time Lord Chancellor and this
legal background was to prove of great value in dealing with
the colonies, since an understanding of the law was basic to
understanding many of their problems. His marriage to the
granddaughter of the second Duke of Richmond strengthened
his claims to high office in a society in which few men were

---

[1] See Appendix II.
[2] *The Greville Memoirs*, eds. L. Strachey and R. Fulford, III, pp. 65–6.
[3] *Ibid.*

admitted to the Cabinet without aristocratic connections.[1] Lord Bathurst was just three years younger than the younger Pitt and entered office for the first time as a Lord of the Admiralty in 1783 when Pitt was just emerging as a major political figure. During Pitt's lifetime he held a series of minor dignified offices, becoming, during Pitt's last years, a close associate on whom the Prime Minister relied in confidential matters.[2] He did not enter the Cabinet or accept an active office in the Government until 1807, when he became President of the Board of Trade in Portland's ministry. For a few weeks in 1809 he acted as Foreign Secretary in addition to performing his duties at the Board of Trade. His experience with the problems of empire at the Board of Trade and the Colonial Office extended over a period of twenty years.

Henry Goulburn, Lord Bathurst's Under-Secretary for the Colonies, was a man of somewhat pedestrian talents but of great industry, an ideal subordinate for Lord Bathurst who, while he did not shirk his responsibilities, was not one to do himself what he could depend on others to do for him. In addition to his industry and aristocratic connections Goulburn had two qualifications for high office that were of considerable significance in the early nineteenth century: he was very religious and he was the intimate friend of Robert Peel, the rising young man in the Tory party. 'Of all the men with whom I was ever acquainted he approaches the nearest to perfection,' wrote Peel in a letter to his fiancée in 1820.[3] The 'perfect' man duly rose to be Chancellor of the Exchequer in Wellington's ministry—'Goldburn' was a pun that the Duke could not resist—and Home Secretary in Peel's. For more than nine years he shared with Lord Bathurst a growing burden of correspondence amid a postwar colonial restlessness and an unwelcome interest of the home public in some aspects of their work. Mrs. Helen Taft Manning has devoted two chapters of her book *British Colonial Government after the American Revolution* to a study of these years and is full of high praise for Goulburn's achievements.[4]

'In-letters' from all parts of the Empire have drafts of Goul-

[1] Aspinall, A., 'The Cabinet Council, 1783–1835', p. 199.
[2] *Bathurst Papers*, 'Introduction' by Francis Bickley, pp. X–XI.
[3] *Private Letters of Sir Robert Peel*, ed. G. Peel, p. 32: for Lord Liverpool's opinion of Goulburn see *The Correspondence of Charles Arbuthnot*, p. 45.
[4] Chapters XV and XVI.

burn's concise replies on their turned-up corners. Other letters
have details of the nature of the reply to be made or are marked
'Put-by' for later consideration. Goulburn kept all threads of
correspondence in his own hands, advised Lord Bathurst on
what required his attention, and directed his clerks in their tasks.
Letters, such as those which appear in the Colonial Office
records after 1821 between Lord Bathurst and Goulburn's successor,[1] must also have been exchanged between Bathurst and
Goulburn when the former was away from Downing Street, but
Goulburn probably followed the example of many statesmen of
his day by taking these documents from office with him.[2] Since
the Colonial Office records from 1822 onwards clearly reveal
that it was Lord Bathurst's habit to write his reply in the form
of a minute on the letter received by him, it is not surprising
that the Historical Manuscripts Commission's report on the
papers in the Bathurst family archives at Cirencester contain
few letters from Goulburn on matters pertaining to the office.
Within the office Lord Bathurst, like most of the statesmen of
his time,[3] preferred the interview to the memorandum in the
normal course of business. No evidence exists to show that any
of the clerks composed letters except in Goulburn's absence.
There is much evidence that their role was the minor one of
finding the papers relating to a question and copying letters
and despatches, for answers even to routine queries are frequently drafted in his hand complete from formal introduction
to complimentary close.

The second Under-Secretary in the office when Goulburn
received his appointment was Major-General Sir Henry Bunbury[4] (31 October 1809–5 July 1816). Napier credits him with
reforming the War Office.[5] Registers, recording letters received
and the action taken on them, but restricted to military business and the affairs of British possessions in the Mediterranean
and Heligoland, were instituted in 1810. From these it is

---

[1] See C.O. 324/75.
[2] There are some Goulburn manuscripts in the Surrey County Record
Office but there are no official papers among them.
[3] See Webster, Sir Charles, *The Foreign Policy of Castlereagh 1815–1822*,
pp. 32–3.
[4] See Dundas, Sir C. J. F., *Memoir and Literary Remains of Lieutenant-
General Sir Henry Edward Bunbury, Bart.*, particularly Chapter IV.
[5] *History of the Peninsular War*, vol. V. Book XVII, Chapter I.

apparent that the office was divided into 'war' and 'colonial' departments at least from 1810, and very probably some such division existed earlier. A report submitted to the House of Commons in 1816[1] stated that the war department had consisted in 1814 of an under-secretary, three clerks, four extra clerks, and an Arabic interpreter. The colonial department, responsible for all colonial business outside the Mediterranean area, had an under-secretary, nine clerks, and two extra clerks. In addition there was a general department with a chief clerk, a précis writer, a translator, and a keeper of the papers and librarian, the last two officials also serving as extra clerks in the war department. There appears to have been no overlapping of the duties of the two under-secretaries except with respect to the war in Canada (1812–1814). Since there would have been obvious difficulties in making a distinction between military and civil correspondence, the correspondence of the Canadian campaign was handled by the colonial Under-Secretary. Bunbury's name does appear from time to time on letters sent out by the colonial department of the office but only when Goulburn was absent from the office. Normally Goulburn signed all colonial and general correspondence that did not require the signature of the Secretary of State.

The wartime establishment of the office reached its maximum size in 1812 when it comprised a secretary of state, two under-secretaries, a private secretary, thirteen clerks, and a précis writer; there were six full-time extra clerks. In addition a provision of £80 a year had been made in 1804 for an Arabic interpreter but the post fell vacant in 1806. When it was revived in 1809 it was as a sinecure to satisfy the claims of a Polish emigré (his father-in-law was the Russian governor of Kamchatka who had entertained Captain Cook)[2] who could neither speak nor write Arabic.[3] It was intended that the military Under-Secretary should retire early in 1815 but his retirement was delayed by the events arising out of Napoleon's return from Elba and he did not leave the office until July 1816. Three clerks, the précis writer, the Arabic interpreter, and four extra

[1] See Appendix IV.
[2] C.O. 323/187 Petition of Charles de la Garde and Charlotte Christina, his wife, 1817. See also C.O. 537/43, No. 12, f. 124.
[3] C.O. 323/198, f. 133.

clerks had left the office three months earlier. The entrench-
ment thus effected did not satisfy the Opposition in Parliament,
some of whom pretended to believe that colonial business could
be handled by an under-secretary and four clerks who would
be attached to the Home Office. The expense of the salary of
the Secretary of State for War and the cost of maintaining his
office would thus be saved.[1]

The amount of specifically military business that remained in
the hands of the Secretary of State was very small. After Sir
Henry Bunbury's retirement the chief task that remained
was the arranging with the Commander-in-Chief and the First
Lord of the Admiralty for the reduction of the Army and of the
Navy. The Secretary of State's war function had been to co-
ordinate the activities of the various military and naval departments in their active operations against the enemy. In the
twenties when he directed the Navy into action the orders to
the naval commanders were given by the Admiralty, except in
1827 when William Huskisson assumed direct responsibility for
issuing orders to the fleet in the eastern Mediterranean.[2] Apart
from thus putting into official form decisions of the Government,
the Secretary of State's responsibility for military matters outside the colonies was probably little greater than that of any
other member of the inner circle of cabinet ministers.[3] Nevertheless, Lord Bathurst's long association with the military
departments was a great advantage in negotiations over the
defence of the Empire, where a large part of the military force
available to the Crown was dispersed.

Most of the war correspondence that remained to the office
after 1816 concerned very human problems of men and women
whose lives had been enriched or broken by the war—claims
for compensation, for decorations, for authority to spend money
long spent, for a mite to keep body and soul together—a motley
collection filed with many other letters under the designation
'Miscellaneous and Colonies General'.[4] French royalists, many

[1] *Parl. Deb.* XXXIII, 892–921 and XXXVI, 51–82.
[2] C.O. 323/196 Bathurst to Lords Commissioners of the Admiralty, Dec.
3, 1822, copy, ff. 25–33. C.O. 537/89 Bathurst to Lords Commissioners
of the Admiralty, most secret, Feb. 1826 (copy), ff. 81–2. Huskisson to Vice-
Admiral Codrington, secret and confidential, (copy), ff. 92–8.
[3] See *Bathurst Papers*, pp. 600, 627–8.
[4] Series C.O. 323/185–212.

of whom had been paid pensions on the secret service funds,[1] inquired about further pensions and made claims for compensation for property destroyed during British campaigns in France. In endless letters they discussed the state of France and urged the need to refute the scurrilous publications of Napoleon's supporters who held Lord Bathurst, as the minister through whom the orders of the Government passed, responsible for his harsh treatment on St. Helena. Army officers wrote requesting the Secretary of State's sanction for the expenditure of money disbursed irregularly in old campaigns, for many of them were held responsible for large sums when the Treasury auditors finally examined their accounts, many years after the war was over. Applications for the Order of the Bath appear frequently, at times pressed with great fervour, but Lord Bathurst wisely armed himself against the importunity of old army men by limiting his selection to officers recommended by the Commander-in-Chief, the Admiralty, or the East India Company. There are many other letters—from scoundrels and soldiers of fortune, from Corsicans affected by the British occupation of 1794, Sicilians employed in Lord William Bentinck's campaigns, and Spanish guerilla chieftains; from the needy and from the letter-writing cranks of half a dozen nations. Despite their numbers and fatuity, only occasionally does a note of impatience enter into the polite consideration given to garrulous and sometimes rude queries.

It would require the pen of Jane Austen to describe the status of the Colonial Office clerks, to put them in their place as she did the impecunious young officers who were their brothers and cousins. Of the three careers open to a gentleman with limited independent means, the Church, the Army or Navy, and the Government, an appointment in one of the higher civil offices offered the surest road to promotion and an adequate income for life. Two of the clerks in the Colonial Office in 1812 received salaries greater than those received by all but the most senior officers in the Army and, in addition, held sinecures and other offices from which the income was greater than the extra allow-

---

[1] These were paid at the direction of the Secretary of State by a special agent also paid and later superannuated from the secret service funds. Most pensions were discontinued early in 1815. C.O. 324/136 Goulburn to W. H. Brooke, April 29, 1814: C.O. 323/195 Brooke to Goulburn, April 13, 1821, f. 34.

ances which such officers were likely to receive. And they had not been forced to buy their commissions at every stage of promotion as the army officers had. In fact, the purchase of civil office under the Crown was forbidden by statute.[1] Nevertheless, the concept of property in office still operated to the extent of giving a clerk security of tenure and guaranteeing him compensation for the loss of income should his place be abolished after he had served for a few years. Thus, granting a young man a clerkship was the equivalent of presenting him with a small estate for life. And there were other small estates that he might add to the original through influence or assiduous attention to duty.[2] Lord Bathurst took steps to ensure the gradual abolition of colonial sinecures,[3] but several colonial agencies at the disposal of the Secretary of State were granted for life to clerks or former clerks in the office.

A note on colonial agents is perhaps advisable, for three different sets of officials were referred to as colonial agents, with considerable subsequent confusion among observers of the colonial scene. (1) Agents were appointed by the colonial assemblies as their representatives in London.[4] (2) Agents were appointed by the Treasury for each of the colonies receiving parliamentary grants; they were frequently Treasury clerks and were responsible for paying out the moneys provided for their colonies. (3) Agents were appointed for the conquered colonies, who were responsible for the financial transactions of those colonies in the United Kingdom;[5] these were the agencies that were held by Colonial Office clerks and former clerks. A dispute arose between the Treasury and the Colonial Office in 1806 over their appointment but the Secretary of State succeeded in retaining the patronage. They were consolidated in 1833 into a single office that later became the Crown Agency Office. The

[1] 49 Geo. III. C. 126, Sect. 3 and 4 was one of the acts forbidding it. For an enquiry into an alleged attempt to sell an office in Demerara that ended tragically, see C.O. 537/40 Case of Captain Tetley; also C.O. 323/209 C. G. Issitt to Murray, Dec. 27, 1828 and C.O. 323/211 Chas. Jones to Hay, Jan. 1, 1829.

[2] For a list of appointments held by Colonial Office clerks see: H.C. 1821 XIV (602) 135–7.

[3] Manning, H. T., *British Colonial Government*, pp. 495–7.

[4] See below, pp. 35-6.

[5] See Penson, L. M., 'The Origin of the Crown Agency Office', *E.H.R.*, XL (1925), pp. 196–206.

Lower Canada agency was essentially an agency of this last type. Some of the agencies were out-and-out sinecures. A miscellaneous undated minute by Lord Bathurst in the early 1820s states of the agency for Demerara, 'if there be any difficulty made in paying Mr. Gordon as agent, on account of Mr. Holmes being permitted to act as one, I shall be obliged to refuse considering him in that Capacity.'[1]

Constitutionally, under-secretaries and clerks were no more than so many extra arms attached to the official person of the Secretary of State. By tradition, however, clerks were attached to the office and not to the Secretary of State holding the office for the time being, and once appointed to the establishment their security was almost absolute. Even extra clerks were so certain of their places that one at the Foreign Office objected vigorously when Canning forced him to retire on a generous pension.[2] Promotion was likely to be slow, but it was certain, for when a vacancy occurred all clerks lower on the establishment moved up a place. This rigid system, with all its disadvantages, was not a complete bar to efficiency. The Secretary of State could raise the status of useful clerks by a judicious distribution of favours, and even at this period there were instances in government offices where men already established in professions accepted the security of a guaranteed moderate income under government.

There was a minor inconsistency in the constitutional position of clerks in the offices of the Secretaries of State in that, while their existence emanated from the Crown and rested on tradition, the only official document of appointment was required by a parliamentary statute. This anomaly arose when the privilege enjoyed by the clerks of sending and receiving packets free of postal duty was so restricted by an act of 1764[3] that it became virtually worthless. In order that they might receive compensation a parliamentary Act of 1769[4] instructed the Postmaster General to set aside £1,500 annually from the postal revenues to be distributed equally among the three Secretaries of State. Under this act a secretary of state was required to issue to each

---

[1] C.O. 324/75, f. 251. For references to the agency of Curaçao, see Br. Mus. Add. Mss. 37906 Windham Papers, ff. 275 and 277.

[2] Temperley, H., *The Foreign Policy of Canning*, pp. 262–3.

[3] Act 4 Geo. III. Cap. 24.

[4] Act 9 Geo. III. Cap. 35.

clerk a warrant under the sign manual, countersigned by three or more of the commissioners of the Treasury, authorizing him to receive quarterly from the Postmaster General his share of the compensation. In practice, secretaries of state did not adhere strictly to the provisions of the Act, but a letter was always sent to notify the Postmaster General that a new clerk had been appointed and to request that he 'may enjoy the privileges allowed him by Act of Parliament.'[1] These allowances were never mentioned in the returns to Parliament and are not included in the tables of salaries given in the appendixes (IV, V and VI). They must have varied according to the size of the establishment from about twenty-five to over fifty pounds a year. Moreover, the loss of privilege did not prevent clerks from sending and receiving personal letters free of charge since they were able to make use of the franking privileges of the under-secretaries.

Parliament also recognized the existence of the clerks on other occasions. The manner of their appointment was questioned in 1785 by a committee whose concern would not be out of place in the mid-twentieth century. It reported:

> That considering that these offices are the Channel of the most Secret correspondence of the Government they were surprised to find that the persons employed therein were not bound to secrecy by oath; and that a trust of such importance required caution in the extreme and ought to call in aid every fence and guard of which the Constitution would admit.[2]

In 1810 the concern was not with appointment but retirement, and generous provision was made for superannuation.[3]

Conditions of service were not onerous. Throughout the government offices work began at eleven o'clock in the morning. In the Foreign Office clerks received rolls and butter every morning, paid for out of the fund for contingencies.[4] There are no references to this practice in the Colonial Office and certainly no entry in the account books of the contingency funds

[1] The letter referring to Henry Taylor's appointment is in C.O. 324/139, Feb. 1, 1824.
[2] Quoted in C.O. 324/144 Wilmot to Lushington (Treasury), Jan. 14, 1822.
[3] 50 Geo. III. Cap. 117.
[4] Hertslet, Sir E., *Recollections of the Old Foreign Office*, p. 164.

for these items, though of course they could easily have been concealed as payments to the tin and oil man or the tallow chandler. In some private offices more generous fare was provided. At one time early arrivals at East India House had received free breakfast, and higher officials, such as J. S. Mill, could still do so at mid-century. Clerks, however, were allowed only tea and two biscuits.[1] It was an India House clerk who described his routine in rhyme;

> From ten to eleven, ate a breakfast for seven;
> From eleven to noon, to begin 'twas too soon;
> From twelve to one, asked What's to be done?
> From one to two, found nothing to do;
> From two to three, began to foresee
> That from three to four would be a damned bore.[2]

In most government offices early in the century, clerks were expected to remain until four or 'until the business of the office be over'. In 1831 Lord Goderich stated that clerks in the Colonial Office were normally expected to remain until six in the evening.[3]

In the Goulburn office one gets the impression of work being done in tremendous spurts. A mail packet sailing from the east might bring dozens of despatches in a single day from all the colonies from Ceylon to Malta and Gibraltar.[4] The business arising from these despatches, consultation with the Treasury and other departments, and letters and instructions to departments and private individuals must at times have required overtime from the staff. A similar burst of activity usually accompanied the sailing of a packet as last-minute despatches were hurriedly copied and franked in time for the eight o'clock mail coach for Falmouth.[5] While Parliament was sitting there were also busy periods, but the session of 1824, when some clerks worked on at least one occasion until one or two o'clock

---

[1] Foster, Sir W., *The East India House its History and Associations*, p. 230.
[2] *Ibid.*, p. 229.
[3] C.O. 324/146 Hay to J. Stewart, July 22, 1831, pp. 316–21.
[4] Letters reaching the Colonial Office on March 11, 1823 included despatches from Ceylon (July–Nov. 7, 1822), Mauritius (July–Nov. 27, 1822), Cape of Good Hope, Gibraltar, Malta (five despatches, the last dated Jan. 7, 1823), the Barbary States and the Ionian Isles, See P.R.O. Index 8388.
[5] See below pp. 142–4.

in the morning,[1] was probably unique. If we may judge by
reports made in the thirties, there was a tradition of driving the
clerks with a light rein in the hope that the 'temptations to inaction incident to such a condition of life' might be overcome
by 'an habitual appeal to those feelings which a liberal confidence is calculated to excite.'[2] The appeal was apparently not
particularly effective in the earlier years. Of the sixteen clerks
in the office at the beginning of 1809 (see Appendix III) only
two were still serving in 1825; one had died, one was appointed
to a higher office, two served for only a few months, and the other
ten were superannuated. Of those ten none had reached the age
of sixty, and five were superannuated before reaching the age of
forty. The appeal may have been more effective with clerks
appointed from 1809 onwards. All of the seven appointed between 1809 and 1824 either had reasonably good records in the
Colonial Office or were given lucrative appointments in the
colonies after short periods of service.

When the office of the Secretary at War, the financial office
of the Army, was reduced after the war, the principle adopted
was to retire those who wished to retire and then 'to select those
who . . . were individually the least good and useful.'[3] The same
principle seems to have been adopted in the office of the Secretary of State for War and the Colonies. Although little information is available on individual clerks, at least three of the persons who were superannuated in 1816 were deficient in some of
the qualities required in a good clerk. Two of them were of
mature years when appointed to the financial haven of clerkship; Hugh Stuart was twenty-nine[4] when he first entered the
office in 1799 and John Strachan was twenty-two in 1805. Henry
Cutler was eighteen when he was appointed in 1806. Stuart was
completely worthless. When he was retired after fifteen years'
service he was given a pension of £562/10 and in addition held
the sinecure of secretary and registrar in St. Lucia which paid

[1] Taylor, H., *Autobiography*, I., p. 67.
[2] C.O. 324/146 Hay to J. K. Stewart, July 22, 1831, pp. 320–1.
[3] Br. Mus. Add. Mss. 40862, Ripon Papers, Palmerston to Robinson,
June 11, 1826, f. 181.
[4] The ages of retired clerks given in different documents vary by as much
as six years. Those given here are from C.O. 324/133, pp. 87–8, which give
an appearance of precision by stating the pensioners' ages in years and
months on April 1, 1822.

him £375 a year.[1] Yet, soon after his retirement he was lodged in King's Bench prison for a debt which he declared he would not pay.[2] In 1819 he applied for and was granted permission to live in a 'cheap' town on the coast of France in order to pay his creditors,[3] but in 1829 he was again residing comfortably within the bounds of King's Bench prison and refusing to pay his debts.[4] Henry Cutler was also a spendthrift. Shortly after he retired in 1816 on a pension of £213/6/8 he received the agency of Trinidad at a salary of £250 a year.[5] His defalcation for the sum of £3,000[6] in 1827 led to a revision of the regulations governing colonial agents;[7] for up to that time no security was required of them. One person may have taken some satisfaction in Cutler's downfall. John Strachan, gentleman usher and quarterly waiter to His Majesty,[8] had been forced to eat humble pie in 1816 when his father had applied to have the same privileges extended to him as had been received by Cutler, his junior on the establishment. Henry Goulburn had written on that occasion:

> . . . Lord Bathurst must reserve to himself the right of deciding upon the respective Merits of the Gentlemen who have been removed from the Establishment of the Office and the Claims which they in consequence may have on the Liberality of Government.[9]

When the office was established in 1795 the position of chief clerk was given to William Huskisson, who regarded it as a 'contemptible occupation'. He found his role acceptable only because the Under-Secretary allowed him to 'outstep the sphere of my duty as one of your clerks.'[10] He soon exchanged it for the

[1] C.O. 701/14, p. 94 (+71).
[2] See the letter from Francis Lambert in C.O. 323/189, Jan. 17, 1818, f. 238.
[3] C.O. 323/191, f. 543.
[4] C.O. 323/211 George Sawyer to Sir George Murray, June 10, 1829.
[5] C.O. 701/14, p. 94 (+71).
[6] C.O. 323/208 Planta (Treasury) to Hay, Nov. 15, 1828, ff. 145-152.
[7] Letters to various colonial agents, C.O. 324/146 Aug. 27, 1830, p. 260.
[8] N.L.S. Sir George Murray Papers, Memorandum, March 9, 1830, vol. 171, ff. 78-9.
[9] C.O. 324/137, p. 213.
[10] *The Huskisson Papers 1797-1830*, ed. Lewis Melville, I, pp. 23 and 25.

post of Under-Secretary (see Appendix III) and was succeeded by James Chapman, the second clerk on the original establishment. Chapman entered the government service in 1784 at the age of seventeen, and received his high appointment from Henry Dundas in 1795, who also, a few days before he left office in 1801, gave him the sinecure of 'secretary and registrar and clerk of the council' in Trinidad. In 1814 Chapman received a salary of £1,325/8/4 plus £42 Agency on passing commissions under the Great Seal.[1] The income from his sinecure depended on fees which increased through the years: in 1816 he received £701;[2] in 1821, £990;[3] and in 1829, £1,427.[4] For these adequate emoluments he handled all office finance, including the payment of the salary of the Secretary of State, kept the accounts, ordered supplies, and supervised the clerks and office servants. The post of chief clerk was abolished as unnecessary in 1833 but in 1839 Lord John Russell recommended its restoration on the ground that the duties were sufficient to occupy full-time the able and conscientious clerk who had performed them for six years.[5]

The most important clerk in colonial affairs in the early days was Adam Gordon. He was a man of some activity, and his name appears more frequently in the records and the account books than that of any other clerk. As early as 1799 he was receiving a special allowance 'for Extraordinary Services by direction of Mr. Huskisson,'[6] who was then under-secretary, and in 1804 a special increment of salary was allowed him by order in council (Appendix IV). In 1814 he was receiving £1,375/8/4 for his Colonial Office duties, a higher official emolument than the chief clerk: in addition he held the sinecure of naval officer in Trinidad (1801) and the agencies for Demerara (1805) and Lower Canada (1814–1828). His annual income from government posts was over £2,500 annually for many years. He was the son of an American loyalist who, according to a statement by Lord Bathurst, had a claim on government, having received no compensation for his losses in

---

[1] See Appendix IV.
[2] H.C. 1817 XVII (129) 231–242.
[3] C.O. 701/14, pp. 77–8 (+71).
[4] H.C. 1830–31 VII (23) 240.
[5] C.O. 537/22, No. 23.
[6] C.O. 701/1, p. 14.

the Revolution because of the restrictions in the regulations governing compensation.[1] He received his appointment in the office from Henry Dundas whose mother was a Gordon. An entry in the accounts for 1797 records the payment of £50 'his expenses to Scotland and back attending Mr. Secretary Dundas.'[2] Eighteen years later he was still attending the secretary of state, for an entry of 17 May 1815 records the payment of 'his Expenses to Putney at various times by Lord Bathurst's directions.'[3] Lord Bathurst spent much of his time at his house in Putney, and, in 1814, while Henry Goulburn was acting as one of the British plenipotentiaries negotiating with the Americans at Ghent,[4] Gordon served as head of the office. Many of the outgoing letters for this period bear his signature. Gordon's name appears especially frequently in connection with Canadian affairs; he seems to have been on confidential terms with Lord Dalhousie[5] and possibly with other Canadian governors.

Three other clerks who held colonial sinecures or agencies are worthy of mention. Richard Penn[6] was a cousin of Granville Penn[7] and, like him, was appointed by Lord Hobart in 1801. In 1807 he was made librarian with a salary of £200 in addition to his regular salary, and, in 1811, agent for Mauritius at a salary of £500[8] a year. In 1814, and probably much earlier, he was senior clerk in the war department of the office (Appendix IV). Thomas Amyot[9] (1775–1850), member of an old Huguenot family of Norwich, is described in the *Dictionary of*

---

[1] Br. Mus. Add. Mss. 40862, Ripon Papers, Bathurst to Robinson, private, Dec. 25, 1826. Lord Bathurst was writing in support of the application of Gordon's sister for a pension. She was the widow of the British consul at Charleston, South Carolina.

[2] C.O. 701/1, p. 8.

[3] C.O. 701/2, p. 33.

[4] There are a few short notes in the Colonial Office records from American statesmen whom he had met at Ghent. See C.O. 323/191 Henry Clay to Goulburn, Washington, March 1, 1819, f. 68; Albert Gallatin to Goulburn, Paris, May 25, 1819, f. 211.

[5] See P.A.C., L.C. 'Q' Series, Gordon to Horton, July 15, 1823, vol. 167–1, pp. 1–2.

[6] D.N.B. XV 751.

[7] See above. p. 15

[8] C.O. 701/14, pp. 77–8 (+71).

[9] D.N.B. I, 368–9: *Greville Memoirs*, eds. Strachey and Fulford, I, pp. 242–3, 317: *The Windham Papers*, introduction by Lord Rosebery, II. p. 199n.

National Biography as 'a favourite with all who knew him, well informed, accomplished, amiable, industrious.' William Windham knew him as a young attorney in Norwich and made him his election agent. When Windham became Secretary of State he brought him to London. Amyot could hardly have chosen a better patron; for few statesmen so blatantly used their patronage to provide for their friends. In Windham's fourteen months in the Colonial Office (February 1806–March 1807) Amyot became private secretary, clerk, agent for Curaçao, and, on the day before Windham left office, secretary in Lower Canada. His agency came to an end when Curaçao was returned to the Dutch at the end of the war, and his Lower Canada post was later taken from him but he received compensation of £400 in place of his former salary of £454.[1] In 1819 he was promoted from his clerkship to the new post of registrar of colonial slaves at a salary of £800 a year. Amyot belongs to that group of civil servants for whom an official income made possible devotion to literary interests. He was a member of the Royal Society and of the Society of Antiquaries in whose journal he published several papers on archaeology. He is also remembered for an edition of Windham's speeches, which he edited in 1812 and for which he wrote a biographical introduction. George Baillie[2] was appointed by Lord Liverpool in 1810 and, in 1812, Lord Bathurst made him agent for Berbice at a salary of £200 a year.[3] He was one of Bathurst's favourite clerks. Baillie's brother, Thomas, a young army subaltern, was appointed to the first vacant clerkship which Lord Bathurst had at his disposal after the reduction of the office in 1816 (Appendix III).

The extra clerks who served full-time during the war years

[1] H.C. 1817 XVII (129) 231–242 and H.C. 1830–31 VII (23) 229. Concerning this post he wrote to Windham November 14, 1807: 'My Canada appointment (concerning which you have enquired from time to time) is I fear put in jeopardy by the prospect of an American War. I should hope, however, that if the province should be lost I should receive something from Government by way of compensation, as in such cases has been usual.' Br. Mus. Add. Mss. 37906, Windham Papers, f. 275.

[2] Much information on Baillie can be gleaned from the long dispute over his brother's activities as commissioner of Crown lands in New Brunswick. See particularly MacNutt, W. S., 'The Politics of the Timber Trade in Colonial New Brunswick', *C.H.R.* XXX (1949), pp. 51–2. Also Manning, H.T., 'The Colonial Policy of the Whig Ministers 1830–37', *C.H.R.* XXXIII (1952), pp. 233–4.

[3] C.O. 701/14, pp. 77–8 (+71).

seem to have been chosen for their efficiency.[1] In 1812 there were half a dozen of them. Two, who had been serving since 1798, were receiving liberal extra allowances (Appendix IV) in addition to the regular pay of an extra clerk (fifty-two shillings and sixpence a week). Before 1812 only two of the supernumeraries received appointments on the regular establishment: Richard Plasket, who later became secretary in Malta and the Cape of Good Hope, and George Wilder, one of the most conscientious of clerks (Appendix III). In 1814, however, Lord Bathurst selected two more for appointments which assured their remaining in the office after its reduction. George Mayer became librarian in place of Richard Penn,[2] and a new post of translator of foreign languages with a salary of £200 a year was created for Peter Smith. Both retained their salaries as extra clerks until 1816. Their new posts were extra to the establishment but later they received regular appointments, Smith in 1819, Mayer in 1822. The survival of Wilder, Smith, and Mayer in the office long after 1836, when the last of their contemporaries of this early period retired, indicates that personal merit gained them their places on the establishment.

'To build a central machinery which could furnish information for the ministry and parliament on colonial affairs was,' in Mrs. Manning's opinion, 'the first step towards the reorganization of the empire in the nineteenth century'.[3] The office in the Goulburn era moved slowly but steadily towards arming itself with the necessary facts, sometimes urged on by Parliament, at other times initiating comprehensive measures of its own. The greatest sources of information were the governors' despatches with their numerous enclosures. Prompt replies to enquiries and attention to their affairs encouraged governors to write much more frequently and to write more informative despatches than they had written in the first decade of the century, but the despatches could not provide much routine information that would have been available in the records but for the years of neglect. In 1813 the House of Commons requested that six printed

---

[1] Supernumeraries in the Foreign Office had no reputation for efficiency at this time. See Temperley, H., *The Foreign Policy of Canning*, p. 263.

[2] Penn received compensation in the form of an increment of salary of £200 approved by order in council (Appendix IV).

[3] Manning, H. T., *British Colonial Government*, p. 483.

copies of all colonial legislative acts be sent to Great Britain and made provision for all unprinted acts of previous years to be transcribed.[1] This task kept several copying clerks employed intermittently for the next two or three years. A circular was sent out as late as 1818 to urge colonial governors to comply with this request.[2]

An even more useful contribution to the information store was made in 1817 when the House of Commons Select Committee on Finance requested returns of the various civil and military offices in the colonies, the salaries, methods of appointment, the names of the office-holders and the dates of their appointments. Some of the departments had difficulty in providing the Colonial Office with information on their officials. The Judge of the High Court of Admiralty reported that he was unacquainted with the emoluments of the officers of the Vice-Admiralty Courts and had no means of obtaining information, no return being made to the High Court 'or anywhere else that I know of.'[3] Returns for thirty colonies and for Van Diemen's Land, then still a dependency of New South Wales, were made to the House of Commons in March.[4] Impressed by the need to have such information on hand, the office had, in the previous month, prepared printed forms and a circular to governors instructing them to have the forms filled out by all the individual office-holders in the colonies.[5] The need for up-to-date information led in 1819 to an instruction that colonial almanacs[6] be sent regularly and in 1822 a system of regular annual reports was instituted.

In March of that year a large book was sent to each governor accompanied by a circular instructing him to make a return of statistical information for 1821; in future similar returns were to be made 'as soon as possible after the close of every year.'[7] Information was requested under five headings: 'Abstract of the Nett Revenue and Expenditure'; 'Schedule of Taxes, Duties, etc.'; 'Military Expenditure'; 'Establishment'; and 'Schedule of Fees, etc.'. In a circular dated 30 April 1823[8] three

[1] C.O. 323/182 Address of House of Commons, July 13, 1813, f. 60.
[2] C.O. 324/104 Nov. 23, 1818, marked 'Ceylon and Gibraltar'.
[3] C.O. 323/186 May 24, 1817, f. 23.
[4] H.C. 1817 XVII (129) 231–242.
[5] C.O. 324/104 Feb. 24, 1817.   [6] C.O. 854/1.
[7] C.O. 854/1.   [8] *Ibid.*

additional heads were added: 'Population'; 'Exports and Imports', and 'Currency'. These regular and uniform reports were referred to as the Blue Books[1] and were designed to be an easily consulted and readily available source of general information on the colonies.

From time to time additional headings were added to the Blue Books on which reports were required. Other types of reports were also instituted. On 11 September 1826 the governors of the conquered colonies, whose finances were directly under the control of the secretary of state at that time,[2] were instructed to send half-yearly reports on revenue and expenditure.[3] In 1828 Huskisson had a circular drawn up[4] instructing governors of legislative colonies to make use of their annual addresses to the legislatures, their throne speeches, to make extensive and accurate surveys of the state of their colonies. These statements, which were to unite 'an exact summary of facts with a careful though brief enquiry into their causes and probable results', were to be sent to the Colonial Secretary where they would 'supply a deficiency which is daily felt.' The Colonial Office could never get adequate reports from the colonies with legislatures. G. R. Porter, head of the statistical department of the Board of Trade, giving evidence before a House of Commons committee in 1837, reported that the information from the Crown colonies was good, that from the colonies with legislatures frequently inaccurate and incomplete, with the returns from Jamaica being the worst.[5] He was supported in his opinion by the evidence of Peter Smith of the Colonial Office.

Secretaries of state did not, of course, have to depend entirely on governors' letters and reports for information. Most colonial assemblies maintained agents in London who were always available for consultation in Downing Street.[6] These men carried on regular correspondence with the speakers of the assemblies and frequently with other colonial politicians, and were usually in

[1] The returns of 1817 were also referred to as Blue Books.
[2] See Chapter VI.
[3] C.O. 854/1.
[4] C.O. 323/208 Filed under 'Stephen'.
[5] H.C. 1837 VII (516) 407–10. See also the evidence of Peter Smith, *Ibid* pp. 347–353; also pp. 477–9.
[6] See Penson, L. M., *The Colonial Agents of the British West Indies;* also Cockroft, G., *The Public Life of George Chalmers . . .*, particularly Chapter IV.

contact with prominent colonials visiting Britain. They were treated as the ambassadors of the assemblies, and it was as such that James Stephen described them before the Canada committee of the House of Commons in 1828:

> Making all due allowance for the disparity of the two offices, the agent of a colony is accredited in the Colonial Department in the same way in which a foreign minister is accredited in the Foreign Department.[1]

The Canadian (i.e. Upper and Lower Canada) assemblies did not appoint agents and some of their troubles may have stemmed from this lack of a direct channel of communication with the colonial secretary. In the twenties they did on a few occasions send special representatives to Downing Street who were usually well received.[2]

Several critical problems arose after 1815 that required much closer study than could be given to them in Downing Street. One of the most urgent was the need for the establishment of a new system of government in New South Wales. The autocratic system that had served when the colony was primarily a convict settlement became unsuitable when the country began to attract a population of free settlers. The powers exercised by the governor were also unconstitutional in a colony of free settlement. In April 1817, Lord Bathurst proposed sending 'forthwith' a royal commission of enquiry[3] with extensive powers to investigate complaints and make recommendations for the alteration of the system of government. Almost exactly two years later John Thomas Bigge, a former chief justice of Trinidad, sailed with full powers as commissioner.[4] In the same year radical politicians in the House of Commons turned their attention to securing the extension of British principles of government to the colony.[5] From this beginning, radical interest in the colonies and criticism of colonial policies continued

---

[1] Quoted in Manning, H. T., 'The Civil List of Lower Canada', *C.H.R.*, XXIV, p. 36.

[2] See Smith, William, 'Sidelights on the Attempted Union of 1822', *C.H.R.*, II (1921) 38–45.

[3] C.O. 324/138 Bathurst to Sidmouth, April 25, 1817.

[4] C.O. 324/141 Goulburn to Commissioners of the Navy, immediate, April 29, 1819.

[5] Manning, H. T., *British Colonial Government*, pp. 535–41.

for three decades. Bigge's reports on his return two years later were the basis for the New South Wales constitution granted by parliament in 1823.

Earlier, notable commissions of colonial enquiry were sent to Trinidad, in 1802, and to West Africa, in 1811. A Treasury commission reported on the customs service in the American colonies in 1812,[1] as did a royal commission on Malta in the same year.[2] The military departments also sent officers out from time to time to inspect the defences of various colonies. But the New South Wales commission is significant as the first of a series sent out by Lord Bathurst to make independent and comprehensive enquiries. Their reports formed the basis for many important decisions in the years that followed. In the 1820s committees of enquiry of the House of Commons also turned up some useful information on colonial questions, particularly on emigration. By 1829, an easily satisfied under-secretary could boast that even a critical committee of the House of Commons had been forced to concede that ample information on the colonies was available in the Colonial Office.[3] More critical people urged further improvement.

After the reduction in 1816 the office had only nine clerks, a librarian and a translator besides its three political persons, the secretary of state, under-secretary, and private secretary. The amount of extra help in 1817 and 1818 was negligible. However, the most inefficient clerks had been removed and the new hands transferred from the war department of the office brought with them ideas on the filing and indexing of papers that must have been a considerable aid to its efficiency. Old problems of empire, long quiescent, again sprang to life. The zealous group in the House of Commons which had secured the act for the abolition of the slave trade in 1807 was vigorously urging the need for the government to take active measures for the improvement of the lot of the colonial slaves. According to a statement by Goulburn,

---

[1] Manning, H. T., *British Colonial Government,* pp. 351-2, 511-2.

[2] For royal commissions during this period and the dates of their reports see: H.C. 1826-27 XX (301) 499–507: Further reports to 1830 are listed in H.C. 1829 XXI (212) 63: H.C. 1830 XXIX (379) 263: H.C. 1831–32 XXVI (512) 501.

[3] N.L.S. Sir George Murray Papers, R. W. Hay to Murray, private and confidential, May 12, 1829, vol. 169, ff. 89–90.

several clerks were employed on the slavery question alone.[1] But even the demands of the slavery issue and the growing volume of the routine business (see Appendix VIII) did not prevent Lord Bathurst and Goulburn from making a probing tentative approach to several of the general problems of empire; defence, currency, religion, and emigration. Emigration in particular made great demands on the limited administrative resources. The overseas movement of people from the British Isles, which had been reduced to a trickle during the war, began again as shipping became available and economic hardship at home increased.

Lord Bathurst was willing, and even anxious, to give encouragement to emigration where an increase in the population of a colony was advisable in the interests of imperial defence. The two colonies considered to be most in need were the Cape of Good Hope, where it was felt that a larger British element in the population was desirable, and Upper Canada, where the long line of communication with the lower province was to be strengthened by new settlements.[2] Parliamentary grants in 1819 and 1821 were used for assisting emigration to these two colonies.[3] Wherever it was feasible colonial officials and persons willing to lead groups of settlers were employed, but even then the administrative task was such that the personal efforts of Bathurst and Goulburn were creditable. Regulating emigration to New South Wales demanded almost as much work as encouraging it to Canada and the Cape of Good Hope; not only was there the task of sending convicts but also the need to discourage prospective emigrants without capital and to encourage prospective emigrants with capital.[4] For replies to the queries of persons desirous of emigrating and the inquiries of relatives of convicts desirous of proceeding to New South Wales

[1] Manning, H. T., *British Colonial Government*, p. 479.

[2] C.O. 324/75 Lord Bathurst's Minutes 'Miscellaneous' N/D 1822–26, f. 233. See also Lower, A. R. M., 'Immigration and Settlement in Canada, 1812–1820', *C.H.R.*, IV (1923), 37–47.

[3] See: Edwards, Isobel E., *The 1820 Settlers in South Africa* and Cowan, Helen I., *British Emigration to British North America 1783–1837*.

[4] '. . . Lord Bathurst . . . has always considered it his Duty to prevent by every legal means the residence in New South Wales or Van Diemen's land of persons who are not possessed of sufficient means to support themselves, or to cultivate Land with advantage'. C.O. 324/143 Goulburn to Jos. Pinsent, June 29, 1821. See also Appendix X.

special letter forms were lithographed, the earliest use noted of this labour-saving device in colonial correspondence apart from circulars to governors and passport forms.[1]

In 1819 the increasing interest of Parliament in colonial affairs led to the payment of £40 to J. Gudge for keeping a daily account of the orders of the House of Commons.[2] It was also found necessary to hire several extra clerks part time to copy papers demanded in an inquiry into the affairs of the Red River colony of the Hudson's Bay Company. But the hiring of extra help in 1819 was exceptional for this period. In 1820 only one extra clerk was hired and in 1821 only £22 was spent on extra copying.

In the years of greatest distress in the country, 1817 and 1821, the Treasury, pressed on by the House of Commons, instituted several measures designed to reduce expenditure in the public service. One of the most significant developments was the assumption of responsibility for insuring uniformity in the salary scales in all the departments of government. In order that a comparison might easily be made between the pay of clerks in the Treasury and those in the offices of the Secretaries of State, the clerks were divided into classes on the assumption that the duties in the different offices required roughly the same amount of effort and ability. An attempt was also made to lay down the proportion of the establishment in each office that was to fall within a given class.

The Treasury's efforts in 1817 had very little effect on the Colonial Office. The select committee of the House of Commons that reviewed all public expenditures in that year concentrated mainly on urging the abolition of the many sinecures that still remained. Legislation was introduced doing away with most of those remunerative places that had been retained by the reformers of the 1780s, who had argued that some provision was necessary for rewarding persons who had given outstanding service to the state. A pension fund was established out of part of the money saved as a result of the abolition of the sinecure offices; it was intended that it should be used to make provision for the retirement of men of business not covered by the civil service pension act of 1810. The committee's report also empha-

---

[1] Several examples of these letters are contained in C.O. 854/1.
[2] C.O. 701/2.

sized that since the extensive report of a select committee on finance in 1797, which reported in detail the number of persons employed in government departments and their salaries, all departments had increased in size and many increments of salary had been granted to offset the decline in the value of money.[1]

In July 1817, the Treasury instructed department heads to suspend increases of salary for length of service; it had decided 'to revise the whole of the present Establishments in the Civil Offices of the State with a view of ascertaining how far prospective Reductions may reasonably be made therein.' Already, during the session of Parliament, arrangements had been made for all members of the government service receiving more than £1,000 a year to make a contribution of 10 per cent of their salaries to the government.[2] This, in effect, required them to continue to pay, for that year, the income tax that had been abolished by Parliament in 1816. In January 1818, Goulburn was asked to attend a general meeting of representatives of departments to prepare a statement on salaries and emoluments.[3] It may have been out of this meeting that there grew up the 'self-denying committee' that Palmerston later described as having met at the Chancellor of the Exchequer's for the purpose of retrenching the expenses and reducing the salaries of a great variety of public offices. According to Palmerston their enquiries led to the issuing of several Treasury minutes. At the end of 1818, a return of prosperity having eased the pressure for economy, the old regulations for granting increased salaries for length of service were restored.[4] At the same time it was decided that there was no need to introduce a uniform system throughout the government departments:

> . . . the Establishment of every Public Office must be modelled with reference to its own extent and its peculiar Duties, with a general reference only to the Salaries and Emoluments of other Public Offices where the duties are in any degree similar.[5]

[1] A useful summary of the findings of these committees comparing them with a survey made in the late twenties appears in H.C. 1830–31 VII (92) 299–415.
[2] See C.O. 323/186, ff. 259 and 312.
[3] C.O. 323/188, f. 162.
[4] C.O. 323/188 Harrison to Goulburn, Nov. 6, 1818, f. 217. For the regulations, see Appendix IV.   [5] *Ibid.*

Early in 1821 the worthy Sir Henry Bunbury, the former Under-Secretary for War, had his Colonial Office pension taken from him, not as an economy measure but because he had, by calling a meeting of his neighbours and delivering a speech highly critical of the government, added 'the sin of ingratitude to that of treason.'[1] The House of Commons, reflecting in its attitude the discontent of the landowners, was very critical of the Government that year. In April the Treasury once more suspended salary increases and announced its intention of reviewing Civil Service incomes.[2] In August the changes, much more drastic than any that had been previously attempted, were announced. Palmerston gleefully recollected in later years the dissatisfaction of his clerks with his 'vigorous & unsparing Pruning Knife.'[3] The general rules that the Treasury announced that it would follow had little influence on actual policy but do reflect the impractical demands of the House of Commons. They were:

1st. That every office was to be restored to the situation in respect to the number of Persons employed, and of their respective Emoluments in which it stood in 1797 unless some adequate cause continued to exist which rendered some alteration necessary.

2nd. That where increase of Business or the more correct and efficient execution of the Public Service rendered it necessary the Emoluments of the Officers composing those Establishments should be assimilated as nearly as the change of circumstances would admit, to those received by persons in similar situations in 1797.

3rd. Offices no longer necessary to be abolished.[4]

New salary scales calling for a considerable reduction in the salaries of the more highly paid posts were to be introduced in several departments. Persons already holding positions were to receive their old salaries but all promotion after 1 January 1822 was to be governed by the new scale. In a minute dated 10 August 1821 the Treasury[5] ordered that the salaries of all civil

---

[1] Lord Liverpool to Bathurst, private, Jan. 7, 1821, *Bathurst Papers*, pp. 493–4.
[2] C.O. 323/194, f. 165.
[3] Br. Mus. Add. Mss. 40862 Ripon Papers, Palmerston to Robinson, June 11, 1826, ff. 181–2.
[4] C.O. 323/194 Enclosed in Lushington to Goulburn, Aug. 13, 1821, ff. 169–70.   [5] C.O. 324/194, f. 169.

servants receiving more than £100 a year[1] be reduced in the future by five per cent. Where a civil servant was receiving emoluments greater than the salary allotted to his office under the new regulations, ten per cent of the excess was to be deducted. Nominally these deductions were to take the form of a compulsory contribution to a newly established superannuation fund. Since, however, civil servants were already entitled to generous pensions under an act of 1810,[2] and there certainly was no intention of giving them any additional benefits, the payments were recognized for what they were, a deliberate cut in salaries authorized by a simple order of the Treasury.

The new salary scale authorized for the Colonial Office (see Appendix V) considerably reduced the salaries for the senior positions. Henry Goulburn was to continue to receive £2,500 annually as Under-Secretary but his successor would receive only £2,000. The new scale for clerks, subject to the Treasury's five per cent deduction, was to be:

	starting salary	annual increment	maximum salary
chief clerk	£1000	£50	£1250
first senior clerk	700	20	800
two senior clerks	600	20	800
three assistant clerks	350	15	545
three junior clerks	150	10	300

One notable relic of the past disappeared at this time. In the eighteenth century the clerks in the offices of the secretaries of state had shared the proceeds from the sale of the *Royal Gazette*. Towards the end of the century this share of '*Gazette* money' was converted into a fixed allowance of £75/8/4 a year. The new salary scale made no mention of it.

In fitting the existing clerks into the new establishment Lord Bathurst interpreted very liberally a Treasury instruction that the provisions for a reduction of expense were to be combined with

> ... a due regard to the interests of those who are at present in the Office and whose faithful Services entitle them to every possible consideration.[3]

[1] Those receiving between £50 and £100 were to be reduced by two and a half per cent.   [2] 50 Geo. III, Cap. 117. See below p. 162.

[3] C.O. 324/143 Goulburn to Lushington (Treasury), Nov. 30, 1821, p. 364.

Four clerks were classed as senior and four were placed in the assistant class, so there was only one junior clerk in the office. All increases due for length of service to the end of 1821 under the old regulations (Appendix IV) were granted. Three clerks actually received small increases in their net emoluments under the new arrangements (Appendix V). A significant innovation which accompanied the introduction of the classification of clerks was the provision that promotion need no longer be strictly according to seniority:

> On a vacancy occurring in the situation of Chief Clerk, or in either of the two first Classes, the Secretary of State will supply the same by selection of a fit individual from the Class immediately below.[1]

This regulation was later honoured in the spirit of its wording. When clerks were passed over it was because they were unfit; it was exceptional for clerks of particular merit to be singled out from their less able brethren.[2]

An attempt by the Treasury to assimilate Colonial Office salary scales in the junior ranks to its own was opposed by Lord Bathurst in a curt note.

> In the first place his Lordship does not conceive that his office can be compared with that of the Treasury, either with regard to the number of Persons employed, the nature of the duties in which its several members are occupied; or the advantages to be obtained by Service and Promotion.
>
> The pecuniary advantages to which a Junior Clerk in the Treasury may fairly look in the course of time are much superior to those which a Junior Clerk in this Establishment can expect to attain: whilst the duty and attendance which may at all times be required of the latter are much greater.[3]

The negotiations with the Treasury over the proposed reduction of expenditure dominated the scene at the Colonial Office all through the autumn of 1821. Even the clerks who were not faced with an immediate reduction of salary could no longer

[1] C.O. 324/144 Bathurst to Lord President of the Council, Jan. 31, 1822, p. 21; regulations recognizing merit in promotions from one class to another were also introduced in other offices. See Br. Mus. Add. Mss. 40862, Ripon Papers, Palmerston to Robinson, June 11, 1826, f. 184.

[2] Note in Appendix III the exceptional careers of Frederick Elliott and Clinton Murdoch.

[3] C.O. 324/144 Wilmot to Lushington, Jan. 14, 1822.

look forward to succeeding to the attractive emoluments received by those in the higher situations. For the senior clerks who were still receiving high salaries commensurate with their wartime responsibilities there were no increments for length of service to be brought up to date to offset the deductions. Adam Gordon's salary was £475/8/4 above the new scale; he was to be required to pay £92/10 annually. Richard Penn was to be required to pay £72/10, his income being £325/8/4 above the salary for the office he held. After occupying, while still under thirty, the highly confidential post of senior clerk in the war department, he was reduced at the age of thirty-eight to the dull and heavy routine of colonial administration with a lower income and almost without prospects of improving it.

Before the final details of the order in council authorizing the new establishment were settled, Goulburn left the Colonial Office, in December 1821, to become Chief Secretary for Ireland. A series of eight letters[1] that he wrote to Lord Bathurst in the summer before he left the office provide an interesting glimpse of the relations between the Secretary of State and his Under-secretary. The intimate details of government policy that Goulburn, in Westminster, reported to Lord Bathurst, in the country, help to confirm a remark once made by Lord Liverpool, that the 'confidential' Under-secretary of State knew more of the secrets of government than any cabinet minister except his principal and the first minister.[2] The Under-Secretary had a key to cabinet boxes, for which he was responsible when they were sent to the office, and he quite obviously made use of it. The letters contain comments on the current business of the office, gossip about the King and his relations with the Cabinet, reports on decisions of the Cabinet, i.e. those members of the Cabinet who were in London,[3] and of discussions that Goulburn had held with Lords Liverpool and Castlereagh on Mediterranean policy.[4] Lord Liverpool was out of favour with the King and there was an expectation that the government would be dismissed. Goulburn and Charles Arbuthnot, the patronage secretary to the Treasury, were keeping Lord Bathurst posted on developments. Among

[1] *Bathurst Papers*, pp. 503–9.
[2] Aspinall, A., 'The Cabinet Council, 1783–1835', p. 173.
[3] *Bathurst Papers*, p. 508.
[4] *Ibid.*, p. 505.

other matters Goulburn reported that he was preparing to make a 'proper selection' of papers in anticipation of their departure from the office[1] and that he was making representations regarding patronage that Lord Bathurst was endeavouring to obtain in favour of one of his sons.[2]

In his last months in the office Goulburn worked very hard, for he had discovered that colonial business was a plant which thrived enormously on the attention given it. An office beset by economy, an under-secretary besieged with work, and clerks refusing to bear their share of the increasing load form the picture presented by Charles Greville[3] who, after being Lord Bathurst's private secretary for nine years, had left the office in June 1821. In a letter to Goulburn's successor he warned him of his bleak prospects:

> For fear you should be too much elated, I think it right to represent to you that you will find the whole array of clerks in a state of mutiny on account of the proposed reductions, and that you will receive no active assistance in getting through your business, which is beyond belief lonesome and laborious—nothing can equal the stupidity and prolixity of your Colonial Correspondents and you will be assailed with documents of bulk immeasurable without one interval of repose.[4]

The end of Goulburn's under-secretaryship was the end of an era. After the abolition in 1782 of the departments created for the purpose of supervising the old empire, new arrangements had been made for administering the remaining colonies. A new Committee of the Privy Council for Trade and Plantations, given a permanent office in 1786, was expected to work closely with one of the secretaries of state. In the first decade of the nineteenth century this arrangement functioned very badly at a time when the remnant of the old empire was presenting new

[1] *Bathurst Papers*, p. 504.
[2] *Ibid.*, p. 503. He also sought to make provision for another son at this time, *Ibid.*, pp. 511–2.
[3] Charles Greville (1794–1865) the author of the famous diary. He succeeded in June 1821 to a clerkship of the Privy Council to which he had received the appointment in reversion from his grandfather the Duke of Portland. See Appendix II.
[4] Greville to Wilmot, Dec. 4, 1821, quoted in Jones, E. G., 'Sir R. J. Wilmot Horton, Bart., Politician and Pamphleteer', unpublished M.A. thesis, Bristol, 1936, p. 39.

problems and a number of new colonies conquered in war had to be integrated into the British system. A government department devoted entirely to the colonies came into being, not as a carefully designed instrument of colonial government, but in response to needs of the colonies that had long been neglected. After 1812 two unimaginative men with a great capacity for routine business devoted their industry to the task of bringing order to colonial government. By 1821 the Colonial Office had firmly established its place in the framework of British administration. Internally it remained a department of the old type with responsibility and initiative entirely in the hands of the political heads of the office.

2

THE OFFICE REMODELLED, DECEMBER 1821 – JULY 1825

Had the Colonial Office lost its Secretary of State as well as its Under-Secretary in December 1821, it might have reverted to a condition similar to that which existed before 1812. Certainly the handling of colonial business would have suffered until new men trained themselves in colonial affairs, for no attempt had been made to school any of the permanent members of the department in the intricacies of colonial policy. Thus there was no machinery to ease the changeover from one set of political heads to another. The Foreign Office and the Home Office each had a permanent under-secretary who, although not regarded as policy makers, could provide an incoming secretary of state with information and initiate the political under-secretary into the habits of official business. The need for such a person in the Colonial Office was even greater than in those offices; for they dealt in affairs with which statesmen were habitually familiar while the Colonial Secretary directed more than thirty governments of whose problems most statesmen were only dimly aware. During his last months in the office Goulburn was finding it difficult to keep up with his work. Unless steps were taken to improve the administrative structure, his successor would have to be a professional administrator and colonial expert who could excel that paragon of industry.

On the formation of a new ministry, when many posts were vacant, secretaries of state could choose their under-secretaries from numerous aspirants for office: scions of noble families who required training for the high posts to which wealth and influence would raise them, able young 'House of Commons' men who were to be groomed as men of business, and old friends, like Castlereagh's Edward Cooke, with long experience in official positions. When a ministry had been long in office, as in 1821, a vacant under-secretaryship was a rare prize in which the whole ministry took an interest.[1] Lord Bathurst's appointment of Robert John Wilmot (11 December 1821–5 January 1828) to succeed Goulburn has been ascribed to the efforts of Peel, Goulburn, and Lord Harrowby, who had marked him as the man to initiate a scheme of emigration for the relief of Ireland.[2] But his biographer finds little evidence for this.[3] Lord Harrowby, who recommended Wilmot to Lord Bathurst,[4] was the least conservative of Lord Bathurst's intimate friends and the one with the closest ties to George Canning and his friends. Since the letter suggesting Wilmot's appointment also contains the latest news of difficulties that had arisen over the proposed appointment of Canning as Governor-General of Bengal—'Burn this' was added as a postscript—it is quite conceivable that the appointment of Wilmot was intended as a favour to Canning's supporters in the ministry. The likelihood that the recommendation was favoured by Lord Liverpool, and that he was making use of Lord Harrowby's friendly letter as an indirect way of making his opinion known to Lord Bathurst, is strengthened by the fact that Harrowby had just seen the Prime Minister and had discussed the probability of Goulburn's resignation; it is unlikely that they missed the opportunity to mention possible successors.[5] That Lord Harrowby was merely intending to do a favour to a young Staffordshire neighbour is possible, but unlikely.

Wilmot had made himself an obvious choice by deliberately using his considerable powers in debate to support the Government on all possible occasions. Five months earlier he had argued with Lord Ellenborough,

> ... whether it was the surer and easier road to high political office to oppose diligently and malignantly (in the modern sense) or to support energetically and uncompromisingly,[6]

himself maintaining that support was the better course. His for-

---

[1] See the *Croker Papers*, ed. L. J. Jennings, three vols. (1885) I. pp. 187 and 189.

[2] Cowan, H. I., *British Emigration to North America 1783–1837* (1928), p. 146, and Adams, W. F., *Emigration from Ireland* (1932), p. 274.

[3] Jones, E. G., 'Wilmot Horton', pp. 32–3.

[4] Harrowby to Bathurst, Nov. 26, 1821, *Bathurst Papers*, p. 523.

[5] *Ibid.*

[6] Wilmot Horton to Huskisson, Jan. 22, 1828. Quoted in Fay, C. R., *Huskisson and His Age*, (1951), p. 88. In 1828 Wilmot Horton and Ellenborough had not been on speaking terms for four years.

tune by inheritance and marriage was sufficient to sustain him, as Goulburn sometimes feared that his was not,[1] until he could hope to attain the high office to which he aspired and for which he had assiduously prepared himself.

Wilmot is better known as Wilmot Horton, which name he took by royal licence on 8 May 1823 in compliance with the directions of his father-in-law's will[2] and it is by this name that it is most convenient to designate him. He was a cousin to Lord Byron and had a share both of the family wit and of its instability. Extensive and sustained reading had made Wilmot Horton well-informed on general issues, and in addition to speaking well enough to impress the House of Commons, he wrote well enough to be published in *The Quarterly*.[3] But at thirty-seven years of age he was the same age as Goulburn who had already had twelve years in office, and was four years older than Peel who was shortly to become Home Secretary. And to counterbalance the impression he had made on the House of Commons was his reputation as a popular man about town, 'the first punster of the age, addicted to good shooting, good eating and écarté' who would probably be 'a horrid man of business'.[4]

In the literary world Wilmot Horton is remembered for having authorized the destruction of Byron's memoirs. Byron detested him and on occasion expressed his opinion of him in verse, most notable in a rhyming letter sent to his publisher from Venice in 1818 and usually published under the title of *An Epistle to Mr. Murray*:

> Now tell me some news
> Of your friends and the Muse
> Of the Bar, or the Gown, or the House
> From Canning the tall wit
> To Wilmot the small wit
> Ward's[5] creeping Companion and Louse.

[1] Goulburn to Bathurst, Nov. 1821, *Bathurst Papers*, p. 523.

[2] D.N.B. IX. 1284.

[3] For Wilmot Horton's connection with *The Quarterly* beginning March 1813 with an article on Feinagle and Grey's *Artificial Memory* see Jones, E. G., 'Wilmot Horton', p. 47 and pp. 368–72.

[4] Charles Greville to Wilmot, Dec. 4, 1821. Quoted in Jones, E. G., 'Wilmot Horton', p. 37.

[5] John William Ward, later 1st Earl of Dudley, Foreign Secretary (1827–8).

Who's so damnably bit
With fashion and Wit,
That he crawls on the surface like Vermin
But an insect in both,
By his Intellect's growth,
Of what size you may quickly determine.

The one thing about Wilmot Horton that Byron did approve
was his choice of a wife; it was of her he was thinking when he
wrote:

She walks in Beauty, like the night
Of cloudless climes and starry skies.

The popularity of the Liverpool government in the House of
Commons reached its nadir in 1821. Goulburn's departure for
Ireland and Wilmot Horton's installation at the Colonial Office
were sidelights of more significant changes designed to increase
its popularity, namely, the acceptance by Peel of the office of
Home Secretary in January 1822 and the attachment of the
small Grenville party to the ministry by the award of positions
to its leading members. The depression of trade and the very low
price of grain continued into 1822. Servicing the debt still took
more than sixty per cent of the revenue, yet the country gentlemen continued to put pressure on the Government to grant them
relief from taxation—some were urging repudiation of the debt
or a capital levy, while all were supporting Hume's campaign
for further economy in government. By the beginning of 1823,
however, prosperity had returned and in that year grain prices
were double what they had been in the previous year and continued high in 1824; moreover, fortune, having smiled at last,
was lavish in her gifts and sent fine weather and good crops.
With prosperity came contentment in the country and the
return of the country gentlemen to the support of the Government.

The Government itself was further remodelled until, by
January 1823, only two of the old men, Lords Liverpool and
Bathurst, remained in key administrative offices. The new
men favoured change and were much more active than their predecessors had been. On Castlereagh's suicide, in September 1822,
George Canning succeeded him at the Foreign Office; in January
1823, Frederick Robinson succeeded Vansittart as Chancellor of

the Exchequer and was himself succeeded at the Board of Trade by William Huskisson. A new energy infused the Government and a period of reform began, instituted not according to a doctrinaire plan, but aimed at providing practical relief for long-felt evils. Peel undertook a major reform of the criminal law and Canning, while not radically changing the direction of the foreign policy that Castlereagh was pursuing in his last months, was much more aggressive in his support of liberal movements, particularly in South America. In the economic field a great many restrictions on internal and external trade were swept away; the navigation acts were amended, and a reform of the revenue system, begun by the institution of a commission of enquiry in 1818, was carried to completion. Legislation sponsored by the Board of Trade in 1822 and 1825 freed the colonies to export wherever they liked but they retained their heavy preferences in the United Kingdom market. Restrictions on the right of workers to organize were reduced but not entirely removed.

Within the Cabinet a faction critical of Canning's foreign policy and opposed to the freeing of trade came together under the leadership of the Duke of Wellington. Lord Bathurst was attached to the Duke whereas Wilmot Horton was on friendly terms with most of the leaders of the Canning party. He greatly admired William Huskisson and got on well with Frederick Robinson. Canning had little liking for Wilmot Horton,[1] but they were in agreement in supporting Roman Catholic emancipation and opposing parliamentary reform. It was as an earnest advocate of the principles of political economy that Wilmot Horton believed that the dispute over the Roman Catholics was obscuring the more fundamental economic problems.[2] Thus his devotion to the 'dismal science' explains the connection between the two great projects with which his name was associated, an attempt to find a compromise solution to the religious question,[3] and an effort to persuade his countrymen that the problem of unemployment could be solved by a planned large-scale emigration to the colonies, financed by and under the direction and control of the state.[4] In his faith in the efficacy of immediate

[1] Jones, E. G., 'Wilmot Horton', pp. 75–6.   [2] *Ibid.*, p. 134.
[3] *Ibid.*, Chap. VII.
[4] *Ibid.*, Chapters IX–XV.

government planning based on a study of statistics, he was an anachronism in the administrative machine of his day. Because of this impractical pursuit of visions he has been roundly and justly condemned as a policy maker. But his critics have sometimes been extremely injudicious. One veteran historian, in particular, has allowed his personal antipathy for an individual to cloud his historical judgement:

> . . . Robert Wilmot Horton [he writes] . . . (to put it mildly) adorned little that he touched, though he remained with Bathurst till the ministry fell; so, that it seems probable that Bathurst himself, as 'an experienced and energetic administrator', was the new broom—that with his shrewd practicality, he was behind the stock-taking and the reforms.[1]

Giving Lord Bathurst his due, he just did not possess the initiative to institute major reforms. Wellington's good friend, Mrs. Arbuthnot, the wife of the toadying patronage secretary to the Treasury (1809–1823), in criticizing Lord Bathurst, emphasized an aspect of his personality that provides a clue to the very vital part that he did play in bringing the new system into being.

> . . . he is a very bad minister for present times [she wrote], he likes everything to go in the old way, likes a job for the sake of a job, not to get money into his own pocket for there cannot be a more disinterested man, but he hates all innovations and would have done perfectly and been considered a very upright minister in the time of Sir Robert Walpole.[2]

'The old way', as Mrs. Arbuthnot indicated, could be a very old way; it went back to the time when non-parliament men had been active in government. Lord Bathurst saw no constitutional impropriety in taking the advice of his permanent officials or in devolving responsibility on them; to some of his contemporaries this must have appeared not only old-fashioned but dangerous.[3] Before a pronouncement can be made on the other aspect of Mrs. Arbuthnot's criticism, that Lord Bathurst liked a job for the sake of a job, a detailed study of his use of his patronage will be required. But that he was largely 'disinterested' is

[1] Beaglehole, J. C., 'The Colonial Office, 1782–1854', *H.S.A.N.Z.* I p. 181.

[2] *The Journal of Mrs. Arbuthnot 1820–1832*, I, pp. 158–9.

[3] See Pugh, R. B., 'The Colonial Office', p. 720.

obvious from the way in which he allowed Wilmot Horton to use his patronage plums to persuade several clerks to retire and thus to make their places available for more efficient men. Mrs. Arbuthnot was unfair to Lord Bathurst in one respect, for though he did not himself introduce innovations, he had the shrewd practicality not to prevent others from doing so. Wilmot Horton, writing many years later, pointed out the nature of Lord Bathurst's considerable talents and summed up his true stature:

> ... one of the most sensible and honourable of men. The character of Lord Bathurst as an efficient public servant at the head of an important political department, is very imperfectly appreciated by the English public. Undoubtedly his general politics did not respond to the movement of the latter days in which he lived; but in all cases where first rate practical good sense, and a rapid yet discreet view of intricate subjects was essentially required, Lord Bathurst possessed a mind far more able to grapple with difficulties than many of those persons who have underrated his political efficiency. . . . Above all for a sedulous discharge of the peculiar duties of his office as Colonial Secretary, no public man who has ever filled that situation has been more remarkable. . . .[1]

No money was available for additional help in the office when Wilmot Horton stepped into Goulburn's place at the very crest of the economy wave. He had had no previous official or colonial experience but his passion for remaking the world was concentrated on the task at hand and he made good use of existing talent, the clerks, the colonial counsel, and the tolerant Bathurst himself. Business got done in 1822 and 1823 but the brief notes on many letters tell their own story. Instead of Goulburn's neat, concise drafts of his replies there appears, in a bolder hand, 'Mr.——, Speak to me'; the clerks were being consulted. But there are other notes even more revealing than these requests for information. For example:

> I send a blank sheet with my Signature for a letter to the Audit Office, sanctioning in Ld. B's name the sums, or rather I believe, *sum*, in question.[2]

[1] Horton, R. W., *Exposition and Defence of Earl Bathurst's Administration of the Affairs of Canada, during the years 1822–1827 inclusive*, (1838), pp. 39–40.
[2] C.O. 323/196 On a letter from Major Gen. C. W. Doyle, 1822, f. 324.

or,

> Mr. Smith, Inform General Sarrazin that when the pressure of public business will allow me time to answer his last letter it will be answered.[1]

or,

> West Indies—a very concise reply.

This last note shows that Wilmot Horton was not long in the office before he had given it a more formal internal structure. The earliest specific reference to the existence of several departments under the direction of clerks was written by Wilmot Horton on a Treasury letter of 25 December 1822, requesting a list of the bills that were to be submitted to the next session of Parliament.

> MR. GORDON,
>   I have to request that the gentlemen at the head of the different Departments will give me a written list of such Acts of Parliament as they have reason to believe will be required in their Individual Departments.[2]

Individual clerks had for some time, possibly from the beginning, been associated with specific colonies and had been responsible for producing papers relating to their colonies when called upon. Clerks continued to be assigned to individual colonies but at least from 1822 onwards the empire was divided into geographical areas with a senior clerk responsible for each area. Registers of incoming correspondence were started in that year. In the first registers a section was assigned to 'Mediterranean' business, indicating the existence of a department handling the affairs of those colonies that had been under the war department of the office until 1816. The division of North America and West Indian business shows signs of having been arranged on the basis of volume of correspondence (see Appendix VIII) rather than on an identity of interests among the colonies. Under 'America' was included Jamaica, the Bahamas and Hon-

---

[1] C.O. 323/197 1823, f. 545. General Sarrazin was a French royalist general receiving a pension from the British Government who spent much of his time writing to the Colonial Office. The volume C.O. 323/210 is composed entirely of his correspondence, and the notes on it, covering only the years 1825 to 1828.

[2] C.O. 323/196, f. 201.

duras, Newfoundland, and the mainland North American colonies. Sierra Leone and the African Forts were included in the 'West Indies' section. There was a section for New South Wales and one for the other colonies in the eastern hemisphere.

From 1824 onwards the registers divided the Empire into four convenient geographical areas. A memorandum prepared for the new Secretary of State in 1828 shows the grouping and something of the internal arrangement of each department:[1]

Eastern Colonies	H. J. Short
New South Wales	G. Gairdner
Van Diemen's Land	H. S. Kelsey
Ceylon	V. Jadis
Mauritius	J. S. Martin
	(Extra Clerk)
North America	G. Baillie
Canada	E. T. Harrison
New Brunswick, Nova Scotia,	
Prince Edward Island	A. Blackwood
[Bermuda and Newfoundland]	
Mediterranean and Africa	P. Smith
Malta	W. G. Chapman
Gibraltar	W. Unwin
Ionian Islands	J. Walker
[Sierra Leone and the West African Forts. Consulates to the Barbary States.]	
West Indies	H. Taylor
	S. J. Blunt
	H. Drummond
	C. Talbot
	T. W. C. Murdoch
	(Extra Clerk)

[Fourteen Governments]

The Cape of Good Hope, not mentioned in this memorandum, was usually included in the 'Mediterranean and Africa' section, but occasionally it was grouped with the eastern colonies in the registers. Heligoland was also a wanderer, appearing at different times in all departments except the 'West Indies'.

[1] N.L.S., Sir George Murray Papers, June 10, 1828, vol. 168, f. 57. The words in brackets were later additions to the original memorandum.

Beginning in May 1822 all official letters entering the office passed through the hands of a registrar whose duties were later described as 'peculiarly "Confidential" but . . . not such as to demand a "more than ordinary degree of capacity".'[1] The registrar was the first person in the office in the morning so that it seems likely that he received each letter, noted the writer, the date on which it was written and when received, and made a brief note of its contents. Occasionally letters were marked 'Not to be registered'. Beginning in January 1823, each letter was also numbered. It was then sent to the appropriate department, unless it was of a confidential nature in which case it went to the person to whom it was addressed.

The senior clerks were allowed considerable initiative in the preparation of despatches; they drafted replies to routine queries and consulted the Under-Secretary or the Secretary of State on more important matters. It is probable that at this time they made oral inquiries at other departments on their own initiative;[2] certainly they held conversations even with secretaries of the Treasury[3] and the Post Office[4] and with senior officials at the Ordnance[5] on instructions from the Under-Secretary. Before 1822 persons standing in a special relationship to the Colonial Office, such as colonial agents, the secretary of the Colonial Audit Office, and the registrar of colonial slaves, frequently went directly to the senior clerks when seeking factual information. After the setting up of the departments they had even less need to approach the higher officials. With their increase in responsibility, prestige and influence, senior clerks became surrounded by job-seekers,[6] pension-seekers, and persons anxious to cultivate the acquaintance of those who stood close to the chair of colonial authority. Outgoing colonial governors found it useful

[1] C.O. 324/146 Hay to Spring Rice (Treasury), July 22, 1831.
[2] P.A.C. Sir Howard Douglas Miscellaneous Papers, George Baillie to Douglas, Nov. 6, 1824.
[3] *Ibid.*, July 13, 1825.
[4] C.O. 324/145 Horton to Freeling, private, Nov. 26, 1824.
[5] C.O. 323/202 Horton to Ulysses Burgh, Dec. 24, 1825, ff. 380–3; Horton to Hay, Dec. 27, 1825, f. 384.
[6] George Baillie intimated that the importunity of job seekers was a source of annoyance even to lesser members of the establishment long before this. Of one individual of doubtful reputation he wrote: 'Lord Bathurst decided upon confirming his appointment much to my relief as I had been *daily* tormented by him for *five* years.' P.A.C. Sir Howard Douglas Papers, Baillie to Douglas, Nov. 6, 1824.

to cultivate their acquaintance, and at least one governor carried on a private correspondence with the senior clerk responsible for his colony.[1]

The introduction of a system in which a number of individuals took part in the decision-making process made it essential that a record be kept of every decision taken or commitment made. Wilmot Horton insisted that all the scraps of paper on which Lord Bathurst wrote his brief informal minutes be preserved, but he was never able to persuade the noble lord to put the register number on each minute, which he requested William Huskisson to do when he became Colonial Secretary in 1827.[2] Individuals were also occasionally requested to make written reports on their understanding of what had been said at interviews with the Secretary of State or Under-Secretary. John Galt, the novelist, who carried on extensive negotiations on behalf of the Canada Company, later recalled that 'Mr. Horton generally had a shorthand writer in the room',[3] but since there are no reports of such negotiations in the records, it is likely that Galt mistook the function of Wilmot Horton's private secretary, who was forced to remain in the room because there was no other place for him to go in the overcrowded office.[4] Minutes, even brief informal minutes, were too infrequently written, except when the Secretary of State was in the country, to provide anything like an adequate record of how decisions had been reached; it remained for James Stephen to reduce the use of oral communication and put minuting on a regular basis when he became Under-Secretary in 1836. Even the register of papers fell into disorder when Wilmot Horton left the office and it was not until mid-century that an adequate and comprehensive central register was created.[5]

Just where Wilmot Horton got his ideas on office reorganization is not clear. A departmental system was in effect in several government offices and in the East India Company's office in London, which had been thoroughly reorganized in 1819. Pos-

[1] Governors had, of course, in the past on occasion corresponded confidentially with clerks who were the agents for their colonies.
[2] P.A.C. New Brunswick 'A' Series, vol. 39, f. 131.
[3] See P.A.C. Galt Papers, 000232 to 000246. I am indebted to Dr. Frederick Cogswell for this reference.
[4] See below pp. 126–7.
[5] See Pugh, R. B., 'The Colonial Office', p. 721.

sibly this last event, when Edward Strachey, James Mill, and Thomas Love Peacock were brought into the India Office and given high positions,[1] provided him with his model.

When Wilmot Horton was changing the arrangement of the office and making himself familiar with the details of conducting an empire, he found that, in addition to Lord Bathurst, there was another man connected with the office to whom he could turn for expert advice and assistance. This was James Stephen, junior, whom Lord Bathurst had appointed in 1813 'to peruse and report his opinion on the Acts transmitted from the Colonies for the Royal Confirmation.'[2] Stephen, the son of one of the most active workers in the cause of slave emancipation and the nephew of William Wilberforce, himself had a great abiding interest in the welfare of the slaves, so much so that at the time of his appointment Henry Goulburn thought it advisable to caution him not to divulge official information to the 'African Society'.[3] No man was ever more conscientious in maintaining official secrecy. He was to find his medium not in organized agitation but in the influence which his great industry and intelligence gave him in the department responsible for supervising the government of the slave colonies.[4] Until the entry of Wilmot Horton into the Colonial Office this influence was almost entirely confined to his review of colonial legislation, though immediately after the war Goulburn had found it convenient to consult him regarding the colonies ceded by France and Holland and on one or two other legal questions.[5]

Until 1823 Stephen's position was that of a barrister in private practice who was paid a fee of three guineas for each colonial act reviewed[6] (of which one-twelfth was deducted for the payment of the 'gentleman' employed to transmit the act to him). In

---

[1] Foster, W., *The East India House its History and Associations*, pp. 194–7.

[2] Following the abolition of the old Board of Trade by Burke's Act in 1782, a Mr. Selwyn had been appointed by the Home Office to perform this task. James Stephen succeeded a Mr. Baldwin. See: C.O. 323/197 James Stephen to Wilmot, April 21, 1823, f. 162.

[3] C.O. 138/145 Apr. 7, 1813. This letter was drawn to my attention by Dr. Alexander Murray.

[4] See Knaplund, P., *James Stephen and the Colonial Office 1813–1846:* also Taylor, H., *Autobiography*, II, 301.

[5] C.O. 323/197 Stephen to Wilmot, April 21, 1823, f. 162.

[6] *Ibid.*

the beginning he found it to his professional advantage to be in receipt of official business[1] and he expressed a willingness on one occasion to give an opinion on occasional legal questions referred to him without extra charge to the department.[2] By 1820, however, the number of colonial acts being sent to him annually for review was more than double what it had been at the end of the war and he was finding that he had to make 'some considerable sacrifice of general professional business' in order to discharge his official duties.[3] Whereas Goulburn had never taken up Stephen's offer to perform extra services for the office, Wilmot Horton, 'the pleasantest of companions and the most restless of politicians', called so frequently on Stephen's services that it became impossible for him to carry on his private practice. That he made a great financial sacrifice in entering official life is indicated by the fact that in 1824, despite his being extensively employed in the Colonial Office, he had an income of £2,700, of which only £1,000 came from government.[4] A letter to Wilmot Horton of 21 April 1823, which might be regarded as Stephen's application for a permanent appointment in the Colonial Office, is worthy of extensive quotation as an illustration both of his attitude to public employment and of his relations with the office up to that time.

Shortly after the close of the late war Mr. Goulburn requir'd my assistance on some legal questions which had then occurr'd with respect to the Colonies ceded to Great Britain by France and Holland. Under his direction I prepared the Drafts of various Orders in Council relating to the Laws of the Ceded Colonies, & Instructions to the Governor of Mauritius respecting the formation of a Charter of Justice for that Island. Since your accession to office I have been employed in a similar manner under your immediate direction, & during the last twelve months the business which I have thus transacted has been far greater in amount, & more varied in its nature, than at any former period. It has consisted in the perusal of various documents transmitted from the different Colonies relating to legal subjects—in writing opinions on the questions arising on such documents—in preparing the

[1] C.O. 323/187 Stephen to Goulburn, Aug. 6, 1817, f. 510.
[2] *Ibid.* Nov. 18, 1817, f. 528.
[3] C.O. 323/192 Stephen to Goulburn, July 20, 1820, f. 135.
[4] See N.L.S. Sir George Murray Papers, Memorandum of James Stephen, Feb. 16, 1830, vol. 171, f. 55.

drafts of Orders in Council, Acts of Parliament, & Instructions to the Governors of the Colonies on matters of a legal nature—in making searches among the documents preserved in Lord Bathurst's office for papers connected with the various subjects already noticed—& finally in frequent personal conferences with yourself at Downing Street in relation to the different questions thus brought under my consideration. In effect my employments have comprized not only the functions of a Counsel, but many also of those which belong to the Solicitors of the different Boards in other Departments of Government. Like them I have brought the questions laid before me into such a shape & compass as to enable Ld. Bathurst to obtain the opinions of the Attorney and Solicitor General upon any important points, without imposing on them the necessity of perusing a mass of voluminous and partly irrelevant documents.

All the services thus described I have performed since the year 1815 gratuitously, except in a single case, viz. that of preparing the Drafts of Certain Orders in Council relating to the tenure of lands in Gibraltar. The great and increasing demand which these engagements are now making on my time has imposed on me the necessity of requesting your attention to the situation in which I find myself placed.

After an experiment of long continuance, during which my powers of body and mind have been unsparingly exerted, I am satisfied that it is impossible for me, and I think for any man, at once to perform the various duties required of the Counsel to the Colonial Department, & to hold any considerable share of business as a Barrister. I have indeed suffered materially in my health from the exertions I have made to combine the two pursuits, and, as you are aware, have been for the last three months compeld[*sic*] to make a temporary abandonment of my general professional business. Without continuing to make this sacrifice (at least to a very considerable extent) I feel it would be impossible for me, even with health perfectly re-established, to execute to my own or to your satisfaction the various duties with which you have intrusted me. If I should have permanently to relinquish the general practice of my profession, it would be the loss of an income which for some time past has exceeded £1500 per annum, and the prospects which such a measure of success may reasonably be thought to open. This is a sacrifice which of course I could not venture to make without some pecuniary compensation. The question which you desired me to consider was—What ought the nature and amount of that compensation to be?

In answer to this question, I have in the first place to state, that I conceive that any compensation which may be made to me for devoting my time to the legal business of the Colonial Department should be not less secure in its tenure than the Salaries allowed to the Gentlemen permanently placed on the establishment of Lord Bathurst's office. . . .

The *amount* of my official income is less important to me than an assurance of its permanency. In the conversation which took place between us it was suggested that £1000 pr. annum would be a moderate compensation for the whole of my services (the references on the Colonial Acts included)—it being understood that in consideration of such an income I should attend the Under Secretary of State in person whenever he might require it, and should discharge the several duties already mentioned as my first and principal occupation giving to my profession only such portions of my time as could be employed in it, without inconvenience or delay to the public business. These terms I should be content to accept if I might rely on their stability.[1]

Some further letters were exchanged between Stephen and Wilmot Horton in the following months,[2] and at the end of October Stephen's proposals were submitted to George Harrison, one of the secretaries to the Treasury.[3] After conversations, Harrison, on behalf of the Treasury, sanctioned the proposal that Stephen's emolument from the Colonial Office be made up to £1,000 a year, including his fees, and concurred in a letter which it was proposed that Lord Bathurst should send to him guaranteeing the permanence of his appointment.[4] No provision was made for clerical assistance or for his office, but he was allowed stationery.[5] For his services in 1822 he was paid £250 in addition to what he had received for his review of colonial acts.[6]

Wilmot Horton's administrative methods required a greater degree of effort from his clerks than some of them were able or

---

[1] C.O. 323/197 Stephen to Wilmot, April 21, 1823, ff. 162–164.
[2] See C.O. 323/197 Horton to Stephen, Oct. 8, 1823 in reply to Stephen's letter of Sept. 4, f. 248.
[3] C.O. 323/197 Horton to Harrison, Oct. 21, 1823 (draft). This draft is incorrectly dated as 1822, f. 250.
[4] C.O. 323/197 Harrison to Horton, private, Nov. 4, 1823, f. 246.
[5] C.O. 323/197 Stephen to Horton, Nov. 7, 1823, f. 166.
[6] C.O. 323/199 Harrison to Horton, July 6, 1824, f. 254.

willing to give. But the 'mutiny' of which Greville had warned him did not continue, probably because he fought against the deductions for superannuation to which Goulburn and Lord Bathurst had agreed.[1] In doing this he adopted the argument of Joseph Planta, the Permanent Under-Secretary at the Foreign Office,[2] who maintained that the Treasury had not the authority to override the orders in council by which salaries had been set. When a Treasury order was sent 'requesting' that the agreed deductions begin from 5 April 1822 Wilmot Horton replied that:

> ... payments of that nature in this Department being made under authority of the King in Council his Lordship feels that he has no power to comply with their Lordships' request.[3]

This show of resistance was overcome by the passing of a new Superannuation Act[4] authorizing the measure proposed by the Treasury. The deduction of five per cent was made to apply, however, only to salaries of over £200 instead of from £100 upwards. A deduction of two and a half per cent was ordered on all salaries from £100 to £200 whereas the previous arrangement was for a payment of two and a half per cent on salaries from £50 to £100. This Act was very unpopular and remained in force only two years, its repeal[5] being accompanied by a repayment to the persons concerned of all sums deducted from their salaries. Wilmot Horton expressed his opinion on such cheese-paring in a statement to the House of Commons four years later accusing Joseph Hume of being chiefly instrumental in preventing government departments 'from being manned in a way necessary for the efficient discharge of their duty'.[6]

[1] See above pp. 41–4.
[2] Both Horton and Planta were at Eton and Oxford and both were charter members of Grillon's Club, a non-party political organization of friends who met for dinner every alternate Wednesday while parliament was in session. See *Grillion's Club from its Origin in 1812 to its Fiftieth Anniversary* —by P.G.E., London 1880. Copies of two of Planta's letters to the Treasury, one of them dated June 28, 1822, are bound with a Treasury letter of August 13, 1821. See: C.O. 323/194, ff. 165, 167.
[3] C.O. 324/144 Wilmot to Harrison, July 1, 1822.
[4] 3 Geo IV. Cap. 113.
[5] By Act 5 Geo IV. Cap. 104.
[6] *Parl. Deb. New Series*, XIV, 1080, March 3, 1826.

In 1822, however, the financial stringency allowed little scope even for a bold man. But it did not prevent the introduction into the office in October of Thomas Hyde Villiers,[1] an able young Benthamite who had been at Cambridge with Charles Austin, Edward Strutt and John Romilly and formed one of their circle in London of which John Stuart Mill was also a member. At twenty-two years of age Villiers accepted a position as junior clerk at a salary of £150 a year. In order to make even this post available it was necessary to take advantage of a provision in the Superannuation Act of that year which allowed a man to be retired if a saving was produced on the establishment after providing for the retired allowance and for the salary of his successor.[2] Edward Barnard, the first assistant clerk, was thirty-six years of age, had been in the department almost eighteen years, and was receiving £525/8/4 a year. He was given a retired allowance of £200 a year and the agency for New South Wales, a new post the creation of which had been recommended by Commissioner Bigge, which paid him £600.[3] Villiers remained in the Colonial Office until July 1825, then entered upon a political career in the House of Commons; he was secretary to the Board of Control when he died prematurely in 1832.[4] His worth to the Colonial Office during his three years there is clearly indicated by brief minutes on many letters and by his being raised to the status of a senior clerk with a salary of £600 in January 1824. He shared with Wilmot Horton and Major Thomas Moody[5] the authorship of a number of letters defending the government's policy on slavery which appeared in the *Star* newspaper in 1825 under the pseudonym of 'Vindex', and which were later collected and published as a pamphlet.[6]

In 1823 the gloomy shroud of economy suddenly lifted. Frederick Robinson, succeeding Vansittart as Chancellor of the Exchequer, had the good fortune to be able to reduce taxes. The addition of James Stephen to the establishment in that year was only one of the changes in the office resulting from the prosperity of the country, another significant one being that,

[1] See Taylor, H., *Autobiography*, Chapter. V.
[2] 3, Geo. IV. Cap. 113, Sect. 15.
[3] See *Hist. Rec. of Aust.*, Series I, vol. X. p. 728.
[4] Taylor, H., *Autobiography*, I, pp. 146–151.
[5] See below. pp. 71–4.
[6] See Jones, E. G., 'Wilmot Horton', pp. 157 and 368.

whereas only about £100 had been spent on extra clerks and copying in the two years 1821 and 1822 combined, a total of almost £500 was paid out for this purpose in 1823. One item in this expenditure was the payment of a full-time salary to Francis Kelsey[1] from 22 February 1823 to the end of the year. He received £126/7/6 together with his regular pension of £239/10 paid in consideration of his services as extra clerk from 1798 to 1816. His return to the office for the year was in answer to the demand for able and experienced clerks.

By the beginning of 1824 trade had so improved that 'Prosperity' Robinson was able not only to predict a budgetary surplus but to make provision for rebuilding Windsor Castle and for the establishment of a national library and a national gallery. Wilmot Horton, taking advantage of every opportunity that presented itself, was able in the first six months of 1824 to effect the retirement of three clerks, the resignation of a fourth and to introduce eleven new persons into the office.

Henry Taylor described this evacuation thus:

> The business of the Colonial Office was growing every year more important . . . and it was in utter confusion. Several old clerks who took but little interest in it were therefore to be provided for elsewhere, and several new ones to be brought in, who were to be chosen with a view to obtain more effective service.[2]

Wilmot Horton, who had justified a large expenditure on pensions, spoke of it more bluntly:

> When I came into office, some of the old Clerks were positively worn out, & the whole thing must have stood still if serious efforts had not been made to remodel it.[3]

James Stephen, whose judgements of Colonial Office clerks were more frequently harsh[4] than generous, emphasized other aspects of the change:

> The Clerks of the office, when I first became acquainted with it, were engaged in the performance of duties corresponding with the

---

[1] See Appendix III.
[2] Taylor, H., *Autobiography*, I. p. 64.
[3] Horton to Lushington (Treasury), confidential, June 3, 1826, quoted in Jones, E. G., 'Wilmot Horton', p. 39.
[4] See Williams, T., 'The Colonial Office in the Thirties', *H.S.A.N.Z.* (1943) II., pp. 144–5.

appellation they bear. They had little or nothing to do beyond transcribing Despatches and other papers. At a great expence to the public, a great body of Clerks of this description was super-annuated to make room for younger men, who would be able to execute intellectual as well as mere manual labour.[1]

James Chapman, the chief clerk, was within three years of the age at which he could have been granted his superannuation allowance without the certificate of incapacity from infirmity of body that was the ostensible ground for the grant of a pension of £1,100 a year.[2] There can be little doubt that it was not the prospect of a pension at fifty-seven but the opportunity to introduce a certain 'William G. Chapman' into the office that hastened his retirement. William G. Chapman's appointment was not announced until 20 March,[3] two weeks before the retirement of the chief clerk, yet it was made effective from 5 January, thus giving him seniority over three other assistant clerks whose appointments were announced six weeks earlier.[4] Chapman had entered Eton between the election of 1811 and that of 1814 but left before the election of 1814.[5] He remained in the Colonial Office for many years but was considered unfit for promotion.[6]

Thomas Baillie, the ninth clerk, resigned to accept the post of surveyor general and commissioner of Crown lands in New Brunswick. According to his own statement[7] he was first given the consulship of Tunis with a salary of £1,800 and a competent retiring pension after twenty years. He subsequently exchanged this for the post in New Brunswick '. . . with equal or greater advantages and under the same conditions and promises on the part of His Majesty's Government'. His income in his first year in his new office was almost £4,000, a sufficient inducement for him to relinquish his £365 as an assistant clerk; much later, however, he came into conflict with the colonial authorities over his income and pension rights.[8] John Forbes,

---

[1] C.O. 537/22 Memorandum of James Stephen, March 30, 1832, No. I.
[2] H.C. 1825 XIX, pp. 17–18.
[3] C.O. 324/139 Bathurst to the Postmaster General, March 20, 1824.
[4] *Ibid.* Feb. 1, 3 and 5, 1824.
[5] *Eton School Lists 1791–1850*, p. 87.
[6] C.O. 537/22 Aug. 29, 1840, No. 29.
[7] Baillie, Thomas, *Summary of the case of Mr. Thomas Baillie, etc.* (1858).
[8] See MacNutt, W. S., 'The Politics of the Timber Trade in Colonial New Brunswick, 1825–1840', *C.H.R.*, XXX (1949), pp. 47–65.

the fourth clerk, retired at the age of thirty-eight after twenty-two years in the office. He received a pension of £650, considerably above the minimum authorized by Parliament, 'A saving on the Establishment being produced after providing for the retired allowance and for the salary of his successor.'[1] No additional incentive to induce his retirement has come to light; it is possible that none was needed since he was apparently in poor health.[2] He died in 1830 as the age of forty-four.

One of Wilmot Horton's arrangements caused a minor crisis in the ministry. An opportunity to offer an unwanted clerk an alternative office occurred when William Huskisson decided to give up the agency of Ceylon which he had received in 1801 at the time of his retirement as Under-Secretary. His decision, he said later, was prompted by Wilmot Horton, after a debate in the House of Commons in 1823 during which his holding of the sinecure was attacked.[3] They were agreed that the Ceylon agency was a necessary one but that the temper of the House was such that it was advisable to give it a non-political character and reduce the salary of £1,200 which was attached to it. Wilmot Horton immediately stated that the Colonial Office wanted the agency for 'a hard working man'. On a visit to Huskisson in the summer of 1823 he explained in detail the importance of having the agency as soon as possible 'to facilitate a new official arrangement for giving greater efficiency to his office.'[4] Huskisson reported the conversation to Canning[5] but apparently not to Liverpool, from whom he was trying to obtain a pension as compensation for the loss of his sinecure.[6] On the third of October Huskisson wrote to Wilmot Horton 'to hold your Hand and your Tongue for the present', for he was 'positively enjoined not to send the letter or take any step at this moment.'[7] The Prime Minister, unaware of Wilmot Horton's

[1] H.C. 1825 XIX, pp. 17–18.

[2] See C.O. 323/189, ff. 169–70.

[3] Br. Mus. Add. Mss. 38745, Huskisson Papers, Huskisson to Arbuthnot, private and confidential, Dec. 11, 1823 (draft), ff. 143–4. There are two drafts of this letter, much corrected, and an additional copy bound in this volume.

[4] *Ibid.*, ff. 144–5.

[5] *Ibid.*

[6] Liverpool to Bathurst, Dec. 21, 1823, *Bathurst Papers*, p. 555.

[7] Br. Mus. Add. Mss. 38745 Huskisson Papers, f. 5 (draft).

designs on the agency, had his own plans[1] and Huskisson's announcement of his resignation in late November was followed immediately by a letter to Lord Bathurst from the Duke of Wellington urging him to give the post to Charles Arbuthnot, recently retired as patronage secretary to the Treasury and successor to Huskisson as first Commissioner of Woods and Forests.[2] Lord Bathurst immediately announced his intention of obliging his friend and received warm thanks from Lord Liverpool— 'though I could not have brought my mind to have said a word to you about the agency of Ceylon, which I considered as exclusively in your gift.'[3]

Wilmot Horton, breaking the news of Lord Bathurst's decision to Huskisson—'he (Lord Bathurst) would be *displeased* with me if I were to say anything upon the subject, or rather if it were known that I had said anything upon it'—advised him to 'shew the difficulties that will probably attach to the question in the House of Commons.'[4] Huskisson wrote to Arbuthnot[5] and consulted Canning[6]—this was 'the Death blow to Colonial Agency generally'—who reacted with his usual effusiveness, 'In my life I was never more astonished & confounded.'[7] Arbuthnot did not surrender quickly, however. In the end he gave in, on New Year's day 1824, perversely, because Liverpool was arranging for Canning to intercede with Huskisson on his behalf—'I could not consent to be under any obligation to Canning.'[8]

In February 1824 the agency was given to Richard Penn, the third clerk, at a salary of £800 a year; Penn, in turn, gave up the Mauritius agency, with its salary of £500, to Peter Smith. Penn was also given a retired allowance of £750 a year.[9] At the age of forty, after twenty-three years' service, he was able to retire to his easy task at the agency on an income of £1,550 a year. Soon after his retirement he became a Fellow of the Royal

---

[1] Br. Mus. Add. Mss. 38745, Huskisson Papers, Huskisson to Liverpool, Nov. 20, 1823, f. 97 (draft); Arbuthnot to Huskisson, Nov. 23, 1823, f. 117.
[2] *Bathurst Papers*, p. 552.
[3] *Ibid.*, pp. 552–3.
[4] Br. Mus. Add. Mss. 38745, Huskisson Papers, most private and confidential, undated, f. 132.
[5] *Ibid.*, Dec. 3, 1823 (draft), ff. 124–6, 128–30.
[6] *Ibid.*, Dec. 4, 1823, ff. 134–5.
[7] *Ibid.*, Dec. 5, 1823, f. 137.
[8] *Bathurst Papers*, pp. 556–7.
[9] H.C. 1825 XIX, pp. 17–18.

Society and in 1829 published a book on a method of secret writing that he had invented while in the war department. He also wrote humorous works on fishing and chess, illustrated by his friend, Sir Francis Chantrey. He died in 1863.[1] The troubles over the Ceylon agency did not end on his appointment, for Mr. Hoblyn 'of the Treasury', who had been Huskisson's deputy, made difficulties over handing it over.[2] According to Arbuthnot, the work was not performed by Hoblyn but by the deputy's deputy, Mr. Howard.[3]

Six clerks and the librarian remained of the old establishment. Only two of these had been of senior rank under the 1822 classification; Adam Gordon, who now became chief clerk, and George Wilder, a very reliable and experienced clerk whose new post, that of second clerk acting as registrar and as deputy to the chief clerk, was probably created especially to fit his talents. The other four clerks retained were promoted to the senior class, and each was put in charge of a department; Henry Short (Eastern), George Baillie (North American), Peter Smith (Mediterranean and Eastern), and Hyde Villiers (West Indies). The librarian, George Mayer, was also given senior status and received an assistant.

Eight new clerks were appointed, four as assistant clerks and four as junior clerks.[4] There is no indication that any system of examination was used, but the need for able clerks was so great that some care was taken in choosing them; at least one man who was offered a post was told that he would have to retire if his work proved to be unsatisfactory.[5] The time was propitious. The army and the navy lists were choked with experienced officers on half pay, and ancillary military departments were still reducing their establishments as their structure was rationalized under the direction of the Duke of Wellington. Opportunities for young gentlemen in the traditional pursuits of war and government were, therefore, very scarce. But since the

[1] D.N.B., XV, 752.
[2] Br. Mus. Add. Mss. 38745 Huskisson Papers, Horton to Huskisson, Feb. 28, 1824, ff. 209–10.
[3] *Ibid.*. f. 123.
[4] The order in council setting out the new establishment was passed March 19, 1824.
[5] See Appendix VII.

administration was enjoying the favour of the House of Commons at this time there was no pressing need to conciliate members by allowing them to make nominations to the new places.

The most outstanding of the new clerks was twenty-three-year-old Henry Taylor. He had several qualifications to recommend him. He had been twice to the colonies; once to Quebec as a young midshipman in the Navy in 1814,[1] and again, for a few months in 1820, as a clerk in the storekeeper general's department at the headquarters of the Windward and Leeward Islands Command at Barbados.[2] This clerkship he had received when he was sixteen through the good offices of Charles Arbuthnot who was a friend of his father.[3] He had lost his employment in 1821, when the storekeeper general's department was absorbed in the Commissariat, and returned to his father's home in the north of England for two years where he employed himself in extensive reading and writing.

When Taylor moved to London in October 1823, he intended to earn his living by writing. Early in January, however, he was recommended to Wilmot Horton by Dr. Henry Holland, an eminent literary as well as a medical man. Two articles published in *The Quarterly* and his having been 'in official habits' were sufficient testimony of his ability to gain Lord Bathurst's approval.[4] He was elevated to the rank of senior clerk in January 1825, becoming head of the West India department, which post he continued to hold for over forty-seven years.[5] As a minor poet of some distinction Taylor associated with Southey, Wordsworth and Tennyson. In 1836 he wrote a short cynical work on political philosophy, *The Statesman*, which was frowned on in his own day but has brought him considerable posthumous fame. Gladstone, who had been political under-secretary a few months previously, read the original proofs. In 1927, it was republished with an introduction by Harold Laski and reprinted in 1957 with a new introduction by Leo Silberman. The crown of success truly came in 1958 with its publication as a paperback in New York, bearing on its front cover the misleading appeal 'the

[1] Taylor, Henry, *Autobiography*, I, 28.
[2] *Ibid.*, p. 36.
[3] *Ibid.*, p. 33.
[4] *Ibid.*, p. 64.
[5] *Ibid.*, II, p. 297.

famous classic on the art of personal advancement', with an introduction by C. Northcote Parkinson. Taylor was several times considered for higher office and declined the post of Permanent Under-Secretary in 1847 in order to leave himself time for his literary pursuits.[1]

Taylor was, of course, exceptional, as was Chapman. Of the other six clerks appointed at this time, one resigned in 1826, one died in 1829[2] and the other four went on to become senior clerks, all of them achieving that rank by 1840. The resignation of Thomas Hay, the next in rank to Taylor, after two and a half years' service suggests that he may have proved unsuitable. The others were Samuel Jasper Blunt, Gordon Gairdner, Edmund T. Harrison, and Arthur Blackwood, all of whom had creditable records of service in the department. Harrison died, from overwork it was said, in 1840;[3] the rest appear in the early Colonial Office Lists issued after 1860.[4] Blackwood was only sixteen years of age when he was appointed, Gairdner was twenty and Harrison twenty-one.

How welcome the new clerks were and how quickly the able among them would be entrusted with confidential duties is shown by Taylor's report of his introduction to colonial business:

> I plunged into it at once, and by a letter which, though not dated, must have been written in March 1824, it appears that I was working in Downing Street night after night till one or two in the morning, in the preparation of a paper which was immediately printed at the Foreign Office private press and laid before the Cabinet; and in furnishing materials for a speech to be spoken by Mr. Canning on the subject of the measures then in agitation for meliorating the condition of the slaves. My 'remarks nearly in full', I wrote to my father, 'were sent to Canning; cram, cram, cram, and on Tuesday night *evolabat oratio.*'

The paper for the Cabinet seems to have been elaborate and

---

[1] An excellent description of the personality of Henry Taylor may be found in Burn, W. L., *Emancipation and Apprenticeship in the West Indies* (1937), pp. 128–132.

[2] Hugh Drummond was paid up to January 27, 1829. J. S. Martin was appointed in April 1829 in consequence of a vacancy by death. See C.O. 323/211 Hay to J. Stewart (Treasury), July 10, 1829.

[3] C.O. 537/22 August 29, 1840, Nos. 28 & 29.

[4] Gairdner's worth is assessed by Williams. See Williams, T., 'The Colonial Office in the Thirties' *H.S.A.N.Z.* (1943), II., p. 148.

voluminous. 'A clerk was sent to see the types broken up and receive the printer's declaration that he had delivered all the impressions taken off and kept no copy. The impressions delivered I was directed to keep under lock and key and give to no one.'[1]

To his stepmother he wrote:

At this time I have scarcely a word or thought for you but such as are born and die in Downing Street; but I shall be glad to send my thoughts . . . by way of a diversion from foolish governors, furious houses of assembly, methodists, and slaves.[2]

In April Major Moody[3] of the Royal Engineers, a person as controversial as James Stephen, junior, was introduced into the office. He had served extensively in the West Indies going there first as private secretary to Sir James Leith and Lord Combermere successively,[4] and later serving as a member of the commission appointed by Lord Bathurst in 1821 to enquire into the state of certain captured negroes. Moody had made an extensive study of French and Dutch systems of colonial government and of theories of colonization,[5] but it was for his forthright opinions on slavery that he was best known. While acting as commissioner in the West Indies he had quarrelled with his colleague[6] and come under the fire of the anti-slavery group, but he retained the confidence of Lord Bathurst.[7] The *Edinburgh Review* found his talk of 'physical causes and the philosophy of labour' abhorrent.[8] Lord Bathurst, however, was inclined to set some store by 'his doctrine that repose is in truth the governing principle of a black in a Tropical Climate',[9] though he deemed it expedient not to use Moody's arguments too openly.

[1] Taylor, H., *Autobiography*, I, pp. 67–8.
[2] *Ibid.*, p. 68. His own word is confirmed in the records.
[3] The only Major Moody to appear in D.N.B. was the father of Maj.-Gen. Richard C. Moody, first governor of the Falkland Islands, 1841. D.N.B. XIII, 779–80.
[4] C.O. 323/195 Combermere to Wilmot, Dec. 15, 1821, f. 108. He brought himself to the attention of government in 1812, when still a captain, by submitting a report on the shortage of coin; see C.O. 537/151 June 4, 1812.
[5] There were two long unsigned memoranda in the Colonial Office records which reveal Major Moody's wide interests. See C.O. 323/199, ff. 19–23, and C.O. 323/204, ff. 53–8.
[6] C.O. 854/1 Instructions to Moody and Dougan, Sept. 9, 1822.
[7] C.O. 324/75 Lord Bathurst's Minutes, 'Slaves', Jan. 4, 1823, f. 120.
[8] See Jones, E. G., 'Wilmot Horton', p. 158.
[9] C.O. 324/75 Lord Bathurst's Minutes, 'Sierra Leone' 1825, f. 62.

His comments on a paper prepared by Moody on instructions to be given to the commissioners of enquiry sent to Sierra Leone in 1825 clearly reveal this attitude:

> Major Moody's Observations are very sensible, and would make a good Pamphlet, but I doubt very much the sending anything of that kind to the Commissioners: and still more the prudence of laying them in that shape before Parliament, as it would create a flame, & we should be charged with giving a decided bias to the future report of the Commissioners. Major Moody's Observations are founded on certain abstract principles. . . . It would be said that the very last thing which we should wish to infuse into the Commissioners is any system whatever. We want from them an accurate report of the facts, and there is nothing so fatal to investigation of truth, as the having a preconceived System: for we are all too much disposed to bend the facts in some measure so as to make them suit the System. We should have all the Abolitionists in full cry against us, as subscribing to Major Moody's opinions, not only as they might be guarded by your alterations, but as they are known to be or represented to be.[1]

Moody's appointment in 1824 was ostensibly as an additional secretary, resident in Great Britain, to assist in the execution of the details connected with the royal commissions of enquiry in the colonies.[2] He received £800 a year and the services of a clerk paid from the sums voted by Parliament for the commissions. In effect, however, he was an additional senior member of the office with specialized knowledge and interests of great utility. He summed up his position briefly shortly after he left in 1828:

> Although I had been designated as Home Secretary to the Colonial Parliamentary Commissioners, it is well known . . . that my real duties had been more connected with the West India Department, the colonial finance accounts, and the correspondence and details relative to Emigration.[3]

Study of colonial Blue Books of statistics, interviews with the

---

[1] C.O. 324/75, f. 62.

[2] There were two at that time (1) The Commission of Enquiry into the Administration of Criminal Law in the West Indies, and (2) The Commission of Enquiry into the State of His Majesty's Settlements, the Cape of Good Hope, Ceylon and Mauritius. A further commission was sent in 1825 to report on the state of the laws in Sierra Leone.

[3] C.O. 323/209 Moody to Hay, July 14, 1828, f. 139.

auditors, and conversations with the colonial governors in order to explain to them how they might better prepare their returns,[1] revealed the need for a common system for regulating the expenditure of the public revenue in the Crown Colonies.[2] His work on emigration was sufficiently important for William Huskisson to designate him as an intended commissioner of the board which he proposed to set up in London in 1828 for the sale of colonial lands.[3]

In 1824 Major Moody was associated with Stephen in one of Wilmot Horton's great contributions towards bringing order to the administration of the Empire. The general instructions to colonial governors had not been altered for more than three decades,[4] and that summer Stephen was given the task of going through large numbers of documents and proposing amendments.[5] Moody was instructed 'to assist & cooperate with him in the examination of this subject';[6] he was consulted on several questions, but his own great concern was that an article should be included to instruct the governors '... as to the mode & form in which they should prepare their own accounts with the public, & which will facilitate their examination in the Audit Office.'[7]

Major Moody provided the Colonial Office, as James Stephen did in that decade, with an informed mind unhampered by the day-to-day routine preparation of despatches for the eight o'clock mail. They were able to give thought and attention to major issues and to prepare memoranda on technical questions, legal and financial. Each had a philosophic turn of mind which related every detail to the wider aspects of Empire and their opinions were worthy of the respect they received. Moody's work on finance and emigration, while valuable, was not so far-

[1] C.O. 323/200 Moody to Horton, July 20, 1824, ff. 412–3. C.O. 323/204 Memorandum for R. W. Hay, Oct. 13, 1825, f. 337.

[2] See C.O. 323/199, ff. 19–23.

[3] C.O. 323/209 Maj. Moody and Col. Cockburn to Sir George Murray, June 13, 1828, ff. 135–6.

[4] Beaglehole, J. C., 'The Royal Instructions to Colonial Governors', pp. 49–52. Cf. Manning, H. T., *British Colonial Government after the American Revolution*, pp. 81–2.

[5] C.O. 324/145 Wilmot Horton to Stephen, July 31, 1824, p. 18.

[6] C.O. 324/145 Wilmot Horton to Moody, July 31, 1824, p. 18.

[7] C.O. 323/200 Moody to Horton, July 20, 1824, f. 413. The governors' instructions for this period can be found in series C.O. 380 and C.O. 381.

reaching as on the vital question of slavery. His rigid application of the dry principles of political economy to plantation
slavery was resented by the humanitarians, but the emphasis
on the probable economic consequences of emancipation influenced Colonial Office officials from Lord Bathurst to James
Stephen and Henry Taylor to insist on two principles, 'the *right*
of the Planter to *Compensation* and the *duty* of the Public to prepare by Religious Instruction the Minds of the Slaves for such a
change.'[1] When he left the office in 1828 Moody left a testament
to the pleasant personal relations existent there:

> . . . during the period of upwards of four years I never had the
> slightest misunderstanding with any person, nor ever had con-
> veyed to me from any one the slightest censure or reproof.[2]

His connection with the colonies was renewed in 1831 when he
was sent to Van Diemen's Land as a commissioner to investigate claims arising from a war against the aborigines.

About the same time as Moody entered the office there also
became attached to it a most peculiar man, an hour's conversation with whom would have stilled the ardour of any romantic
poet to write an epic on the exotic Mediterranean. His name
was Abraham V. Salamé, and he came into British official life
out of Alexandria, Egypt, via the British embassy at Ankara. A
gifted man with a useful talent can overcome many obstacles,
especially in an alien society where an obsequious perseverence
may be forgiven. When Salamé arrived in England in January
1816 he found the government departments ill-served in their
correspondence with the eastern and southern Mediterranean,[3]
since Mr. Lusignan, the Oriental Colloquial Interpreter to
George III wrote '. . . but his own language the Greek. . . . He
only spoke the Turkish',[4] and the Arabic interpreter in the
Colonial Office was such in name only. Six months after his
arrival in England Salamé went as interpreter with Lord

---

[1] C.O. 324/75 Lord Bathurst's Minutes, 'Sierra Leone', 1825, f. 63: also
Taylor, H., *Autobiography*, I, 121–9.

[2] C.O. 323/209 Moody to Hay, July 14, 1828, f. 139.

[3] For an account of the difficulty of getting adequate translations in the
government departments in the late eighteenth century, see Anderson, M.S.,
'Great Britain and the Barbary States in the Eighteenth Century', *Bull.
Inst. Hist. Res.*, XXIII (1956), p. 106.

[4] C.O. 323/198 Memorial of Salamé to Lord Bathurst, received April 2,
1824, f. 133.

Exmouth's expedition to Algiers, and in 1819 was given an appointment in the Foreign Office at a salary of £200 a year;[1] a request for a similar salary from the Colonial Office was turned down on the excuse that Hume's economy campaign made it impossible. In 1822 his Foreign Office salary was raised to £300. His memorial to the Colonial Office in April 1824 was, he says in the enclosed letter, accompanied by recommendations from the Dukes of York, Wellington, and Rutland, from the Earl of Westmorland and from Viscounts Melville and Exmouth. Of this formidable list only that of the Duke of York appears in the correspondence. Salamé was granted £150 a year effective from the beginning of 1825.

Almost immediately he began to accuse Peter Smith, the senior clerk in the Mediterranean department, who had carried on the negotiations with him on behalf of Lord Bathurst, of having, by astute negotiation, persuaded him to accept £50 a year less than Lord Bathurst had been prepared to grant him— 'I was always timid for my own interests.'[2] Alternatively whining and threatening he tried, first through Smith, then directly with Hay, the Permanent Under-Secretary appointed in 1825, to obtain £50 a year denied to him in 1824. In 1828 John Barrow of the Admiralty, for whom he also did some translating, interceded on behalf of his 'miserable situation' and pointed out how hard it would be to replace him;[3] so his demands were satisfied. One comment in Barrow's letter shows that Salamé did not confine his long petitions to the Colonial Office:

He has written two or three times to me for an amanuensis—his long history proves that he can do very well without one. . . .[4]

According to Salamé's own statements his work for the Colonial Office was consistently greater than that which he had to perform for the Foreign Office, more than half as much again in 1827, and it was more varied:

. . . and curious enough, it was a Correspondence from the 4 extremities of Africa, and of the following mixture. Marochine

[1] C.O. 323/198 Salamé's Memorial, April 2, 1824, f. 135.
[2] C.O. 323/209 Copies of letters written to Smith enclosed in Salamé to Hay, June 12, 1828, ff. 192–206.
[3] C.O. 323/208 Barrow to Hay, June 21, 1828, ff. 16–17.
[4] Ibid.

dialect from the West; Turkish, Algerine and Tunisine Moorish, from the North; African, or corrupt Arabick from the centre and south; and pure Arabick from the East Coast, besides two Greek Documents.[1]

That strange year in Colonial Office history, 1824, brought yet another specialist into the fold. To law, finance and language was added religion. The memorandum drawn up in December at Lord Bathurst's instigation speaks for itself:

It is proposed to form a new establishment for the more efficient supply of a duly qualified Ministry[2] the duties of which will be discharged by a Chaplain General for the Colonies acting under the immediate control of a Board, consisting of the Archbishops of Canterbury and York and the Bishop of London. The primary object of such appointment, and that to which the attention of the Chaplain General is at present to be principally limited is the careful investigation of the characters and attainments of such Clergymen as may present themselves as candidates for Chaplaincies [marginal note: 'professional employment'] in any Foreign Station. . . .

An additional charge may also devolve upon the Chaplain General in a correspondence with all Colonial Chaplains, where ecclesiastical authority has not yet been established and in a general superintendence *of their conduct* [marginal note: 'under the direction of the same Board'].

To carry such a measure into effect it will be necessary to procure an office in some convenient situation for the daily attendance of a clerk, who will be required to preserve copies of all correspondence & the several testimonials produced on behalf of the *candidates*.[3]

This office, which remained in existence until 1831,[4] was modelled on that of the Chaplain General of His Majesty's Forces set up in 1809.[5] The man selected for the post was the Reverend Anthony Hamilton, Secretary of the Society for the

[1] C.O. 323/209 Salamé to Hay, June 12, 1828, f. 197.

[2] 59 Geo. III, Cap. 60, had made provision for persons to be admitted into Holy Orders especially for the Colonies.

[3] C.O. 323/199 December 1824, ff. 439–441: see also C.O. 323/203, ff. 314–8.

[4] C.O. 324/146 Goderich to the Archbishop of Canterbury, Jan. 20, 1831: Hay to Hamilton (Treasury), Jan. 20, 1831.

[5] Copies of the Treasury minutes of Nov. 3, 1809 and Feb. 6, 1810 are included in C.O. 323/203, ff. 306–307.

Propagation of the Gospel in Foreign Parts, a body with wide colonial connections[1] which, aided by parliamentary funds, supported missionaries, churches, and schools in North America and New South Wales, and, until a new body was established in 1824,[2] in the West Indies. He received £500 with £150 for a clerk and office and an allowance of stationery. The impetus for his appointment came with the increased interest in the extension of the Established Church overseas, aroused by the part religious instruction was to play in the 'melioration' policy in preparing the slaves for freedom. In addition to the creation of two West Indian bishoprics and the sending out of two bishops and twenty clergymen to the West Indies, arrangements were made in the autumn of 1824 for the retirement of the Bishop of Nova Scotia, who had been unable to perform his functions for several years, and for consecrating a new bishop in his place. Several new archdeaconries were also authorized, in the West Indies, in North America, and one in New South Wales.

Every summer the British administrative machine braked sharply and then proceeded at a gentle pace without actually stopping. After the strain of the parliamentary session senior ministers spent weeks in the country, farming, visiting, shooting, and dining. Clerks, careless of uncopied letters, went off for long holidays,[3] to visit home, to visit the Continent, or to a house or shooting party which had been earned by a winter's assiduous social cultivation. Even a hard-pressed under-secretary could allow himself some holidays and in the rural quiet gain some recompense for the postponement and delay of business by talking freely with his colleagues from other departments. In the summer of 1824 Wilmot Horton sprinkled his wit with serious talk on Roman Catholic emancipation and emigration which had not yet become his 'amiable weaknesses', but were, with his official preoccupation with slavery, his primary political interests. But his *cri de coeur* that summer was of the strain on his health from excessive work, and the need for a second under-

---

[1] See his evidence before the Canada Committee of 1828: H.C. 1828 VII (569) 559–63.

[2] Incorporated Society for the Conversion and Religious Instruction and Education of the Negro Slaves in the British West India Islands.

[3] See C.O. 537/22 Stephen's Minutes: Oct. 19, 1840, No. 31; Dec. 31, 1840, No. 32; Sept. 28, 1842, No. 34.

secretary to share his administrative burden. His friend Robinson, the Chancellor of the Exchequer, whose own love of ease was notorious, was not too difficult to persuade and, having secured Robinson's consent, he urged Lord Bathurst to take appropriate steps. Early in October 1824 Lord Bathurst wrote to the Prime Minister:

> The inclosed Letter from Wilmot Horton to Robinson is in fact the substance of more than one Letter on the same subject to me, and of many conversations since I return'd to the neighbourhood of London. He assured me that he had conversed with Robinson on the subject when Robinson was with him at Sudbrook,[1] and that Robinson as well as other persons with whom he had conversed agreed in opinion, that there was a necessity of additional assistance in my office. I told Wilmot Horton that I wish'd he would capitulate to Robinson what he had said to him and to me, and that if Robinson's answer was favourable, I would in that Case submit the whole for your favourable consideration.
>
> I am myself quite confident that the business of the office is much increased; and that the best and most efficacious way of obtaining assistance is by the Appointment of a second Under Secretary. My only hesitation has been, how far the proposition would be acceptable in the H. of Commons. Robinson seems satisfied that it will not meet with any serious opposition, and I understand from Wilmot Horton that Canning does not apprehend any; but he had not much communication with him, and the question being one of expense, it falls more under the Chancellor of Exchequer's Office. It is under his sanction that I now submit it for your consideration, and I trust you will give me a favourable answer.[2]

The reply of 'fidgetalis', as Huskisson dubbed the premier, was immediate, cautious, and hedged around with all the possible considerations which could be urged against the increase.

> I could wish the Question as to the additional Under Secretary of State in your Office, to be postponed, till we Meet in Town in December.

[1] Wilmot Horton leased Sudbrook Park in 1824 and bought the house and estate in 1825. It was situated in the village of Petersham near Richmond Park. He kept a town house in Montagu Square. See Jones, E. G., 'Wilmot Horton', p. 34.

[2] Br. Mus. Add. Mss. 38299, Liverpool Papers, Bathurst to Liverpool, Dropmore, Oct. 3, 1824, f. 126.

As far as it is a Matter of Expense, I should make no difficulty about it, if you think the addition of Importance. But I confess I think it a very material Question as regards Parliament.

It is just the sort of Question which might revive the Ill humour in the House of Commons which is fortunately overcome, and will raise again the Question so often agitated, as to the necessity of the office of Third Secretary of State, or the expediency (if it is necessary) of uniting it with the India Board, Board of Trade or some other office.

You will understand that I am far from saying, that the proposed addition is not necessary. If this should be the case, and the Cabinet Ministers in the House of Commons are prepared to defend it, I shall certainly acquiesce in it, but I wish the Decision to be taken after Communication with Canning, Peel and Wynn,[1] as well as with Robinson, and I shall be glad likewise to have it considered, whether additional assistance might be afforded in any other way, than by appointing another Under Secretary, for if it could, it would certainly create less observation & prejudice, than must be expected to arise from that particular appointment.

I throw these observations out now for Consideration. The Question is altogether new to me, and it would never do to decide upon the appointment, and afterwards find some of our Colleagues not satisfied with the necessity of it.[2]

Almost two years later Wilmot Horton described his feeling of frustration when Lord Liverpool's letter arrived:

I remember that, at the time, Lord Bathurst was very much amused at my indignation; but I was suffering so much that I really could not help being splenetic when that answer came.[3]

'Reiterated application',[4] in Horton's phraseology, succeeded in accomplishing the appointment of a second under-secretary by an order in council of 5 July 1825.[5] In the meantime, Lord Liverpool's suggestion that additional assistance be afforded in another way was taken up, most notably by having James Stephen entirely renounce his private practice and devote his

[1] Charles Wynn, President of the Board of Control; the four ministers mentioned were the government leaders in the Commons.
[2] Br. Mus. Add. Mss. 38299, Liverpool Papers, Liverpool to Bathurst, Walmer Castle, Oct. 5, 1824.
[3] Horton to Lushington (Treasury), confidential, June 3, 1826, quoted in Jones, E. G., 'Wilmot Horton', p. 42.
[4] Ibid.
[5] C.O. 324/145 Bathurst to the Lord President, July 1, 1825, p. 148.

full time to the public service. This step was arranged by Wilmot Horton and proposed to the Prime Minister by Lord Bathurst. Lord Liverpool agreed to the payment of a salary of £1,500 a year and that 'the Income should be permanent and free from deduction';[1] it became effective by an order in council passed 2 February 1825.[2] By the same order in council another senior clerk was added to the establishment, Henry Taylor being promoted to the post with salary effective from 5 January.

In 1825 almost twice as many letters were received as in 1824 and papers laid before the House of Commons were three times as long as those presented in the previous year.[3] About the time that he had received the consent of the Treasury to the appointment of a second under-secretary, Wilmot Horton prepared an elaborate printed table comparing the volume of business in the office of the Secretary of State for War and the Colonies in 1806, when a second under-secretary was appointed, in 1816 when the office was abolished, and in 1824 the last complete year before its restoration. Appended is a comparison of the size of the Colonial Office establishment with that of several banking houses in London.[4] This table was evidently intended to be used for the purpose of convincing the House of Commons of the necessity for the larger establishment if questions should be asked. On 2 August, an order in council was passed authorizing further additions to the establishment; an assistant registrar, a clerk of the parliamentary papers and précis writer, an additional assistant clerk, an additional junior clerk, and a fourth class of clerks, known as assistant junior clerks, three in number, 'to obviate in some degree the inconvenience which has been experienced from extensively employing Extra Clerks in the

---

[1] N.L.S. Sir George Murray Papers, Memorandum of James Stephen to Sir George Murray, Feb, 16, 1830, vol. 171, f. 55. Stephen was under such severe attack in 1830 that he found it necessary to defend his appointment; 'This order was *not* drawn up by myself, nor seen by me until it had actually passed.'

[2] C.O. 324/145 Bathurst to the Lord President, Jan. 31, 1825, p. 76.

[3] In 1824 the letters received comprised 35,836 folio pages: in 1825 there were 61,608 folio pages. The increase in returns to the House of Commons was from 22 papers of 780 printed folio pages to 36 papers of 2,200 printed folio pages. See: Horton to Herries (Treasury), December 15, 1826, Section 9. This letter appears without enclosures in C.O. 324/146, p. 63, and with some enclosures in C.O. 701/14.   [4] See Appendix VIII.

Ordinary dispatch of Business.'[1] On the appointment of a second under-secretary it was assumed that James Stephen's duties would be lightened,[2] and he agreed to act as counsel to the Board of Trade in addition to his other duties, it being arranged that that department should pay one-third of his salary and contingent expenses. Provision was also made for a payment of £150 each to two clerks to act as private secretaries to the under-secretaries of state. Since Hyde Villiers resigned about this time it was found convenient to discontinue the fifth senior clerkship provided in the order in council of 2 February. The post of registrar appeared for the first time on the establishment laid down on 2 August, the status being that of an assistant clerk, but George Wilder continued to hold the post, serving also as second clerk and deputy for the chief clerk.

At the end of 1823 the staff of Lord Bathurst's office had consisted of one under-secretary, a private secretary, ten clerks, a librarian, and a part-time legal counsel. In August 1825 there were on the establishment two under-secretaries, three private secretaries, fifteen clerks, two librarians, two registrars, a précis writer, also acting as clerk of the parliamentary papers, and a full-time counsel shared with the Board of Trade. The number of extra clerks employed had more than doubled. In addition Major Moody was employed full time, though disguised under the title of secretary to the commissions of enquiry, and Archdeacon Hamilton carried on ecclesiastical correspondence and advised on religious matters. And Stephen, Moody, and Hamilton received allowances to enable each one to employ a clerk. Of the other main departments of government only the Foreign Office and Board of Trade increased their establishments at this time:[3] the Board of Trade from twenty to twenty-six,[4] the Foreign Office from thirty-four to forty-eight.[5] But in the case of the Foreign Office the increase was largely nominal, resulting from Canning's policy of transferring supernumerary clerks to the establishment.[6]

[1] C.O. 324/145 Bathurst to the Lord President, July 30, 1825, p. 40.
[2] Memorandum to Sir George Murray, Feb. 16, 1830, f. 56.
[3] 'Returns of the Number, and pay or Salaries, of all Persons Employed in Public Departments: 1797–1827.' H.C. 1830–31 VII (92) 299–415.
[4] Ibid., pp. 310–11.   [5] Ibid., pp. 306–7.
[6] Temperley, H., The Foreign Policy of Canning 1822–1827, p. 263.

Yet such was the favour of the Government in the House of Commons, and so much had the colonies come to public attention, that the increased expenditure for the Colonial Office passed in the next session of Parliament almost without comment. Joseph Hume was very agreeable. When Wilmot Horton openly attacked him he mildly replied that:

> He really had a right to expect far different treatment from the hon. Secretary; for last year he had allowed an increase of £1700 in the estimate for the colonial department to pass without observation.[1]

The further increase in the 1826 estimate for the contingencies in the offices of the Secretaries of State drew only the facetious comment that:

> . . . the government kept governors at the Cape of Good Hope and other colonies, against whom so many complaints were made, that nearly the whole time of the persons engaged in the colonial department was occupied in examining those complaints.[2]

Thus the fear expressed by Lord Liverpool in 1824 that the appointment of a second under-secretary in the Colonial Office would bring about a further debate on the necessity of a separate department for the colonies proved to be entirely groundless.

The neat unimaginative efficiency of the Goulburn era ending in 1821 gave way under Wilmot Horton to the 'utter confusion' which Henry Taylor noted on his entry into the Colonial Office in 1824. Wilmot Horton's early supervision of the office was like his speech-making '. . . full of zeal and animation, but so totally without method and arrangement that he is scarcely intelligible.'[3] The school in which he was learning the habits of official business was one of the hardest ever faced by a new administrator. The melioration of slavery was only one of several problems successfully surmounted,[4] but it was the most

---

[1] *Parl. Deb., New Series*, XIV, 1081, March 3, 1826. The increase Hume referred to was that in the estimates for 1825.

[2] *Ibid.*, 1290, March 10, 1826. Lord Charles Somerset's conduct at the Cape was under attack during the session of 1826.

[3] *The Greville Memoirs*, ed. Henry Reeve (1874), II, 98.

[4] An excellent brief outline of melioration may be found in Mellor, G. R., *British Imperial Trusteeship 1783-1850*. (1951), Chap. II.

important one; for the extra burden placed by the Treasury and
Parliament on the Colonial Office by this policy was sufficient
to elicit their sanction for extra expenditure. Emigration, particularly to North America, was strongly urged by Wilmot
Horton with the support of Peel and Goulburn. Parliamentary
grants were obtained, in 1823 and 1825, for pilot schemes, of
which careful records were kept, to show the practicability of
large-scale planned emigration as a means of relieving the distress of the poor[1] of the British Isles. Under the auspices of the
Colonial Office three joint stock companies were projected for
the development of colonial lands in Canada, Van Diemen's
Land, and Australia.[2] Steps towards a settlement of constitutional problems were taken in the Canadas by the abortive
attempt to unite the provinces in 1822 and by the Canada Trade
Act of 1823, in New South Wales by parliamentary legislation
in 1823 following the report of the Bigge Commission, in the
Cape of Good Hope by the despatch of a royal commission of
enquiry, and in Newfoundland. In 1824 an extensive survey of
the customs establishments in North America and the West
Indies was undertaken at the instigation of the Board of Trade.

In three and a half years the change was so great that the
structure of the office was not so much rebuilt as created. The
need had come from the pressure of business, the opportunity
came in the prosperity of the years from 1823 to 1825. Wilmot
Horton boldly wove the new web around the solid core of Lord
Bathurst's good nature. Few public men could have delegated
authority so extensively to inexperienced young men and yet
retained their affection and respect.[3]

[1] Wilmot Horton's part is discussed in Jones, E. G., 'Wilmot Horton',
pp. 185-199.
[2] The policy of developing the colonial lands by the incorporation of
large land companies was defended by Wilmot Horton in the House of
Commons during a debate on joint stock companies. See *Parl. Deb. New
Series*, XVI, 244, Dec. 5, 1826.
[3] Taylor, H., *Autobiography*, I, 68-72.

THE NEW OFFICE AT WORK
1825–1830

As a government department expands, the difficulty of securing
unity of action increases. There is always a danger that it may
become a mere collection of specialized compartments with no
common policy or principles of procedure. In facing this problem of devolving authority the new Colonial Office started with
some advantages. It grew up around the personalities of its experienced political heads, and its unity was established in the
person of Lord Bathurst whose 'office, rank, age, manners and
talents' entitled him to the deference of his subordinates.[1] So
long as they gave him their full confidence, he was able to leave
the stamp of his experience and mastery of detail on those issues
in which he took an interest. But the political stability which
had produced such a minister was an isolated phenomenon, and
in 1825 he was already, at sixty-three years of age, by far the
oldest of the ministers at the head of onerous departments.[2] It
was obvious to an intelligent observer that before long he would
have to retire and, in preparation for that time, Wilmot Horton
intended that the Permanent Under-Secretary should become:

> . . . the depository of all knowledge of which the Secretary of State
> must daily avail himself . . . .[3]

Eight years earlier when Castlereagh had faced the problem
of selecting a permanent under-secretary for the Foreign Office,
he had revived an old practice by appointing a member of the
permanent establishment, Joseph Planta, his private secretary,

---

[1] Taylor, H., *Autobiography*, I, p. 72.
[2] Lord Liverpool, Canning, and Huskisson were fifty-five at that time.
Lord Bathurst survived all of them, and was in fact still in office as Lord
President of the Council when the last of them, Huskisson, was killed on
September 15, 1830. Eldon, the Lord Chancellor, was seventy-four but his
work was notoriously in arrears.
[3] C.O. 537/22 James Stephen's Memorandum, March 30, 1832, No. 1.

who had previously served as clerk and précis writer in the office.[1] In the Colonial Office there was James Stephen, whose experience and ability made him the obvious choice, but his appointment would almost certainly have raised that storm in Parliament which Lord Liverpool had feared from the creation of the post.[2] How great the risk would have been is shown by Joseph Hume's attack in the ensuing session of Parliament on Stephen's attachment to the office as legal counsel:

> Nothing could be more objectionable to the colonies than such an appointment. He was the son of the person whom the colonists supposed to be their greatest enemy; and to put him in an office in which every communication to and from the colonies must pass through his hands, was highly objectionable. The appointment had outraged the feelings of the colonists more than any other act of the government.[3]

Robert William Hay (1825–1836), who became Permanent Under-Secretary, was innocuous enough to escape attention. His father, George William Auriol Drummond, a clergyman, was the son of an Archbishop of York, Robert Drummond. The name of Hay was adopted when the family received the earldom of Kinnoull, which had formerly been in the Hay family.[4] He was born in Westminster in 1786 and matriculated at Christ Church, Oxford, in 1803, receiving his B.A. in 1807 and M.A. in 1809.[5] In 1812 he became private secretary to Lord Melville, First Lord of the Admiralty, and before coming to the Colonial Office was a commissioner of the Victualling Office.[6] Lord Bathurst's friendship for Lord Melville and Hay's conservatism[7] were probably leading factors in his appointment, but he was well known to Wilmot Horton, for they had been at Christ Church together and both were charter members of

---

[1] Webster, Sir Charles, *The Foreign Policy of Castlereagh 1815–1822*, pp. 36–7.

[2] See above p. 79.

[3] *Parl. Deb., New Series*, XIV, 1081, March 3, 1826. Hume seems to have mistaken the appearance of a salary for Stephen in the accounts as evidence of a new appointment.

[4] 'Robert William Hay' in *Alumni Oxonienses 1715–1886*, II, 632.

[5] *Ibid.*, He died May 9, 1861 in Malta at the age of 74.

[6] H.C. 1821 XIV (602) 137.

[7] Taylor H., *Autobiography*, I, 232.

Grillon's Club, of which Hay became secretary in 1831.[1] There are two portraits of him and one of Wilmot Horton in the British Museum's copy of the *Portraits of the Members of Grillion's Club*, which contains portraits of many of the leading statesmen of the nineteenth century. Hay's years at the Admiralty had brought him into intimate contact with John Barrow,[2] Sir Joseph Banks' successor as the great advocate of British exploration of the unknown regions of the globe, and the staunchest imperialist of the day. Barrow's son, George, was appointed a junior clerk in the Colonial Office and became Hay's private secretary. Some precaution was probably taken against the possibility of parliamentary disapproval of Hay's new post, since Henry Taylor states that 'Whilst his friends were in office he had obtained a grant of a dormant retiring pension. . . .'[3]

Taylor dismisses Hay as 'certainly not equal to the office he held',[4] and there is little evidence to gainsay this verdict. In the absence of extensive official minutes to indicate what part of official policy was his own and what originated with the Secretary of State, the political Under-Secretary, the clerks, and other members of the establishment, his private letters in the official records[5] throw some light on his personality and business habits. They are usually short and show a greater concern for personalities than for ideas. While Wilmot Horton was trying to reduce the number of private letters written by colonial governors to supplement their official despatches,[6] Hay instituted a dubious practice by encouraging lesser colonial officials to write to him privately;[7] thus he received and acknowledged unofficial re-

[1] See *Grillion's Club from its Origin in 1812 to its Fiftieth Anniversary*—P.G.E. (1880) and *Portraits of the Members of Grillion's Club. From 1813 to 1863*, (1864), No. 20. Both are mentioned in Jones, E. G., 'Wilmot Horton', p. 15. See also C.O. 537/40 Chas. R. Vaughan to Wilmot, Paris, Aug. 26, 1822 'our friend Hay is here. . . . He talks of leaving on Friday for Brussels.' Lord Bathurst's son, Seymour, was a member of Grillon's Club in 1825.

[2] Barrow wrote his autobiography, Barrow, Sir John, Bart. *Autobiographical Memoir* (1847), and several works on exploration and articles on colonial policy. From letters listed in the calendar of *The Banks Letters* edited by Warren R. Dawson (1958) it is clear that Barrow's enthusiasm helped to sustain Banks' interest in overseas projects.

[3] Taylor, H., *Autobiography*, I, p. 232.

[4] *Ibid.*

[5] C.O. 324/89, 91, 93, 94.

[6] C.O. 854/1 Circular of Sept. 1823.

[7] There is an interesting example of Hay's ingratiating himself with an outgoing colonial official in the Sir George Murray Papers. Major T. L.

ports on colonial governors, a practice that was subversive of the trust traditionally reposed in those officials. There was no deep dark purpose in this. To him the colonial civil service in its many branches was like a club with whose members he kept in touch by means of personal letters. He was a very sociable person and an enthusiastic botanist who encouraged outgoing colonial officials to send him specimens for his own collection and those of the societies of which he was a member.[1] The use of these friendly letters betrays an attitude to colonial government that was a carryover from the English system where the informal social ties of the race meets and the country-house parties were important in binding the centre to the extremities. This attitude had no place in the new centralized colonial system and James Stephen, when he became Permanent Under-Secretary, very properly took steps to suppress such letters.

Stephen and Henry Taylor had no liking either for Hay, his philosophy of government, or his methods of business. They emphasized the positive role of the Permanent Under-Secretary in making policy on all issues except those where politics and parties were affected by the matter in question.[2] Hay accepted the traditionalist position that the Permanent Under-Secretary should give advice only when called upon to do so; even trifles should be handled by the Secretary of State. In a memorandum prepared for Lord Goderich, on 2 April 1832,[3] he made it clear that his concept of the Under-Secretary's role did not differ substantially from that described by the Permanent Under-Secretary of the Foreign Office in 1870 who wrote, 'the under-secretary of State is merely a channel . . . he has no independent action at all.'[4] The only duties which Hay regarded as peculiarly his own were the supervision of the internal affairs of the office, the preparation of routine reports and of circular despatches and

---

Mitchell, a protégé of Murray's, was sent to New South Wales in 1827 to become Surveyor General. He sent private letters, intended for Hay, to Murray, to ask his opinion whether they might with propriety be sent to Hay. By the time these letters arrived in England Murray had become Secretary of State. N.L.S. Sir George Murray Papers, vol. 168, ff. 1–4, 8–11, 47–8, 105–6, 130–1.

[1] Burn, W. L., *Emancipation and Apprenticeship in the British West Indies*, p. 127.

[2] Taylor, H., *The Statesman*, p. 101; C.O. 537/22 Stephen's Memorandum on the Colonial Office, Mar. 30, 1832, No. 1.

[3] C.O. 537/22, No. II.   [4] Craig, Sir J., *A History of Red Tape*, p. 73.

notices, and the preparation of all papers relating to the secret service money, the last presumably because such papers were kept under his personal care.

If Hay left any mark on the colonial empire during his career as Permanent Under-Secretary, it must be looked for in the Mediterranean and Africa division which he kept under his personal direction throughout his eleven years in the office. On his entry in July 1825 the Eastern division was also put under his supervision. Wilmot Horton, by retaining the West Indies and North America, kept for himself the more troublesome self-governing colonies and most of the business arising from the great issues of slavery and emigration, also the new questions of persuading North American assemblies to undertake the expense of supporting their own civil establishments[1] and of arranging for the payment of salaries to the Custom House officers in North America and the West Indies in lieu of the fees that had recently been abolished.[2] He also continued to handle most interdepartmental questions of a general nature and to supervise the work of the chief clerk, the registrar and the librarian. In the number of letters written and received by the two Under-Secretaries the division of labour was fairly even[3] under this arrangement, but in later years supervising the internal affairs of the office was considered to be the duty of the Permanent Under-Secretary, weighing in the balance against the parliamentary duties of his political colleague.[4]

While Hay was cutting his teeth on the relatively tractable eastern hemisphere, Wilmot Horton attempted to make him familiar with the tougher problems of the legislative colonies. Since personal intercourse, rather than a written exchange of views, was the preferred method of conducting both interdepartmental[5] and intramural business, it was easy to arrange for Hay to sit in on conferences and to take part in conversations. He was present at the discussions with the Treasury and Board of Customs over Custom House salaries,[6] and a whimsical minute

[1] For the complicated problem of the 'civil list' see: Manning, H. T., 'The Civil List of Lower Canada', *C.H.R.*, XXIV (1943), pp. 24–47, also Harvey, D. C., 'The Civil List and Responsible Government in Nova Scotia', *C.H.R.*, XXVIII (1947), p. 365.
[2] See Chapter VII.   [3] See Appendix VIII.
[4] See: C.O. 537/22 James Stephen's Memorandum, Mar. 30, 1832, No. I.
[5] See Webster, Sir C., *The Foreign Police of Castlereagh, 1815–1822*, p. 33.
[6] See Chapter VII.

of Lord Bathurst's also reveals his presence when his former patron was the central figure:

Wilmot Horton:

> I presume that your Lordship will acquiesce in this proposition, which Lord Melville came & read over one day here to Hay and and myself.

Lord Bathurst:

> I am not capable of forming an opinion but am ready to acquiesce, altho' I should prefer first asking the opinion of Hibbert & Carrington, if they would call & have the Paper read to them by you or Hay, as nearly as possible in the tone of voice in which Lord Melville read it to you both & thereby conciliated your acquiescence.[1]

Under-secretaries had many lessons to learn in the art of official correspondence. How well Lord Bathurst was qualified to teach is shown by his handling of the volatile Wilmot Horton. The busy Under-Secretary was guilty of slipshod writing at times, so Lord Bathurst made a practice of checking his letters whenever it was feasible to do so. Sometimes he drafted letters himself for Wilmot Horton's signature, quite properly since the formal introductions always ascribed to the secretary of state the opinions expressed. Differences occasionally arose because Lord Bathurst was inclined to be more forthright than Wilmot Horton who, early in his official career, had become over-cautious after finding himself in difficulties through the giving of too hasty directions to a clerk and the too hasty signature of an unread letter. On that occasion he had expressed '. . . a peculiar, perhaps an unreasonable unwillingness ever to say a harsh thing in an official letter that the Receiver cannot take notice of.'[2] Lord Bathurst's drafts, therefore, did not always go unquestioned.

[1] C.O. 324/75 Lord Bathurst's Minutes, 'West Indies', Apr. 15, 1826, f. 256. George Hibbert was the agent of the assembly of Jamaica and George Carrington the agent of the assembly of Barbados.

[2] C.O. 323/201 General Thomas to Wilmot Horton, October 12, 1824, f. 375. Goulburn had no such compunction about using an official letter to express an honest opinion. His answer on one occasion could hardly have been more direct: '. . . the offer . . . would justly subject you to prosecution and punishment if I did not suppose it to originate in very gross ignorance. . . ." C.O. 324/137 Goulburn to John Malcolm, Jan 13, 1816, p. 126.

Wilmot Horton:

> I understand that your Lordship drew up this letter to Watson. Is not your representation rather too strongly expressed in the third page?

Lord Bathurst:

> I have no objection to leave out the words 'and strongly disapproves' but you will recollect that the whole band of missionaries will make common cause against the spirit of this Act.[1]

But once, at least, a blow to Wilmot Horton's pride caused him to draft a sharp reply which Lord Bathurst urged him to reconsider:

> On looking over your letter again after the first surprise of seeing Lord Chatham's shall have been over, you will I think be inclined to soften some expressions.
> I have marked what I think had better be alter'd or omitted. If you wish to introduce the suggestion that persons of as high if not higher Rank correspond with an Under Secretary, it may perhaps be better to introduce it at an earlier part of the Letter, but I am inclined to think it is below *your* dignity to do so.[2]

There were many lessons in the art of judicious double talk and evasion:

> You have gone further than is necessary in saying that the Directors are '*in no degree* responsible for the delay'. They are responsible for some part of the delay in the *progress* of the business. The accurate Statement is that the Cause of the delay did not originate with the Directors, but if you wish to cavil you may say that the Directors ought not in justice to be considered as having given occasion for the delay.[3]

And an adequate mixture of praise and humour:

> I think your letter to Mr. Gladstone a very good one, & the Question an unpleasant one. This is not the occasion on which you might introduce another Question but watch your time when you may ask him. When he made his late large purchase in Demerara?[4]

[1] C.O. 324/75 Lord Bathurst's Minutes, 'W. Indies Generally', Sept. 22, 1826, f. 73.
[2] *Ibid.*, 'Miscellaneous', N/D f. 243. The Earl of Chatham was Governor of Gibraltar.
[3] *Ibid.*, 'Canada Company 1825–6.' f. 187.
[4] *Ibid.*, 'Slavery 1826–7', N/D f. 149. The reference is to John Gladstone, M.P., father of William Ewart Gladstone, a prominent Liverpool merchant with West Indian interests.

These informal minutes appear regularly in the records only for those months each year which Lord Bathurst spent in the country, leaving Wilmot Horton responsible for the cares of the office in London. Their method of consultation is well illustrated by the following exchange of minutes concerning a matter which appears to have been brought to Lord Bathurst's attention by somebody else in the office, possibly by the head clerk in the West Indian department:

Wilmot Horton:

> As the case of Pamela Munro (which bye the bye I had never seen until it returned from your Lordship) appears to me to involve more important results than any other case which has been sent from the West Indies since I have been in Office you will forgive me inundating you with papers.

Lord Bathurst:

> I must *submit to* but cannot possibly *forgive* the inundation proposed.
>
> As I go to Mr. Bathurst's at Sydney tomorrow beyond the reach of Answers by return of Post, and shall have little time to attend to *many* Papers while I am there, you will act accordingly. Send a messenger if there should happen to be anything *very urgent.* My direction will be Sydney Park Newnham Glostershire. I return Saturday Ev^g or possibly Sunday Ev^g.
>
> I keep the McMillan Papers in expectation of the Inundation.[1]

The good humour, the clear memory, and the ability to say exactly what he wished to say remained part of the evasive personality of Lord Bathurst to the end of his years in the Colonial Office. From 1819 onwards he found himself in disagreement with the financial and economic policies of the Government and, where these affected the colonies, he tended to leave decisions to his colleagues and subordinates or to resort to tactics of obstruction and delay.[2] On defence, religion, and law his observations were always acute. Long experience and sound political sense had also given him a far more just appreciation of colonial susceptibilities than any of his subordinates except James Stephen. When unable to study a question per-

---

[1] C.O. 324/75 Lord Bathurst's Minutes, 'Compulsory Manumission', Oct. 10, 1826, f. 145.
[2] See Chapters VI and VII, particularly pp. 219–20, 286–91.

sonally he preferred Stephen's opinion to that of any other person, though, if a question was vital, he insisted on examining the papers relating to it and formed his own opinion. After 1820 he probably spent more time in the country than he had hitherto, but he continued to attend to his duties at least as regularly as most of his colleagues in other departments. A rooted dislike of controversial issues became more intense, and as business increased, a habit of procrastination became much more pronounced. Fortunately, the relations between him and Wilmot Horton were such that the Under-Secretary dared to remind his superior that allowing an issue to lie forgotten did not dispose of it.[1] The old man, tired, impatient of the burden of reading endless official papers,[2] and inclined to relax too thoroughly on social occasions,[3] sat on his coach and held the reins; he could choose the direction but he could not stop the horses from galloping on.

By judiciously selecting their subordinates and trusting them Lord Bathurst and Wilmot Horton succeeded in devolving on the senior clerks a large part of the administrative load. Senior clerks were men of privilege. They had no set hours of attendance,[4] and usually wrote their drafts at home, since the frequent interruptions made composition difficult at the office. Henry Taylor could talk with his Benthamite friends at breakfasts, which sometimes went on until three o'clock in the afternoon,[5] without feeling that he was neglecting his duties; his serious work was done at home in the evenings. While at the office senior clerks spent their time seeing people on business, conferring with their superiors, and giving directions to assistants and juniors.[6] When the Treasury sought to improve the efficiency of the civil service after 1830 by insisting on regular hours of duty for all clerks, the Colonial Office strenuously defended its attitude:

[1] See, for example, the note on C.O. 188/31 Sir Howard Douglas to Bathurst, Dec. 29, 1825.

[2] There are many indications in the records of his dislike of reading in his last years in the office. Greville described him in 1830 as 'stone-blind', *The Greville Memoirs*, eds. Strachey and Fulford, I, 376.

[3] His drinking had become a topic for jest and there is more than one reference to his becoming drunk at cabinet dinners.

[4] C.O. 324/146 Hay to J. K. Stewart (Treasury), July 22, 1831, p. 317.

[5] Taylor, H., *Autobiography*, I, 159.   [6] *Ibid.*, I, 143.

So long as certain definite tasks are required of any Public Servants as the fixed and indispensable measure of their duty, it will be vain to look to the same persons for any additional voluntary exertions. . .

. . . no person filling the Office of Senior Clerk in this Department could neglect his duties for a single day, without the fact attracting the attention of the Secretary or one of the Under Secretaries of State. The daily intercourse which takes place with them upon every branch of Public business transacted in this Department, affords their immediate Superiors a far more certain test of the amount & efficiency of their exertions than could be supplied by the most exact Registry of the number of hours passed under this roof. Nor should it be forgotten, that the Officers in question are engaged in a service which holds out to them no hope of further advancement and opens no prospect of celebrity and distinction.

To counteract the temptations to inaction incident to such a condition of life, it seems necessary to make an habitual appeal to those feelings which a liberal confidence is calculated to excite, and which would unavoidably be repressed by the appearance of suspicion and distrust.[1]

Another letter maintains that

. . . but for the spontaneous labours at Extra hours of the higher Clerks of this Office and but for the general talents and capacity for business by which some of those gentlemen are eminently distinguished, this branch of the Public Service must have been involved in a state of inextricable confusion.[2]

It is interesting to compare these statements with Herman Merivale's description of the senior clerks and their work in 1854, when he stressed that in the Colonial Office the duties imposed on clerks involved more intellectual exertion than in almost any other department.

It is, in fact, difficult [he said] to over-rate the ability and knowledge required to perform a portion of the functions of its first-class clerks with complete effectiveness.[3]

[1] C.O. 324/146 Hay to J. Stewart (Treasury), July 22, 1831, pp. 318–321. This letter fills eleven pages in the entry book, and reveals the verbosity which began to afflict official correspondence at that time. Another long letter, also signed by Hay, and entered just before this one in the entry book, is marked 'No date to Mr. Gordon's Draft 22nd July 1831'. Its style is much more simple and direct.

[2] C.O. 324/145 Hay to Spring Rice (Treasury) 1831, p. 303.

[3] H.C. 1854-5 XX (1870) 314-5.

Senior clerks frequently consulted the Secretary of State directly so that under-secretaries sometimes found that they had not been informed even on important questions. Though sometimes inconvenient for the under-secretaries, this was a small penalty to pay for the speedy despatch of business. The disadvantage of this flexible system was that it would not work when a secretary of state was unfamiliar with colonial affairs, unless an able and prudent under-secretary could tactfully provide the necessary background of knowledge and bring matters for decision to the attention of the secretary of state. Hay proved unable to do so, and Stephen, with all his brain power and energy, lacked the gift of delegating work and '. . . preferred to engross it into his own hands and not to be much helped.'[1] When he became Under-Secretary, in 1836, a new pattern requiring extensive written minutes was evolved to suit his personality and habits of business. Stephen's achievement in perfecting the office machinery has in the past received much attention and praise, but there is now a tendency to assess his role more critically in the light of administrative developments in the twentieth century. One authority has recently written:

> The fuller and more careful minutes that begin about 1836 were certainly an aid to clear thought, and were perhaps indispensable when Ministers spent much time in their country houses. Short minutes, semi-official letters and abundant devolution are all, however, aids to swift action and by enforcing a more formal system Stephen decelerated the machine and so brought some discredit upon his department.[2]

Senior clerks were sometimes consulted on general business as well as on the affairs of their departments. Peter Smith's proficiency in languages was of greatest utility in his Mediterranean and Africa department, but his services were also called for at times in other divisions. He appears, for example, to have been the clerk most intimately acquainted with the military business remaining in the hands of the Colonial Secretary. George Baillie was called upon at times to give advice on matters not strictly concerned with his own department; his North America department had, in terms of despatches sent,[3] the least business of any

[1] Taylor, H. T., *Autobiography*, I, 233.
[2] Pugh, R. B., 'The Colonial Office', p. 721.
[3] See Appendix VIII. For a time in the 'thirties this department was entrusted to a clerk of the second class. See C.O. 537/22, No. 23.

of the geographical divisions of the office. Not only was the volume of correspondence relatively small, but much of it was so important as to demand the attention of an under-secretary, the Secretary of State, or even of the Cabinet. Both Smith and Baillie were employed by Wilmot Horton to conduct preliminary negotiations with other departments on various occasions on matters of general concern to the office. Henry Short's chief task outside his own Eastern department was the franking of outgoing despatches in the name of the Secretary of State. Until 1824 this had been done by Adam Gordon; when Gordon became chief clerk it was at first arranged that it should fall to each senior clerk for a month in turn[1] but, in practice, the other senior clerks were seldom authorized to perform the task. An extra £100 a year which Short began to receive after 1825 was probably in consideration of the long hours of attendance imposed on him in carrying out this duty. In 1828 he also received the agency of Trinidad, which paid £344 annually.[2] Smith and Baillie already held colonial agencies[3] which, like that of Short's, were for colonies not immediately under their supervision.

Of the clerks who entered the office between 1825 and 1830 (Appendix III) the most outstanding was Thomas Frederick Elliot. He was only seventeen when he was appointed, '. . . a lively and engaging boy, with a head in which youth and age had met and come to terms.'[4] In 1827 he became précis writer and clerk of the parliamentary papers, with a salary only slightly less than that of an assistant clerk.

> The duties of the Precis Writer [according to a letter to the Treasury in 1831] are in fact of a much more 'confidential & important' nature than the name of the Office would imply, or than was perhaps originally contemplated.[5]

The creation of this post made it possible for an exceptionally able junior to be given duties and training commensurate with his abilities. However, it was not immediately allowed to develop into an alternate system of promotion; for although in 1833 Elliot was chosen to succeed to the first senior clerkship

---

[1] C.O. 324/139 Horton to Freeling, Apr. 17, 1824.
[2] See Appendix VI.
[3] *Ibid.*
[4] Taylor, H., *Autobiography*, I, 162.
[5] C.O. 324/146 Hay to Spring Rice, N/D 1831, p. 310.

vacant after 1825, the office of précis writer was abolished and not restored for several years.[1] In 1835 Elliot went to Canada as secretary of a commission of enquiry; later he became an assistant under-secretary.

Although ability earned Elliot his promotion it was social position that gained him his original appointment as clerk; he was a son of Hugh Elliot, who as a young man was minister at the court of Frederick the Great and later held governorships in India and the West Indies. At least one other new clerk, Robert Stopford, was a member of a noble family[2]; he was the youngest brother of the Earl of Courtown. It seems probable that Stopford's Eton education and family influence gained him the post of private secretary to the political Under-Secretary in June 1828,[3] but this was the only type of promotion within the office likely to be influenced by such considerations. Some of the new clerks were relatives of prominent officials or persons well known in official circles. George Barrow was the son of Sir John Barrow, second secretary to the Admiralty, and the name of Vane Jadis suggests Henry Jadis, clerk in the India Board Office and paymaster of exchequer bills, a suggestion that is reinforced by the fact that Jadis was appointed by Lord Goderich who had recently resigned as Chancellor of the Exchequer. Charles Cox, who became a probationer in 1829, is described in the register of Eton College as 'son of the Army Agent'[4]; since the Cox family had been army agents at least since the reign of Anne they were almost indigenous to the official scene. There is no indication of the existence of a regular practice, such as that followed in some departments of government, of exercising a certain proportion of the patronage for the benefit of the office staff.[5] However, the frequent appearance of the surnames of clerks and office servants in the lists of copyists indicates that minor patronage was used to benefit the sons of office personnel.

[1] The usefulness of such an office in attracting men who could not be expected to be satisfied with a junior clerkship can be inferred from certain passages in Henry Taylor's *Autobiography*. See I, p. 235.

[2] There may have been others. Two letters sent to the fathers of prospective clerks in September 1828 were addressed to the Hon. E. Stewart and the Rev. Dr. Lamb. Co. 324/146, p. 203.

[3] He died three months later at the age of twenty-six. *Eton School Lists 1791–1830*, p. 93, mistakenly gives the date of his death as 1825.

[4] *Eton School Lists*, p. 116.

[5] Gash, Norman, *Politics in the Age of Peel* (1953), p. 360.

If a name alone is sufficient evidence, one of the clerks appointed to the establishment in 1825 may have been the son of an extra clerk. His name, Hugh Stuart Kelsey, suggests two clerks who retired in 1816, Hugh Stuart and Francis Kelsey (Appendix III). He became a full-time copying clerk in 1823 when he was only fifteen years old, and there is some proof that merit had won him his promotion to the establishment, for in 1835, when a small sum was available for distribution among the office clerks, he received a share along with several of the more efficient junior clerks.[1] In addition to being born to the office he lived on the premises for several years.[2]

There is little information in the records to indicate whether the choice of clerks, as well as the power of appointment, always rested with the Secretary of State. It seems likely that there was no overt interference by the ministry but the requests of some powerful persons for the right to name candidates could hardly be denied. One such request came directly from George IV himself. On 20 October 1825 he wrote to Earl Bathurst:

> I wish in the course of a year you could give one, the lowest junior clerkship's place in your office, for a lad of eighteen. A year hence will do.[3]

The only vacancy in the next twelve months was filled by Clere Talbot who was nineteen when appointed; beginning in 1828 he served as private secretary to a succession of political under-secretaries in the office. It has been suggested that the Duke of Wellington, when First Lord of the Treasury, undertook to dispose of some of the patronage of other public offices.[4] The only indication that he may have done so in the Colonial Office is a reference, in a private letter to the Treasury in 1829, to the 'Duke of Wellington's candidate as Extra Clerk',[5] but this may refer to some personal favour extended by Sir George Murray to the Duke. This, of course, does not exclude the possibility that he may have taken over the making of some appointments in the colonies.

Extra clerk in this instance meant probationary clerk, the

---

[1] C.O. 701/10.
[2] C.O. 537/22, No. 25.
[3] Hist. Mss. Comm. *Bathurst Papers*, p. 588.
[4] See Foord, A. S., 'The Waning of "The Influence of the Crown"', p. 504.
[5] C.O. 324/91 Hay to Jos. Planta, Sept. 8, 1828, p. 192.

only type of appointment that could be made to the establishment at that time. A regular system of probation was instituted by Huskisson in 1828; John Martin was the first person to be notified that, at the end of twelve months service as an extra clerk at a salary of £100, he would, if he proved suitable, be eligible to succeed to the first vacancy on the establishment.[1] The terms of Martin's probation were observed, for, though a vacancy occurred in January 1829, he was not appointed to fill it until April, exactly a year after his entry into the office. From that time onward there were a number of probationers in the office. Early in 1830 a regulation was introduced under which the two juniors of the extra clerks employed were not entitled to salaries. A youth named Walpole was the first prospective clerk to be notified that he would be required to serve without salary.[2] He was asked to attend at the office, on Monday 22 March 1830, and to report to Mr. Baillie;[3] he remained in the office as a supernumerary for seven years before a place became available on the establishment in January 1837. Charles Cox, who had become a probationer in 1829, succeeded to a vacancy in 1836. Other supernumeraries came and went, among them the future Cardinal Manning, who, after an outstanding career at Oxford, was forced to seek an official appointment in 1831. The practice of not paying salaries to junior probationers seems to have been waived in his case.[4]

The institution of the regular system of probation was the first step taken towards ensuring that clerks appointed to the Colonial Office had the requisite ability. No better indication of the need for selection can be cited than the last appointment under the old system, Lord Goderich's appointment of Vane Jadis in August 1827. In the office at that time were two able copying clerks who were later appointed to the establishment, James Walker, who had already served for two years, and Clinton Murdoch, who had served for one. Walker resigned in 1837, apparently in anger over the slowness of his advancement. Murdoch served with great distinction and eventually became an assistant under-secretary; in the 1860s, when the first

[1] C.O. 324/146 Hay to John S. Martin, March 28, 1828, p. 191.
[2] *Ibid.*, Hay to Thomas Walpole, Mar. 9, 1830, p. 251.
[3] *Ibid.*, March 15, 1830.
[4] Purcell, E. S., *Life of Cardinal Manning*, I, Chapter V.

Colonial Office lists were published, Jadis was still an assistant clerk.[1]

The informality that allowed senior clerks to attend the office at their own convenience extended down to the lower ranks in the office. In 1831 Lord Goderich, at Treasury insistence, agreed to keep a record of the attendance of all clerks below senior rank,[2] but as late as 1842 James Stephen was finding it difficult to prevent clerks from taking their annual six weeks' vacation at their own convenience without consulting the needs of the office:

> . . . our little commonwealth [he wrote to the Colonial Secretary, Lord Stanley] is a pure democracy. The sense of Social equality gets the better altogether of the sense of official inequality. No man gives *orders*, in the proper sense of the word, because no man thinks of himself as one on whom Orders may be properly laid. Living apart from the Junior Members of this Office, I find the difficulty of breaking up this feeling almost insuperable. Living daily with them, Mr. Blackwood and his brethren of the 1st. Class, must, and certainly do, feel the difficulty so strongly that any attempt to govern by authority is, I am well convinced neither made nor thought of by them. In fact your Lordship's authority is the only one which can silence controversies on any question of Office Regulation . . . .[3]

When Wilmot Horton was relieved of the burden of the eastern half of the Empire, by the appointment of a second under-secretary in 1825, he plunged headlong into his great plans for emigration to North America. The emigration committees of the House of Commons in 1826 and 1827 were moved and chaired by him, and he obtained the necessary witnesses, including many from the colonies. His friend, Lord Granville, wrote him a letter in January 1827 which is a good, though exaggerated, illustration of his interests and activities:

> I suppose that you are by this time returned from your Staffordshire visits, & instead of killing or shooting at pheasants etc., are penning articles for the Quarterly or inditing Letters to West India Governors. I marvel how you find time to be under-secretary

[1] *The Colonial Office List for 1864; or General Register of the Colonial Dependencies of Great Britain* (1864), p. 7.

[2] C.O. 324/146 Hay to J. K. Stewart (Treasury) July 22, 1831, p. 316.

[3] C.O. 537/22, No. 34.

of a laborious department, to be the most voluminous contributor to a Review, to be author of pamphlets upon all the interesting Questions of the day . . . to write articles for the daily journals, to write Letters to your Constituents & to secretaries of Boards, to be chairman of committees in the House of Commons, to preside at Mendicity and Chimney Mechanical Sweeping Societies, & at the same time faire la cour aux dames, & shoot both in autumn & winter like any dandy who has no other occupation—surely the 24 hours expand themselves for you.[1]

With a parliamentary under-secretary of such boundless and undisciplined energy creating far more work than he could handle, James Stephen's duties were not reduced as had been expected when it was agreed that his services were to be shared with the Board of Trade. A survey of the registers reveals that he wrote about a hundred letters to the under-secretaries in the last six months of 1825,[2] a prodigious number when the amount of attention and study required for almost every reference is considered. Early in 1826 he was ill and Wilmot Horton told the House of Commons that he had been employed:

> . . . for not less than ten hours a day. That was too much for any man. Unless the House would furnish him with assistance, the public business must, in a case of illness, stand still. He pledged himself, when the colonial estimates should be brought forward, to show that it was impossible that the public business could be transacted without an augmented establishment.[3]

In June an allowance of £200 a year was provided for an assistant,[4] but it was withdrawn, after the payment of £100, and the individual selected was discharged when it was discovered that the expense for contingencies, largely for copying, was exceeding the parliamentary grant.[5] In his place Stephen received the full time services of the précis writer of the department.[6] In 1826 Stephen reported on 480 colonial acts. At the rate of payment prior to the arrangement of 1823 this would have entitled

---

[1] Quoted in Jones, E. G., 'Wilmot Horton', pp. 46–7.
[2] P.R.O. Indexes 8379 and 8398. About half the letters were to Hay.
[3] *Parl. Deb., New Series*, XIV, 1080, March 3, 1826.
[4] C.O. 324/146 Wilmot Horton to Stephen, June 15, 1826, p. 21.
[5] *Ibid.* Horton to Herries (Treasury), Dec. 15, 1826, Section 10. The name of the assistant was Samuel Elijah Blunt. He was selected by Stephen.
[6] *Ibid.* The precis writer, Edward Winslow, left the office in July, 1827. Whether he resigned or died from overwork is not clear.

him to a sum about equal to his salary from both the Colonial Office and the Board of Trade; but, in addition, in 1826 he had been required in the Colonial Office alone to report on 145 cases. '. . . some of them of extreme length & of the greatest importance.'[1] Shortly after Huskisson became Colonial Secretary, Wilmot Horton sought to have Stephen's position properly recognized by giving him the title of assistant under-secretary with the privilege of franking, but Huskisson opposed definite action at that juncture.[2]

When Lord Liverpool suffered a stroke in February 1827, the party that he had kept together for so long immediately fell apart.[3] All its members were still agreed in opposing any general reform of the House of Commons but on the more immediately urgent questions of 'corn and Catholics' and foreign policy they were divided into hostile camps. The 'Protestant' Duke of Wellington was the dominant figure among those who opposed relief for Roman Catholics and favoured high protection for agriculture and support for Metternich in Europe. Opposed to them was the 'Catholic', George Canning, who, with his supporters, supported Roman Catholic emancipation, greater freedom of trade and a liberal foreign policy. Even before Lord Liverpool's death the alliance of these factions had been in imminent danger of breaking down.[4] It had held together since 1822 only because the 'Protestants' had regarded Lord Liverpool as their only sure guarantee that restrictions on Catholics would not be removed, while the Canningites had found in Liverpool a man who shared their interest in economic and financial reform and loyally supported Canning's foreign policy.[5] Robert Peel was the only other prominent member of Liverpool's cabinet who was not attached to one faction or the other. Like Liverpool he was a 'Protestant' and, like him, he was interested in economic reform; he was also the only 'Protestant'

[1] C.O. 324/146, Horton to Treasury, Dec. 15, 1826, Section 10.
[2] Br. Mus. Add. Mss. 38751 Huskisson Papers, Huskisson to Horton, private and confidential, Oct. 18, 1827, ff, 267–70.
[3] For the detailed history of these events see Aspinall, A., *The Formation of Canning's Ministry, February to August 1827*, Camden Third Series, LIX, 1937.
[4] See Feiling, K. G., *The Second Tory Party 1714–1832*, pp. 345–7.
[5] Lord Liverpool's interest in economic matters comes out clearly in Brock, W. R., *Lord Liverpool and Liberal Toryism 1820–1827*, Cambridge, 1941.

on the front bench in the House of Commons. In the crisis Peel finally, after some initial hesitation, chose to follow the Duke of Wellington. Personality counted for more than principle in the final break between the factions, for the Duke's distrust of Canning had become an obsession. When, after several weeks of indecision, the King, in April, designated Canning as First Lord of the Treasury, the Duke and Peel led a 'Protestant' secession by immediately resigning their offices.

Canning spent the next four months attempting to form a government that would have the support of the House of Commons. He died very suddenly in August and the King, angry with the seceders who had resigned in April and anxious to assert his right to name his own chief minister, asked Lord Goderich to lead the government. Goderich proved to be absolutely incapable of leading anything—one noble lord said he was not fit to manage a poultry yard—and after five months of weeping indecision the 'transient and embarrassed phantom' left the stage in January 1828.[1] The Canningites, but not the Whigs who had accepted office under Canning, agreed to serve in a ministry headed by the Duke of Wellington. After four months of constant bickering they resigned at the end of May, leaving the Duke to carry on for two and a half years with only one first-class man in the House of Commons, Peel, and with few efficient men of business in his government. Ironically, this 'Protestant' ministry was to be remembered chiefly for its removal of Roman Catholic disabilities in 1829. Otherwise, apart from Peel's activity at the Home Office—he instituted the metropolitan police for London in 1829—and the reversal of Canning's foreign policy, these two years were noteworthy for a singular lack of energy and initiative in all departments of government. In June 1830, George IV died, unlamented, and when, in November, the Government met the Parliament elected after his death, it became apparent that it could not command a majority in the House of Commons, so the Duke resigned. The Canningites, out of office since May 1828, then joined the Whigs to form an administration, thus putting their talents and experience at the disposal of a new government, a new King, and a new decade.

Earl Bathurst resigned the seals of the Colonial Office on

[1] See Feiling, K. G., *The Second Tory Party 1714–1832*, pp. 357–60.

30 April 1827. By inheritance and inclination a King's man, by habit an executive, he was the last of the seceders to resign when Canning became Prime Minister.[1] Although one of Wellington's closest supporters in the Cabinet, he did not deal in personalities, and did not fully share the antipathy to Canning; he had as a matter of fact been a supporter of Canning after Pitt's death two decades earlier.[2] Always conservative, he became even more so when freed from the necessity of working with more liberal colleagues. From January 1828 to November 1830 he again held office as president of the council. Sir John Fortescue in his analysis of military administration, Francis Bickley in his edition of the *Bathurst Papers* prepared for the Historical Manuscripts Commission, Sir Charles Webster in his work on Castlereagh, and Mrs. Helen Taft Manning in her studies of colonial government have assessed most aspects of his official career. 'There never was tolerated a worse colonial minister than the unrespected Lord', commented *The Times* when he left the Colonial Office, and this epitaph on his career went largely unquestioned at the time.[3] Another comment on his resignation, in a lighter vein than *The Times*, indicates what is apparent from other sources,[4] that few outside his immediate circle took his talents seriously: 'I do not mean to dispute Lord Westmorland's eye for women, or Lord Bathurst's for Burgundy,' wrote Col. Willoughby Cotton to Sir Herbert Taylor, 'but Robinson and Dudley are more likely to benefit the State.'[5]

Frederick Robinson, who was elevated to the peerage as Lord Goderich when he became Colonial Secretary (30 April— 3 September 1827), had been Under-Secretary in the office for six months in 1809 and later had been President of the Board of Trade (1818–23) and Chancellor of the Exchequer (1823–27). He was head of the Board of Trade when the 1822 acts liberalizing the trade laws of the Empire were passed. His interests were, however, centred more on financial administration than on empire development, which so much fascinated his friend and subordinate Wilmot Horton. Both his interests and his ex-

---

[1] See Feiling, K. G., *The Second Tory Party 1714–1832*, p. 352.
[2] *Ibid.*, p. 260.
[3] Tucker, H. F. G., 'The Press and the Colonies, 1802–1833', pp. 39–40.
[4] *The Greville Memoirs, 1814–1860*, III, pp. 65–6.
[5] *The Taylor Papers*, p. 197.

perience admirably fitted Goderich for tackling several urgent financial questions which Lord Bathurst had largely ignored.[1] Despite a reputation for laziness, he had some capabilities as an administrator and might well have performed his tasks quite creditably under the eye of a strong prime minister and with able colleagues at the Treasury and the Board of Trade. George Baillie found him 'very agreeable to transact business with *except* in Money Matters',[2] and when Goderich again became Colonial Secretary in 1830, Henry Taylor, who had apparently not noted his passage in 1827, found him 'a man of more activity than I had expected, and easy and good humoured in personal intercourse.'[3] His term in the office was too brief to produce any very significant measures but he did take steps towards settling a quarrel with the Jamaican assembly over financial policy[4] and gave umbrage to the governor of a North American colony by refusing to support the carrying out of a policy authorized by Lord Bathurst.[5]

Lord Goderich under a strong prime minister might well have been an adequate colonial secretary. His successor, William Huskisson (3 September 1827–30 May 1828), would almost certainly have been outstanding under any circumstances except those that prevailed during his nine months in the office. Writing many years later James Stephen, who served under him both at the Board of Trade and the Colonial Office, declared that of all the statesmen under whom he had served only Huskisson had a 'dominant understanding.'[6] He is usually regarded as the most able man to hold the post of colonial secretary before the advent of Joseph Chamberlain in 1895. Huskisson had one great defect as Secretary of State in the era in which he served; he had no great aristocratic connections except by marriage and had received his higher education not at Oxford or Cambridge but in liberal circles in France on the eve of the Revolution. Moreover, he had served as chief clerk

[1] See Chapter VI.
[2] P.A.C. Sir Howard Douglas Miscellaneous Papers, Baillie to Douglas, Aug. 2, 1827.
[3] Taylor, H., *Autobiography*, I, p. 118.
[4] See below p. 231.
[5] See James Kempt to Sir Herbert Taylor, Oct. 10, 1828 in *The Taylor Papers*, pp. 236–7.
[6] Stephen, Caroline Emelia. *The Rt. Hon. Sir James Stephen. K.C.B., LL.D., Letters with Biographical Notes* (Gloucester, 1906), p. 99.

when the office that he was now to head had first been established in 1795. He had been brought to the attention of Pitt by
Lord Gower,[1] whom he had served as secretary at the British
embassy in Paris, and had become Dundas' protégé, serving
him first as clerk and later as under-secretary. Pitt made him a
secretary to the Treasury in his last ministry, and he held
the same office under Portland. Because of his attachment to
Canning, Huskisson did not again hold an important office until
1823, when he became President of the Board of Trade. He was,
however, Lord Liverpool's most intimate adviser on economic
affairs for several years. At the Board of Trade, from 1823 to
1827, he earned the right to be called a great economic reformer
and a great imperial statesman.[2] His difficulties during his brief
term at the Colonial Office were, in part, due to the very bad
state of his health; he was in Germany consulting physicians
when Canning died and in the strenuous months that followed
he had no opportunity to recover his strength.[3] From September
to January, he was the leader-designate of the Government in
the House of Commons serving under 'weak, undecided and
utterly helpless' Goderich; from January to May he was the
leader of the Canningite faction in the Wellington Cabinet,[4]
squabbling constantly with the Prime Minister and spending
much time in cabinet and in the House of Commons.[5]

The excellence of Huskisson's abilities is apparent in the
records of his term at the Colonial Office. Yet, if his reputation
as an imperial statesman rested on his work as Secretary of State,
it would be based on promise and intention rather than performance. When he entered the office, public opinion in Britain
was at variance with public opinion in the North American and
West Indian colonies on several matters, and every colonial
assembly was quarrelling bitterly with the Colonial Office over
slavery or financial policy, or both.[6] The financial questions
could be tackled but the process of working out solutions was

[1] Fay, C. R., *Huskisson and His Age*, p. 66.
[2] See Brady, A., *William Huskisson and Liberal Reform* (1928).
[3] Bulwer, H. L., *The Life of Henry John Temple, Viscount Palmerston*, I,
pp. 216, 286; also Fay, C. R., *Huskisson and His Age*, p. 87.
[4] Bulwer, H. L., *The Life of Henry John Temple, Viscount Palmerston*, I,
pp. 195, 199.
[5] *Ibid.*, Book V.
[6] See Chapter VII.

bound to be slow and the assemblies and their agents in London were impatient. The slavery problem defied solution at that juncture. Within a few days of taking office, Huskisson wrote to George IV expressing great uneasiness about the deep rift that had developed between the legislatures of Great Britain and Jamaica,[1] but there was little that could be done since the Government could not agree to come down firmly either on the side of the planters or the saints. 'These slave questions' he wrote to Wilmot Horton on one occasion, 'I verily believe will drive me mad.'[2]

He moved firmly, however, to try to get at the root of the internal quarrel between the French and English in Lower Canada by having a parliamentary committee set up to study the problem, thus deliberately bringing into the limelight a colonial issue that had no British ramifications except those involved in the usual ties between the Mother Country and a colony. But such a revolutionary departure from previous practice brought further difficulties in the form of discontented colonial governors; the most able man sent to the North American colonies in this era, Sir James Kempt, quoted with approval one of his colleagues who stated that if the system should continue 'no man who values his character and his honour will accept of a Colonial Government.'[3] Huskisson's bold approach to the problems of government was also shown by his insistence on the appointment of a select committee of the House of Commons in 1828 to enquire freely into and report on public income and expenditure.[4] Some of the committee's far-reaching recommendations applied to the colonies.[5] The emphasis on obtaining more adequate information that is revealed in the setting up of these committees of enquiry is also evident in the existence of a draft circular instructing governors to send more statistical information in their reports.[6]

Huskisson continued the development of a new public lands

---

[1] *Letters of George IV, 1812–1830*, ed. A. Aspinall, III, 312–13. See also Manning, H. T., 'Colonial Crises before the Cabinet, 1829–1935', p. 45.

[2] Br. Mus. Add. Mss. 38752, Huskisson Papers, Huskisson to Horton, Nov. 7, 1827, f. 26.

[3] Kempt to Sir Herbert Taylor, Oct. 10, 1828, *The Taylor Papers*, p. 237.

[4] Fay, C. R., *Huskisson and His Age*, p. 110.

[5] See below pp. 191–5.

[6] C.O. 323/208 Circular filed under 'Mr. Stephen'.

policy for the colonies which had been begun by Lord Bathurst and Wilmot Horton in 1825,[1] when they had introduced a new system for alienating Crown Lands in New South Wales; new regulations were introduced in the North American colonies in 1827. He was making arrangements for the establishment of a land board in London for the sale of colonial lands[2] when he left office. Another innovation introduced in his brief term is worthy of note. By a circular despatch of 1 May 1828 he announced his intention of restricting the terms of colonial governors to six years in order to open posts '. . . for the employment of others who may have claims to the notice of His Majesty's Government.'[3] Whether this was intrinsically an improvement on the long terms of most of Lord Bathurst's governors is questionable.[4]

Wilmot Horton continued as Under-Secretary until the end of 1827;[5] while admitting his private debt to Lord Bathurst he disagreed with the public grounds which Bathurst had given for his resignation. When Canning became Prime Minister Horton hoped to become chief secretary for Ireland, a post for which he felt himself to be well qualified, but Canning is reported to have said that he had 'spoilt himself' for Ireland by his pamphlets on the Catholic question.[6] Canning did make him privy councillor—the first time that the rank of privy councillor had been conferred on an under-secretary of state,[7] according to Henry Hobhouse who had just retired as Under-Secretary at the Home Office.

[1] Riddell, R. G., 'A Study of the Land Policy of the Colonial Office 1763–1835', *C.H.R.*, XVIII, 389–391.

[2] C.O. 323/209 Maj. Moody and Col. Cockburn to Sir George Murray, June 13, 1828, ff. 135–6. George Baillie, the senior clerk in the North American department was strongly opposed to it. 'I do not conceive that they would sell land enough in England in a year to pay the Salary of a Clerk independent of which I am certain it would create universal *disgust* in the Colonies to draw £5,000 a year to pay a Land Board in London, which instead of being of any advantage would create great inconvenience in the Provinces.' P.A.C. Sir Howard Douglas Miscellaneous Papers, Baillie to Douglas, July 3, 1828.   [3] C.O. 854/1.

[4] See Hall, H. L., *The Colonial Office* (1937), p. 92.

[5] Br. Mus. Add. Mss. 38762, Huskisson Papers, Wilmot Horton's statement regarding his political conduct, private and confidential, July 6, 1828, f. 173.

[6] Littleton to Wilmot, October 20, 1827, quoted in Jones, E. G., 'Wilmot Horton', p. 78.

[7] Aspinall, A., *The Formation of Canning's Administration*, p. 247.

When Lord Goderich became Prime Minister, Wilmot Horton could have become vice-president of the Board of Trade but was unwilling, or unable because of the extravagant scale on which he had been living, to undergo the expense of the election contest which would be necessary if he accepted the new office.[1] His real wish was to become Governor of Canada, but he over-rated his claims; the King did, however, make him a tentative offer of the governorship of Jamaica which later fell through.[2] He placed himself on the shelf when he left the Colonial Office, and the fall of the Goderich ministry a few days later reduced his opportunities. Huskisson failed to obtain a place for him in the Wellington administration formed in January 1828.[3] After the Canningites left the Wellington ministry at the end of May, Wellington, at Lord Bathurst's suggestion, tried several times to induce him to accept office but without success.[4] When Lord Bathurst again pressed for his inclusion in the government in 1830, Lord Ellenborough refused to allow his name to be considered.[5] For three years he devoted himself to the propagation of his ideas on Roman Catholic emancipation, the West Indies, and emigration. Palmerston met him in Paris in December 1829, '. . . indefatigably hammering at emigration, and writing his shorthand scribe down to a skeleton.'[6] He did not offer for re-election to the House of Commons in 1830, and in 1831 he accepted Lord Goderich's offer of the governorship of Ceylon where he had a successful term of six years.

While Wilmot Horton was trying to decide what course to pursue in the autumn of 1827, Huskisson appointed as his successor a twenty-eight-year-old Whig, Edward Geoffrey Smith-Stanley (15 October 1827–5 February 1828) heir to the Earl of Derby, who was later to become twice Secretary of State for the Colonies[7] and three times Prime Minister.[8] During his first two and a half months in the office Stanley served as third under-

---

[1] Jones, E. G., 'Wilmot Horton', pp. 82 and 86.

[2] Fay, C. R., *Huskisson and His Age*, p. 88, N.1.

[3] *Ibid.*, pp. 87–88.

[4] Jones, E. G., 'Wilmot Horton', pp. 90–91. See Wellington, *Despatches, Correspondence and Memoranda*, vol. IV, p. 455.

[5] See Fay, C. R., *Huskisson and His Age*, p. 88.

[6] Bulwer, H. L., *The Life of Henry John Temple, Viscount Palmerston*, I, p. 355.

[7] 1833–4; 1841–1845.

[8] 1852; 1858–9; 1866–8.

secretary without pay.[1] Wilmot Horton, by arrangement with Huskisson, remained in the office until the end of the year and retained the West Indies department and the salary, while Stanley administered the North American colonies. When Wilmot Horton retired Stanley took over the Eastern division from Hay who, for a few months, undertook the administration of the West Indies.

When the Duke of Wellington became Prime Minister, Stanley resigned with the other Whigs in the Goderich ministry. Huskisson took advantage of the vacancy to repay an old debt by appointing Lord Francis Leveson Gower (5 February–30 May 1828), a member of the family that had launched him on his official career.[2] Lord Francis, a brother-in-law of Charles Greville, had a very brief official career, but his rise was rapid. After resigning with Huskisson in May, he became, a few weeks later, chief secretary for Ireland. In 1830 he was Secretary at War for a short time. He did not again hold office although he was a member of the House of Commons from 1835 to 1846, when he was created Earl of Ellesmere. He had a reputation among his friends as a writer of original poems, was interested in drama and contributed to the *Quarterly Review*. Like Hay and Wilmot Horton he was a member of Grillon's Club, having been elected in 1825.[3] While in the Colonial Office he administered the Eastern department, including the Cape of Good Hope and Heligoland; Hay undertook the responsibility for all other business.[4]

Whereas in 1827 colonial problems were considered to be of such importance that men of great political experience and worth were appointed colonial secretaries, in 1828 the Duke of

[1] Br. Mus. Add. Mss. 38571, Huskisson Papers, Horton to Huskisson, confidential, ff. 323–8. Jones ('Wilmot Horton', p. 84) regards this letter as an appeal by Horton to be allowed to continue in office while recommending that Stanley should be appointed without pay. But Stanley was already serving when the letter was written (C.O. 324/146 Huskisson to the Post Master General, Oct. 15, 1827, p. 172). Huskisson had announced his intention to appoint Stanley before he himself had received the seals of office (Br. Mus. Add. Mss. 38750 Huskisson Papers, Huskisson to Lansdowne, Sept. 1, 1827). See also Br. Mus. Add. Mss. 38762 Huskisson Papers, Wilmot Horton's statement, July 6, 1828, f. 173.

[2] Fay, C. R., *Huskisson and His Age*, pp. 63–66 and 90.

[3] *Portraits of the Members of Grillion's Club*, 1864, No. 64.

[4] C.O. 854/1.

Wellington chose as Huskisson's successor his old Quartermaster-General and Chief of Staff, Lieutenant-General Sir George Murray (30 May 1828–22 November 1830). Murray was a fine '. . . old soldier and a high-bred gentleman, whose countenance and natural stateliness and simple dignity of demeanour were all that can be desired in a Secretary of State, if to look the character were the one thing needful.'[1] At the time of his appointment he was a member of the House of Commons and Commander-in-Chief in Ireland, but he had never held civil office except for a term of six weeks as Lieutenant-Governor of Upper Canada in 1815.[2] Although Murray was popular in the country for his reputation for freedom from jobbery,[3] and in Parliament for his liberal views, Wellington's appointment of military men to his Cabinet was much criticized. Murray was, for Wellington, the perfect successor to the restless Huskisson; for the Duke, it was alleged, preferred to run his administration as one big department, with Peel an intimate and trusted under-secretary and Lord Chancellor Lyndhurst the legal adviser.[4] On colonial questions Lord Bathurst, President of the Council, and Henry Goulburn, Chancellor of the Exchequer, were called in for expert advice. Murray was treated as a senior clerk not too capable of keeping his department in order. With a magnificent lack of guile Wellington on one occasion stated to Murray his stubborn conviction that he alone should dictate policy:

> I am always very sorry to differ in opinion from any of my Colleagues particularly when I know that I am right.[5]

It is hard to condemn Sir George Murray; the simple sincerity of his character stands out in his every act and word. But sympathy for a thoroughly fine man, too weak to refuse a post for which he was plainly unsuited, is the only complimentary gloss which can be put upon his career in the Colonial Office.

[1] Taylor, H., *Autobiography*, I, p. 117.

[2] See Graham, G. S., 'Views of General Murray on the Defence of Upper Canada, 1815', C.H.R. XXXIV (1953), pp. 158–165.

[3] Tucker, Henry F. G., 'The Press and the Colonies 1802–1833', p. 40.

[4] See Walpole, S., *A History of England from the Conclusion of the Great War in 1815*, II, p. 486. Compare Aspinall, A., 'The Cabinet Council 1783–1835', pp. 207–8.

[5] N.L.S., Sir George Murray Papers, Wellington to Murray, June 27, 1830, vol. 171, f. 133. Wellington, *Despatches, Correspondence and Memoranda* VII, p. 95.

He proved totally incapable of grasping the details of the mass of business that confronted him.[1] Apart from two or three very rough drafts of speeches and records of conversations, his private papers contain almost nothing in his own handwriting on colonial subjects. There are many memoranda on military affairs which reveal his competence in his own field. This deficiency and the scarcity of official minutes lends substance to the popular rumour which prevailed in the small official circle at Westminster. According to Greville, Hyde Villiers had repeated to him a statement which supposedly emanated from James Stephen seven months after Murray entered the office:

> Murray did nothing—never wrote a despatch—had only once since he had been in office seen Taylor, who has got all the West Indies under his care.[2]

With such a Secretary of State at the helm, the political Under-Secretary had an unexcelled opportunity to exercise his talents and reveal his imperial vision. But Murray's political Under-Secretary was not a rising young statesman but a man rejected for the same position in 1821[3] and now selected by Peel[4] not for his interest in empire but in order to give the Government more debating strength in the House of Commons. His name was Horace Twiss (30 May 1828–22 November 1830); he appears in John Doyle's cartoons, a big, dark, handsome man.[5] He was the son of the older Fannie Kemble and a nephew of Mrs. Siddons, but his own Thespian powers were reserved for the drawing-room and the House of Commons. Twiss supervised the administration of the West Indies during his two and a half years in the office, with the Eastern department, minus the Cape of Good Hope, being added to his responsibilities after he had gained some administrative experience. Henry Taylor, not an unbiased observer, found him timid and indecisive '. . . of all

---

[1] Compare, however, Manning, H. T., 'Colonial Crises Before the Cabinet, 1829–1835', pp. 46–49.

[2] *The Greville Memoirs, 1814–1860*, I. 227, Dec. 31, 1828. See also *The Journal of Mrs. Arbuthnot*, pp. 229 and 381.

[3] In 1821 he had been considered as a possible successor to Henry Goulburn, Croker advised against it: '. . . Twiss has not yet weight enough with the House.' *The Croker Papers*, ed. L. A. Jennings, I, p. 187.

[4] Peel to Bathurst, May 30, 1828, *Bathurst Papers*, p. 654.

[5] Trevelyan, G. M., *The Seven Years of William IV, a Reign Cartooned by John Doyle* (1952), Nos. XIV, XV, XXXVII.

the Under Secretaries who had ever laid the weight of their authority upon the transactions of the Colonial Office, "the fleshliest incubus" ',[1] a reference to Twiss's bulk as well as to his ineptitude. Hay, who was serving with Twiss, Taylor characterized as 'obtuse but bold', and he pictures the two of them:

> The one was for ever occupied with details and incapable of coming to a conclusion—routing and grunting and tearing up the soil to get at a grain of the subject; the other went straight to a decision, which was right or wrong as might happen. I remember applying to him the proverb that 'mettle is dangerous in a blind horse'.[2]

Shortly after leaving office Sir George Murray made a statement in a debate in the House of Commons which Walter Bagehot would have relished as a classic statement of that Tory scepticism which would leave things as they were lest they might get worse. 'I have always supposed until this moment,' he stated, 'that to abstain from any extraordinary activity in the measures to be carried into effect with respect to the colonies was a merit rather than a defect.'[3] Wellington was aware of Murray's shortcomings and at one time asked the able Lord Ellenborough, the Lord Privy Seal, to assist him, but Lord Ellenborough was not interested in colonial business.[4] Later, Wellington talked of giving Murray a military assignment[5] but, in the end, nothing was done. Within the office, even a matter so vital to the colonies as land policy was neglected. Despite the accumulation of a wealth of advice and criticism of the system instituted by Lord Bathurst, no decision was made either to continue the system, to amend it, or to replace it. When Lord Goderich re-entered the office at the end of 1830, there were despatches on land policy from the Governor of New South Wales, written in 1828, still unanswered.[6] Hay, commenting on new proposals for reform in 1831, could only deplore the delay:

[1] Taylor, H., *Autobiography*, I, p. 117, quoting from a letter to his mother.
[2] *Ibid.*, p. 118.
[3] Hansard (1830) I, 1060. He was speaking on slavery.
[4] *A Political Diary 1828–30*, by Edward Law, Lord Ellenborough, ed. by Lord Colchester, I. p. 127.
[5] Aspinall, A., 'The Cabinet Council, 1783–1835', p. 158.
[6] Riddell, R. G., 'A Study of the Land Policy of the Colonial Office 1763–1835', *C.H.R.*, XVIII (1937), 391.

I have long thought [he wrote] that the land granting system needed a complete revision and it would have been undertaken had not various causes combined to defer it.[1]

Under such feeble leadership the clerks lost interest, but one man worked steadily on, shouldering the burdens which others dropped. On 16 February 1830, James Stephen prepared a statement of his services. Twice in the previous four months Wellington had protested to Murray against the influence which Stephen exerted through his drafting of the slave ordinances. On 10 October 1829 Wellington had written:

In general I should say that the Gentleman whoever he may be who has drawn the Order in Council is a partisan in favour of the Abolition of Slavery. Government must act upon the Principle of carrying into Execution fairly the Intentions of Parl^t, but must avoid the extreme views of both parties and the hasty measures of the one and those of the other which are calculated to defeat the views of Parl^t. . . .

We must look at it seriously ourselves and oblige those under us to carry into execution our Intentions, and not their own Fancies.[2]

On 27 January 1830 he had written:

I want very much to see the ordinance as amended before it will pass the Council.

I must say in Confidence that the Gentleman who draws these papers for your Office serves the Gov^t very ill.[3]

Whether Stephen was aware of Wellington's censures or not, he was hurt by popular criticism of his working for the Colonial Office and refers to it in his memorandum:

That connection, without any fault, so far as I am aware, of my own, has brought upon me unceasing contumely, reproach and ill will from a most powerful body of persons. In short I made a most improvident and foolish contract, if my interests and comfort only were to be considered.[4]

[1] Riddell, p. 391.
[2] N.L.S., Sir George Murray Papers, Wellington to Murray, Oct. 10, 1829. Vol. 169, ff. 154 and 157. The whole of this long letter is devoted to an analysis of Stephen's introduction of 'enthusiastic' doctrines into an order in council. Published in Wellington, *Despatches, Correspondence and Memoranda*, VI, pp. 206-7.
[3] *Ibid.*, vol. 171, f. 15 and Wellington VI, p. 444.
[4] N.L.S., Sir George Murray Papers, Statement of James Stephen of his services to the Colonial Office, Feb. 16, 1830, vol. 171, f. 55.

The description of the sheer physical extent of his activity makes one wonder how business could apparently stand still despite such industry:

> With respect to the Clerks who are employed on my account. I must in the first place observe, that this is a charge from which the Order in Council[1] relieved me. In point of fact, however, I have generally kept an extra Clerk at my own expence.
>
> As some proof of the quantity of labour which my Clerks have to perform, I may mention that from the 1st June 1828 to the 29th Sept. 1829 there were consumed in my office no less than ten Reams and a half of Folio Paper, every Sheet of which was filled with close writing. The average quantity employed by other Gentlemen in the office during the same time was about *two* Reams and a half.
>
> I must in justice to my Clerks add, that one of them habitually rises at 5 o'clock every Morning to his work, and is engaged 'till 9. He is again occupied for some hours every evening in addition to occasional employment during the other parts of the day. My other Clerk passes the entire day in this Office and performs duties with respect to the Acts of the Colonies scarcely inferior in difficulty or importance to any duty which is placed in the hands of any Gentleman in the Department below the rank of a Senior Clerk. Each of my Clerks receives £100.
>
> For myself, I trust it is not necessary to prove, or even to assert that I am sedulously engaged in my public duties. I can with strict truth declare, that I begin my business daily at 6 o'clock, and continue it till night with no deduction of any part of my time for amusements or for studies of a different nature. It is in truth a very laborious as well as a very invidious calling. Were I to bring a Bill against the Public drawn out upon the same principle as that of a common Attorney's Bill, I am confident I understate the fact in saying that I should make an annual charge of £6000 or £7000.[2]

At the request of Sir George Murray, he prepared a further statement, which included this summary of duties performed 'in the twenty months since Sir George Murray took office'.

---

[1] See above pp. 80–1, 100.
[2] N.L.S., Sir George Murray Papers, Statement of James Stephen, ff. 56–7.

Col[1] and Legislative Acts reported at an average of 331 per ann.	559
Despatches and letters connected with these Acts	76
Reports on general subjects	193
Despatches	220
Commissions and Instructions	4
Cases for the Law Officers of the Crown	13
Orders in Council	13
Acts of Parliament	8
	1086

Amongst the Reports above noticed several are included each of which would separately have formed a Pamphlet of no inconsiderable bulk, as for example some Papers on the subject of Canada, and some connected with the question of the New South Wales Act and the controversies of that Colony, and others respecting the Slavery question.[1]

Wellington's conception of what the role of a counsel should be was far different. In June 1830 he wrote to Murray about a proposed Canada Act:

This is a question of law upon which I confess that I should have been happy to see Mr. Stephen's opinion instead of upon Questions of Policy with which according to my Notions he ought to have nothing to do.[2]

In a prolix criticism of the structure of the Colonial Office in 1832[3] James Stephen cited two great faults: the 'chronic evil of lack of punctuality in administering colonial affairs', and, the failure to co-ordinate the efforts and policies of the different sections of the office. By such phrases as 'it was certainly his design', and, 'was intended to be', the memorandum clearly reveals that Stephen had been in Wilmot Horton's confidence when the office structure was being remodelled. It was with a view to continuing the improvement in administrative organization that Wilmot Horton had begun that he made his recom-

[1] N.L.S., Sir George Murray Papers, Statement of James Stephen of further facts added by Sir George Murray's desire, February 1830, vol. 171, ff. 59-60.
[2] N.L.S., Sir George Murray Papers, Wellington to Murray, June 27, 1830, vol. 171, f. 133.
[3] C.O. 537/22 Memorandum of James Stephen, March 30, 1832, No. I.

mendations, and pointed out where unforeseen difficulties had created weak points that needed reinforcement. Stephen, perhaps for the sake of argument, over-rated the independence of the Colonial Office in framing policy, and, in his anxiety to blame deficiencies in colonial government on the internal organization of the office, rather than on individuals, he did not always choose his examples wisely. For example, he used the situation in Canada as an illustration of the effect on policy of dividing the colonial Empire between the two Under-Secretaries; according to Stephen's argument, policies of firmness alternated with policies of weakness as one under-secretary succeeded another until the local politicians, observing the lack of consistency, attempted to take matters into their own hands.[1] In making such an over-simplified judgement, Stephen ignored two facts. First, few changes had been made in the supervision of the North American department—Wilmot Horton had kept it until October 1827, Stanley then supervised it for three and a half months, and was followed by Hay who was officially responsible for the four years from February 1828 to January 1832.[2] Secondly, the Canada question had been many times under the attention of the Cabinet, which did not always heed the advice of a colonial under-secretary.

Hay's stolid comment on Stephen's memorandum reveals an emphasis on the political, a factor that Stephen, at this stage of his career, tended to ignore:

> I fear that the evils pointed out by him are too much the natural result of the frequent changes of government which have of late years occurred, & of the diversity of opinion which have prevailed among the different individuals to whom the management of Colonial affairs has been entrusted;—to be entirely removed by any scheme which can be suggested; but they certainly may be very much mitigated . . . .[3]

In Stephen's conception of the role of the Permanent Under-Secretary can be recognized the character he later gave to that office. A few scattered sentences will provide a sufficient sketch:

[1] C.O. 537/22 Memorandum of James Stephen, private and confidential, March 30, 1832, No. I.

[2] C.O. 854/1 Printed circulars 1827–1832.

[3] C.O. 537/22 Memorandum of R. W. Hay, private and confidential, Apr. 2, 1832, No. II.

... the Secretary of State has always been, and I apprehend, must ever continue, dependent upon others for information and assistance in the discharge of his duties to an extent scarcely known in other departments, which are conversant with topics with which statesmen are, from the nature of their ordinary pursuits, habitually familiar.

The two under-secretaries have scarcely more intercourse with each other than if they were in different offices. The senior Clerks have become virtually Under Secretaries, and are often drawn into personal and direct communication with the Secretary of State. Hence there is much important knowledge in their exclusive keeping . . . .

The permanent Under Secretary of State fills a station of which the real importance and responsibility far exceeds its avowed and ostensible character.

The permanent under-secretary was intended to be the depository of all that knowledge of which the Secretary of State must daily avail himself . . . .[1]

Hay expressed his agreement:

... that the Senior Clerks should be less called into counsel, & that the Juniors should be kept more closely to the task of copying; but here again, all must depend upon the view of the subject taken by the Secretary of State.

If it be of the first importance (as I think it must be admitted) that both Under Secretaries should be cognizant of all the material arrangements which are determined upon by the Colonial Minister there are many minor matters which seem more exclusively to belong to the Permanent Under Secretary, & which cannot be taken out of his hands altogether without mischief;—I allude to the preparing for the consideration of the Secretary of State, of all Papers relating to the internal management of the office, or to proposed alterations in its Establishment—of the proposed disposal of the Secret Service Money & the amount of the vote,—of the Colonial Estimates which are annually laid before Parliament, & of all Circular Dispatches & Notices which are generally distributed either at home or abroad.[2]

The clash of opposed personalities, never overtly admitted, lurks behind these memoranda. It is tempting to make more

[1] C.O. 537/22 Memorandum of James Stephen, March 30, 1832, No. I.
[2] C.O. 537/22 Memorandum of R. W. Hay, April 2, 1832, No. II.

use of them but there is a danger of drawing too many general conclusions from a specific situation. Much more refreshing is Henry Taylor's empirical philosophizing in *The Statesman*. His book does not cavil over details nor make observations with a view to obtaining immediate action. He wanted abundant devolution:

> The most important qualification of one who is high in the service of the state is his fitness for acting *through others* . . . .[1]

Instead of one permanent under-secretary there should be four or six, of whom two at least should be endowed 'with some gifts of philosophy and speculation', in addition to their practical abilities.[2] The head of an important department '. . . ought to be relieved from all business which is not accessory to the performance of his duties as councillor and legislator.'[3] But in addition to soaring freely into the future *The Statesman* had a facetious analysis of how an under-secretary might reduce the business of an office 'within a very manageable compass' without creating a public scandal[4] that was quite obviously intended as an ironical comment on Hay's conduct of business.

Stephen's concern was not how a permanent under-secretary might reduce business without reproach from his colleagues but the 'chronic evil of the lack of punctuality in administering colonial affairs'. It is one with which his successors are still wrestling.[5] In 1832 it was the internal structure of the office that he blamed; in later years he criticized the delays due to the division of powers that gave other departments so much voice in colonial affairs. Of the weaknesses of the office in 1832, its inefficiency in getting papers copied appeared to Stephen the most unforgivable: '. . . the deficiency of Labourers working with their hands is the constant source of the most inconvenient and discreditable delays.'[6] The fourth class of clerks had been added in 1825 'to obviate in some degree the inconvenience which had been experienced from extensively employing Extra Clerks in the Ordinary dispatch of Business.'[7] Some excuse may

---

[1] Taylor, Henry, *The Statesman*, p. 33.
[2] *Ibid.*, p. 106.   [3] *Ibid.*, p. 100.
[4] *Ibid.*, p. 101.
[5] Parkinson, Sir C., *The Colonial Office from Within 1909–1945*, pp. 38–42.
[6] C.O. 537/22 Stephen's Memorandum, Mar. 30, 1832, No. I.
[7] See above pp. 80–1.

be found for Wilmot Horton's failure to anticipate the difficulties that arose as a result of the change in the status of clerkship. No doubt, he was using the generosity of the Treasury and Parliament in the prosperity of 1825 to guard against the possibility of a return to the conditions of 1820, when money for extra clerks was unobtainable. There was also an insistence on uniformity of structure for all departments that made it difficult to suggest, at that time, any radical innovation that might be reminiscent of the old practice of overloading offices with extra clerks.

When senior clerks were given intellectual duties the routine dog-work at the lower levels seemed beneath the station of men who would some day succeed to intellectual tasks. Stephen observed this psychological change in the junior's attitude to copying:

> The change thus made in the nature of the duties of the senior Clerks, required a corresponding change in those below them. Being required on accidental emergencies of absence or illness, to act for their immediate superiors, and looking forward to succeed to their stations, the younger Clerks naturally betook themselves to thought and composition on every possible opportunity, until the humble labour of the desk & pen at length became irksome, as carrying with them some indication of inferiority to associates belonging to the same general rank, and bearing in common with themselves the name of clerks.[1]

If men of the requisite ability and education for the high office entered at the bottom of the ladder that was the only method of access, their initiative and abilities would be blunted in years of performing manual tasks while they were awaiting the opportunity to do the type of work that they had entered the office with a view to perform. Henry Taylor, who had himself been fortunate in beginning near the top rung of the ladder, commented on the frustration of an able person caught up in such a system.

> If he revolt from mechanical labour (as may be expected of a highly educated man of good abilities) and yet find that there is the only task assigned to him, he will lapse into idleness.[2]

[1] C.O. 537/22 Stephen's Memorandum, Mar. 30, 1832, No. I.
[2] Taylor, H., *The Statesman*, pp. 109-110

This is what Stephen also observed in 1832 and without urging, as Taylor did in 1836,[1] that there should be two grades of civil servants, one for manual tasks and one for intellectual duties, he observed that men from the higher ranks of society would not perform manual duties:

> One man writing at 1d/per folio would do more work and do it better than twelve young Gentlemen copying Papers in the interval between their morning Rides and their Afternoon Dinner Parties.[2]

On his recommendation a copying department was instituted shortly afterwards, with the copying clerks paid on a piecework basis—twopence a sheet. According to Taylor copying by the piece was done at five times the speed of copying performed by salaried clerks, and at a third of the cost.[3]

It would be ridiculous to assume the validity of Wilmot Horton's assurance thrown out in the heat of a House of Commons debate in 1826,[4] that every person in the office was fully employed, and to compare it with the chapter in a biography of Cardinal Manning entitled 'The Colonial Office—Love in Idleness',[5] but there is some support for Wilmot Horton's statement. The teen-aged youngsters, who entered on new duties with youthful enthusiasm in the mid-twenties, became bored and lax during the 'years of torpor', as Henry Taylor aptly described the years 1828 to 1830.[6] In part, this was a natural reaction after the initial enthusiasm; in part, as Stephen maintained, the result of the change in the status of clerkship but, in great measure, the failure to provide a material incentive must have been responsible for their lack of interest. From January 1829 to January 1836 the whole establishment of clerks of the assistant, junior and assistant junior classes was completely static, except for the appointment of one of the assistant junior clerks as private secretary to the Earl of Aberdeen from 20

---

[1] Taylor, H., *The Statesman*, pp. 109–10.
[2] C.O. 537/22 Stephen's Memorandum, Mar. 30, 1832, No. I. He expressed the same conviction without sarcasm in 1839 when, on the death of his private secretary, he refused to appoint a successor from the establishment. C.O. 537/22, No. 16.
[3] Taylor, H., *The Statesman*, pp. 110–11.
[4] *Parl. Deb.*, *New Series*, XIV, 1080, March 3, 1826.
[5] Purcell, E.S ., *The Life of Cardinal Manning.*, I., Chapter V.
[6] Taylor, H., *Autobiography*, I, 117.

December 1834 to 24 July 1835. James Walker, who received £140 as a copying clerk in 1826, received £150 as an assistant junior clerk in 1835. When Adam Gordon and George Baillie retired in 1833, the posts of chief clerk and précis writer were abolished as an economy measure, thus further blocking the possibilities of promotion. So intent was the urge to economy that the registration department, one of the most important sections in a well-regulated office, was allowed to become so inefficient that the registers were inadequate.[1] But the only under-secretary who had ever dared to challenge administrative economy in the name of administrative efficiency was off in Ceylon, building roads through the mountains and then sending home for permission to pay for them.[2]

A rough picture of the activity of the Colonial Office following its reorganization is given by the expenditure on extra clerks and copying beyond the regular establishment.[3]

1825	..	..	..	..	£1,125
1826	..	..	..	..	1,285
1827	..	..	..	..	1,400
1828	..	..	..	..	800
1829	..	..	..	..	700

In 1828 seven full-time extra clerks were employed and fourteen other copyists appeared in the office, some of them for considerable periods. Of the sums paid out in 1829 and 1830 over half went in salaries to probationers; apart from them, only one full-time extra clerk was employed and, in 1830, five other copyists, most of them for very brief periods.

In 1830 the office faced the consequences of the too extensive hiring of new clerks in the twenties. There were thirteen young gentlemen under the age of twenty-five, of varying abilities and capacity for business, on a permanent establishment that counted only twenty-three persons who might be classified as clerks. Two of the clerks of the second class were only twenty-

[1] C.O. 537/22, 1835. Nos. 5 and 23.
[2] Mills, L. A., *Ceylon under British Rule 1795–1932*, p. 223.
[3] These figures are taken from the contingent accounts (C.O. 701/2). Totals given by Wilmot Horton in a report to the Treasury in 1826 are slightly different but show the same pattern. See C.O. 701/14 Dec. 15, 1826, enclosure.

two years of age; one of the senior clerks was still under thirty. In 1826 the sixth clerk in the Colonial Office had completed only two years' service; in comparison the sixth clerk in the Home Office had completed twenty-two years, and the sixth clerk in the Foreign Office twenty-five years.[1] In addition to being unable to offer the incentive of promotion, the structure was out of balance because clerks had begun to regard themselves as intellectual workers. It was a poor training school for administrators; recruits had not been selected for merit or education and supervision was irregular and inadequate. But a few able and conscientious individuals were eventually distinguished from the mass and became the leaders of the office in the next forty years.

A glaring weakness, revealed by the years of torpor, was the inadequacy of the Permanent Under-Secretary. When the political leadership was weak he became the centre of the administrative machine. Robert W. Hay displayed neither the powers of leadership nor the initiative necessary for the situation. The legal counsel was forced by his sense of duty to shoulder an even greater burden than he had been carrying, and to suffer abuse for engrossing business that did not normally fall to a legal counsel. And in addition to the increased employment of James Stephen on routine duties, the other extra adviser whom Wilmot Horton had kept near him, Major Moody, was not employed after 1828. Thus, there was a loss of flexibility because all the intellectual workers in the office were employed on day-to-day business instead of giving thought to the more general problems of empire.[2]

[1] Wilmot Horton to Lushington, confidential, June 3, 1826, quoted in Jones, E. G., 'Wilmot Horton', p. 40.

[2] There may have been another adviser on slavery questions in the office. It is not absolutely clear from the account books whether William Matheson, the assistant registrar, is the Matheson who received £200 a year as an extra clerk. On one or two occasions the name is entered as G. Matheson, sometimes as W. Matheson, but more usually as Mr. Matheson. The name disappeared from the payroll about the time that William Matheson left the office in 1828. There is a pamphlet, listed in the British Museum catalogue entitled *A critical Review of a pamphlet (by Sir R. J. W. H.?) entitled 'The West Indies Question practically considered.'* ... *in a letter* ... *to* ... *R. W. H.* (1827), which is ascribed to Gilbert Mathison, who also is listed as the author of a travel book on South America and the Sandwich Islands published in 1823. W. Matheson was appointed secretary and clerk of the Crown in Nevis in October, 1828 (See Appendix III).

But the deficiencies must not be allowed to conceal the fact that a new structure had emerged. At the beginning of the twenties no permanent member of the establishment, with the possible exception of Adam Gordon, was consistently employed on intellectual duties. By 1830, in addition to the Permanent Under-Secretary, there were half a dozen clerks who had been executing responsible duties for a number of years, two or three of whom were men of considerable worth. Some of the assistant and junior clerks were preparing themselves, though haphazardly, to succeed to the senior positions. And James Stephen had been tempered and hardened by almost continuous employment for nine years. Even though his new machine had gone awry in places Wilmot Horton would undoubtedly have repeated, with conviction, in 1830 a statement that he had made in 1826:

> The Department by the greatest degree of labour & pains—by the exertions of the old working Senior Clerks, & (I must say) by the exertions which I myself have made with every assistance from Lord Bathurst, has acquired a very considerable & improving degree of competency to execute the duties imposed on it. Therefore my successor will have a 'beau jour' of it in comparison with me.[1]

[1] Horton to Lushington (Treasury), private, June 3, 1826, quoted in Jones, E. G., 'Wilmot Horton', p. 40.

CHAPTER

4

'THE OFFICE'

When Disraeli, in his last novel,[1] decided that his hero should
begin his political career in a public office, he led him through
'several chambers . . . all full of clerks seated on high stools and
writing at desks.' Despite the lack of detail, the general impression is clear; for the mechanical centre of every office was the
quill pen, driven over endless sheets of durable official note-
paper by the arm of the copying clerk. Such an office had no
mechanical efficiency problems, no equipment which needed to
be carefully placed to facilitate business. Its difficulties were
rather those of providing the minimum conditions in which
administrative work can be carried out in a temperate climate:
adequate space for the storage of large numbers of books and
papers, lighting for a profession which ignored the mornings but
worked late in the evenings, heating in the cold, damp Thames-
side winter, and servants to provide those timeless services
essential in all ages in all houses of business.

The Colonial Office lay amid the tiny cluster of government
offices between St. James's Park and the Thames, conveniently
close to the Houses of Parliament. When his office was created
in 1794 Henry Dundas moved into rooms in the Horse Guards,
thence to a leased house in Parliament Street in 1795.[2] In 1798
a Crown house, No. 14 Downing Street,[3] became available. In
location, No. 14 was ideal, for it stood where the steps now lead
from Downing Street to St. James's Park, conveniently close to
the Prime Minister's residence. Its comfort was marred, however, by a damp basement that had to be pumped out at inter-
vals, and by the generally shoddy construction of the building.[4]
Nevertheless, there were some fine fixtures to provide an air of
elegance, including a famous eighteenth-century chimney-piece

[1] *Endymion.*
[2] C.O. 701/1, p. 4, Entry of April 9, 1796.
[3] *Ibid.*, p. 12, Entry of November 15, 1799.
[4] Williams, T., 'The Colonial Office in the Thirties', p. 141.

124

that was incorporated into the Secretary of State's room when the new Colonial Office was built in 1876.[1] This, according to a rather dubious legend, came from the waiting room, 'the little waiting-room on the right hand', in which Nelson and Wellington, who chanced to call on the Secretary of State at the same hour, met for the first and only time, in the autumn of 1805.[2] At that time the house served as the official residence as well as the office of the Secretary of State. Also residing on the premises were two office keepers and a housekeeper, so it is not surprising that at times additional rooms had to be hired whenever the volume of wartime business required the employment of special clerks.[3]

The post-war reduction of staff in 1816[4] should have provided some spare room, but the space fell prey to a ubiquitous paper hoard as the office was 'assailed with documents of bulk immeasurable without one interval of repose'. By 1822 the accumulated documents were invading even the private quarters of the office keepers.[5] Space had to be found not only for the flood of incoming letters, but also for the additional persons brought into the office in order that it might keep abreast of the task of answering them, and papers had to be moved to give them room to work. When, therefore, in July 1824, Major Moody asked permission to have his office in his own house provided he could find one near Downing Street, his wish was encouraged, so '. . . that many papers only occasionally referred to might be placed therein, and the rooms therefore would be accessible to the Gentlemen of your office.'[6] Moody was unable to find a suitable house in the vicinity, so he set up his office at No. 18 Downing Street, to which the West India department was moved at about the same time. Lord Bathurst's private rooms were also made available for official purposes, chambers being rented for him in Whitehall.[7] On the eve of the further increase in the establishment, in June 1825, four hundred and

[1] Parkinson, Sir C., *The Colonial Office from Within, 1909–1945*, p. 13.
[2] Jeffries, Sir C., *The Colonial Empire and its Civil Service*, p. 207.
[3] C.O. 701/1, p. 101.
[4] See above pp. 21–2.
[5] C.O. 323/196, f. 304.
[6] C.O. 323/200, f. 413.
[7] C.O. 324/146 Horton to Herries, Dec. 15, 1826, pp. 75–6, Nos. 13 and 14.

sixty-nine volumes of official correspondence were removed to the State Paper Office.[1] These moves were accompanied by alterations in the structure of the building.[2] Perhaps some of the alterations were not dictated strictly by the need to provide for more clerks and more papers. A short note in the 1823 accounts, 'To paid Porters for moving Books and Book Cases from the Upper Rooms',[3] may record the transfer of the library to the basement and ground floor, recommended because the weight of the papers was threatening the rickety walls.[4]

Negotiations for taking over a second house were begun in 1826 after notice was received that No. 18 was to be demolished.[5] Next door to the office there was a convenient Crown house, No. 13, occupied by the Judge Advocate General. However, when the Judge Advocate sent a very rude reply to Wilmot Horton's initial query,[6] it became necessary for the Under-Secretary to adopt some other expedient. He therefore proposed to ask the Chancellor of the Exchequer '. . . whether he will be disposed (otherwise we would not apply to him officially) to sanction the appropriation of an eligible second House for the Department.'[7] The Chancellor must have been sympathetic; for, in December, Wilmot Horton took advantage of the usual Treasury request for a reduction in the departmental estimates to emphasize the crowded state of the office. The only room which could be used as a waiting room was a small and inconvenient room, twelve feet by thirteen, which had been 'separated from the space which ought to belong to the Office Keepers and Messengers.'

Into this room [he asserted], every person, whatever his Rank or Station, may be from a Governor General down to a Lascar, is obliged to be shown and it frequently happens that when several persons are there, a Deputation consisting of a number of persons, arrives for the purpose of seeing the Secretary of State or one of the Under Secretaries, and its members are obliged to quarter

[1] C.O. 323/202, f. 358.
[2] See C.O. 324/145, p. 38.
[3] C.O. 701/2 April 8, 1823.
[4] See H.C. 1839 XIII (466) 244 and 252.
[5] C.O. 324/75 Lord Bathurst's Minutes, October 1826, f. 272.
[6] *Ibid.* Wilmot Horton was vexed but Lord Bathurst, with his usual equanimity, minuted '. . . no man is pleas'd with being turn'd out of a good House.'
[7] *Ibid.*

themselves in the passages of the Office. I am also directed by
Lord Bathurst that neither of his Under Secretaries have adjoining
rooms in which their Private Secretaries can sit; and with respect
to the Under Secretary of State who sits on the same floor with his
Lordship,[1] if any person wishes to speak to him confidentially he
has no other alternative than to impede the business of the day by
removing from the room his Private Secretary who is obliged to
sit there, or to receive the individual who may wish for such conversation upon the Staircase which is the alternative to which it
is generally necessary to resort.[2]

Whatever alleviation of these conditions may have been contemplated by Robinson, the Chancellor of the Exchequer, the
real decision was made when the change of government in 1827
deprived the Judge Advocate both of his office and of his 'good
house'. Robinson, who became Lord Goderich and Secretary of
State in April 1827, was able to obtain by default what he had
hitherto been unable to grant.

With the two houses incorporated into one, more than enough
space was available to meet the immediate needs of the office,
so the Secretary of State gave his consent that the basement and
ground floor of No. 13 should be appropriated to the use of one
of the under-secretaries, since

In many supposable causes and particularly in time of War, the
greatest advantage would obviously arise from the residence within the Office itself of a person to take immediate charge of any
business which might require dispatch.[3]

Apparently the Treasury frowned upon this effort to obtain a
house at the government's expense, for, in 1831, Hay reported
to the House of Commons that both houses were

. . . entirely appropriated to the business of the Department,
except part of the basement of each House, which is occupied by
an Office-keeper, with the necessary female servants.[4]

[1] This was Wilmot Horton.
[2] C.O. 324/146 Horton to Herries (Treasury), December 7, 1826, pp.
77–8. This letter also appears with enclosures in C.O. 701/14, p. 154 (+71)
et seq.
[3] Ibid. Hay to Herries (Treasury), July 19, 1827, p. 151. One of the clerks,
Hugh Stuart Kelsey, was allowed to occupy a room during the thirties.
He was required to give it up during a rearrangement of the office in 1840.
See C.O. 537/22 Stephen to Wilder, Jan. 6, 1840, No. 25.
[4] H.C. 1831–32 XXVI (194) 566. At the Foreign Office two clerks lived
on the premises, p. 565.

The expanded building of 1827 continued to serve as the Colonial Office for fifty years. By 1876, when a new building was erected, the office was occupying all the spare rooms in Downing Street,[1] and was mother to a numerous brood of sub-departments scattered around Westminster. By a study of its accommodation alone there is a clear record that the ragged fledgling, which so timidly joined the war department in 1801, had grown to lusty independence in the twenties.

Although the office had increased in size, the original maintenance staff was large enough to meet most of the new needs. The housekeeper seems to have been truly 'the necessary woman', common to public accounts of the period. As Maria Caldwell she appears in the first accounts of the establishment in 1795; as Mrs. Pillochody (she had been married, or remarried, in 1809), she was still housekeeper in March 1837.[2] Her salary from first to last remained at £100 a year, but she received certain perquisites. In 1814 these amounted to £50, out of which she was to pay the salaries of two female servants and some other minor expenses.[3] In the reduced office of 1818 her perquisites amounted to only £32/5/9,[4] but with the growth in the twenties this sum was increased to make allowance for additional female servants.[5] There were two porters in the office,[6] each receiving £136/17/6 annually.[7] One was employed as a doorman. The other evidently had more complicated tasks to perform. There is a memorandum of James Stephen's in 1839 directing that two of the porters then on the staff be required to exchange duties, since the 'upstairs' man, while having an excellent personality for a doorman, was too stupid for the tasks

---

[1] See Pugh, R. B., 'The Colonial Office', p. 749.

[2] C.O. 701/8, 9 and 10. A new housekeeper, Sarah Acland, was appointed by Lord John Russell in 1841. C.O. 537/22 No. 33.

[3] See Appendix IV.

[4] T1/1817/9710 Bathurst to Treasury, May 15, 1819.

[5] C.O. 324/146 Wilmot Horton to Herries (Treasury), Dec. 15, 1826, p. 75.

[6] A third porter 'to perform laborious duties' was hired on a temporary basis in 1825. He received only £40.

[7] Porters are frequently listed as receiving £137 5s. 0d. but, since their basic pay was 7s. 6d. per day, the larger sum would only apply to a leap year. At least till 1820 perquisites in the form of New Year's gifts amounting to £15, were also given. C.O. 323/192 Harrison (Treasury) to Goulburn, April 8, 1820, f. 168.

assigned to him.[1] A proficient porter might, if an opening occurred, become an officekeeper or a messenger. The two officekeepers, who lived on the premises, were responsible for fires, lighting, and the general care of the building. Their constant presence in the office also brought them many small tasks, such as paying the coachman from their own pockets when the Secretary of State found it necessary to use a hired conveyance. Other tasks of considerable importance that they performed were the keeping of accounts of messengers' journeys,[2] and, after 1823, accounts of all issues of stationery.[3] Each officekeeper was entitled to a salary of £100 a year, a New Year's gift of £20, and perquisites of £60, 'with Coals and Candles'.[4] There is even a record of an officekeeper's being asked by a correspondent to obtain information on the progress of a petition that he had sent to the Colonial Secretary.[5]

The day-to-day discipline of the office servants was the responsibility of the chief clerk, but their circumstances and working conditions depended to a great extent on the Secretary of State, who alone could authorize the expenditure of small sums for extras, and who made the recommendations for pensions. Under Lord Bathurst's genial rule conditions were undoubtedly good. There are no positive statements to this effect, but a Treasury stricture in June 1816 against the expenditure of £48/9/0, 'for Wine allowed to the Office Keepers and King's Messengers on Illumination nights', reveals his benevolent attitude.[6] The Treasury solemnly pointed out that no such allowance was made in other government departments, but must have agreed that some concession could be made to the War Office for the great illuminations of Westminster in the year of Waterloo.

In times of adversity the Secretary of State used public money to treat the office servants as he would treat servants in his own house. In 1818 £75 was paid for the medical treatment and funeral of Thomas Robinson, one of the office porters, and a further £5, 'towards Mourning for the Servants of the Office';[7]

---

[1] C.O. 537/22, ff. 54–5.
[2] See below. Special printed forms were provided in 1829.
[3] C.O. 854/1. Printed forms, Jan. 1, 1823.   [4] See Appendix IV.
[5] P.A.C., L.C. 'Q' Series, Black to Allsopp, Feb. 16, 1819, vol. 153, p. 40.
[6] C.O. 323/185, f. 162.
[7] T1/1817/9710, Colonial Office contingent accounts for 1818, enclosed in Lord Bathurst to the Treasury, May 15, 1819.

in 1822 a similar payment was made for the funeral of James Gray, an office porter, '. . . he having died in the execution of his duty'.[1] Children of deceased servants were also frequently assisted from official funds. In 1820 Lord Bathurst ordered the payment of an apprentice fee of £105 for the orphan son of William Lewis,[2] a late officekeeper, and Thomas Robinson's son was frequently employed to copy papers. So many servants died in office that the question of superannuation scarcely arises in this period. Two porters, however, did receive pensions: John Stewart, £70 per annum in 1802, and Arnauld Le Sage, £100 per annum in 1820.[3] The superannuation act of 1810[4] gave pension rights to all civil servants and, in the abortive attempt to establish a superannuation fund in 1821–24, provision was made for contributions from office servants, as from other personnel.[5] This right of lesser civil servants to superannuation, instead of a pension 'during pleasure', was questioned in a report of the finance committee of the House of Commons in 1828, which made a recommendation that no pensions be allowed to artificers and messengers, except under special circumstances.[6] The concern for economy was leading to the adoption of a less considerate attitude towards the lower ranks of the government service.

Occasionally, the veil of the official record lifts sufficiently to reveal a touch of drama in the private lives of these persons who otherwise survive only in name. Arnauld Le Sage, who retired as porter in 1820, 'being no longer capable from age and infirmity of executing the duties of his office which he had hitherto fulfilled with zeal and attention',[7] fled to France to escape his creditors. In 1821 Lord Bathurst, harassed by the importunate demands of the creditors, minuted on one petition:

This is another complaint against Arnauld Le Sage the late Messenger [sic]. He seems to have been a great Rogue & tho' we

[1] C.O. 701/2 p. 99.   [2] C.O. 701/2 p. 75, Aug. 4, 1820.
[3] C.O. 323/192 f. 194.
[4] 50 Geo. III, Cap. 117.
[5] C.O. 323/194 Extract of Treasury minute dated Aug. 10, 1821, enclosed in Lushington to Goulburn, Aug. 13, 1821, ff. 172–8.
[6] H.C. 1828 V(480) 493–4.
[7] C.O. 324/141 Letter to the Treasury Dec. 17, 1819 marked 'Cancelled': also C.O. 323/192 Harrison (Treasury) to Goulburn April 8, 1820 and Sept. 7, 1820, ff. 166 and 194.

cannot undertake to settle his debts, I hardly think that his scandalous Conduct will make it fit to continue Him his pension.[1]

A further note written as an afterthought (not uncommon in Lord Bathurst's minutes) gave a more positive directive:

To be cautioned to come to England & pay his debts [or] to stop his allow[ance].

Le Sage, who was evidently a French refugee, must have mended his ways, for he was still drawing a pension in 1831.

Messengers occupied a niche in the Civil Service peculiarly their own, but since they were drawn from the same ranks of society as the office servants[2] and, like them, ranked a bit below the 'gentlemen' who occupied positions as clerks, observations on their duties will not be out of place at this point. They belonged to a corps designated Messengers of His Majesty's Great Chamber, thirty of whom were assigned to the offices of the Secretaries of State when those offices were remodelled in 1795,[3] the arrangement being that they were to attend in rotation, a fortnight at each office. Each messenger received a salary of £60 annually, paid from the State Paper Office, and board wages of seven shillings and sixpence a day on home service, or thirteen shillings and fourpence a day on foreign service, paid by the office to which he was assigned.

Profits from expense accounts provided a legitimate addition to these emoluments. For letters delivered in the metropolis that could be conveniently carried in the pocket there was no payment unless they were sent express,[4] but foreign journeys were very profitable. They were assigned in rotation to the men fit to travel. At one period during the war each messenger had only one foreign journey in three years, but usually each member of the corps had about one journey a year. A messenger unable to travel abroad could expect a profit on his expense account of

[1] C.O. 323/195 Petition of Stephen Ulderic de Labertauche to Bathurst, (March) 1821, f. 137.

[2] 'There are thirty-eight messengers, most of them retired Army officers of about the Lt.-Col. rank, with a high incidence of D.S.O.'s.' *The Observer*, April 25th, 1954.

[3] C.O. 323/198 Abstract of Sixteenth Report of Select Committee on Finance of 1797, enclosed in Lewis Hertslet's (Foreign Office) Memorandum on the Salaries of the King's Messengers, Dec. 12, 1822, ff. 335–6; see also 323/203, f. 21.

[4] C.O. 323/198 Hertslet's Memorandum, Dec. 12, 1822, f. 329.

about £50 a year, while an individual stationed abroad, or employed frequently on the Continent, might make £300 a year in addition to his salary and board wage. For purposes of the pension act of 1810 the average emoluments of a King's Messenger were taken as £400 per annum, the sum being fixed by reference to the total amount of the bills of the whole corps on an average of several years, '25% on the journies as in the case of the Property Tax being estimated as profit'.[1] This was generous treatment:

> . . . it being considered that, as each messenger is entitled to an equal participation of service and emolument, it would be unjust to calculate the Income of the proposed Pensioner at the low ebb at which it may possibly have arrived, owing to his inability to undertake Foreign Journies in consequence of age and infirmity, and thereby to deprive him of the benefit of his former active services.

The passion for reorganization in the interest of efficiency overtook the messenger corps in the twenties. In 1825 eleven messengers were superannuated, four because of age and infirmity and seven 'for the advantage of the public service';[2] three others had been superannuated on the Colonial Office funds in the previous year.[3] A new establishment of thirty-eight was set up. Eighteen, to be generally employed on foreign service under the immediate orders of the Foreign Office, were to be British subjects under thirty-five with a knowledge of French and qualified for performing journeys on horseback. Twenty messengers, for home service, were to be under forty-five at the time of appointment, and were to be separately attached to the Secretaries of State's offices, six at the Home Office, eight at the Foreign Office, and six at the Colonial Office. The patronage was shared, the three Secretaries of State nominating alternately to vacancies in the list of foreign messengers.[4]

---

[1] C.O. 323/198, ff. 330–1.
[2] C.O. 323/203 Herries (Treasury) to Horton, Feb. 11, 1825, f. 17: the recommendations were made by Peel, Canning and Bathurst, June 30, 1824.   [3] H.C. 1826 XXII (220) 505.
[4] C.O. 323/203 Herries (Treasury) to Horton, Feb. 11, 1825, f. 17. Colonial Office Messengers listed as: Smith, Pegler, Aves, Lack, Pratt and Patten, Messengers on Foreign Service; Hunter, Mestes, Latchford, Littlewood, Dykes, Draffin, Erotch, Newman, Waring, Trylecote, Moore, Fennessy, Hunter, Holmes, Kraus, Kaye, Haviland, and Clews. The last three were appointed by Lord Bathurst.

Lewis Hertslet, librarian at the Foreign Office, who had previously acted as their agent, became superintendent of the messengers with a salary of £350 a year, £100 of which was provided by the Colonial Office. No change was made in their emoluments but a certain 'irregularity', which had crept into the custom of charging coach-hire in the metropolis, was corrected.[1]

The establishment of a Post Office 'express' reduced the number of messengers' journeys on home service outside London.[2] There was sometimes a delay and inconvenience when papers failed to reach the Secretary of State during his peregrinations among the lordly country houses, but, on the whole, the postal service must have been satisfactory or complaints would have been much more frequent. Less urgent messages within London were entrusted to the twopenny post. The employment of six messengers is, therefore, indicative of the extent of communication with other government departments and with individuals within the metropolis.

Travelling in all types of conveyances at all seasons of the year, and sleeping in inns that would rate less than a star in Michelin, imposed a severe strain on the health of the messengers. Added to the discomforts and dangers of the roads were the dangers to which the carrying of confidential information exposed them; violent deaths and even murders were reported from time to time.[3] Since older men were usually appointed, because of the responsible nature of the duties, the strain of foreign journeys was especially great. The appointment of men in their forties was not uncommon and, before the introduction of the new regulations in 1825, appointment of men over fifty years of age was not unknown. The family responsibilities of these men were recognized, widows of messengers appointed before 1821 being entitled to pensions of fifty or seventy-five pounds a year, according to circumstances.[4] Messengers appointed after 4 January 1821 were given to understand that they must provide for their widows and families, 'either by means of

[1] C.O. 323/198 Note on Hertslet's Memorandum, Dec. 12, 1822, f. 332.
[2] *Ibid.* Lewis Hertslet's Memorandum, Dec. 12, 1822, f. 330.
[3] See Hertslet, Sir Edward, *Recollections of the Old Foreign Office*, Chapter VIII.
[4] C.O. 323/212 Foreign Office to Dawson (Treasury), Nov. 12, 1830. (Unsigned draft of a letter), ff. 164–5.

their Savings or by Insurances upon their lives.'[1] Pensions of one hundred pounds a year were still to be awarded to the widows of messengers killed on duty.[2]

Retired messengers were treated more generously. Two, superannuated in 1824 because of ill-health after fourteen and five years of service respectively and a third, who had reached the age of sixty after fourteen years service, were awarded £200 annually.[3] This was considerably more than their entitlement under the act of 1822.[4] Following the drastic reorganization of 1825 there were no further pensions granted until 1830, when there were two, both after long service: John Aves, afflicted with gout at forty-nine, had served the department for eighteen years; Richard Pegler had reached the age of sixty-five and had served twenty-six years. Both of these awards were questioned by the Treasury. Strong representation was made by the Colonial Office before Aves' pension was raised from £100 to £120.[5] The retirement of Pegler on his statutory pension of £230 was still being questioned months after his successor had been appointed, despite a report of the superintendent of messengers stating that he was 'in a state of complete helplessness and imbecility.'[6] A new era had arrived which adopted a strictly economic approach to the reward of civil servants.

While porters ushered in returning governors and messengers hastened out with notes for the Treasury or Ordnance, or while they lazed easily in their attenuated quarters, the chief clerk had frequently to turn his attention from the governing of colonies to the mundane task of ensuring that arrangements for heating and lighting were adequate and supplies satisfactory. Lighting was important in a vocation which made such a fetish

[1] C.O. 323/212, f. 165.
[2] *Ibid.* A pension fund to which messengers contributed was set up by the secretaries of state in 1795 and appears to have continued at least till 1819. C.O. 324/153 Memorial of Sarah Pegler, Jan, 23, 1832, pp. 129–30 (Copy).
[3] H.C. 1826 XXII (220) 505. Two of them died before the year was out.
[4] 3 Geo. IV. Cap. 113.
[5] C.O. 323/212 Aves' Memorial, Feb. 23, 1830, f. 224; also C.O. 324/146 Stewart (Treasury) to Hay, Nov. 17, 1830 and C.O. 701/14, pp. 235 and 238.
[6] C.O. 324/133 Lord Goderich to Stewart (Treasury), Aug. 20, 1831, pp. 110–114. See also Lord Goderich to Treasury, Feb. 10, 1832, requesting a pension for Pegler's widow, pp. 128–30.

of its gentility that, in winter, many hours of natural daylight were ignored, while office hours extended to eight in the evening. Gas lights were used for outside lighting of the office within a decade of their introduction into London,[1] but the inside lighting continued to be provided by oil and candles. For heating, coal fires were used. While general responsibility rested with the chief clerk, the officekeepers looked after the lesser details of ensuring that oil for internal lighting was on hand and that the inadequate coal bins were restocked frequently.[2]

The coals and candles served the clerk, who copied each overseas despatch thrice over, an original to be sent immediately, a duplicate to be sent by a later mail, and an entry in the book of 'Out-Letters' for the official record. With his pens, ink, ruler, sand and penknife the clerk was typewriter, duplicator and calculator. Where many copies of a letter were required, other methods of duplication, such as printing and lithography, were available, but they were expensive and of less wide application than the clear hand of the copying clerk. Pens were expended in enormous quantities. Two thousand were ordered in three lots between April 1795 and January 1796,[3] when there were only nine persons in the office. Later they are seldom listed separately from stationery, but the bills for that item record the increasing business of the office almost as surely as a quantitative table of the letters despatched.[4]

When Wilmot Horton was reorganizing the office the perennial problem of the excessive use of stationery came to his attention, and a regular system of issue was adopted. The officekeepers were instructed to prepare a book, and to receive a signature for every issue of stationery. All articles were to be issued in the following proportions:

> 100 pens
> 1 quire of Crown Paper, Gilt, or Black
> $\frac{1}{2}$ ream Folio Paper $\frac{1}{2}$ ream Folio Envelope
> $\frac{1}{2}$ ream Quarto Paper $\frac{1}{2}$ ream Quarto Envelope

[1] C.O. 701/2 July 25, 1816, 'To paid Gas Light Company for Lighting Lamps to 24th June last . . . . £1:17:9.' Gas lighting was first used in London streets in 1807.

[2] For a discussion of coal supplies to government offices see below pp. 154–5.

[3] C.O. 701/1, pp. 1–5.

[4] See below pp. 155–6.

½ ream Note Paper
3 quires Blotting Paper
1 lb. sealing wax
1 box wafers [dried paste used for fastening letters, holding
    papers together, etc.]
1 dozen of pencils
12 pieces of Tape or Silk
Knives, erazors, scissors, etc. when required.[1]

The length of tape is not specified but, anyway, the quantity
was hardly relevant when Carlyle was seeking a metaphor in
which to tie up the delays and endless formalities of mid-
nineteenth-century government administration.[2] Wilmot Horton's deprecatory word was not 'redtape' but 'pinnery', with
its participial form, 'ad-pinned'.

Where aids were available the War Office had not been
slow in adopting them. A simple map-making machine was
acquired soon after the office was established,[3] and in 1799 a
'copying machine' was purchased.[4] The so-called copying
machine was a press invented by James Watt in 1780. It used
dampened sheets of very thin paper which, when pressed on a
letter, took up sufficient ink to make a readable copy. It was, of
course, a copy in reverse and had to be read by holding the
paper up to the light. Besides the unattractiveness of the copies,
there was also the disadvantage that the copies could be taken
only after the ink had firmly set on the original letter, a matter
of several days or weeks. In addition the number of copies was
limited. The copying press had its uses, especially in the military
departments during the war when the liaison between departments was very close and one department had frequently to
consult the records of another. An indication of the extent of its
use is given by the one hundred and forty-seven press copy
books, 'All Subjects & Departments, various dates 1793–1816,'
sent by Wilmot Horton to the Deputy Keeper of State Papers
in 1825.[5] By the number of times that it was repaired it is

[1] C.O. 854/1 Printed form, Jan. 1, 1823.
[2] Murray, Sir James, ed., *A New English Dictionary on Historical Principles*,
Part 1 Vol. IX, (1919), 'Redtape'.
[3] C.O. 701/1, p. 8.
[4] *Ibid.* p. 14. 'October 30, 1799–To paid Messrs Folgham for a Copying
Machine £13:4:9.' There is one of these copying machines, sold by Bra-
mah's, in the Science Museum in South Kensington.
[5] C.O. 323/203 Robt Lemon to Horton, June 2, 1825, f. 358.

evident that the Colonial Office also found it very useful. Some departments,[1] however, frowned on its use, so there is a tinge of apology in a letter sent by Wilmot Horton to the Treasury in 1826:

> The impossibility of copying on a sudden by the means of the present Establishment of Clerks all papers which require to be copied has made it absolutely necessary in this Department to resort to the daily use of the Copying Machine by which an extreme saving of time and labour is made in the Public Service.[2]

'Few questions are well considered till they are largely written about,' wrote Henry Taylor in 1836,[3] thus giving succinct expression to the philosophy that dominated colonial administration in the years that followed. The frequent conferences and interviews of the twenties he deplored as time-wasting, and they had the added disadvantage that adequate minutes were seldom kept so no records were available for later consultation. Nevertheless, although officials in the twenties did not make a fetish of keeping records of all intra-departmental discussions, Wilmot Horton did insist that scraps of paper containing official comments should be carefully preserved, and thus prepared the way for the systematic minuting and record-keeping introduced in the thirties. Other improvements were also effected, notably an insistence on a regular system of preparing and docketing the despatches[4] sent home by the governors, with consequent advantages in storing and filing them. Because of this serious effort to preserve all written records relating to official business and to keep careful indexes of incoming correspondence the official memory of the Colonial Office for a time in the mid-twenties was much better than it

[1] A copying press was introduced into one department of the Board of Trade in 1850. The Treasury did not have one at that time. The Ordnance, a very progressive department, had one in 1786. See Cohen, E., *The Growth of the British Civil Service*, p. 125.

[2] C.O. 324/146 Horton to Herries, December 15, 1826, pp. 66-7, No. 6. For the cost of copying in general see Chapter V. Carbon paper was tested by Sir Humphrey Davy in 1818. It was carboned on both sides, the intention being that the writing be done with a stylus—the 'original' becoming a reverse copy. It was not used in the Colonial Office in this era.

[3] *The Statesman*, p. 103.

[4] See below; also Appendix IX.

had been previously and indeed better than later writers have credited.

The man responsible for looking after the papers was George Mayer, the librarian. Incoming correspondence did not concern him until it had accumulated in such quantity in the departments of the office that it became necessary to turn it over to his care. In the thirties departments kept despatches for two years before handing them over; earlier, when the numbers were smaller, they may have held on to them for a longer time. For some reason never explained, the librarian seems to have had a special responsibility for out-going correspondence and Mayer was expected to remain at the office every evening until the eight o' clock mail had left. It is likely that he had to make sure that an accurate copy was kept of each out-going letter and a record of its being sent; he may also have been responsible for ensuring that duplicates of overseas letters were sent by a later mail. One senior clerk remained with him to frank the despatches.

In an official letter to the Treasury, dated 22 July 1831, the duties of the librarian were described as requiring 'knowledge of a peculiar nature, and an unusual degree of Memory, punctuality and method. As Keeper of all the Records from the earliest period of British Colonization, the Chief Librarian is entrusted with duties which are both "Confidential and Important" and which demand an extreme degree of attention and labour.'[1] The nature of these duties made it inevitable that he should bear a large share of the responsibility for preparing papers for Parliament; as Parliamentary interest in the colonies increased, his duties became proportionately more arduous[2] with the result that in the thirties and forties the library itself was badly neglected[3]. The commission of enquiry into the Colonial Office in 1849,[4] of which Sir Charles Trevelyan was a member, recognized Mayer's significant but peculiarly personal contribution to the work of the office, and some of the papers prepared by him in answer to Parliamentary questions bear witness to his diligence. Even the historically-minded

[1] C.O. 324/146 p. 310.
[2] See H.C. 1839 XIII (466) 252–9.
[3] Pugh, R. B., 'The Colonial Office', p. 721.
[4] H.C. 1854 XXVII (1715) 79–97.

individual who asked for 'a list of members of the House of Commons in the first Parliament of George I (1715–22) and in the first Parliament of George II (1727–34) who held any office, place, pension, contract, or reversion thereof during the time he sat in Parliament' was provided with an answer after a check of old grants and warrants.[1]

In the twenties it was already assumed that the newspapers provided a very useful supplement to the official records. In addition to the colonial newspapers, which governors were encouraged to send, a number of English and continental newspapers were subscribed to by the office. Librarians were instructed to extract articles on colonial subjects and to form them into commonplace books for easy reference.[2] In 1818, the newspapers and stamps for their receipt cost the office £142.[3] In 1826 the larger department was attempting to glean information from a wider variety of sources; its expenditure on this item was £297.[4] When, in the following year, the estimates of the department had to be reduced, several continental newspapers were discontinued.[5] In 1837 governors were instructed to send home copies of leading colonial newspapers and the files of these were kept in the office.

The acquiring of books for the library was not a major consideration since so few were published on the colonies in this era. Patrick Colquhoun's book *A Treatise on the Population, Health, Power and Resources of the British Empire in Every Part of the World*[6] (1814) was one of the few significant works on the colonies to appear before 1820. A more ambitious, though not original, work was G. A. Thompson's *Alçedo—Dictionary of America and the West Indies*—five volumes quarto, ten guineas—published in 1816 with later supplements. Two copies were acquired by the Colonial Office.[7] Less voluminous works were sometimes purchased in larger quantities. Ten copies of the fourth edition of J. Marshall's 'revised and enlarged' *Statistics of*

---

[1] C.O. 323/197, ff. 210–11.
[2] C.O. 324/146 Horton to Herries (Treasury), Dec. 15, 1826, pp. 65–6, No. 3.   [3] T.1/1817/9710 Bathurst to Treasury, May 15, 1819.
[4] C.O. 324/146 Horton to Herries, Dec. 15, 1826, pp. 65–6.
[5] C.O. 324/146 p. 117.
[6] C.O. 323/182 Colquhoun to Gordon, Aug. 24, 1814, f. 282.
[7] C.O. 323/185, f. 137 and C.O. 323/209, f. 219.

the British Empire were ordered by Twiss in July 1829.[1] One or two statistical studies of individual colonies also appeared during this period, notably Wentworth's on New South Wales in 1819[2] and Gourlay's on Upper Canada in 1822.[3] But most books acquired by the Colonial Office were of a more general nature. Books by travellers, missionaries, and publications of government departments added to the volume of information in the library. In 1831 Jared Sparks sent Mayer several copies of his *Diplomatic Correspondence of the American Revolution* to be distributed among various government departments and acknowledged the many civilities that he had received in the public offices in London.[4] Congressional papers giving information on American land policy were obtained for the library in 1830 by Major Moody.[5]

Financial assistance was occasionally given to aid the publication of works which would be of special value or in which the Colonial Office had some interest. In 1826 £100 was given to Major Denham in aid of a publication on his explorations in West Africa, and £160 to Mr. Johnston 'towards the publication of a valuable work on Spanish Law'.[6] George Mayer was consulted not only on books to be purchased for the library but on the merits of works for which assistance was requested.[7] The most notable instance of assistance towards publication during this period appeared in the Colonial Office estimates for 1830; £400 to Captain Franklin 'towards defraying the expense of publishing prints for illustrating the botanical and zoological specimens collected in North America by the expedition lately under his command'.[8]

[1] This book or pamphlet must have depended largely on the patronage of government departments and Members of Parliament for according to Marshall's circular Hume took ten copies, the Treasury fifty, the Mint five, the East India Company ten and the Admiralty ten. C.O. 323/211 July 20, 1829.

[2] Wentworth, W. C., *A Statistical Description of the Colony of New South Wales*, 1819.

[3] Gourlay, R., *General Introduction to a Statistical Account of Upper Canada*, 3 vols. 1822.

[4] P.A.C., L.C. 'Q' Series, vol. 200–2, p. 327. Other historians who consulted the records of the department in this era were Napier and Thomas Southey.   [5] *Ibid.*, vol. 195, p. 216 and vol. 192, p. 580.

[6] C.O. 324/146 Horton to Herries (Treasury), Dec. 15, 1826, p. 67, No. 7.

[7] C.O. 323/209, f. 92.

[8] H.C. 1830 XVIII (127) 546. The expeditions of both Denham and Franklin had been sent out by direction of the Secretary of State.

As part of the reorganization of the office in the twenties an effort was made to provide a more adequate map collection, there having been in the office in 1820 only 'a very few maps other than those general maps which have been from time to time published'.[1] In 1826 alone about £400 was spent on new books and maps, chiefly maps, large numbers of which were obtained from the Admiralty.[2] At that time a geographer was employed in the duty of copying and constructing maps and plans. In 1827 Mr. Thompson, who held this post originally, was appointed to a situation in New South Wales. His successor, Mr. Hebert, was recommended to the Colonial Office as the best geographer in London.[3] The *Catalogue of Maps, Plans, and Charts in the Library of the Colonial Office* (1910) lists several maps as his work. In addition to the expenditure from Colonial Office funds governors were, in several cases, directed to spend colonial money for the preparation of adequate maps of their colonies.[4]

George Mayer must have been well pleased during the 'twenties by the insistence on a uniform system of preparing and docketing despatches. Certainly the new devotion to regularity must have been invaluable to him in arranging the departmental records. Instructions were sent in 1818[5] requiring the numbering of official despatches and the sending of a letter on December 31 each year stating the number of letters addressed by the writer to the office in the course of the year. Despatches not immediately connected with the series of official correspondence, or on private matters, were not to be numbered but marked 'separate' or 'private'. In 1823 Wilmot Horton requested governors to keep public and private correspondence entirely distinct:

> . . . and the practical test of this distinction will be, simply to consider whether there is *any* objection as affecting the public interest that the subject discussed, or proposed, should appear in the Archives of the Department. If *no objection* should exist, it is

---

[1] C.O. 323/192, f. 237.

[2] C.O. 324/146 Horton to Herries (Treasury), Dec. 15, 1826, No. 4, p. 66. See also C.O. 323/205, f. 11.

[3] C.O. 323/207, ff. 424-7.

[4] A circular dated Jan. 1, 1827 requested governors of the West Coast of Africa, the Cape, and Eastern colonies to make half-yearly reports on the advance of geographical knowledge. See C.O. 854/1.

[5] Appendix IX.

infinitely more convenient for the despatch of public business that the matter should be expressed in a public letter and kept with the other records of the Department, and that for this purpose the letter should begin 'Sir' and not be marked 'private'.[1]

In addition to sending the regular duplicates of despatches, governors were instructed to send to the Under-Secretary a short summary of separate points contained in any series of them, '. . . this summary not to go into details but merely sufficient to revive the recollection of any person who has carefully read the despatches.'[2] Wilmot Horton's circular accompanied an official instruction from Lord Bathurst directing governors to confine each despatch to a single subject. Specific 'heads' were listed: 'Executive Government', 'Finance', 'Trade', 'Judicial Affairs', 'Military Affairs', 'Slavery', 'Civil Servants' (including all questions on their appointments, promotions, claims, leaves of absence, and resignations), and 'Miscellaneous'.[3] Instructions on the numbering of despatches and on use of paper of uniform size to facilitate binding were also included.[4] Another circular dated 26 July 1825[5] complained of the inconvenience of governors' not following 'private directions' on the preparation of despatches. In addition to repeating previous instructions in a new form, this circular urged that 'strictly' private letters for the consideration only of the Secretary of State or Under-Secretary should be marked 'secret and confidential'.

Even the arrangements for despatching the official mail were of administrative significance, since much of the organization of empire was determined by the time that elapsed between an order and its execution, between the sending of an enquiry to a colonial governor and the receipt of his reply. The months that a letter spent aboard ship were governed by the irrevocable decisions of the winds; the hours that a packet remained in port were hours granted to man's control. If a letter should miss the sailing of a packet it might be delayed for several weeks, or even months. During the war difficulties sometimes arose in finding sufficient packets to maintain an attenuated schedule;[6] sometimes postal officials were lax under the stress

---

[1] C.O. 854/1 Circular signed by Horton, Sept. 1823.
[2] *Ibid.*   [3] *Ibid.*   [4] *Ibid.*   [5] *Ibid.*
[6] See for example C.O. 323/181, f. 51.

of war conditions. In January 1809 a ship's captain reported finding a bag of despatches addressed to the secretary of state for war and the colonies in a passenger's 'bed place' when the ship was being inspected after the passengers had disembarked.[1] Four months later a bag of despatches for Halifax was returned to England in one of the portmanteaus containing the English mail.[2] With the peace, delays in receipt seem to have been largely confined to those caused by customs officials at the outports who, in their zeal to prevent smuggling, sometimes held up parcels addressed to the Secretary of State. Each individual offence called forth a vigorous protest from the Colonial Office until, in 1819, regulations were made requiring customs officials to obtain a receipt from persons entrusted with despatches for the heads of government departments,[3] who in turn were required to acknowledge receipt of the parcels.

The system of despatching mail from the Colonial Office was on a very unsatisfactory basis all through the twenties. The overseas mail left the Lombard Street Post Office at eight o'clock in the evening. Letters from government departments were supposed to be delivered to the Post Office by a quarter to eight. As early as 1802 there was a protest that precious time required in preparing despatches after the close of the office was not available, because the mail from two or three public offices was being collected by one man instead of being despatched by messenger from each office.[4] Evidently no action was taken on this, for the complaint was made in 1824 that one messenger was collecting the mail from all the offices and that frequently the mail arrived at the Post Office as late as a quarter to eight, thus making it difficult to despatch the mail coaches punctually.[5] The Colonial Office was prepared to admit itself the principal offender and to accept the justice of the postal secretary's rebuke.[6] Overwhelmed by the increasing volume of business, and suffering from the defects of a largely youthful and inexperienced staff, whose keenness did not always compen-

[1] C.O. 323/179, ff. 96–8.
[2] Ibid., ff. 147–8.
[3] C.O. 323/190 Lushington to Goulburn, Feb. 15, 1819, f. 218.
[4] C.O. 323/176 Freeling to Sullivan, Feb. 6, 1802, f. 25.
[5] C.O. 323/198 C. Dawson (Home Office) to Wilmot Horton, Nov. 3, 1824, enclosing F. Freeling to Hobhouse, Oct. 30. 1824, ff. 350–2.
[6] C.O. 324/145 Horton to Freeling, Dec. 22, 1824, p. 59.

sate for their lack of knowledge of official habits, it could not find a remedy within its own organization. It therefore begged to be allowed for its own use all the spare minutes which could be wrung from the system by having a postal official attend at the office in the evening to accept the mail and place it on the mail-coach as it passed by on its way westward to Falmouth.[1] A personal conference between the Postmaster-General and Lord Bathurst must have decided that Horton's proposal was impracticable, for complaints continued that the mail was being delayed by the late arrival of Colonial Office despatches.[2] Although Wilmot Horton did not cease to press for a new arrangement the situation must have improved, or he must have charmed Freeling, the secretary to the Post Office, for the exacerbation that had crept into Freeling's letters in 1824 had given way in 1826 to helpful co-operation.[3]

It was not until 1830 that the Post Office, still protesting the difficulty of punctual despatch of mail coaches 'from the Late Hour, at which the bulk of the Letters from the Public Offices are received at the General Post Office', made new arrangements for the collection of letters from the offices of the Secretaries of State. A person from the General Post Office was to collect letters at 5.45 p.m., and a 'Despatch Cart was to call at 6.55 p.m., by which time the bag was to be in readiness. Any letters remaining were to be forwarded by a Colonial Office messenger.[4] A few weeks earlier arrangements had been made for the collection of despatches from the branch post office at Charing Cross, instead of from the main office in St. Martin's-le-Grand.[5]

The suspicion of the customs officers that the official mail was being used as a means of defrauding the revenues has already been noted. A much more persistent loss of revenue arose from the minor patronage exercised by ministers in permitting their friends to send private letters and parcels by the official mail. At one time, clerks in the secretaries of state's offices had had

---

[1] C.O. 324/145 Horton to Freeling, Dec. 22, 1824, p. 59.
[2] C.O. 323/203 Freeling to Horton, Jan. 19, 1825, f. 336 and Sept. 15, 1825, f. 410.
[3] C.O. 323/205 Freeling to Horton, private, Sept. 15, 1826, f. 375.
[4] C.O. 323/212 Freeling to Hay, Mar. 16, 1830, f. 206.
[5] Ibid., Feb. 3, 1830, f. 202.

the same privilege, but their right of franking had been taken from them in 1764 and compensation provided by an Act of Parliament of 1769.[1] They were still able, however, to send and receive their personal letters under franks provided by the Secretary of State and the Under-Secretaries. Thomas Amyot, in a letter to one of his antiquarian friends who lived outside London, advised him to save postage by addressing his letters to the Under-Secretary of State with the initials 'T.A.' at the left-hand corner of the envelope, the inner cover to be addressed to him personally.[2] On the other hand, official letters were sometimes addressed to persons in the office who had not the right to receive their mail postage-free; in 1829 the secretary of the Post Office complained that the covers of packets were being frequently returned to the Post Office with a claim for the recovery of postage, or a certificate that the contents were largely official.[3] Each incoming despatch bag from the colonies con-contained its quota of private letters. These, divested of their outer covers, were entrusted to the internal postal system, the twopenny of London, or the more expensive system outside town. Outgoing personal letters were also numerous; since colonial postal rates were high, there were many requests to have letters sent in the official mail. Refusals to these requests were rare, though officials sometimes complained about the number of people who took advantage of the privilege.[4] The actual franking of despatches was performed by one of the senior clerks who acted as deputy for the Secretary of State under an informal agreement with the Postmaster-General.

In all its internal arrangements the office of 1812 was a gentleman's house in which the clerks, like youthful relations, went about their tasks under the kindly, paternal eye of the Secretary of State. As business grew the house became inadequate. Not only was it not sufficiently roomy to provide space for additional personnel and for the storage of documents, but the structure was not designed to bear the weight of the papers that had to be

[1] See above pp. 25–6.
[2] Br. Mus. Egerton Mss. 2660, Correspondence of the family Hutchinson, Aug. 24, 1825, f. 189.
[3] C.O. 323/211 Freeling to Hay, Aug. 3, 1829.
[4] See C.O. 323/209 Minutes on a letter from S. M. Edgecumbe to Horton, Aug. 18, 1828, f. 72.

kept at hand. The problem of space was solved when the house next door became available in 1827. The two houses, converted into one, provided accommodation which, although not ideal, was more adequate than that of some other government departments.[1]

If administrators were to be free to devote themselves to their tasks many services had to be provided for them. Most of the commonly accepted comforts of a household were arranged by the office servants. They looked after the heating, lighting, and cleaning; ushered visitors in and out; carried books and papers; procured supplies; kept minor accounts; and carried messages, within the office, to other government departments in the vicinity, and, when necessary, to Malta or the Ionian Islands. In general the Government was very indulgent in its treatment of these servants, but a trend away from paternal care towards the impersonal justice of large organizations was apparent towards 1830.

At another level were the services provided for the administrators by the library and the Post Office. As the volume of papers grew the librarian's importance increased. More order was required in the papers when they became too numerous for individual memory to recall; insistence on a uniform method of preparing official correspondence aided in filing the documents in a more orderly fashion. Books, newspapers and maps were acquired by the library to supplement the official sources of information. The Post Office service for carrying colonial despatches was not always easily fitted into Colonial Office routine. In an age of sailing ships and stage coaches it may seem strange to find departments quarrelling over delays of a few minutes, but minutes might mean months if they were the minutes between the end of business for the day and the leaving of the mail-coach with the overseas mail.

[1] The two Colonial Office houses were described by the Surveyor of Works and Buildings in 1839 as merely 'decrepit to a certain degree', while some of the five occupied by the Foreign Office, in addition to being inconveniently arranged, were not only unsound, but were sinking into the alluvial soil of the ancient watercourse over which they were built. H.C. 1839 XIII (466) 241–4.

5

THE FINANCIAL SYSTEM
OF THE OFFICE

The persistence into the nineteenth century of the traditional independence of government departments is clearly apparent from an examination of the account books of the Colonial Office. Instead of being a unit in an accounting system, the office was an independent institution that merely reported its expenditures annually to the Treasury and observed, within limits, the principles of economy that the age enjoined on all departments. It received its own revenue, it paid its own bills. The revenue, admittedly, was not enough to meet all the bills but in drawing on the Exchequer for block grants, the department paid for the services of the clerks of the Exchequer according to a form prescribed centuries before the Treasury assumed the central role among the government departments, and thus, in form at least, it did not prejudice its independent and equal status.

Distinctiveness the office certainly had, but changes in the financing of the public service, begun before the office was set apart in 1795 and continued in the years that followed, made the appearance of independence to a considerable extent illusory by 1830. The size of salaries and the number of persons receiving them were, nominally in 1795 and definitely in 1830, determined outside the department. By 1830 the awarding of pensions and the determination of their size had also passed out of the hands of the Secretary of State. In addition, by 1830, the provision of accommodation for the office was decided by the Treasury, stationery and printing were obtained through prescribed channels and even the supplying of coal had come under parliamentary scrutiny. Many of the old customs and prejudices that had developed in the office of the Secretary of State over the centuries were still retained but the trend was definitely away from an independent departmental service in the direction of a single integrated Civil Service.

The official accountant for public money received and expended by the office was the chief clerk. Adam Gordon reported in 1829 that he kept the Colonial Office funds 'in the Bank of Messrs Coutts & Co. in a separate Public Account';[1] the authority of the Secretary of State or of an Under-Secretary was obtained for every expenditure. Three separate accounts were made up to the fifth of January[2] in each year under the heads of 'Fee Fund Account', 'Contingent Account', and 'Messengers Account', and transmitted to the Treasury,'. . . after having been examined, approved & signed by the Secretary & Under Secretary of State and sworn to by the Accountant before one of the Barons of the Exchequer'.[3] Occasionally the chief clerk held other public money for services executed under the direction of the Colonial Office. In January 1828, Gordon reported a balance of over two thousand pounds in the hands of 'the Bankers, Messrs Drummond', which was being used to meet the expenses of 'the Land Arctic Expedition under Captain Franklin'.[4]

Ancient practice permitted officeholders to take fees in return for the official services they provided, thus, incidentally, assuring them a large measure of freedom from control. Fees, 'charged according to immemorial usage', were still taken in the Colonial Office but they were no longer distributed in the traditional way. Instead, by a reform that was gradually extended throughout the public service, in the departments of the Secretaries of State before the setting up of the third division of the office in 1795, in the Board of Trade by 1810,[5] and in the Slave Registry Office on its creation in 1819,[6] fees were paid into a general fund, the 'Fee Fund,' out of which the salaries and pensions of the members of the establishment were paid. The income from fees collected in the Colonial Office was not large but the Colonial Secretary was also entitled to a share of the fees received in the offices of the other Secretaries of State, the fees received in the three offices being shared equally among

[1] C.O. 323/211 Gordon to Hay, June 3, 1829. Under 'G'.
[2] The practice of having the financial year coincide with the calendar year began in 1833.
[3] C.O. 323/211 Gordon to Hay, June 3, 1829.
[4] *Ibid.*
[5] Cockroft, G., *The Public Life of George Chalmers . . .*, p. 114.
[6] See C.O. 323/212, f. 204.

them. In several of the war years the fees, swollen by the large number of military commissions, were more than sufficient to meet the bill for the salaries and pensions of the establishment. From 1812 onwards, however, it was always necessary to meet the deficiency of the fee fund by a Treasury warrant on the civil list, which at that time supplied many government salaries as well as meeting the expenses of the royal household.

Of the fees received in the Colonial Office those charged on patents to governors were largest in amount; this is the scale given in a report to the House of Commons in 1833:[1]

Warrant to Attorney General	£ 7	13	6
If a Reference £2 2 6 additional			
If a Revocation £2 15 0 additional			
Bill, if only one skin	7	13	6
For every additional skin £6 7 6			
Gratuities	6	6	0
Gratuities of office	53	15	0
Plantation Office	37	16	0
Instructions	6	7	6
If a letter to the Treasury £2 2 6			
If a letter to the Admiralty £2 2 6			

In addition to the fees paid to the Colonial Office, governors paid various other fees on their commissions. The stamp duty alone, regulated by an act of 1815, was £200 on an appointment with an income of £3,000 a year and upwards, and the total expenses of letters patent, including the stamp, might range from £450 to £600 depending on the number of sheepskins used. In the older colonies patents required several skins, in some of the conquered colonies only one skin was needed.[2]

In contrast to the large fees paid by governors,[3] which were swollen by following the ancient practice of passing their commissions under the Great Seal, lieutenant-governors paid only £9/15/6, exclusive of *ad valorem* stamp, all of it to the Colonial

---

[1] H.C. 1833 VII (516) 360.

[2] There was some return. Outgoing governors received a grant of £122/12/6 for chapel plate and chapel furniture, also a portrait of the reigning monarch, which cost about £400. These allowances to governors, paid from civil contingencies of the Treasury, came to an end during Sir George Murray's term of office. H.C. 1830 XVIII (127) 551.

[3] H.C. 1833 VII (516) 360.

Office.[1] Colonial bishops paid about seventeen pounds[2] to the office on their warrants, archdeacons usually about thirty pounds.[3] Upper Canada College paid £42/16/6 in fees to the office for its charter,[4] the 'West Indies Company' £131/11/6.[5] Occasional fees were also obtained for licences to cut timber in Canada, on charters for the various commissions of enquiry, on warrants for the distribution of booty and warrants for trials for piracy, for colonial passports, for passing colonial estimates (ten shillings each), and for the signature of the Secretary of State (two pounds, two shillings and sixpence). A considerable sum was also received in the form of fees on military commissions issued to officers of the army of the East India Company.

The Colonial Office paid fees as well as receiving them. When drawing bills on the Exchequer it paid £34/10/2 on a bill for £1,000, while on £4,000 the payment was £109/10/2, made up as follows:[6]

On £1,000			
Treasury	£ 8	6	
Auditor & Pells	21	19	
½ Tellers	3	15	
Receiver & Stamp		10	2
	34	10	2
On £4,000			
Treasury	£ 8	6	
Auditor	25	7	
Pells	15	7	
Tellers	60		
Receiver & Stamp		10	2
	109	10	2

Since Lord Bathurst was a teller of the Exchequer (with an income of £2,835/2/0 a year in 1830;[7] he also held the post of clerk to the Crown with an income of £1,105/18/10), he nominally

[1] C.O. 701/1 p. 127.
[2] C.O. 701/9 Bishop of Nova Scotia, 1825; Bishop of Quebec, 1826.
[3] *Ibid.* Three appointments in 1825.
[4] C.O. 701/9 p. 72.
[5] *Ibid.*, p. 62.
[6] T.1/1817/9710 Bathurst to Treasury, May 15, 1819.
[7] H.C. 1830–31 VII (23) 229.

received fees on bills drawn on the Exchequer and authorized by him in his capacity of secretary of state. The paying of fees on Exchequer bills may have been the height of contradiction, but it was not the only contradictory feature in the fee system. On occasion the Colonial Office indirectly paid fees even to itself. This occurred whenever a governor-in-chief was appointed for British North America, on which occasion three patents were issued, one as governor-general of the Canadas, one as governor of Nova Scotia, and one as governor of New Brunswick. Since the governor-in-chief's duties in these last two colonies were almost entirely nominal, and no salary was attached to them, the Colonial Office reimbursed him for the expense of taking out the patents. Fees paid into the 'Fee Fund' were reimbursed from the 'Contingency Fund'. The Duke of Richmond received £702/16/0 in 1818[1] and Lord Dalhousie £729/19/6 in 1820;[2] the payment of only £519/1/0 to Sir James Craig in 1807 seems to indicate that, at times, the payment of fees to the Colonial Office did not even constitute a book entry. The expense of the fees was repaid to outgoing colonial officials in a few other instances, but rarely to colonial governors.[3]

Fees received annually by the Colonial Office in the years from 1812 to 1830 varied irregularly from slightly over eight hundred pounds to almost three thousand pounds, the average being about eleven hundred and fifty pounds a year.[4] Its share of the fees received in the offices of the three Secretaries of State was less variable. In 1812 it was about sixteen thousand pounds; at its lowest in 1818 it was less than seven thousand pounds, having declined gradually in the intervening years. It remained between seven and eight thousand pounds from 1819 to 1823, then declined again in 1824 and 1825. In 1827 it reached another peak of close to eleven thousand pounds and declined once more, to about eight thousand five hundred pounds in 1829 and 1830.

The total expenditure for salaries and superannuation on the establishment authorized by order in council was £17,616 in 1812, of which £1,086 was paid by Treasury warrant. In 1815,

---

[1] T.1/1817/9710 Bathurst to Treasury, May 15, 1819.
[2] C.O. 701/2, p. 73.
[3] See, however, C.O. 701/1, p. 127.
[4] The account books giving details of the fee fund are Series C.O. 701, Nos. 8, 9 and 10.

the last year of the wartime establishment, the total was £18,915, of which £6,835 was met by a warrant on the Treasury. The lowest expenditure for salaries and superannuation was £17,150 in 1821, of which £9,572 was drawn from the Treasury. From 1826 onwards the expenditure was more than £26,000 a year, reaching £26,820 in 1830. The largest amount drawn from the Civil List account at the Treasury to meet the 'deficiency on the fee fund' was £19,397 (plus the fees on Treasury warrants) in 1827. Since the fees were also large in that year, a surplus of over £6,000 was built up in the fee fund account, a considerable part of which was still retained in 1830. The actual deficiency of the fee fund in 1829 and 1830 was over £18,000 annually. By that time fees covered only a fraction of the total salary bill so the term 'fee fund' was scarcely applicable. Beginning in 1831 superannuation was paid directly by the Treasury and no longer appears in the Colonial Office accounts.

The bills drawn by the chief clerk to meet the deficiency of the fee fund were officially described as 'Sums issued without account except that required by the Secretary of State'. An annual return was, however, submitted to the Treasury[1] giving details of their expenditure. In addition an annual return was required by Parliament giving details of the increase and diminution of salaries and pensions in the public offices.[2]

Glimpses of the hand-to-mouth existence of the Treasury occasionally come to light in the records. One in 1814, is especially revealing:

> Mr. Cotton's Compliments to Mr. Chapman and requests he will have the goodness to send the Certificate of the different Governors abroad to 5th July last, as there is nearly money in the Exchequer sufficient for the Payment of their Salaries to that Period.
> Treasury Chambers
> 21 October, 1814.[3]

---

[1] Most of these have apparently been destroyed but there is a record of them in the Treasury indexes. That for 1818 is preserved in T1/1817/9710 Bathurst to the Treasury, May 15, 1819.

[2] Act 50 Geo. III Cap. 117 amended by Act 3 Geo. IV. Cap. 113. Such accounts had frequently been called for before 1810.

[3] C.O. 323/182, f. 348.

In 1816 the position was so precarious that James Stephen was in doubt whether the government would be able to pay the interest on the national debt.[1] In later years the difficulty was usually that of a delay in the voting of annual estimates. On such occasions it was usual for the Colonial Office to obtain loans from the agent for commissariat supplies.[2]

In noting the expenditure from the contingent account it is convenient to adopt the main heads used in making it up: rent and taxes; tradesmen's bills; salaries and other payments to office personnel not authorized by order in council and so not covered by the fee fund account; stationery, books, maps, seals, and printing; and, finally, special expenditure. Payments for contingencies averaged considerably more than nine thousand pounds a year from 1812 to 1815, less than seven thousand from 1817 to 1825, rising to an average of slightly less than eight thousand pounds from 1826 to 1830. In 1830 only £5,825 was expended from the account.

Rents, rates, and taxes varied little from year to year, and formed only a minor item of expenditure. In the Crown property occupied by the Colonial Office the only rent was the ground rent. In 1823 that was £16/11/4[3] and in 1828, when two Crown houses were occupied, it was twice as much. Rent on the Parliament Street house in the 1790s was £120 a year[4] and on No. 18 Downing Street in the 1820s somewhat less.[5] This may provide some indication of the saving to the office in occupying Crown premises. The poor rate constituted the largest item on the tax bill; in 1818 it amounted to £75/12/6.[6] Paving rates, land tax, assessment towards the repair of the church of the parish of St. John, Westminster, and the water rate in that year totalled less than forty-five pounds. Taxes increased as the office expanded but were never a major item of expenditure.

The coal merchant, the 'woodman', the wax chandler, the tallow chandler, the turner, the potter, the oil and tin man,

---

[1] Stephen, Caroline E., *The Rt. Hon. Sir James Stephen, K.C.B., LL.D.* (Gloucester 1906), p. 9.

[2] See for example C.O. 323/207 Treasury to Hay, June 12, 1827 where a repayment of £8,400 is requested, f. 141.

[3] C.O. 701/2, p. 95.

[4] C.O. 701/1, p. 4.

[5] C.O. 701/2, p. 144.

[6] T1/1817/9710 Bathurst to Treasury, May 15, 1819.

the linen draper, the ironmonger, and the chimney sweeper received, among them, about four hundred pounds a year from the office in the early postwar years. When the office grew in the mid-twenties their bills grew with it, reaching over six hundred pounds a year in 1826, 1827, and 1828, then declining to about five hundred pounds in the 'years of torpor' when the office had settled down after its rapid expansion. In the postwar 'economy' atmosphere the payment of over twelve hundred pounds to the 'tin and oil man' in 1815 would have looked very much out of place. That sum must be read in conjunction with the payment of almost fifty pounds for wine, already mentioned,[1] as part of the cost of the illuminations in celebration of Napoleon's defeat.

Treasury questioning of these expenses was confined, apart from the wine, to an attempt to reduce the cost of heating and lighting in government offices. In 1817 a survey was made of the cost of lighting external lamps 'distinguishing those lighted with Gas from those lighted with Oil'.[2] No action seems to have been taken on this information but an enquiry, begun in 1828 by the finance committee of that year,[3] resulted in the introduction of a uniform system into the purchase of coal supplies that has continued until the present day.[4] The Treasury introduced its reform in a carefully worded order that was unlikely to offend departmental susceptibilities:

> . . . My Lords observe that in some departments Coals are obtained by Tender or Contract and in others without resorting to competition, and that the variations in price paid by the different offices is so considerable as to induce a belief that a material saving might be effected if all the Departments of Government were to adopt a general system of calling for Tenders, and of entering into periodical contracts for such supplies as they might require during the year.[5]

The only modification proposed by the Colonial Secretary was that a merchant who had supplied coal for many years should

[1] See above p. 129.
[2] C.O. 323/186 Lushington to Goulburn, Feb. 15, 1817, f. 245.
[3] C.O. 323/208 Stewart (Treasury) to Hay, Oct. 17, 1828, f. 138.
[4] Jennings, W.I., *Cabinet Government*, p. 109: '. . . household coals are obtained by concurrent contracts placed by the departments after joint comparison of tenders. . . .'
[5] C.O. 323/211 Stewart to Hay, May 22, 1829.

have the preference.[1] A letter from the regular supplier, expressing a willingness to accept a price set by the Colonial Office on a basis of the cost in other departments, indicates that this modified procedure was followed.[2] The cost of coal in 1818 was one hundred and twenty-six pounds;[3] in 1826 and 1827 it was about two hundred pounds.

The item of salaries and pensions not authorized by order in council was an extremely variable one to which reference has already been made frequently in the first three chapters of this study. Until 1822 the librarian and two porters, their positions being authorized by the Secretary of State only, were paid from the contingent account. So was the translator of foreign languages until he became a clerk in 1819, and the Arabic interpreter whenever there was one attached to the office.[4] Extra clerks, supernumerary clerks, and copyists were also paid from this account; the largest amount paid to them in any one year was fourteen hundred pounds in 1827.[5] Pensions to two extra clerks,[6] two porters,[7] and the widow of a former chief justice of Newfoundland[8] were also granted on this account at various times.

The cost of printing and stationery in public offices always seemed to exceed all reasonable expectations. It was only natural, therefore, that it should come under scrutiny. An early indication of this was the transference, in 1796, of the account for printing and stationery in the Secretaries of State's offices from the civil list to the parliamentary estimate for contingencies.[9] A government Stationery Office was set up in 1786, as a measure of economy, to purchase all parchment, vellum, paper, and other supplies and to undertake to contract for binding and printing. Although the Colonial Office obtained most of its supplies from the Stationery Office, it seems to have been free to make purchases or to have printing done elsewhere if it chose to do so. Until 1823 it paid for these items from the contin-

---

[1] C.O. 323/211 Minute on Treasury letter, May 22, 1829.
[2] C.O. 323/211 Luard and Co. to Gordon, July 25, 1829.
[3] T.1/1817/9710 Bathurst to Treasury, May 15, 1819.
[4] See Appendix III.   [5] See above p. 121.
[6] See Appendix III.
[7] See above p. 130.
[8] See T1/1817/9710 Bathurst to Treasury, May 15, 1819.
[9] F.O. 366/344, p. 46.

gency account, but in that year provision was made for the Stationery Office to receive a parliamentary grant for the supply of stationery to government offices. There were few complaints in the following years about the service or the quality of supplies but the new arrangement does not appear to have been conducive to economy. The bill for stationery and printing was running at around six hundred pounds a year in 1820,[1] of which the bill for printing was negligible.[2] In 1830 the estimate for the Colonial Office was sixteen hundred and fifty pounds.[3] The estimates for comparable departments were:

Treasury and Commissariat	£2,400
Admiralty	2,900
Navy Office and Yards	4,500
Home (& Alien) Office	600
Foreign Office	1,800
Board of Trade	300

No cure was found for extravagance in the next decade; for, in 1840, the Treasury, in an effort to keep a closer check on consumption, offered to make an allowance of forty or fifty pounds a year for keeping store in the Colonial Office, and still expected to save money.[4] Small sums were still spent for printing, lithographing, and small articles of stationery after 1823. In fact, the Colonial Office papers for Parliament were not usually printed by the Stationery Office; bills for up to one thousand pounds were sometimes received[5] but must have been paid from parliamentary funds, since they do not appear in the office accounts. One item classed with the stationery should be noted in passing. Office seals were very expensive; in 1817 a new set cost nearly one hundred pounds[6] and, in a year like 1827 when new sets

[1] C.O. 701/2, pp. 42, 71 and 100.

[2] C.O. 701/14, p. 98.

[3] H.C. 1830 XVIII (88) 486. 'Estimate of the probable Expense of providing Stationery, Printing and Binding, for 1830.'

[4] C.O. 537/22 Stephen to Wilder, May 1840, No. 27.

[5] C.O. 323/206 R. G. Clarke to Wilmot Horton, Sept. 1826, f. 121. See also C.O. 323/211 Stewart (Treasury) to Twiss, Jan. 7, 1829 pointing out that although Clarke's charges were warranted by the general usage of the trade, they were considerably higher than charges made for similar work by the Stationery Office.

[6] T.1/1817/9710 Contingent account for 1818, enclosed in Bathurst to Treasury, May 15, 1819.

were necessary for each of the new secretaries of state, they could add a considerable sum to the account for stationery.

Very little was spent on books and maps until the mid-twenties when the expenditure reached several hundred pounds a year.[1] Newspapers in 1826 cost three hundred pounds. Bookcases, office boxes and locks, other furniture, and repairs usually cost somewhat more than three hundred pounds a year before 1815.[2] By the late twenties these expenses had considerably increased though, like most Colonial Office expenditures, they were not so great as those of the Foreign Office.[3] Furniture was traditionally supplied to the secretaries of state by the Lord Chamberlain but the ancient practice does not appear to have been extended to the Colonial Office.

Many other minor items of interest are scattered through the account books such as payments of fair-sized sums to office-keepers,[4] who frequently found it necessary to make small payments out of their own pockets, and the generous payments on behalf of deceased office servants noted in the last chapter. Other 'human interest' stories must be disguised behind the payments 'to relieve the necessities of a Blackman named Polidore from the Mauritius',[5] or 'on account of T. Roberts an indigent Black Seaman a native of the West Indies.'[6] The Colonial Office did not make itself a charity institution but the lot of any poor African was too potent a public issue to be ignored. Gifts of books to clergymen in the colonies and other minor expenditures of a like nature also appear from time to time.

Gifts to minor potentates in many parts of the globe were provided by means of 'imprests for Casual Services'.[7] The presents given by the British consuls-general on their appointments to posts in North Africa were generous, and special additional presents were given from time to time to facilitate the entry of explorers attempting to reach the interior of Africa

[1] See above pp. 139–41.
[2] C.O. 701/1, June 8, 1813, p. 153 and C.O. 701/2, p. 25.
[3] H.C. 1830 XVIII (127) 551.
[4] T.1/1817/9710 'To Tos. Allsop, Office Keeper his Bill for Disbursements £63/4/3'.
[5] C.O. 701/2, p. 62.
[6] *Ibid.*, p. 157.
[7] A list of these covering a seven-year period may be found in C.O. 323/192 Harrison (Treasury) to Goulburn, March 21, 1820, ff. 163–5.

from the north.[1] The Emperor of Morocco, the Bey of Fezzan, the Sultan of Boncon, the Bashaw of Tripoli, and the Bey of Algiers, all accepted gifts; the most important of these, the Bey of Algiers, received £1,582/9/0 in 1813, £1,268 in 1819 and £1,500 in 1827.[2] The king of the Sandwich Islands, Indian chiefs in North America, and chieftains in Borneo received less generous presents; in the case of the North American Indians these were supplementary to the much larger grants from the military chest. Imprests for casual services also included direct grants to the exploring expeditions in Africa and the Arctic, such as, £6,597 for equipment to Captains Franklin and Lyon in 1824 and 1825, £1,500 to Franklin in 1826, and £8,000 in 1827. Franklin also received four hundred pounds from the contingency account in 1830 towards the publication of the report of his North American expedition.[3] Mungo Park received grants from the contingency account for equipment and travelling expenses.[4] A sum advanced to Dr. Thiacke in 1819, 'to enable him to proceed to America for the purpose of making Astronomical Observations',[5] undoubtedly had a more direct connection with the American boundary dispute than with abstract scientific investigation.

In any list of expenses closely connected with Colonial Office activity, the cost of the various commissions of enquiry sent overseas must have a place. The fact that Major Moody served the office for four years while drawing his salary and the money to support his establishment from funds voted for the commissions[6] is also a sufficient reason for mentioning them. The most costly, £35,244/6/9, was the one sent to the Cape of Good Hope, Ceylon, and Mauritius.[7] Second was the Commission for inquiring into and reporting upon the Administration of Criminal Law in the West Indies, £20,902/19/7.[8] All told seven commissions sent to the colonies between 1812 and 1830 cost over ninety-three thousand pounds.[9]

[1] See C.O. 323/207, ff. 119–20, C.O. 323/208, f. 106 and C.O. 323/211 Stewart to Hay, Jan. 5, 1829.　　[2] *Ibid.*
[3] See above p. 140.
[4] C.O. 701/1, pp. 47–8.
[5] C.O. 323/192, f. 209.
[6] See above p. 72.
[7] 'Account of the expense of Commissions of Enquiry . . .', H.C. 1826–27 XX (301), 499–507 No. 34.　　[8] *Ibid.* No. 37.
[9] *Ibid.* Nos. 12, 28, 29, 32, 34, 37 and 38.

Perhaps the most important service not indicated by the official accounts kept by the chief clerk was the payment of the legal counsel before 1824. A fee of three guineas was paid for each colonial act sent to him for review. This payment came from the law fund of the Treasury, the payment being sanctioned by the Secretary of State. The average annual payment from 1815 to 1822, inclusive, was almost six hundred and forty pounds; the counsel reckoned his net income to be about one hundred pounds less than this.[1] Details of the change in his status have already been given.[2] After July 1825 he received a salary of fifteen hundred pounds annually; one thousand pounds from the Colonial Office fee fund and five hundred from the Board of Trade.

The messengers' account was fairly straightforward. Messengers' salaries were paid by the State Paper Office; their allowances,[3] from which most of their income was derived, were paid by the office employing them. During the war years the cost of messengers in the war and colonial departments sometimes exceeded six thousand pounds.[4] In the years following the war the average was probably about four thousand pounds; reports in 1820 and 1821, indicating an expenditure of less than twenty-five hundred pounds,[5] are deceptive, since large arrears of unpaid bills were being accumulated in those years.[6] In 1826 it was estimated that the annual cost was almost five thousand pounds; twelve hundred pounds for pensions following the reorganization in 1825, twenty-one hundred and sixty pounds for messengers on home service, and sixteen hundred pounds for foreign service.[7]

In addition to the sums already mentioned in the various accounts, £164,107/1/0 was 'imprested' to Lord Bathurst for

---

[1] A small sum was paid to the person carrying the documents from one office to the other. The legal counsel provided his own stationery. See above pp. 58–61.

[2] See above pp. 80–1.

[3] See above pp. 131–3.

[4] C.O. 323/198 Lewis Hertslet's Memorandum on the Salaries of the King's Messengers, Dec. 12, 1822, f. 337.

[5] *Ibid.*

[6] C.O. 324/146 Horton to Herries, December 1826, p. 113.

[7] *Ibid.*, pp. 113–115. The acute situation in the Mediterranean in the mid-twenties made it essential to maintain a frequent service to Malta and the Ionian Islands.

foreign secret service during his first four and a half years as Secretary of State,[1] and further sums were received by secretaries of state in later years. A few of the names of persons receiving payment appear in the correspondence from time to time. W. H. Brooke acted as agent in paying pensions to French refugees.[2] Charles Brennan, who lived in Brussels, wrote regularly to acknowledge his pension of two hundred pounds a year and to offer his services.[3] A Dutchman named Van Noort, 'lately employed under the Sanction of H.M.'s Government in corresponding with this Department furnishing information during the period that Holland was occupied by the French', wanted a certificate of his activities so he could get out of prison in Groningen.[4] Imprests for the foreign secret service appear from time to time after 1817, but there is only one case of real interest, and it was scarcely connected with Colonial Office finance. The daughter of a former general in the British army was recommended for a pension because of 'her great degree of intimacy with the King of France'. Wilmot Horton, in returning papers to her, made the error of enclosing the private letter in which the recommendation was made. She obtained her pension.[5]

In the upper reaches of the Civil Service there was some danger that economy would undermine efficiency by reducing the salaries in important offices to a level that would dissuade able young men from trying to make a career in the government service. This, however, was more a danger in the eighteen-thirties than in the period covered by this study. Although one effect of the changes made in 1821 was to reduce drastically the salary to which a clerk could aspire when he reached senior status,[6] the clerk's prospects were more significantly reduced by the abolition of absentee office-holding, which had provided generous supplements to salaries in the

[1] C.O. 323/186 J. L. Mallet (Audit Office) to Lord Bathurst, July 11, 1817, f. 401. On which he paid more than forty-one hundred pounds in Exchequer fees.

[2] See above p. 23.

[3] C.O. 323/211 Brennan to Hay, April 14, 1829. He claimed to have been attached to the war and colonial department since 1809.

[4] C.O. 324/135 Goulburn to Cooke (Secret), Dec. 23, 1813, p. 283.

[5] C.O. 537/40, Section I.

[6] See above pp. 41–2.

early days of the office.[1] In 1822 only the chief clerk's office was maintained at the old level, and the chief clerkship was abolished in 1833.[2] The ultimate salary of an under-secretary was reduced in 1822 from twenty-five hundred pounds to two thousand pounds. In 1833 the salary of the parliamentary under-secretary was further reduced to fifteen hundred pounds;[3] at the same time the salary of the secretary of state was reduced to five thousand pounds.[4] Nevertheless, although these reductions were resented, the social prestige of the Civil Service was not undermined so that, when, later in the century, it was opened exclusively to talent, outstanding persons from the schools and universities were attracted to the service of the Government.

The House of Commons committee on finance of 1828 urged that salaries should be kept down to the rate current in commercial establishments. Except in special circumstances where the duties required 'a more than ordinary share of intelligence' a top salary for clerks of four hundred pounds a year was recommended. However, the committee advised against any systematic reduction at that time.[5] There is no definite indication that its members foresaw the later division of the civil service into intellectual and manual grades. Like most earlier parliamentary enquiries, the 1828 committee was more interested in pensions than in salaries. Although the office of the Secretary of State for War had been in existence only seven years before it took over the administration of the colonies in August, 1801, a pension was already being paid. It had been granted to a clerk on the establishment[6] by an order in council dated 17 March 1801. In 1802 a pension was granted to a porter and in 1806 an extra clerk received a large pension on the fund for contingencies, after correspondence between the secretary of state and the prime minister.[7] Edward Cooke, Castlereagh's Under-Secretary, received a pension while out of office during the Talents administration, and again for a time after 1809; his pension in both instances was approved by an order in council.[8]

[1] See Appendix III.   [2] H.C. 1833 XXIII, p. 345.
[3] *Ibid.*   [4] *Ibid.*
[5] H.C. 1828 V (420) 20.
[6] See Appendix III. William Huskisson, who was Under-Secretary until May 1801, also received a pension while out of office.
[7] See above p. 15.
[8] See C.O. 701/14 Shee to Harrison (Treasury) Mar. 10, 1807, p. 52.

Thus, little more than a decade after coming into existence, the office was encumbered with pensions amounting to more than fifteen hundred pounds a year. The habits of generosity to friends and servants were not easily broken despite the many reports of financial committees urging economical reform.

An orderly system of superannuation, though at first not an economic one, was, however, coming into existence. The finance committee of 1828 dated its commencement from a Treasury minute of 10 August 1803 that laid down a plan for customs officers.[1] The first legislative action of Parliament[2] came in 1810, following an enquiry by a committee on public offices in 1809. The aim of the Act of 1810 was to reduce expenditure by having the Treasury exercise firm control over the scale of compensation granted on removals from office and on retirements in every department of government.[3] The immediate effect of the Act was to establish a general system of superannuation allowances throughout the Civil Service. The grant of any retired allowance, compensation for any office abolished, or special allowance or remuneration 'for any good services', whether charged 'upon the Incidents or any other Fund of any Publick Office or Department', could be made only with the concurrence of the Commissioners of the Treasury. One loophole was left, however, that was to frustrate the Treasury's efforts to exercise control over retirements in the offices of the Secretaries of State; that was the insertion in the act of the clause, in brackets: '(except such as may be granted by any Order of His Majesty in Council)'.[4]

Despite the existence of the 1810 Act, Lord Bathurst treated the reduction of his official establishment in 1816 as a purely departmental matter. Clerks were selected for retirement, and the scale of pensions arranged, by the department, the Treasury merely being informed in a routine manner that the principle adopted in awarding compensation had been that

> Such as have been borne on the regular Establishment and have served 5 years or upwards, to receive from the Office an Allowance equal to one half of their Salaries; such as have served 10

[1] H.C. 1828 V (480) 490.
[2] 50 Geo. III Cap. 117.
[3] C.O. 323/179 Harrison (Treasury) to Cooke, Sept. 11, 1809, ff. 188–9.
[4] 50 Geo. III Cap. 117, Sect. II.

years or upwards an Allowance equal to two Thirds; and such as may have served 15 years or upwards an Allowance equal to three Fourths of their respective Salaries.[1]

In a circular sent out a few months later the Treasury called for further reductions in official establishments and drew the attention of the heads of departments to the provisions of the 1810 Act:

> ... you will not upon the occasion of this, or any future reduction hold out any promises or expectations of Superannuation or Retired Allowance being granted to any Persons whose Services may no longer be necessary in consequence of any Reductions which you may be able to recommend, but in case any of the Individuals proposed to be reduced should in your opinion have a Claim for a Retired Allowance, My Lords desire you will bring the Claim either under consideration of this Board, by whom alone Superannuation, Retired, or other Allowance to Servants in the Civil Service of the Country can be granted, previously to your making any communication to the Party upon the subject.[2]

A Treasury minute of August 1821, outlining proposals to be submitted to Parliament for amendment of the superannuation Act of 1810, reasserted that no superannuation could be granted except by the Treasury, and informed the departments that superannuations would only be granted at four periods in each year except in cases of immediate urgency.[3] In the 1822 Act, however, the authority of the Privy Council was continued. Both the Foreign Office and the Colonial Office opposed any extension of the authority of the Treasury at that time.[4] When, in 1831, the Treasury sought to stretch the interpretation of the 1822 Act, by ruling that the Treasury alone could sanction superannuations, Lord Goderich challenged the ruling by pointing out that, if this interpretation was correct, retirement grants made since 1822 by order in council would be invalid, and questioned 'how far it would be judicious to exclude His Majesty from the exercise of those Powers which with the advice of the Council Board, His Majesty has for a long series of years

[1] C.O. 324/137 Goulburn to Lushington, March 12, 1816, p. 163.
[2] C.O. 323/185, f. 243. This is a very early use of the phrase 'Civil Service'.
[3] C.O. 323/194, f. 175.
[4] See above p. 62.

exercised.'[1] Nevertheless, it is obvious that by 1831 even secretaries of state were finding it impossible to circumvent the Treasury in the interests of their departments. An order requiring heads of departments, when they recommended any individual 'whomsoever' for superannuation, to state the number of days on which that person had been present in the office during each of the preceding ten years, and which required the keeping of a 'perfect record' of the attendance of all persons eligible for superannuation, drew only a grumbling protest about the extension of the latter provision to senior officers.[2]

Departmental recalcitrance in the early twenties was partly responsible for the failure of an attempt to cover half the cost of superannuations by means of contributions from personnel eligible for pensions.[3] Since civil servants were already entitled to generous superannuation in addition to their salaries, the principle of a contributory pension fund was not so much at issue as the propriety of reducing salaries by indirect means. Clerks expressed their resentment by adopting an unco-operative attitude;[4] resentment was also expressed in several pamphlets appearing at that time. With the return of prosperity in 1824 the scheme was abandoned and all contributions restored by a parliamentary Act[5] that the 1828 committee on finance regarded as 'wholly ill-advised'.[6] In 1829, the Treasury, in announcing anew its support of the principle of contributions, was more diplomatic than in 1822:

> . . . it appears . . . to be advisable that a distinct intimation should be given to every Individual who may hereafter enter into the Civil Service of the Crown, at the time of his admission to office that he will be subjected to a deduction from his annual Salary and Emoluments and to such regulations with respect to Superannuation as my Lords may hereafter lay down.[7]

The generosity of the terms of the superannuation acts served to encourage the Colonial Office to make use of them in getting

---

[1] C.O. 324/146 Hay to J. Stewart, July 22, 1831, p. 314.
[2] *Ibid.*, pp. 316–21.
[3] See above p. 62.
[4] See above pp. 42 and 45.
[5] Act 5 Geo. IV. Cap. 104.
[6] H.C., 1828 V (420) 8 and (480) 483.
[7] C.O. 323/211 Stewart to Twiss, Aug. 11, 1829.

rid of inefficient clerks. Under the act of 1810 any civil servant over sixty years of age could, after only fifteen years' service, be granted a pension equal to two-thirds of his salary and emoluments. Any officer under sixty could receive a pension equal to half his salary after ten years service, upon receiving a certificate from the head of his department certifying that, having served 'with Diligence and Fidelity', he was no longer capable, 'from infirmity of mind or body', of discharging the duties of his office.[1] The act of 1822 reduced the pension that could be received at the end of ten years to a third of the salary, and required the certificate of two medical practitioners in addition to that of the head of the department.[2] Such a certificate was unnecessary if a saving was produced on the establishment after providing for the retired allowance of a clerk and for the salary of his successor.[3] Little arithmetical calculation is required to figure out that the difference between the salary of one of the old clerks and the salary of a new junior clerk would provide a small allowance for promotions and still permit a generous pension under this clause.

One of the Treasury's suggestions for the administration of the superannuation fund in 1821 was, that the annual amount payable to retired servants of the public should at no time exceed ten per cent of the aggregate amount of the salaries of all the officers eligible for pensions.[4] The degree to which the Colonial Office fell short of that ideal is a mark of the justice of Parliament's dissatisfaction with the regulations in force. Although in 1814 the office had been in existence for only two decades and had begun with a very small establishment, the ratio of salaries to pensions had already reached the proportion suggested by the Treasury. Salaries to permanent officials amounted to £11,700; the amount paid in retired allowances was £1,140.[5] In 1818 for a salary bill of about seven thousand two hundred and fifty pounds the corresponding payment was over thirty-four hundred pounds. In 1822 the figures were £8,578/13/4 and £2,685/6/8. In 1826 salaries of approximately thirteen thousand seven hundred pounds were paid to

[1] 50 Geo. III. Cap. 117.
[2] 3 Geo. IV. Cap. 113.
[3] *Ibid.*, Section 15.
[4] C.O. 323/194, ff. 174-5.
[5] These figures have been extracted from the account books.

personnel eligible for superannuation; pensions in that year amounted to £5,335/6/8.[1] Messengers' incomes and pensions have not been included in the above totals.[2] In 1826 when there were six messengers on home service and one on foreign service (at an average emolument of four hundred pounds each for purposes of pension), pensions paid from the Colonial Office account amounted to almost twelve hundred pounds.[3] The full expenditure on pensions in the Colonial Office, compared to that for the Home and Foreign Offices, was:[4]

	Home Office	Foreign Office	Colonial Office
1814	£1,330	£1,894	£1,489/7/7
1818	1,417/10/0	5,239/14/8	3,967
1822	1,885	3,067/14/9	3,472
1826	2,109	5,661/11/8	6,427

The comparable figures for the number of persons on the official establishments were:[5]

	Home Office	Foreign Office	Colonial Office
1815	31	34	21
1819	30	34	16
1827	29	48	33

These figures serve to confirm the truth of a statement made in a report of the 1828 committee on finance, that heads of departments had taken advantage of the superannuation system to rid their offices of the less useful of their clerks.[6] There can be no doubt that an improvement in the quality of the establishments was essential, but the method could hardly recommend itself to the Treasury or Parliament.

Taking the three main accounts of the office—fee fund, contingencies and messengers' expenses—as a guide, the cost of

[1] These figures have been extracted from the account books and checked against various sources in the Colonial Office records and parliamentary papers.
[2] The method of estimating their income for purposes of pension was given in Chapter IV. The position was further complicated by the payment of pensions to widows.
[3] C.O. 324/146 Wilmot Horton to Herries, Dec. 1826.
[4] H.C. 1828 V (480) 506-7.
[5] 'Returns of the Number, the Pay or Salaries, of all Persons Employed in Public Departments; 1797–1827,' H.C. 1830–31 VII (92) 306-9.
[6] H.C. 1828 V (480) 491.

maintaining the Colonial Office, including the war department, was approximately:

1814	£35,100
1817	27,500
1820	29,400
1823	30,100
1826	40,500
1829	37,800

Some fairly prominent items of expenditure do not appear in these accounts. One, not mentioned in this chapter, was a payment of five hundred pounds annually by the Post Office to the clerks of the office.[1] Others not included were the small official salaries of the messengers, the incomes from sinecure offices that supplemented official salaries, a reasonable allowance for rent of the Crown property, fees to the legal counsel before 1825, expenditure for stationery and printing after 1823, and the salary of Thomas Moody for four years. Of the cost of postage that would form such a large item in any statement of the expense of administering the colonies, some portion should he added to the totals listed above to cover franks received by members of the office. On the other hand, a sizable portion of the contingency account was expended on items that should not be considered as administrative costs. Among these should be listed a payment of two or three hundred pounds yearly from the contingency fund to supply the deficiency in the fee fund of the Slave Registry Office.[2] On balance, possibly, some small sum should be added to the above totals to give a true picture of the cost of supporting the office.

It is obvious that the increase in cost was in no way proportional to the office's increased capacity for business. The crowded office of 1830 required little more heating and lighting than the office of 1820. Virtually the same office servants served the new establishment as the old. The cost of messengers had increased but little. A counsel of perfection might urge that the establishment was larger than business demanded but the salaries of a

---

[1] See above pp. 25–6.

[2] This payment continued by Treasury order despite protests that the Slave Registry Office had 'no immediate connection' with the Colonial Office. See C.O. 324/146 Horton to Herries, Dec. 15, 1826, pp. 78–80.

few extra junior clerks added little to the expense, and there was always the possibility of finding an able man among them.

Parliament continually urged that national taxation be kept at a reasonable level, and the Treasury, in response to public demand, intermittently tried to introduce more businesslike methods into government. In vital matters, neither supported the niggling economies suggested by some of the radicals in this era; in fact, with regard to retired allowances, both were extremely generous. It was departmental irresponsibility that forced the Treasury in the twenties to new and stricter controls by awarding pensions on a lavish scale in order to overcome their own errors in the selection of personnel. By their intervention Parliament and the Treasury had by 1830 introduced a measure of uniformity into the departmental structure. The classification of clerks introduced in 1822 made possible a comparison of salaries. The measures adopted for stationery, printing, and coal made possible a closer comparison of the costs of these important items. In 1828 enquiries were set afoot with a view to introducing a uniform system of keeping departmental accounts.[1] Uniformity of departmental structures was certainly becoming a feature of government organization by 1830. Just how effectively the centralized control operated in keeping down expenses is problematical; business was expanding so rapidly that no simple comparison can be made between one decade and the next.

[1] H.C. 1829 VI (290 and 325).

INTERDEPARTMENTAL
RELATIONS

'Memorial first given to Sir Herbert Taylor.
                                    —by him
Referred to Lord Sidmouth.
                        —by him
Referred to Lord Bathurst.
                        —by him
Referred to Lord Castlereagh.
                        —by him
Returned.'
                        —Note on memorial of Sir John Clarke,
                        4 October 1820

In the two decades after 1800 the office of the third Secretary of State exercised unusually wide powers. The combining of the military and colonial functions in a single office meant that, particularly in the conquered colonies, there were few really effective checks on the Colonial Secretary's authority. Parliament, the British public, and statesmen were so busy with their own wartime and post-war problems that, except for a flurry of interest in colonial slavery, they were hardly aware that a new empire had been acquired and was being governed from No. 14 Downing Street.[1] The independence of the Colonial Secretary was assured both by public apathy and by the absence of an integrated government policy. In the fifteen years following the death of Pitt, in 1806, few questions outside the fields of war and foreign affairs were regarded as 'cabinet' questions; each department head managed his own department with a minimum of interference from his colleagues.[2] In the 1820s, however, a number of questions arose that attracted general interest, the chief of these being colonial slavery, the need to reduce expenditure in the colonies, and the quarrel between the 'French' and

[1] See Tucker, F. G., 'The Press and the Colonies 1802–1833', unpublished M.A. thesis, Bristol, 1936, pp. 2–3.
[2] Aspinall, A., 'The Cabinet Council, 1783–1835', pp. 204–8.

the 'English' in Lower Canada. By the mid-twenties the Treasury had begun to assume a very active role in the determination of colonial financial policy and, in 1829 and 1830, the cabinet spent a good deal of time discussing colonial questions. The newly-aroused interest in colonial problems was to be sustained throughout the thirties.[1]

While the Secretary of State could handle many issues without consulting his colleagues, he did have to observe many ancient forms. He and his department had frequent contact with other departments, and with the King, Privy Council, and Parliament. In one of its aspects the Colonial Office was merely a post office between the governments of the colonies and those offices of government in Westminster whose authority extended to the colonies and was complementary to the powers of colonial governments. The defence of the 'nation at large'—Wilmot Horton's phrase—was the responsibility of the Army and Navy and their controlling ministers, the foreign policy of 'the nation at large' was the responsibility of the Foreign Secretary, the postal service of the 'nation at large' was the responsibility of the General Post Office, prisoners sentenced in the United Kingdom were the responsibility of the Home Office no matter where they might be dispersed throughout the 'nation at large', the regulation of trade of the 'nation at large' was the responsibility of the Board of Trade. The Attorney-General and Solicitor-General provided legal advice on the nature of the constitution of the 'nation at large'. Most significant of all, the responsibility for supervising the collection and disbursement of the revenue of the 'nation at large' was the responsibility of the Treasury. When another department failed to assume its responsibility, or when no other department could claim authority, the Colonial Secretary was recognized as a sort of residual legatee of the prerogative of the Crown. But he had to do far more than fill administrative gaps. In particular, as the only minister authorized to correspond with colonial governors,[2] he had the great responsibility of ensuring that those officers maintained

---

[1] Manning, H. T., 'Colonial Crises Before the Cabinet 1829–1835', *Bull. Inst. Hist. Res.*, XXX (1957), pp. 46–9.

[2] A colonial governor in his military capacity of commander-in-chief corresponded with the Treasury and military departments. With the permission of the Secretary of State he might correspond directly with other ministers on matters concerning his colony.

the internal tranquillity of their colonies. Since the activities of other departments might have an important bearing on the political situation in a colony, the Colonial Secretary also assumed a co-ordinating authority and insisted that he be kept informed of all government activities within colonial territories; and he sometimes made representations to other departments, insisting that their colonial officials be subject to the political authority of the governors.[1]

At some time or other every department of the British government had something to contribute to colonial government; sometimes several official letters were written to the Treasury in a single day, while to the office of the Duchy of Lancaster only one reference has been noted in two decades, a request for information on the precise proportion of minerals reserved by the Crown out of the produce of leased lands,[2] (the Colonial Office was preparing a charter for an Australian land company). Treasury indexes in the Public Record Office show five hundred letters received from the Colonial Office in 1825 (slightly fewer than the number received in 1813); in 1826 the number was five hundred and sixty-five and in 1831 over six hundred. The number of letters sent directly to the Treasury by colonial agents, governors, and officers commanding at stations abroad shows an almost identical progression in those years. Other departments received from one to two, to several dozen letters a year. The military departments individually and as a group accounted for a large amount of correspondence; Admiralty, Navy Office, Ordnance, Commander-in-Chief's Office, Secretary at War's Office (the 'War Office'), Army Medical Board, and a host of lesser offices that were gradually absorbed after the war into the larger departments, formed a maze ideally suited to the purpose of curcumlocution.[3] The great attention paid to trade policy required reference to the Board of Trade. So also did the review of colonial legislation, for

---

[1] Manning, H. T., *British Colonial Government* . . ., pp. 511–2; also H.C. 1837 VII (516) 350.

[2] C.O. 324/145 Horton to Lord Bexley, Apr. 19, 1825, p. 119.

[3] Fifteen offices were concerned with Army affairs at the time of Waterloo. See Hampton, G., *The War Office* (1935), p. 43. Of these the Commander-in-Chief's Office, the Ordnance and the Admiralty had the greatest interest in the colonies. The office of Secretary at War, responsible for pay, allowances and pensions, had less need to consult the Colonial Secretary.

which the Board of Trade was officially responsible. Some correspondence on the latter was carried on through the office of the Privy Council.[1]

Several departments maintained their own officials in the colonies. In the military departments this seldom gave rise to any friction except that arising from the need for a strict definition of the distinction between a governor's powers as a civil officer and his powers as commander-in-chief.[2] Most governors were military men accustomed to the division of authority in the military departments; they were also aware of their own positions in the military hierarchy and knew to whom they should appeal in case of doubt. Potentially fruitful as sources of friction, however, were the chaotic arrangements for the supervision of colonial revenue. Most officials concerned with the collection and expenditure of colonial funds held Treasury patents; some received articles of appointment both from the Treasury and from the governor of a colony, and received instructions from both. In some of the legislative colonies, provincial treasurers responsible for collecting and disbursing large sums of money were employed by the local legislatures and supervized by the governors; in outports some local revenue officers served as deputies both to imperial customs officers and to provincial treasurers. In several of the conquered colonies, the Treasury was largely excluded for several years and the Secretary of State had almost complete control in his own hands. In Mauritius, New South Wales, Van Diemen's Land, and Sierra Leone even the officers employed in the collection of customs revenue were under the control of the Colonial Office until 1825;[3] and in Ceylon and Malta until 1837 or later.[4] In Mauritius in 1816 the Secretary of State named the governor and the commissioner of justice, and the governor granted articles of appointment to sixty-six other officials under mandamus from the Secretary of State;[5] the only appointments not controlled by the Secretary of State were those of the eight Ordnance officers. In St. Lucia, also a former French colony, fourteen officials were appointed directly by the Secretary of State, nine by the

[1] See below pp. 197–200.
[2] See C.O. 323/198 Memorandum of Commander-in-Chief's Office, August 30, 1824, with pencilled notes by the Colonial Office, ff. 200–204.
[3] C.O. 323/203 Herries to Horton, Aug. 8, 1825, ff. 108–11.
[4] H.C. 1837 VII (516) 371.   [5] H.C. 1817 XVII (129) 231–242.

commandant, four by the Treasury (all customs officers), one by the Paymaster-General, and six by the Ordnance.[1]

The web of ancient practices in which the Colonial Office operated was protected from decisive reform by the veneration expressed in Burke's aphorism counselling statesmen to '. . . approach to the faults of the state as to the wounds of a father'. In the esoteric maze of traditional forms the inexperienced minister or civil servant had to tread warily as he learned to thread his way through tortuous administrative pathways. The impossibility of containing all business in the official channels forced the creation of an extensive informal system of contacts between the various branches of government and gave the whole executive framework an underlying flexibility that belied its rather rigid superstructure. To expedite business an administrator might seek out the clerk or Under-Secretary in another department who was the real author of official policy; but he must be discreet lest he offend a sensitive chieftain resentful of any slight to his official authority. The form of official action might have little relation to the reality of power—the polite fiction, 'I am directed by His Majesty', was only a small part of the ritual that made it difficult to distinguish the fact from the make-believe—in a never-never land where petulant lions roared when industrious mice were observed in their lairs. Nevertheless, the forms were, as Lord Bathurst declared, 'frequently the substance too',[2] and their ritual observance gave cohesiveness to the executive structure.

Form and substance were not easily distinguishable at the apex where the King was both the symbol of absolute authority and the possessor of an undefined residuum of power. In his name ministers negotiated with governments abroad and gave orders to a host of officers, civil and military. Since in all matters affecting his authority he had a right to be consulted, he might be forgiven if he sometimes attempted to decide, especially when ancestral memories were stirred by the persistence of ancient deference. George IV, as Prince Regent and as King, was the sovereign in the most eventful years of this study.[3]

[1] H.C. 1817 XVII (129) 231–242.

[2] C.O. 324/75 Lord Bathurst's Minutes, 'Misc.', Aug. 25, 1826, f. 257.

[3] For George IV's relations with his ministers see Aspinall, A., 'The Cabinet Council, 1783–1835', especially pp. 221, 237, 248.

Lazy, luxurious, and not unintelligent, he had the gentleman's interest in foreign affairs and war and his lack of interest in the colonies. Colonial patronage sometimes engaged his attention, especially if a possibility existed that one of his friends might be provided for. Prospective colonial governors,[1] at least for important posts, were paraded for his approval, and when it became necessary to recall a governor Lord Bathurst informed the King of a disturbance in his 'family'.[2] Other 'colonials' might be honoured by presentation at a levee.[3] Even some of the memorials addressed to the Secretary of State for submission to the King may have received his personal attention.[4] There is, however, no indication that he had any serious advice to offer the Colonial Secretary when the minister was called into the royal presence; no minutes were kept of these audiences and George had a notorious aversion to letter writing.[5] On one matter the King's initiative was definitely decisive, the designing of uniforms for colonial governors and superior civil officers;[6] on the subject of uniforms George was an expert.

Greville's picture of the King in the Privy Council, chattering away to the clerk while his ministers were conducting business,[7] indicates how much of a formality were the meetings of that body. Constitutionally, it was the supreme legislature for the conquered colonies and, in addition, could veto the acts of colonial legislatures. In practice it merely gave formal approval to decisions made elsewhere, and debates at top level took place in the cabinet rather than in the council chamber.[8] The Judicial Committee, which became responsible for hearing appeals from colonial courts, was established by statute in 1834.

It is unlikely that Lord Liverpool's Cabinets devoted very much time to the internal affairs of the colonies. It is difficult

---

[1] Victoria insisted on seeing her personal representatives. See Hall, H. L., *The Colonial Office*, p. 91.

[2] *Hist. Mss. Comm., Bathurst Papers*, Bathurst to the King, May 27, 1824, pp. 570–1.

[3] *Ibid.*, Goulburn to Bathurst, July 25, 1821, p. 506.

[4] See C.O. 323/193 Memorial of William Prevost, Feb. 6, 1820.

[5] Lord Bathurst was the recipient of very few of his carefully composed letters. See Aspinall, A., ed., *The Letters of George IV. 1812–1830*.

[6] C.O. 323/199 Warrant signed by the King dated Nov. 9, 1824, f. 413.

[7] The Greville Memoirs, ed. Strachey and Fulford, I, pp. 227–8.

[8] See for example, N.L.S. Sir George Murray Papers, Wellington to Murray, Jan. 27, 1830, vol. 171, f. 15; also May 28, 1829, vol. 169, f. 94.

to be precise, for the subjects of Cabinet deliberation as well as the decisions were supposed to be secret and, due not only to the absence of formal minutes but also to the extreme informality of most of the meetings, few details have survived. Even the arrangements for meeting were carelessly made; no pains were taken to ensure that each minister received his summons and sometimes even the Prime Minister had no idea why the members of the Cabinet were being summoned or who had sent out the summonses.[1] Any member of the Cabinet had the right to summon a Cabinet meeting.

> There are no precise laws or rules [wrote Lord Holland (*c.* 1812–16)], nor even any well established or understood usages which mark what measures in each Department are or are not to be communicated to the Cabinet. . . . There is nothing but private agreement or party feeling generally, or the directions of the King accidentally, which obliges even a Secretary for Foreign Affairs to consult his colleagues on any of the duties of his office before he takes the King's pleasure upon them. . . . In the other branches of Administration, such as the Treasury, the Home Secretaryship, the Chancery, the Admiralty, the discretion is yet larger as to the matters in their respective Departments on which the Ministers take the King's pleasure directly or previously consult their colleagues before they advise him.[2]

It was usual for a Secretary of State to have his Under-Secretary send out the summonses. The only Cabinet meetings known definitely to have been called to discuss specifically colonial questions before 1829 were those called to discuss the slavery issue in 1823,[3] when the Government was preparing to counter the anti-slavery group by introducing its 'melioration' proposals in the House of Commons. It is quite probable, however, that the Cabinet was summoned to discuss the internal affairs of the colonies on other occasions. On 17 January 1826, for example, Lord Liverpool wrote to Lord Bathurst:

> I will . . . be prepared on the Canada question before we meet on the 25th. It will be quite useless to circulate the papers till our colleagues are assembled.[4]

[1] Aspinall, A., 'The Cabinet Council, 1783–1835', p. 187.
[2] *Memoirs of the Whig Party*, II, pp. 85–6 quoted in A. Aspinall, 'The Cabinet Council, 1783–1835', p. 174, f.n.2.
[3] For a reference to a summons issued by Lord Bathurst and Horton at that time, see A. Aspinall, 'The Cabinet Council, 1783–1835', p. 183.
[4] *Bathurst Papers*, p. 599.

This could scarcely refer to anything except a proposed Cabinet meeting, probably to discuss the sale of a large amount of land in Upper Canada to the Canada Company. The negotiations with the Company had become very involved.[1]

It is unlikely, though always possible, that this letter of Lord Liverpool's refers to a meeting of a smaller group than the full Cabinet. Lord Liverpool had a few chosen colleagues whom he consulted frequently and who formed an 'inner cabinet'.[2] One historian has, in fact, distinguished two 'inner cabinets', one of which he has designated the 'economic cabinet'.[3] Lord Bathurst was not a member of the 'economic' cabinet but he was always a member of the 'inner' cabinet, being both a friend of the Prime Minister and one of the chief spokesmen of the conservative wing of the Government. In addition to the 'inner' cabinet, or cabinets, *ad hoc* committees were sometimes formed to look after such questions as the planning of new legislation; these might contain members of the ministry outside the Cabinet as well as Cabinet Ministers.[4]

The advantage to a minister of having his policy approved by Cabinet was that, according to the principle of Cabinet solidarity that was becoming generally accepted,[5] his colleagues were then bound to support him if his policy was attacked in Parliament. It follows that only issues on which there was a probability of division of opinion among the ministers, or on which there was likely to be a major debate in the House of Commons, were likely to receive the attention of the full Cabinet. At most times when the Colonial Secretary found it advisable to consult his colleagues, it is likely that he did so individually, either in London or during the long season of rustication in the summer and autumn when those Cabinet members who were intimate friends spent a good deal of time in one another's company. Naturally, the Prime Minister was consulted most frequently,

[1] See C.O. 324/75 Lord Bathurst's Minutes, Miscellaneous, ff. 181 and 187. Compare, however, Mrs. Manning's excellent article 'Colonial Crises before the Cabinet, 1829–1835'.

[2] Aspinall, A., 'The Cabinet Council, 1783–1835', p. 210, f.n. 4; see also Webster, Sir C., *The Foreign Policy of Castlereagh 1815–1822*, p. 15.

[3] Brock, W. R., *Lord Liverpool and Liberal Toryism, 1820–1827*, p. 55.

[4] See Chapter VII where there is a reference to the committee that discussed the colonial aspects of the customs legislation of 1825.

[5] Aspinall, A., 'The Cabinet Council, 1783–1835', pp. 216–7; but see also p. 223.

since he had an interest in all departments of Government. In the case of Lord Liverpool this interest was reinforced by the fact that he had been Lord Bathurst's predecessor as Colonial Secretary. Although Liverpool did not normally intervene in departmental affairs, as Wellington did during Sir George Murray's tenure in the Colonial Office,[1] he did insist that one colonial appointment, namely the governorship of Jamaica,[2] should be made 'upon consultation with the person at the head of the Government, though upon the recommendation of the head of the department'. The Duke of Wellington was frequently consulted regarding the appointment of colonial governors, since so many of them in this era were military men who had served under his command. When he was Commander-in-Chief his consent had, of course, to be obtained for all such appointments.

The only effective restraint on arbitrary government and irresponsible spending in the colonies was provided by the House of Commons; administration was always carried on in the shadow of its powers of enquiry and censure. In the drafting of official papers, officials had to keep in mind that Parliament could demand that they be produced for inspection and, therefore, care was taken to anticipate unfavourable reactions by expressing sentiments and, where feasible, framing policies to which members of the House of Commons would not take exception. To please all members was, of course, impossible. To give but one example, the inclination of the colonial department was, rightly, to employ military officers, many of whom had reached high rank as a result of their abilities, as senior administrators in the colonies. Saving was made on salaries by counting military pay as part of a governor's income, and the extensive experience gained in the course of the Napoleonic Wars was usefully employed. Radical politicians, with some justification, saw in the employment of military men as governors a danger to free institutions. They were, therefore, very alert in pointing out instances of arbitrary government. Their attacks on the conduct of Sir Lachlan Macquarie in New South Wales[3]

---

[1] Manning, H. T., 'Colonial Crises before the Cabinet, 1829–1835', pp. 46–9. [2] *Bathurst Papers*, pp. 605–6.

[3] Manning, H. T., *British Colonial Government . . .*, pp. 535–41.

and on Lord Charles Somerset at the Cape[1] were effective in leading to constitutional changes in those colonies.

Lord Bathurst, with his old-fashioned attitudes,[2] resented any interference by the House of Commons in his conduct of colonial affairs. Wilmot Horton and Huskisson, on the other hand, who were both House of Commons men and who were reformers both by inclination and conviction, believed in building up parliamentary interest and directing it into constructive channels. Wilmot Horton organized, chaired, and was the leading spirit in the emigration committees of the House of Commons in 1826 and 1827.[3] Huskisson was responsible for the creation of the Canada Committee of 1828, which aroused the interest of the House of Commons and the country in the affairs of Lower Canada.[4] In general, however, although it was constitutionally necessary to employ the legislative powers of Parliament from time to time,[5] the colonial department did all that it could to avoid and discourage parliamentary interest. As a result, comment on the administration of the colonies was almost always critical and came, by and large, from radical 'Parliamentary Orators' whose questions were intended to set the colonies 'into a flame'.[6]

Debates, when they did take place, lacked the stimulus of the healthy self-interest that got discussions of United Kingdom affairs away from an undue emphasis on abstract principles. Very few members were competent to pass judgement on colonial affairs. When Hume put forward his proposal for colonial representation at Westminster in 1831, most newspapers opposed it on the ground that colonial agents always had enough influence to induce some member to advocate the colonial point

---

[1] Roberts, M., 'Lord Charles Somerset and the Beaufort Influence', *Archives Yearbook for South African History*, 1951, II, pp. 1–34.

[2] See Dicey, A. V., 'The Period of Old Toryism or Legislative Quiescence', in *Law and Opinion in England* (1914), Lecture V.

[3] Jones, E. G., 'Wilmot Horton', Chapter X.

[4] Manning, H. T., 'Colonial Crises Before the Cabinet, 1829–1835', p. 45.

[5] See C.O. 323/211 for an interesting memorandum by James Stephen, dated January 16, 1829, listing eight topics on which it would be necessary to legislate or report to Parliament and giving a short history of each. There are similar memoranda in later years. The heads of the departments within the office were usually also asked to report on the need for parliamentary action in the colonies under their supervision.

[6] C.O. 324/75 Lord Bathurst's Minutes, 'N.S.W. 1824–6', f. 35.

of view. In this way, it was reckoned that practically every dependency had indirect representation, there being, according to one estimate, 104 members who watched over colonial interests.[1] Most of these, however, were merchants and absentee estate owners whose interests were imperial rather than colonial, and they seldom, if ever, truly represented colonial opinion.

Throughout most of the early years of the nineteenth century the political Under-Secretary of State was the spokesman for the department in the House of Commons. Henry Goulburn was primarily an administrator, belonging to the 'class of under-secretaries', said Lord Ellenborough.[2] Towards the end of his decade in the office parliamentary affairs did begin to take up a great deal of his time. Wilmot Horton, his successor, was chosen for the office not from any likelihood of his being an outstanding administrator but because of the reputation that he had established for himself as a debater.[3] Horace Twiss also was chosen because of the need to strengthen the Government bench in the House of Commons. He was selected for office by the leader of the House.[4] Sir George Murray, the Secretary of State, was in the Commons but was so ineffective in general debate that the Duke of Wellington at one time considered the advisability of giving him a military appointment.[5]

The Government's desire to avoid questioning was well understood by the public and was exploited by various interested groups and individuals. Shipowners, planters, West Indian merchants, Scots Presbyterians anxious to receive similar privileges to those extended to the Church of England in the colonies, colonial land companies, and other groups attached to the Government, or seeking privileges, were usually not disposed to embarrass the Government[6] though the Government was seldom left unaware of their ability to do so. Also working with the Government at most times, but much more difficult to handle, were the anti-slavery people. Accepting enthusiastically the senior James Stephen's teaching that '. . . we shall do nothing

---

[1] Tucker, H. F. G., 'The Press and the Colonies, 1802–1833', pp. 54–5.
[2] *Political Diary*, 1828–30, I, 3.
[3] See above pp. 47–8.
[4] *Bathurst Papers* pp. 653–4.
[5] Mrs. Arbuthnot's *Journal*, II, pp. 229, 381, 389.
[6] For one miscalculation see C.O. 324/75 Ld. Bathurst's Minutes 'Canada Company 1825–6'.

effectual to check colonial crimes till we blazen them to the English public, and arm ourselves with popular indignation,'[1] they attained such strength in the Commons that they had to be conciliated rather than managed. In 1823 the leader of the House took the question of slavery firmly under his personal direction and the spokesman for the colonial department was not even allowed to express his opinion in debate.[2] Buxton, the spokesman for the London Society for the Mitigation and Gradual Abolition of Slavery throughout the British Dominions, agreed to withdraw the emancipation resolution that he had intended to press and the Cabinet, in turn, agreed to bring proposals designed to 'meliorate' the condition of the slaves.[3]

There were several special categories of correspondence between departments: 'Private', 'Confidential', 'Secret', 'Private and Confidential', all appear. 'Secret' letters, intended only for the eye of the Secretary of State or Under-Secretary, were also sometimes, though very rarely, bound in the departmental records. 'Private' was not used to distinguish personal letters, although personal remarks might on occasion be tacked on as a postscript; it was rather a precaution used to prevent certain discussion, usually preliminary, from being published should the House of Commons call for papers; such letters were registered and were available to the clerks in the office. In fact, on one occasion George Baillie took the liberty of making a copy of a 'Private' letter from the Archbishop of Canterbury to Lord Bathurst, and of enclosing it in a personal letter to the governor of New Brunswick.[4] Some 'Secret' correspondence regarding matters under discussion in the Cabinet may not have been seen by the clerks, but the description of the duties of the registrar as 'peculiarly "Confidential" '[5] indicates that most letters passed through his hands.

Most interdepartmental correspondence originating in the Colonial Office was signed by an under-secretary, and, unless the subject concerned was at the 'Private' stage of negotiation,

[1] Howse, E. M., *The Clapham Sect*, p. 153.
[2] Jones, E. G., 'Wilmot Horton', p. 45.
[3] See Mellor, G. R., *British Imperial Trusteeship, 1783–1850*, pp. 87–8.
[4] P.A.C. Sir Howard Douglas Miscellaneous Papers, Baillie to Douglas, July 13, 1825.
[5] See above p. 56.

each letter began by formally stating that the writer had received his instructions from the Secretary of State. Before such official letters were written, however, many questions were discussed orally between representatives of the departments. As has already been noted, senior clerks[1] frequently performed this duty, a procedure apparently quite acceptable to the heads of most departments. Occasionally, however, someone did take exception to it; in November 1824, Wilmot Horton apologized for having delegated a senior clerk to carry out preliminary negotiations with the Post Office on a question connected with the foreign mail service.[2] Two months later the Post Office secretary wrote to Wilmot Horton agreeing to a meeting between Lord Bathurst and the Postmaster-General to discuss another subject, that of the twopenny postal service in Downing Street.[3] Fortunately no other department insisted that a twopenny matter required personal intercourse between departmental chiefs.

Personal intercourse and the exchange of 'Private' letters, then, normally preceded the official broaching of an important question. In 1825 the Customs carried on long and complicated negotiations with the Colonial Office covering three months, at the conclusion of which they proposed '. . . to open a correspondence with your Department through the proper official channel of the Treasury.'[4] During preliminary discussions great care and anxious attention were sometimes paid to the wording of the proposed official letters, with both senders and receivers attempting to find an acceptable form. One of Lord Bathurst's minutes shows how complicated the negotiations could become.

I think [he wrote] there will be full as many objections to allow Mr. Galt to answer the unsigned letter *after* it has been perused, as there were to receiving his answer *before* it was perused. Is the unsigned letter to be alter'd with reference to such an answer?[5]

When letters drafted with such care were called for by the House of Commons they usually revealed sentiments acceptable to that body.

[1] See above p. 56.
[2] C.O. 324/145 Horton to Freeling, private, Nov. 26, 1824.
[3] See C.O. 323/203, f. 336.
[4] C.O. 323/203 R. Dean to Horton, private, Nov. 15, 1825, f. 432.
[5] C.O. 324/75 Lord Bathurst's Minutes, 'Canada Company', Dec. 13, 1825, f. 181.

The Treasury welcomed preliminary discussions at all levels; the difficulty was to get its decisions into official form. Business sometimes dragged on for months.[1] At least part of the perpetual delay in the mid-twenties was due to the character of Frederick Robinson, the Chancellor of the Exchequer, who was notorious for his indolence. References to Treasury dilatoriness in the handling of routine business certainly do not appear frequently during the terms of office of his predecessor, Vansittart, or of his immediate successors, Herries and Goulburn. It was almost impossible to persuade Robinson to come to London in the off-season.[2] Wilmot Horton spoke, on one occasion, of a 'field day at the Treasury'[3] when he did come to town for a day, but such days were too rare for the efficient conduct of business, though they did allow the Treasury secretaries to get on with their tasks of writing official letters to sanction what the Chancellor of the Exchequer had agreed to. Treasury delay was notorious but it was almost certainly not so hampering as in later years, when the written word was not so frequently abetted by oral communication. In 1840 James Stephen complained that it took not less than two months on an average to obtain an answer from the Treasury, and that in several cases there had been a delay of a year or more.[4]

The contrast in attitude between the Post Office and the Treasury indicates an individuality in the departments that allowed a considerable variety in the pattern of interdepartmental relations. That of the Colonial Office with the Admiralty is particularly interesting in its similarity to the 'joking' relationship that exists between certain individuals in some primitive societies and in university common rooms. Its origin

[1] The memorandum suggesting the Rev. Anthony Hamilton's appointment as chaplain general for the colonies was drawn up in December 1824, apparently with the sanction of the Treasury (see above p. 76). In February 1826, Hamilton was still requesting that provision should be made for his salary and expenses, which were to date from the first of January 1825 (C.O. 323/205). He had been assured in July 1825 that the delay was of no importance (C.O. 323/203, ff. 314–8 and f. 104).

[2] *Bathurst Papers*, p. 550.

[3] C.O. 324/75 Lord Bathurst's Minutes, 'Canada Company', No Date, (1825), f. 185.

[4] See Parkinson, Sir Cosmo, *The Colonial Office from Within 1909–1945* (1947), p. 41. By 1909 the average time had been reduced to four weeks. Later when exploitation of the telephone revitalized the oral tradition communication between departments was further improved.

probably lay in the friendship of Lord Bathurst and Lord Melville, the First Lord of the Admiralty (1812–27), and in their close association during the war. One of the most amusing compositions was a facetious reply by Admiralty Secretary Croker to a letter from Under-Secretary Bunbury urging that orders be issued to put a stop 'to the injurious practice of wantonly and needlessly turning upon their backs the innumerable turtle which are found in the island of Ascension', and protesting against the hundreds that 'were left to perish in a supine position, which appears to be little agreeable to their nature'.[1] In Croker's mock serious reply, marked 'Immediate and Confidential', 'My Lords' urged that, 'in a matter of such vital moment', Lord Bathurst 'receive and communicate officially to their Lordships, the pleasure of His Royal Highness the Prince Regent as to the steps which are to be pursued.' After this sally he saw fit to comment on two points: first, that since the last vessel to visit the island had seen only one turtle, they were certainly in danger of becoming innumerable, and secondly, that their Lordships 'entirely concurred with Lord Bathurst, that it may be inferred, since the turtle invariably die when placed in a supine position, that this position is but little agreeable to their nature.' Later the presence of Wilmot Horton, who much fancied himself as a wit, added to the levity of official exchanges. Sometimes Lord Melville was the butt of the Colonial Office[2] though the enthusiastic John Barrow lent himself even more readily to ridicule. On one of Barrow's proposals for expanding the Empire Lord Bathurst minuted:

Barrow is a great authority, but it has been often said that if coveting Islands or For. [eign] Settlements is a breach of the Tenth Commandment he is the greatest violator of the Decalogue in the Kingdom.[3]

On another occasion, when Barrow was pressing Lord Bathurst to send the newly married Captain Franklin to explore the north-west passage, one of his letters, containing some cynical comments on marriage, was shown to Georgina Bathurst, the Colonial Secretary's daughter. Her minute was forthright and sensible.

[1] *Bathurst Papers*, Jan. 11, 1816, pp. 408–10.
[2] See above p. 89.
[3] C.O. 324/75 Lord Bathurst's Minutes, 'Misc.', f. 266.

If Mrs. Franklin finds her husband a bore then I think he had decidedly better be sent *but* not if she don't approve. Mr. Barrow is very impertinent———.[1]

But good humour alone could not overcome all the obstacles to the efficient conduct of business. One trivial example of the 'emergency-order-that-was-never-rescinded' type wasted many man-hours in the Admiralty. In 1811, at a time when a shortage of shipping was causing a crisis, the Secretary of State for War and the Colonies had arranged for a weekly report on shipping to be prepared for him. A protest from the Navy Office in 1829 about the time wasted in its preparation[2] finally led to its being discontinued in 1831.[3]

While, in theory, the Treasury claimed the right to supervise the collection and spending of all public money throughout the colonies and the right of auditing all accounts, in practice before about 1825 it exercised these functions perfunctorily when it performed them at all. Even on supplies voted by the British Parliament for the civil government of the colonies Treasury supervision did not extend beyond the auditing of accounts, and these were frequently submitted late and in such a confused state as to be difficult to evaluate. In some colonies, notably New South Wales and Sierra Leone, governors were at times given virtual *carte blanche* to draw on parliamentary funds, the form of proceeding being for the Secretary of State to authorize bills drawn on the Treasury in the same manner as he authorized military expenditure in time of war:

> . . . and I am directed to acquaint you for their Lordships' information that Lord Bathurst is of opinion it may be proper to pay the said Bill upon account.

Financial authority was also almost entirely in the Colonial Secretary's hands in the colonies acquired during the Napoleonic wars. In some of them institutions were preserved as before the conquest, some taxes being levied and applied by local authority, others being paid into the government treasury.

---

[1] C.O. 324/75 Lord Bathurst's Minutes, 'Misc.', Barrow to Horton, private, Nov. 21, 1823, f. 223.

[2] C.O. 323/211 Boyle (Navy Office) to Hay, Sept. 25, 1829; also C.O. 323/186 Croker to Goulburn, Apr. 10, 1817, f. 19.

[3] C.O. 324/146, p. 298.

In some, revenue was collected as before the conquest, in others, old taxes and duties were abolished and new ones imposed in lieu of them. In some instances almost every branch of military expenditure was defrayed from colonial funds under the authority of the Secretary of State; in others only minor portions, and these differing in different colonies according to the regulations in force before the conquest.[1]

In 1812, even the auditing of such accounts as were received from the colonies appears to have been very haphazard. There were three auditing offices responsible for different types of colonial accounts.[2] The commissioners of audit for the United Kingdom, the Audit Office, handled all grants made by the British Parliament for colonial purposes and Treasury auditors attempted to check the expenditure of local revenues in the colonies without legislatures. In addition to these, a relic of the first empire,[3] the Deputy Auditor-General of the Plantations, performed labours in inverse ratio to the grandiosity of his title by passing the few accounts received from the legislative colonies in North America and the West Indies. The real check, in most cases the only check, on local expenditure was that provided in the colonies themselves. In 1814 a new office was established for auditing colonial accounts[4] in the United Kingdom after Treasury auditors had declared their inability to cope with the accounts of Ceylon, which were prepared on the Indian pattern.[5] A three-man commission of colonial audit, the Colonial Audit Office, was authorized by Parliament[6] to audit the accounts of the conquered colonies of Ceylon, Mauritius, Malta, Trinidad and the Cape of Good Hope, the expenses to be met from the colonies concerned.

The commissioners of colonial audit were not expected to keep a close check on the internal expenditure of the colonies,

---

[1] See C.O. 323/203 Brande (Colonial Audit Office) to Horton, Feb. 25, 1825, ff. 362–5.

[2] For reports of the accounts audited by the various auditors in the United Kingdom concerned with colonial revenue in 1826 and 1827, see C.O. 323/208, ff. 175–182. There is no reference in these reports to an audit of the Crown revenues of Lower Canada.

[3] See Manning, H. T., *British Colonial Government* . . ., pp. 97–8.

[4] It was suggested by Clement Martin Edwards, who claimed to have Sir Thomas Maitland's support. See C.O. 323/182 Edwards to Goulburn Sept. 19, 1813. He also submitted a memorandum a few months later.

[5] Manning, H. T., *British Colonial Government* . . ., p. 516.

[6] 54 Geo. III. Cap. 184.

for which task local auditors were considered to be more suited, but they did attempt to keep an overall check on those accounts in addition to their regular duties of checking bills drawn on Great Britain and India.[1] Under a parliamentary Act of 1820[2] authority was given to the Treasury to extend the duties of the commissioners and, by a Treasury minute of 20 December 1822, the examination of the accounts of New South Wales, Van Diemen's Land, Sierra Leone, Gold Coast, Demerara, and Berbice was assigned to them.[3] These colonies were, however, not required to pay towards the cost of maintaining the office.[4] In 1828 the commissioners of colonial audit were reporting on twelve colonies, St. Lucia and Newfoundland having been added to those previously mentioned.[5] The Colonial Audit Board was merged into the Audit Office of the United Kingdom in 1832.[6]

From the beginning Lord Bathurst showed little desire to assist the commissioners of colonial audit. He failed even to co-operate with the Treasury in drawing up the original instructions for their guidance[7] and later he exerted himself conspicuously in attempting to prevent the commissioners from being too searching in their enquiries. In 1818 the auditors were refused access to the general correspondence of the colonies.[8] In 1819 a Treasury request that governors be instructed to notify the Colonial Audit Office of new colonial appointments was reluctantly granted,[9] but the Colonial Office steadfastly refused to furnish copies of appointments on the grounds that

---

[1] Manning, H. T., *British Colonial Government* . . ., pp. 517–8.
[2] I Geo. IV. Cap. 1. [3] C.O. 323/197, ff. 208–9.
[4]

	Establishment	Salaries
1815	17	£5,850
1827	23	7,140
1829	23	7,450

H.C. 1830–31 VII (92) 318–9.

[5] C.O. 323/208, ff. 179–182. The accounts of Van Diemen's Land had been merged with those of New South Wales.
[6] 2 Wm. IV. Cap. 26.
[7] Manning, H. T., *British Colonial Government* . . ., pp. 516–520. See also C.O. 323/183 Lushington (Treasury) to Goulburn, March 17, 1815, f. 103 complaining of a Colonial Office failure to answer a letter sent four months earlier.
[8] C.O. 323/188 Brande to Penn, undated, ff. 275–6, Brande to Goulburn, June 16, f. 272, and Aug. 10, 1818, f. 277.
[9] C.O. 323/190 Lushington to Goulburn, June 14, 1819, f. 271. Reproduced with enclosures as a circular, see C.O. 854–1.

... the Introduction of such a practice cannot be necessary and can have no effect but that of compelling his Lordship to augment the Establishment of the Office in order to provide for the new, and as their Lordships may well imagine, this extensive Branch of Labour.[1]

In 1820 there was an apparent lull when the Colonial Office and Treasury co-operated in preparing regulations requiring governors to draw up annual estimates on which colonial budgets could be based. However, on this occasion Lord Bathurst did not allow the Treasury to infringe on his authority in the conquered colonies, for, contrary to the original intention of the Treasury, the instructions were drafted in the Colonial Office and issued in the name of the Secretary of State.[2] In 1825 the Colonial Office refused the auditors permission to correspond directly with colonial governors,[3] who were the official accountants responsible for all the revenue collected. The commissioners were, therefore, unable to question individual items in the accounts except by corresponding with the governors through the Colonial Office. Even when colonial treasurers were made officially accountable for the expenditure of colonial funds[4] all orders from the commissioners to the treasurers had to go through the Secretary of State.[5] Direct correspondence between the secretary of the Colonial Audit Office and the treasurers was concerned only with the delivery of accounts.[6]

The constant aim of the Bathurst office was to keep as much authority as possible in its own hands. The limits of Treasury authority were not always clear, and where there was any doubt about the need to consult the Treasury, Lord Bathurst studiously avoided referring a question to that department. On at least one occasion he stated his philosophy very explicitly:

But before you leave the Treasury to decide, consider what may be the consequence of referring to them. ... I am afraid that wherever the sanction of the Treasury is legally necessary, the

[1] C.O. 324/143 Goulburn to Harrison, Aug. 15, 1821, p. 245, quoting from his letter of Feb. 24, 1820.
[2] Manning, H. T., *British Colonial Government* ..., p. 520.
[3] C.O. 323/203 Harrison (Treasury) to Horton, Feb. 16, 1825, f. 43. Brande (Colonial Audit Office) to Horton, March 8, 1825, ff. 366–7.
[4] C.O. 323/203 Brande to Horton, May 6, 1825, f. 385.
[5] H.C. 1837 VII (516) 324.
[6] *Ibid.*, f. 355.

responsibility rests with the Treasury. If the sanction of the Treasury is necessary to complete a Grant, the Treasury is responsible for that Grant, altho' the Secretary of State may be deeply responsible also for having recommended it. If the sanction of the Treasury is necessary for the appropriation of any Money, the Treasury is responsible for such appropriation. The responsibility of the Secretary of State is discharged by the recommendation, & if his recommendation is not accepted, his responsibility ceases. Care therefore must be taken not to apply to the Treasury for their sanction, except in those cases, in which their sanction is legally required. It is one thing to confirm a Grant, it is another to appropriate any Revenue arising from that Grant, if there be nothing in the Grant, which specifies the fund into which the Money shall be placed. It will therefore be very desirable to ascertain accurately what are the appropriations of Crown Revenues which require the legal sanction of the Treasury, & what do not require this Sanction, before you can come to any Understanding with the Treasury, who seem more anxious to extend their duties than to discharge them.[1]

At least one of Lord Bathurst's protégés was unable to distinguish between this subtle legalism and a resort to illegality and petty mendacity in support of departmental independence. This is revealed in a letter from George Baillie, head clerk in the North American department, to Sir Howard Douglas, the governor of New Brunswick, at a time when a large sum had accumulated in the Crown Revenue fund of that colony:

I have not sent you answers to some of your letters respecting the Receiver of the Crown Revenue & some other arrangements because we ought not to do it without the Treasury & if we send the Papers then they may take a fancy to some of the Money or at all events claim a control over it. I had some conversation with Mr. Harrison yesterday & I found he was very much disposed to interfere more than would have been *useful* & I therefore put him off by saying that when the accounts arrived we would send them off which I have not the least intention of doing unless Lord Bathurst desires me.[2]

When this letter was written, in July 1825, the Treasury was becoming increasingly disposed to interfere more than Lord

[1] C.O. 324/75 Lord Bathurst's Minutes 'N. America' undated, f. 160. The minute was concerned with the disposal of the Cape Breton coal mines.
[2] P.A.C. Sir Howard Douglas Miscellaneous Papers, July 13, 1825.

Bathurst considered 'useful'. In that month the Commission for inquiring into the state of His Majesty's Settlements, the Cape of Good Hope, Ceylon, and Mauritius made its first report;[1] this and a subsequent report, which was laid before Parliament in the following year, revealed the laxity of the management of colonial revenues.[2] The Colonial Secretary at that time authorized expenditures in several colonies without consulting the Treasury and, as Peter Smith succinctly stated to a parliamentary committee of enquiry in 1837, 'a great deal of money was expended.'[2] To be more precise, the deficiency of revenue over expenditure over a ten-year period in the five colonies most completely under the Secretary of State's control—Ceylon, Mauritius, Cape of Good Hope, Trinidad and Malta—was stated by the Treasury to have been over two and a half million pounds, most of it in Mauritius and Ceylon.[4] In Lower Canada, the only other colony in which there was a large expenditure not sanctioned by an independent local authority, the governor borrowed for the use of the civil government over £114,000 between 1820 and 1827 from funds voted by Parliament for the military services.[5]

A few tentative suggestions for, and efforts directed towards, bringing order into the colonial financial systems were made from time to time. The appointment of an able young man, G. W. Brande, as secretary of the Colonial Audit Office in 1818 led to an effort to introduce a uniform method in the preparation of colonial accounts, and to an insistence on greater promptitude in the submission of accounts for audit. In 1823 William Hill, Assistant Secretary to the Treasury, revealed unusual insight into the financial problems of Lower Canada in a letter to the Colonial Under-Secretary[6] but his ideas appear to have had

---

[1] See H.C. (1826–27) XX, 499–507, No. 34. I have found no explicit evidence to show that Lord Bathurst's support for the sending out of this commission was motivated by a desire to postpone Treasury and parliamentary enquiry.

[2] See H.C. 1830–31 IV (194). Report of Commissioners of Colonial Enquiry on Mauritius.

[3] H.C. 1837 VII (516) 353.

[4] Herries to Horton, Mar. 24, 1827, published in H.C. 1830 XXI (212) 173–4.

[5] Creighton, D. G., 'The Struggle for Financial Control in Lower Canada, 1818–1831', p. 129.

[6] C.O. 323/197 Hill to Horton, private, Dec. 17, 1823, ff. 259–262.

little influence either in his own department or in that of the
Secretary of State. In 1824 an effective step was taken towards
obtaining a much larger Crown revenue in New Brunswick by
the appointment of an energetic Colonial Office clerk as commissioner of Crown lands. This appointment, made jointly by
the Treasury and the Colonial Office, was dictated, however,
more by considerations of patronage than by a concern for the
revenue. A much more significant move was the appointment
of Major Thomas Moody as home secretary to the overseas
commissions of enquiry in 1824. He was immediately instructed
by Wilmot Horton to attempt to prepare a common system for
keeping colonial accounts and was detailed to co-operate with
Stephen in drawing up new financial instructions for colonial
governors.[1] This was the only attempt made to bring the financial affairs of all the colonies under a single head within the
Colonial Office.

Major Moody, soon after his appointment, consulted G. W.
Brande and it may have been as a result of their co-operation
that Brande penned a proposal for a thoroughgoing reorganization of the machinery for supervising colonial expenditures. On
25 February 1825 he sent his suggestions to Wilmot Horton.
The primary need, as he saw it, was for some measure for ensuring prompt and efficient control in Great Britain over the
financial operations of the colonial officers:

> This end would be best attained by placing the supervision of all
> matters of Colonial Revenue and Expenditure under *some com-*
> *petent officer* attached to the Treasury or to the Colonial Depart-
> ment; *whose duty it would be to see that all proper Accounts and Financial*
> *Documents are regularly transmitted from the Colonies—to superintend the*
> *collection of the Colonial Revenues—to see that the regulations respecting*
> *them are duly observed—and to prepare all necessary information for His*
> *Majesty's Government or for Parliament relative to them*; and also to
> make such immediate inspection of all accounts received from the
> Colonies as shall enable *him to ascertain that no Expenditure has been*
> *incurred which has not been authorized by His Majesty's Government.*[2]

Lord Bathurst's tart comment on this letter shows that he

---

[1] See above pp. 72-3.
[2] C.O. 323/203, ff. 362–5. The underlining was added in the Colonial
Office.

did not share his Under-Secretary's interest in the need for reform:

> The neglect and incompetency of the Treasury & the Colonial Department being thus established [he wrote], the remedy is perfectly clear and simple. Appoint the writer to the Office here proposed & *transfer to this Gentleman & the B^d of Audit all correspondence with H.M.'s Governors, which can in any manner relate to Expenditure.*[1]

With unerring perception Lord Bathurst had in a couple of sentences summarized Brande's proposal. Seven years later Brande was appointed to an office patterned on the lines that he had suggested.[2]

A letter laid before the House of Commons select committee on finance on 24 June 1829 clearly shows that time did not soften Lord Bathurst's casual contempt for Treasury officials nor weaken his waspish obstruction of attempts at reform. In a letter written on 24 March 1827 the Treasury had expressed 'their decided opinion that some alteration is urgently required in the system under which the financial arrangements of the Colonies (not having legislatures) had hitherto been conducted.'[3] Maintaining that the Treasury 'has been uninformed, not only of the measures which have from time to time led to occasional and extraordinary expenses in the Colonies, but even of the state of their ordinary revenues and the permanent charges upon them', the Treasury secretary had asked for information on the state of the revenue in those colonies since that possessed by the auditors was not up-to-date. The Colonial Office reply, penned only a few days before Lord Bathurst gave up the seals of office, was stingingly abrupt. Referring apparently to the order permitting the Colonial Audit Office to correspond with the colonial treasurers, he wrote:

> ... as a direct communication has for some time been established between the Board of Treasury and the Colonial authorities abroad, his Lordship could not but have imagined that the Lords Commissioners had availed themselves of the means which were open to them for obtaining such information as they required.[4]

[1] C.O. 323/203, f. 365.
[2] See below p. 195.
[3] H.C. 1830 XXI (212) 173–4. The original is in C.O. 323/207.
[4] H.C. 1830 XXI (352) 169–70.

Treasury officials, notably J. C. Herries,[1] began to take active steps to improve the efficiency of the administration of the revenue departments at least as early as 1818.[2] The reduction of the military forces also presented them with an opportunity to rationalize the operations of the military departments and establish a more efficient control over expenditure.[3] All approaches to the Colonial Office were rebuffed, however, as has been indicated, until after the retirement of Lord Bathurst. Herries, whom C. R. Fay has described as 'a veritable Sidney Webb' in the diligence of his minuting, was the champion of the idea that, in the interests of good administration, the control of expenditure should be firmly in the hands of the Treasury.[4] In 1828 he was Master of the Mint with a seat in the Cabinet and almost no departmental responsibilities; the prestige of his office, and his reputation as an administrator with a fervent interest in increasing the efficiency of the financial administration, gave him great influence in the House of Commons select committee on finance of that year. The reports of that strong and independent committee brought about a great increase in the demand for reform of the financial administration of the colonies. It was not, however, until 23 April 1830 that the Treasury followed up the recommendations of the committee by appointing two commissions of enquiry, one to enquire into the revenue of Great Britain and Ireland, the other 'into the Receipt of the Revenues, collected within His Majesty's several Colonies & Foreign possessions and into the expenditure both of the said Revenues, and of the supplies provided out of the Revenues of the United Kingdom for the maintenance of the said Colonies and Foreign Possessions.'[5]

The commission of colonial enquiry was very weak and was so constituted that it could do little except echo the opinions of the Treasury. It was evidently considered fitting that a com-

[1] J. C. Herries (1778–1855) was Commissary-in-Chief to the Army during the last years of the war, then successively Auditor of the Civil List, Secretary to the Treasury, Chancellor of the Exchequer (Sept. 1827–Jan. 1828), Master of the Mint (1828–1830), President of the Board of Trade (1830), Secretary at War (1834–5) and President of the Board of Control (1852).

[2] Fay, C. R., *Huskisson and his Age*, pp. 286–90.

[3] See the interesting Treasury minute of May 24, 1822. There is a copy of it in C.O. 323/211 under 'Treasury'.

[4] Fay, C. R., *Huskisson and his Age*, pp. 113–4.

[5] T 29/304 Treasury minute No. 7214 (Sixth Division).

mission on finance should not cost anything, for no money was provided either for salaries or secretarial work. Two of the members were cabinet ministers, two were nonentities and the fifth, Sir Willoughby Gordon, who was obviously named because of his knowledge of military affairs in the colonies, regarded the whole set-up as a farce designed to forestall more searching enquiry:

> A Commission to enquire into the expenditure of the Colonies with a view to reform it [he wrote], a Parliamentary Commission with only one of the Commissioners who has ever been in the Colonies, or who has perhaps ever thought twice upon the subject of them![1]

His remark was not strictly accurate, for one of the members was the Chancellor of the Exchequer, Henry Goulburn, who had been Colonial Under-Secretary for almost a decade.

Four reports were laid before Parliament,[2] of which at least two were published.[3] There was also a fifth report, dated 13 December 1830, which contained the general observations of the commissioners, who had not completed their investigations when the warrant under which they were appointed expired on the death of George IV.[4] These reports reflected faithfully the views expressed in the report of the 1828 parliamentary committee on finance, which had deplored the fact that

> ... the ancient and wise control vested by our Financial Policy in the hands of the Treasury, over all the Departments connected with the Public Expenditure, has been in a great degree set aside.[5]

and urged that it be re-established. Thus fifty years after Burke delivered his great speech on economical reform of 11 February 1780, his proposal that this 'ancient and wise control' be established was being vigorously pressed. The commission also emphasized the need for a greater measure of private enterprise and competition in the obtaining of supplies for the military forces stationed in the colonies, the renting of accommodation whenever it was feasible, and the employment of contrac-

[1] Letter to Sir Herbert Taylor, April 15, 1830 in Taylor, Sir Herbert, *The Taylor Papers*, ed., Ernest Taylor, 1913, p. 317.
[2] See H.C. 1831–2 XXVI (512) 501.
[3] H.C. 1830–31 IV (64 and 194) 1–179.
[4] C.O. 323/212, ff. 177–183.
[5] H.C. 1828 V (420) 5.

tors by tender for the erection and maintenance of buildings. The emphasis on 'private enterprise' was part of Herries' programme for administrative improvement. By the extensive employment of contractors the administrative burden would be reduced and a more effective control of expenditure could be maintained.

The final report of the commissioners was not a full general report, which they did not feel competent to submit on the basis of their incomplete investigations. It did, however, make several specific recommendations, the tone of which may be judged from these two:

1. It appears to be above all necessary that the Treasury should exercise a strict & efficient control over every branch & every article of Colonial Expenditure.

   We know that many salutary regulations exist upon this point but we trust that we may be excused for urging it still more strongly, & recommending, not only that the present orders be rigidly enforced; but that such further directions should be given as will ensure the attention of the Colonial Governments to this important object.

2. We recommend that the Accounts of all the several Colonies without exception should be made up & certified in the manner directed by your Lordships, & regularly & punctually transmitted to this Country for examination at the Colonial Audit Office.[1]

On his copy of the report Lord Goderich, the Colonial Secretary, noted on the first clause, 'Quite right.', and on the second, 'Is this practicable in its full extent, in those Colonies which have independent Legislatures?' On a further proposal, that demands for stores should be certified as necessary by a colonial governor, he minuted:

A copy of such requisition sh^d be sent at the same time to Sec^y of State & the Treasury sh^d not comply with it untill the Colonial Depart^t has been consulted.

Thus the pattern of the future was outlined; the colonies with legislatures were not brought under Treasury supervision, and for the control of expenditure of the other colonies a dyarchical system was established with frequent consultation and the

[1] C.O. 323/212, f. 177.

resultant delays. The Treasury assumed primary responsibility but everything relating to the revenue or expenditure of the colonies was referred to the Colonial Office.[1]

In its letter to the Treasury incorporating Lord Goderich's comments on the final report of the commissioners of colonial enquiry, and incidentally translating his remarks into officialese, the Colonial Office expressed its satisfaction that the report contained scarcely anything of importance that had not been the subject of 'much anxious deliberation, and in many cases of positive instructions from the Department.'[2] This agreement between the departments on the need for improving the system of regulating colonial expenditure soon led to several changes in addition to the one referred to in the last paragraph. The most important of these were the establishment of a joint agency in 1833 to replace the old system of individual agents for each Crown colony, the merging of the Board of Colonial Audit into the Audit Office of the United Kingdom in 1832, and the appointment in the same year of an official in the Treasury with specific responsibility for the colonies. G. W. Brande, the secretary of the Board of Colonial Audit at the time of its dissolution, was appointed to the newly created post of clerk for colonial accounts at the Treasury. In 1834 his title was changed to that of principal clerk for colonial business.[3] Giving evidence before the select committee on the preparation of colonial accounts in 1837, he reported that he took the directions of the secretary and the board of the Treasury on all papers relating to colonial matters and superintended the preparation of abstracts of colonial accounts for the House of Commons.[4]

The setting up of the select committee on colonial accounts in 1837 indicates that the system of colonial accounting was still unsatisfactory despite several efforts to improve it. Carrying out another recommendation of the 1830 commission, the Treasury in 1831 and 1832 called on all the departments of government for annual returns of every branch of their expenditure on transactions relating to the colonies. Crown colonies were also

[1] See H.C. 1837 VII (516) 325.
[2] C.O. 324/146 Hay to J. Stewart, Dec. 31, 1830, p. 272.
[3] Of the six sections into which the Treasury was divided colonies were included in the fourth division, which also handled the affairs of the Channel Isles, Isle of Man, and the Commission on Woods and Forests.
[4] See H.C. 1837 VII (516) 309.

required to make quarterly returns and the legislative colonies were requested to make a return annually, for information only.[1] In his evidence before the 1837 committee, G. R. Porter, head of the then recently created statistical department of the Board of Trade, reported that his statistics for the Crown colonies were good, for the legislative colonies, not so good, with Jamaica being the worst.[2] The committee also heard the evidence of an auditor who was not at all satisfied with the accounts sent from the Crown colonies.[3] But, then, another witness, P. H. Abbott, who had been a member of an 1828 committee that looked into the making up of public accounts and in that capacity had examined the accounts of twenty-eight government departments, gave evidence that 'the Treasury is . . . as imperfect in its mode of keeping accounts, if not more so, than many of the inferior departments of the Government.'[4]

Whereas in the twenties the Colonial Office resented the Treasury's justified efforts to extend its control over colonial finance, it was reluctant to allow the Board of Trade to surrender its responsibility for reporting on colonial laws. The Board of Trade, legally a committee of the Privy Council, had been responsible since its origin for examining all acts of the colonies with legislative assemblies and recommending them to the King in Council for confirmation or disallowance. The 'pleasure of the King' on acts of the conquered colonies was, however, signified directly by the Secretary of State. James Stephen thought this distinction a valid one since

> The Acts of a Legislative Assembly assented to by the Governor and his Council in a Country governed by English Law may properly exact a more solemn form of proceeding for their confirmation or disallowance than Ordinances emanating entirely from the representatives of the King, . . . assisted only by Councils nominated by His Majesty.[5]

This reflected the official view of the Colonial Office, and presumably also of the Board of Trade. At no time was it officially

[1] See H.C. 1837 VII (516) 312.
[2] *Ibid.*, 407–10.
[3] *Ibid.*, 355.
[4] *Ibid.*, 438.
[5] C.O. 323/205 Memorandum of September 26, 1826, f. 219.

suggested that the Privy Council should cease to have formal authority to disallow colonial legislation.

From the very early days of the revived Board of Trade, colonial acts were referred to John Reeves, its law clerk, for an opinion. By 1823, Reeves, who was a greatly respected figure among extreme conservatives, a well-known writer on legal subjects, and the first chief justice of Newfoundland, was nearing retirement.[1] At this time, also, the Board of Trade was undertaking the task of overhauling the trade laws of the Empire and had little desire to make new provision for the time-consuming routine business of passing its opinion on the acts of the colonial legislatures. In January 1823, there was a suggestion that the Board of Trade be divided, with the review of colonial acts being put under a separate department in the Board of Trade office.[2] This was probably considered impractical and in July, with Lord Bathurst present as a member of the Board, a solution was adopted that, in effect, recognized the right of the Colonial Office to be the effective reviewer.[3]

Colonial acts relating to trade were to be transmitted privately to the Board of Trade and an answer returned to the Colonial Office. Acts involving points of law, accompanied by a statement from the legal counsel of the Colonial Office, were to be similarly submitted to the Privy Council Office, with a request that the opinion of the law officers of the Crown be secured.

> . . . with respect to all other Colonial Acts which involve points of policy or administration, the responsibility of deciding upon which must rest exclusively with the Colonial Department, it is to be understood that no examination need take place by the Board of Trade, but that Lord Bathurst will attend at the Board, and give his opinion generally as to the propriety of their being sanctioned.

From 1823 onwards, the Colonial Secretary formally attended Board of Trade meetings three or four times a year for the purpose of giving assent to the acts.

---

[1] See Fay, C. R., *Life and Labour in Newfoundland*, Cambridge, 1956, pp. 105–9 for a few remarks on Reeves' career.
[2] Arbuthnot, Charles, *The Correspondence of Charles Arbuthnot*, ed. A. Aspinall, Camden Third Series, LXV, 1941, p. 44.
[3] B.T. 5/31 Minute of July 14, 1823, pp. 363–4, cited in Cockroft, G., *The Public Life of George Chalmers . . .*, p. 122.

But even a formal acquiescence proved irksome to the Board of Trade. Since the acts were allowed to accumulate for months at a time before being disposed of, the task of listing the numbers and titles in the preparation of the formal Board of Trade minute and of preparing formal letters for the Privy Council and the Colonial Office was soon regarded as a tedious chore. Since the routine had no connection with the other Board of Trade business, there was probably a tendency to postpone action as long as possible. In 1826, in pressing for the setting up of a new committee of the Privy Council to review the acts, the vice-president of the Board declared with utilitarian fervour that he did not wish to be

> required by his sacred Majesty gravely to address him & advise him on subjects on which he is misled if he thinks it is in our power to offer an opinion.[1]

At that time the process of reviewing colonial legislation required eight steps:

1. All acts were supposed to be transmitted by a colonial governor to the Secretary of State.
2. Upon arrival at the Colonial Office they were referred by the Secretary of State to the legal counsel of his department for his opinion 'in point of law'; i.e. whether they were consistent with a governor's instructions and commission, whether repugnant to the law of England, and whether the Act would have the effect intended.[2]
3. Acts were then returned to the Secretary of State with the counsel's report on them.
4. The acts along with the reports were transmitted to the Lord President of the Council with a request that they be brought under His Majesty's consideration.
5. They were laid before His Majesty at the next meeting of the Privy Council.
6. An order was then made by which the King in Council referred the acts, with the letter from the Secretary of State, 'to the Right Honourable the Lords of the Committee of Council appointed for the consideration of all matters relat-

---

[1] C.O. 323/205 Grant to Horton, private, Aug. 22, 1826, ff. 126–7.
[2] H.C. 1825 XV, p. 8, quoted in Manning, H. T., *British Colonial Government . . .*, p. 77.

ing to Trade and Foreign Plantations, to consider the same, and report their opinion thereupon to His Majesty at this Board.'

7. 'It would seem as if the next step in the process should be a Report from the Lords of the Committee of Trade to His Majesty in Council, in obedience to His Majesty's Reference to them. But, in point of fact it is not the habit to make any such report, except when it is necessary that any Act should be disallowed, or expressly confirmed. In those cases a Report is made to His Majesty and an Order in Council is thereupon issued, disallowing or confirming the Act. In general however their Lordship's make no report at all upon the Reference to them.'[1]

8. 'They communicate through their Secretary, to the Secretary of State, such observations as they are pleased to make on the subject. In many recent cases this communication from their Lordships is confined to the remark that they are not officially competent to express an opinion on the Acts thus referred to them.'[2]

About forty-nine out of every fifty of the acts of the older colonies were 'left to their own operation'. At one time no colonial act had been valid unless it had been sanctioned by order in council, but this practice had fallen into disuse. In James Stephen's opinion the irregularity of this arrangement placed the Secretary of State in an embarrassing situation:

He cannot signify to the Colony the decision of His Majesty in Council; for no such decision has been made. He cannot signify His Majesty's pleasure in any other form; because the Law and the Constitution require that the King should decide upon such Acts only with the advice of His Privy Council. Neither can the Secretary of State bring the subject again under the consideration of the Council, without manifest impropriety. The consequence, in point of fact is, that in a great number of cases the Acts remain at the Colonial Office without any measure being taken upon them.[3]

The procedure for changing the form of reviewing colonial acts was, according to Lord Bathurst, for the Board of Trade to pro-

---

[1] C.O. 324/146 Wilmot Horton to Lack (Board of Trade) June 23, 1826, pp. 23–40, draft in C.O. 323/205 under 'Stephen', f. 199.
[2] *Ibid.*   [3] *Ibid.*

pose a plan to the Lord President of the Council and through him to the Cabinet.[1] In 1828, when Lord Bathurst was Lord President, a small but significant change was made in the formal reviewing process; the Privy Council Office was instructed to refer the acts to the Board of Trade without first obtaining authority by order in council.[2] By 1830 no further headway had been made in the attempt to simplify procedure.[3] The effective reviewer of all but the laws affecting trade was still James Stephen; almost all else was formality.

Only by an examination of all the correspondence between the Secretary of State and other ministers, and between the Colonial Office and other departments, would it be possible to give an exact picture of the part played in colonial government by the interlocking sections of the British government. Even the choice of a colonial governor, usually considered to be a function of the Secretary of State, might require consultation with the King, the Prime Minister,[4] and the Commander-in-Chief;[5] in fact, if the governor was likely to be dealing with matters in which Parliament took an interest, the approval of all the leading members of the Government might be sought.[6] The seeking of the advice and support of the Cabinet, or of its leading members, was a common practice when a question was likely to arouse Parliament's interest; on the slavery issue in 1823 and on the situation in Canada following the report of the Canada Committee of 1828, the Prime Minister and the Cabinet insisted on taking the lead. Support from the King and Privy Council for colonial policy was largely a formality, except that the personal idiosyncrasies of the King had always to be taken into account. The Foreign Office had many colonial cards to play at Ghent and Vienna in 1814 and 1815 and in the Mediterranean in the twenties. Attempts at international control of the slave trade, suspicion of French designs on Western Australia, West Africa,

[1] C.O. 324/75 Lord Bathurst's Minutes, 'Misc.', Aug. 25, 1826, f. 257.
[2] C.O. 323/208 Privy Council Office to Colonial Office, May 30, 1828, f. 45.
[3] N.L.S. Sir George Murray Papers, Statement by James Stephen, Feb. 16, 1830, vol. 171, f. 58.
[4] *Bathurst Papers*, Liverpool to Bathurst, secret, July 16, 1826, p. 605.
[5] See Br. Mus. Add. Mss. 38751, Huskisson Papers, Huskisson to Goderich, Oct. 10, 1827, f. 184; Horton to Huskisson, Oct. 12, 1827, ff. 218–28.
[6] *Bathurst Papers*, p. 605.

and various islands in the Pacific, and the long negotiations on the boundary in North America also brought it into close touch with colonial affairs. The Home Office was constantly consulted on various aspects of government in New South Wales and handled colonial judicial appeals in Great Britain. But though the jurisdictions of the Secretaries of State sometimes overlapped a spirit of amiable co-operation existed among them. As a result of his function as Secretary of State for War, the head of the Colonial Office also had an intimate relationship with the many departments concerned with the defence of the nation. The long tradition of working together facilitated negotiations with those departments, several of which had extensive colonial responsibilities.

A stout resistance to all change either in the form or substance of his authority gave consistency to Lord Bathurst's relations with other departments and with Parliament. His wartime role had left the Secretary of State supreme in the newer colonies acquired by the Crown; Lord Bathurst placed obstacles in the way of the Treasury in its attempt to assume its constitutional control of their revenues. The development of the Board of Trade into a department responsible for economic affairs made it anxious to free itself of a relic of its past responsibility for the colonies, the review of colonial laws; Lord Bathurst insisted that the old form of carrying out the business be retained. Parliament increasingly took an interest in colonial matters, fired by humanitarian ideals, a desire to reduce expenditure, and a concern to prevent the growth of arbitrary government in the British possessions overseas; Lord Bathurst saw in the interest of the House of Commons a threat to internal order in the colonies.

His successors either adopted changes or were forced to accept them. Huskisson, like the colonial secretaries of the thirties, had respect for the House of Commons and made use of its powers of enquiry. Wellington and Peel allowed Sir George Murray very little say in two of the leading questions of policy in the department. And the Treasury by 1830 had made it plain that it intended that a dyarchical system should operate to control colonial revenues; the supervisory power was to be in the hands of the Treasury but it was not to make decisions without consulting the Colonial Office.

7

THE COLONIAL OFFICE AND THE TREASURY – THE DISPUTE WITH THE LEGISLATIVE COLONIES OVER CUSTOM HOUSE SALARIES

'I have no objection to the Treasury giving directions . . . on the Question respecting the Custom House Officers, provided I am neither called upon to give the Instructions, or by communicating them, appear to support them.'

LORD BATHURST, September 1825.

If the purpose of constitutions is to discourage initiative and frustrate administrators, then the constitutions of the legislative colonies were masterpieces of design. Whereas in the new empire acquired after 1783 the administrator was supreme, in the tag end of the old empire in the western hemisphere governors, responsible to the British government, had to exercise great tact and political skill in managing assemblies in order to avoid becoming bogged down in a morass of local issues. Even when possessed of patience, good will, and political acumen a governor could not look forward to a peaceful and effective administration if there was disagreement between his superiors in Whitehall and the politicians in the assembly. Wrangling was endemic in the system since there was no basic agreement on the question of the extent to which the political and social institutions of the colonies should be required to conform to those of the United Kingdom. On the one hand, the Pitt doctrine that colonial institutions should be 'assimilated' as nearly as possible to those of the Mother Country prevailed against colonial attempts to initiate changes that might weaken the control of the British government or the position of the Church of England. On the other hand, the pressure of the humanitarians for alteration of those aspects of the West Indian social system that outraged moral principles accepted by the British community was effectively resisted by the assemblies. In its control of the governor and its authority to disallow acts of colonial legislatures the government had overwhelming power with which to stifle independent action by the assemblies; the assembly of a larger colony could, in turn, by a persistent refusal to co-operate with the governor, effectively veto any measure that did not meet the approval of its members.

The Achilles' heel of the administration in dealing with the assemblies was finance. When the 'economists' in Parliament began to concentrate on colonial expenditure in the early 1820s, relations with the assemblies became very critical. Since Parliament voted funds in the United Kingdom and the assemblies controlled internal taxation and appropriation in the colonies, administrators were forced to rely on one or the other for almost all the expenses of government. Persistent attacks on departmental estimates in the early 1820s led the Treasury to insist on a reduction of the votes for the colonies and it became necessary to apply to the assemblies of North America for grants. On 8 October 1825 the lieutenant-governors of Upper Canada, Nova Scotia, and New Brunswick were instructed to request the assemblies to make permanent provision for the salaries of officials previously paid out of parliamentary funds,[1] the new demand being linked with the improvements in colonial revenues expected to result from the removal of restrictions on colonial trade. The attempt to persuade the assembly of Lower Canada to place funds at the disposal of the Crown had begun earlier. Since 1818 the assembly had been asked several times to make a grant to supplement the revenue reserved to meet the ordinary expenses of government in the Canada Act of 1791.[2] Astute politicians in the assemblies, well aware of the power that the ability to withhold salaries would give them, insisted on concessions from the government in return for permanent votes. The issue plagued the colonies for several years. In the West Indian colonies the quarrel over financial arrangements was in some ways the reverse of that in North America. Several colonies petitioned regularly against a duty of

[1] Circular printed in the Report from the Select Committee on the Civil Government of Canada, H.C. 1828 VII (569) 686–7.

[2] See Creighton, D. G., 'The struggle for Financial Control in Lower Canada, 1818–1831', *C.H.R.* XII (1931) 120–144.

four and a half per cent paid to the British exchequer on all their exports under an agreement entered into in the very early days of the colonies.[1] Under another agreement, dating from just before the American Revolution, Jamaica provided barracks and paid for the supply of troops stationed on that island.[2] The arrangement was in the nature of a treaty between the island and the British government and, since the assembly voted the necessary funds annually, it could at its own convenience abrogate the agreement and embarrass the government. 'Any payment by a Colony', Henry Goulburn wrote on one occasion, 'is an instrument in their hands always used against the Mother Country.'[3]

The Colonial Office, long accustomed to the intransigence of the assemblies, moved cautiously when their constitutional sensibilities were affected. Although it was generally asserted in Britain that Parliament had the legal competence to legislate in the internal affairs of the legislative colonies, the government, in its efforts to improve the condition of the slaves, made little use of this authority.[4] Because it was aware of the antipathy of the assemblies to parliamentary interference, the Colonial Office preferred to use persuasion and example to induce them to make the desired changes in their slave codes. There can be little doubt that the government had no desire to test the efficacy of Parliament's theoretical authority. The Prime Minister, who had obviously sensed the temper of the assemblies, urged his colleagues on one occasion to have a decided policy should violence ensue even from the moderate approach that was contemplated.[5]

The Treasury was not nearly so circumspect as the Colonial Office. In the tense situation of December 1825 it issued an order which could be, and was, interpreted by colonials as a step in a deliberate campaign to abridge their constitutional rights. In Lower Canada at that time the two nations warring in the bosom of the state were finding in the struggle over

[1] See Ragatz, L. J., *The Fall of the Planter Class in the British Caribbean, 1763–1833*, New York, 1928, p. 101.

[2] See C.O. 138/53 Murray to Belmore, Sept. 15, 1830, pp. 136–157, for a history of the arrangement.

[3] C.O. 137/173 Goulburn to Murray, private, Aug. 19, 1830.

[4] Schuyler, R. L., *Parliament and the British Empire*, Chapter 4.

[5] *Bathurst Papers*, p. 560.

financial policy an issue that crystallized their fundamental difference of outlook and embittered relations between them; in the West Indies all of the assemblies were sullenly devising obstructive tactics to impede the attempts of the governors to have new slave codes enacted. The arrival of the Treasury order in the midst of this unrest brought forth a furious outburst of indignation. The assembly of Jamaica, outstanding in the high quality of its vituperation, characterized the new order as 'too oppressive to be borne and calculated to destroy those chartered rights most solemnly conceded.'[1]

The fiscal regulation so described was an innocent-looking instruction sent to the colonial customs officers authorizing them to deduct from the duties they collected under parliamentary acts a sum large enough to cover their salaries and expenses. Though Treasury officers were responsible for the collection of duties, the revenue received was turned over to the assembly of the colony in which it was collected. Hitherto the expenses of collection had been very small. Colonial customs officers had been paid only nominal salaries, their incomes having been derived almost entirely from fees levied on ships entering and leaving colonial ports. The fees were abolished from 5 January 1826, the officers being compensated for their loss of income by the award of fixed salaries. The expense to which the assemblies objected was, therefore, a new one, and the Treasury's right to authorize the deductions from colonial revenue was of sufficiently doubtful validity that it was questioned, not only by every colonial lawyer who expressed an opinion, but also by James Stephen.[2] Under the new order a sum of over one hundred thousand pounds[3] a year was to be paid by the colonies to officers whose main function was admitted to be, not the collection of colonial revenue, but the control of imperial trade.

No issue, not even the slavery question, so clearly illustrates the basic dilemma of the British government in its relations with the legislative colonies as does its handling of this dispute. It is of equal, perhaps of even greater, interest for the light that it throws on relations between the Colonial Office and the Treasury. It is as a study in that relationship that it is examined here.

[1] C.O. 137–163 Manchester to Bathurst, Dec. 23, 1826, No. 72.
[2] See below pp. 216–8.   [3] See C.O. 323/208, ff. 163–4.

The customs service had never been popular in the old empire. The customs officers in the colonies, being directly under Treasury control exercised through the commissioners of customs in Britain, had never been susceptible to the pressure of colonial opinion to the same degree as officials directly responsible to the governor and the Secretary of State. Criticism continued in an unbroken tradition from the first empire into the second. Even during the American Revolution the loyal colony of Nova Scotia lodged protests against the customs service and at least once every decade thereafter the local assembly conducted an enquiry into the customs establishment.[1] In the West Indies, too, it was looked upon as an impediment to trade and a drain on the revenue. In 1811 the Treasury took notice of the many protests by sending a commission of enquiry to the West Indies. The report of this commission, while admitting some shortcomings, did not go very far in recognizing the validity of colonial criticism,[2] and minor changes instituted by the Treasury in 1817 did little to still colonial protests. The question was the subject of correspondence between the departments concerned on several occasions, but it was either quietly shelved or lost in the routine of interdepartmental consultation.

Colonial criticism was concentrated on what were regarded as the exorbitant incomes received by customs officers. The Treasury in 1817 considered that the chief customs officer, the collector of customs, in one of the larger colonial ports was entitled to £2,500 a year.[3] In the absence of accurate reports of fees received there was much speculation in the colonies on the size of the incomes. It was frequently alleged, for example, that the collector at Quebec received around £5,000 annually,[4] and incomes of £2,000 or more were certainly not unusual. The Treasury jealously guarded its right of appointment to these highly paid posts and they were seldom, if ever, held by colonials. It was natural, therefore, for a colonial legislature to compare the collector's income with that of the highest post to which a colonial could normally aspire, that of chief justice. In New Brunswick in 1818, for example, the chief justice received a salary of £750 voted by the British Parliament be-

[1] Gilroy, Marion, 'Customs Fees in Nova Scotia' *C.H.R.* XVII (1936), pp. 9–22.   [2] *Ibid.*, p. 13.
[3] Manning, H. T., *British Colonial Government . . .*, p. 255.
[4] P.A.C., L.C. 'Q' Series, vol. 174–1, p. 33.

cause the colony was considered unable to support its own officers; in the same year the assembly of the province asserted that the collector of customs received a personal income of £2,900 from fees levied on shipping entering and leaving the colony's ports.[1] Even the governor's income, according to the assembly's report, was considerably less than that of the collector of customs.[2]

While colonials objected to the exorbitant incomes of the customs officers, shipowners and merchants, both in Britain and the colonies, protested against the burden of the fees. In the West Indies it was the practice to collect full fees at each of the small islands at which a ship called, adding greatly to the expenses of the shipowners and, it was alleged, contributing to the ill-service from which those islands suffered.[3] In North America there were frequent complaints that differing scales of fees prevailed at different ports;[4] at some ports coastal vessels paid full fees every time they entered port, at others they paid annual fees. Both colonial assemblies and shipowners complained that the table of fees had not been reviewed since before the American Revolution. In a few cases there were complaints that fees had suddenly been increased; on the other hand, customs officers sometimes defended their high incomes by asserting that they were not taking fees to the full extent to which they were authorized.

Legally the fees were regulated by a British act of 1765[5] and by later acts renewing the provisions of that act.[6] In practice the 1765 act, which authorized customs officers to receive the same fees as they and their predecessors had received before September 1764, proved unworkable, since there was no agreement on what the standard had been. Several West Indian legislatures passed local acts to remedy the inconvenience. A Jamaica act of 1809 was, in James Stephen's words, 'allowed by the Crown without difficulty.'[7] Acts of 1815 and 1821 were also left to their own operation.

[1] Hannay, R., *History of New Brunswick*, vol. I, p. 360. The second officer of the Custom House, the comptroller, received about £1,500.
[2] *Ibid.*   [3] C.O. 323/194 Memorial of James Hume, Nov. 9, 1820, ff. 43–8.
[4] See for example P.A.C. N.S. 'A' Series, Vol. 158, p. 121.
[5] 5 Geo. III Cap. 47, Sect. 27.
[6] 10 Geo. III Cap. 37, Sect. 2 and 45 Geo. III Cap. 68.
[7] C.O. 323/202 Stephen to Horton, private, Sept. 15, 1825, f. 195 *et seq.*

In 1823, however, the assembly and council of Jamaica passed a bill reducing the fees. To this the governor refused his assent and he was upheld by the Secretary of State.[1] A Colonial Office memorandum, dated 5 April 1824, admitted that the fees taken under the colonial acts, 'with the acquiescence, if not under the sanction of the Departments by which those Officers are appointed', considerably exceeded the legal fees established by the act of 1765, but denied the right of the colonial legislatures to regulate the scale of fees. 'Established practice seems to have long furnished the only rule of proceeding,' the memorandum asserted.[2] James Stephen, dissenting from this opinion, maintained that, although the colonial acts could have been disallowed as contrary to a British act already in force, they had been attended with such practical convenience that no action had been taken and that, in consequence, colonial legislatures had in fact been regulating fees.[3]

There is no evidence that the claim of the Jamaica legislature had any direct bearing on the decision of the Treasury and the Board of Trade to undertake a study of Custom House fees with a view to reducing them. It is not even mentioned in a letter of the Board of Trade to the Treasury dated 16 March 1824, which formally opened a review of the question. The Board of Trade urged a reduction of the fees on purely commercial grounds:

> with a view to the maintenance and encouragement of our own shipping and trading Interests in the competition which they have to sustain with the Merchants and Ship Owners of other States.[4]

It was, then, the prospective benefit to the shipowner and merchant that was emphasized when the subject first came under discussion, and only later, when the colonies protested that the shipowners had received benefits at their expense, was it maintained that the reform had been intended primarily for the relief of the colonies.

The documents for this period provide only a bare outline of the beginning of the administrative process. Six weeks after this

---

[1] C.O. 137/157 Manchester to Bathurst, Oct. 18, 1824.
[2] C.O. 137/157 Bound with October correspondence.
[3] C.O. 323/202 Stephen to Horton, private, Sept. 15, 1825, f. 195 *et. seq.*
[4] C.O. 323/198 Lack to Herries, f. 237.

Board of Trade letter was written, the Treasury asked the Colonial Office to obtain detailed information on the nature and extent of the fees.[1] A printed circular, dated five weeks later, requested the colonies to send the desired information.[2] Few, if any, replies to the circular had been received when, on 21 March 1825, the President of the Board of Trade, William Huskisson, announced to the House of Commons that the fees were to be abolished.[3] The papers examined do not reveal when, or by whom, the decision to abolish the fees was taken. What the Board of Trade had requested in opening the question and what the Treasury had later suggested was a reduction in the fees. This may have been opposed by the Colonial Office as impracticable, since the colonial assemblies contended that by the Declaratory Act of 1778[4] Parliament had given up the right of passing further legislation for the regulation of fees.[5] Some details of the new arrangements were settled at conferences held at the Prime Minister's residence at which, in addition to Huskisson and Lord Bathurst, Wilmot Horton, and probably officials of the Customs, Treasury, and Board of Trade were present.[6]

The Customs Consolidation of 1825 owed its origins to a royal commission on customs and excise that presented a series of reports between 1818 and 1824.[7] In the Treasury it was referred to as the Herries Consolidation,[8] after John Charles Herries, one of the most prominent members of the commission, who in 1825 was a secretary to the Treasury; but the initiative in 1824 and 1825 came from Huskisson at the Board of Trade. It was in his department and under his direction that the new legislation was drawn up; it was he who introduced the new legislation in the House of Commons and pressed the Treasury in order to ensure that the legislation was carried through Parliament in the session of 1825.[9] The details of the abolition of fees and the arranging for the payment of salaries were outside

[1] C.O. 323/199, f. 230.
[2] C.O. 854/1 June 4, 1824.
[3] *The Speeches of William Huskisson* (1831) Vol. II, pp. 323–4.
[4] See below p. 210.
[5] C.O. 137/157 Memorandum of Apr. 5, 1824.
[6] C.O. 323/203 Horton to Huskisson, private, Sept. 15, 1825, ff. 137–8.
[7] Fay, C. R., *Huskisson and His Age*, pp. 113 and 287–9.
[8] *Ibid.*, p. 285.
[9] See C.O. 323/202 Huskisson to Horton, Mar. 24, 1825.

the scope of his department, yet he had a clearly defined policy in mind in drawing up the legislation; whereas the Treasury and the Colonial Office, who shared the responsibility, had held no official discussions on the matter and had not even agreed on the source from which the salaries were to be paid when the time came to make arrangements for their payment.[1] Lord Bathurst and Wilmot Horton, after insisting on certain general principles, obviously gave the matter little further consideration until faced with the task of implementing the legislation. The bills submitted to Parliament were not closely examined in the Colonial Office and when, in May, the Treasury asked for Lord Bathurst's opinion on whether any principle of colonial government was violated by their provisions, Wilmot Horton maintained that

> It would take three months' hard study to answer the question safely. It is therefore most safe not to answer it at all in the present exigency about time.[2]

While the technical character of customs regulation contributed to the complexity of the legislation, the clauses which it would have taken 'three months' hard study' to examine were those that repealed the old laws regulating customs and the customs service. One reason for not instituting a general repeal was the Government's decision not to surrender to the assemblies any portion of the limited income, the Crown revenue, under its control. In an Act passed in 1778,[3] usually referred to as the Declaratory Act, designed to appease the rebellious thirteen colonies, Parliament had asserted its right to pass legislation for the control of the trade of the Empire and, at the same time, declared that the 'net' revenue received under parliamentary acts should be placed at the disposal of the legislature of the colony in which it was collected. The principle was, however, only regarded as prospective; all the pre-1778 acts continued to be in force and their revenue remained at the disposal of the Crown. Apart from funds raised under the Quebec Revenue Act of 1774 and specifically allotted to meet the costs of government in that colony, the Crown income from this source amounted in all to only about £15,000 a year.[4] In only four colonies,

---

[1] See below. [2] C.O. 323/203, f. 117. [3] 18 Geo. III Cap. 12.
[4] C.O. 323/203 Report of J. Woodhouse, Inspector and Examiner Plantation Account (Customs), Jan. 14, 1825, f. 253; also C.O. 323/212 E. Stewart to Hay, Dec. 17, 1830, ff. 18–19.

Jamaica, Barbados, Nova Scotia and Lower Canada did it consistently amount to more than £1,000 a year. There was general agreement that if a pre-1778 act should be repealed, its proceeds would be lost to the Crown, for, even if Parliament should re-enact the provisions of an old act, duties collected under the re-enactment would have to be turned over to the colonial legislatures.[1] In order to insure that no colonial pre-rogatives were being surrendered it would have been necessary to examine in detail the hundreds of old acts and parts of acts which were being repealed individually. Act 6 George IV Chapter 105 listed four hundred and forty-five such acts and sections of acts.

The abolition of fees on colonial shipping, in so far as these depended on statutory legislation, was effected by a repeal of the statute of 1764 and all other acts that authorized the practice of fee-taking by officers concerned with the regulation of commerce and shipping in the colonies. Colonial as well as British acts were repealed—'a strong measure indeed; but one which Mr. Huskisson was not afraid to take', was James Stephen's comment.[2] Fees taken by governors, colonial secre-taries and other officials authorized by colonial statutes were not mentioned, it being the intention of the framers of the Bill to call on colonial legislatures to repeal the enabling legislation and compensate the officials concerned.

Although the term 'customs officers' has been used exclusively up to this point, there was, in fact, a group of officials, the 'naval officers' responsible for the regulation of colonial shipping, who were not actually members of the customs service. Each of the West Indian and North American colonies, including Upper Canada, had such an officer appointed by the governor, under a mandamus from the Secretary of State. Naval officers were responsible for seeing that the provisions of the navigation acts were observed. Some of the legislation governing their office went back to Charles II's time when the post was created.[3] By the beginning of the nineteenth century, and probably much

---

[1] See P.A.C., L.C. 'Q' Series, Law Officers of the Crown to Bathurst, Nov. 13, 1824, Vol. 169, p. 87; also Kempt to Murray, private, Dec. 15, 1829, vol. 190–1, pp. 201–6.

[2] C.O. 323/202 Stephen to Horton, private, Sept. 15, 1825, f. 195.

[3] See P.A.C., N.S. 'A' Series, Kempt to Bathurst, No. 5, Feb. 12, 1826, Vol. 168, p. 40, where the legislation is reviewed.

earlier, the office was a sinecure in most colonies.[1] Even where the holders took their duties seriously, their work depended on the co-operation of the customs officers and could have been performed by them without an undue addition to their other duties. Naval officers were paid small salaries but most of their income came from fees on shipping. To the colonists their presence was a persistent annoyance and the shipowners objected to paying fees for their support. The abolition of these offices which had long been urged was finally effected by Huskisson's legislation.[2]

In strictly legal terms the fees of customs officers were not abolished by Parliament. This fact was clearly stated by James Stephen when the Colonial Office began its consideration of how the acts should be administered.

The case, therefore, as far as respects the Officers of Customs remains at present upon the most simple footing; disembarrass'd of all former Laws whether Parliamentary or Colonial. It rests with the Treasury to continue these fees or to abolish them, or to increase, or to diminish them.[3]

This clearly expresses the legal position and indicates the extent of the discretionary powers left to the administrators. In fact, however, Huskisson had asserted in the House of Commons that the fees would be abolished and his statement was considered to be binding.

In drawing up the new legislation, the Board of Trade assumed that the colonies would be willing to pay the expenses of their customs establishments in return for the many advantages accruing to them under the acts:

Relaxation, almost to abandonment, of the old Colonial System, was the valuable consideration for which they were expected to give their concurrence: but their concurrence was always deemed

---

[1] Manning, H. T., *British Colonial Government* . . ., p. 253. In New South Wales and the other eastern colonies, where the customs service was under the direction of the Secretary of State, until this time, the naval officers' posts were not sinecures.

[2] The abolition had not been decided in July 1824, apparently, for in that month Major Moody was instructed to report on means of increasing the utility of naval officers in the West Indies. See C.O. 323/200, ff. 412–13.

[3] C.O. 323/202 Stephen to Horton, private, Sept, 15, 1825, f. 191.

to be necessary; and in the event of a refusal, the only alternative ever contemplated was the withdrawal of the benefits of the new liberal system.[1]

This straightforward course, despite the threat lurking in the background, had the merit of making an appeal to the generosity and sense of gratitude of the members of the colonial assemblies and to the assemblies' desire, perhaps one should say the universal desire, for recognition and for greater authority in local matters. Arrangements could undoubtedly have been made in nearly all colonies had governors been given some discretionary powers to negotiate salary scales. But colonial leaders had so long emphasized the extravagance of the customs establishments that they could not easily have agreed to any arrangement that did not incorporate some reduction, or prospective reduction, in the incomes of the more highly paid officers.

On the subject of negotiation with colonial assemblies, however, the Treasury was firm. It insisted on itself setting the new salary scales as a necessary adjunct to that complete control of the customs officials by the British government that was deemed essential.[2] It also refused, wisely, to consider allowing the colonial legislatures to make any temporary provision for the officers, since this would leave to the legislatures the power of withholding the salaries or of regulating them according to colonial views.[3] But this is to anticipate positions and attitudes that only became clear to the participants themselves in the months that followed.

On 5 July 1825 the statutes forming the new consolidated law of customs received royal assent and, on 8 August, the Treasury officially brought to the attention of the Colonial Office the need for instituting a new system for the payment of colonial customs officers and for making arrangements for the compensation of naval officers whose posts had been abolished.[4] Discussions were also begun on the transfer of the customs service in the eastern colonies to Treasury control. For the historian the time was propitious, for most Cabinet ministers and many senior

[1] Memorandum in Huskisson Papers, March 16, 1826, quoted in Fay, C. R., *Huskisson and His Age*, pp. 295–6.
[2] C.O. 323/203, ff. 108–111.
[3] C.O. 323/208 Treasury Minute No. 1229, Dec. 2, 1828, f. 161.
[4] C.O. 323/203, ff. 108–111.

departmental officials had left Westminster for the country and letter writing of necessity replaced oral reports on the progress of negotiations between departments.

Shortly after the end of the parliamentary session Wilmot Horton sent for James Deacon Hume, who explained to him what the Board of Trade had in mind in drafting the legislation. Hume,[1] who is recognized as one of the greatest nineteenth-century civil servants, was a customs officer on loan to the Board of Trade. It was he, under Huskisson's direction, who searched the statute books and framed the bills for the House of Commons. He was, therefore, well able to present Huskisson's views and to make it clear to Wilmot Horton that the Board of Trade believed that the colonial assemblies should be frankly requested to make permanent provision for the salaries of the customs officers and the pensions to naval officers. For a time Wilmot Horton accepted this policy and he incorporated Huskisson's ideas in the draft of a very long letter which he proposed to send as a circular to the governors of colonies with legislatures.[2]

Then, at the end of August, he suddenly changed his mind and decided to by-pass the assemblies if it was legally possible to do so. On August 31 he suggested to James Stephen that the salaries for customs officers and compensation for naval officers might be deducted from the customs revenue of the colonies by a simple Treasury order.[3] He asked Stephen to give his opinion on whether under the declaratory act the British government had not the right to consider the proposed salaries as 'necessary charges of management', which it would be legal to deduct from the gross proceeds 'under the letter and spirit of that act.' Accompanied by the newly-appointed permanent under-secretary, R. W. Hay, he had been holding discussions with two of the commissioners of Customs and with Treasury officials. Under their influence he had been weaned away from his original support for Huskisson's proposals.[4]

[1] See Fay, C. R., *Huskisson and His Age*, pp. 276–96. James Deacon Hume (1774–1842) was Comptroller Inwards and Outwards of the Port of London (salary £1,000). He was paid for part-time services to the Board of Trade from mid-summer 1825, went permanently to the Board of Trade in January 1828 and became joint secretary in 1829.

[2] C.O. 323/203, ff. 145–148.

[3] C.O. 323/203 Horton to Stephen, Aug. 31, 1825 (draft), ff. 117–19.

[4] C.O. 323/203 Horton to Huskisson, private, Aug. 30, 1825 (draft), f. 137.

On the first of September Wilmot Horton finally informed Lord Bathurst of his 'sundry tedious conversations with the Treasury and Customs' and sent to him the Treasury letter of 8 August, which had initiated the formal administrative process. He also sent him a copy of his letter to Stephen. His correspondence with Huskisson was not mentioned, and in place of the circular that he had drafted a few days earlier, he proposed to frame the public despatch upon his letter to Stephen.[1]

Lord Bathurst's reaction was immediate and his opinion certain. Years of dealing with colonial legislatures had made him an expert in their idiosyncrasies and nobody in authority could have been more careful in trying to avoid offending them.

It will be certainly very desirable that your letter should go to Mr. Stephens [sic], because if I am to do anything in the business, the Questions you have proposed to him ought to be answer'd, so that I may know what I am about, when I embark in executing the late Act. But I confess to you that I think it rests with Parliament to make compensations for the fees they have abolish'd, and that the Treasury should make out the amount, and propose it in the next Budget. It is the British Merchant who will be much more benefited than the poor Planter by this arrangement, and it should be paid for by the British Treasury, not from the Colonies. As the fees are to be abolish'd, there can be no fee fund out of which this compensation can come. I am quite sure that the Revenue of the Colonies cannot afford to be charged with it: for there is scarcely a Colony, certainly none which have Legislative Assemblies, which have a Revenue equal to the due maintenance of the Civil Establishments. If then the Colonies are to pay for this Act, it must be by new Taxes, and I hardly need tell you that we can look only to a refusal from Legislative Assemblies: in which case I should protest against the other Colonies being charged with what the Colonies with Legislative Assemblies are exempt. I am sure you must understand my reluctance in being called upon to stir in the Colonies all the unpleasant Questions, to which your Letters [sic] to Mr. Stephens very properly refers.

The answer which I should propose to give to the first part of the Treasury Letter . . . would be something in the way of what I shall sketch in a separate Paper. I am sure that Mr. Huskisson's Pledge will not be redeem'd if all the fees, as well those of the

[1] C.O. 323/203, f. 112.

Governors and their Secretaries (who are specially mentioned) as others, are not abolish'd: and as this was done for the relief of the British Merchant, can Parliament expect that the Colonies should pay for it. It must come to Parliament at last and I shall be only creating ill humour by asking them in the first Instance to pay for it. At the same time do not let this view of the subject prevent your Letter going to Mr. Stephen.

(Postscript) I am most anxious not to be involv'd in a second Battle with all the Colonies, in addition to the Slave Question. I see no reason, why the Grace is to belong to one department, and the odium cast on another.[1]

By enclosing a draft of the reply that Wilmot Horton was to send to the Treasury letter of 8 March, Lord Bathurst showed that he had no intention of abdicating his function of directing colonial policy. In contrast to his frank letter to Wilmot Horton, he assumed in this official letter an amusingly bland tone, giving to his simple unadorned language the exact nuance he desired.

... Lord Bathurst will lose no time in complying with the request of their Lordships to transmit to them a list of those officers whose present Emoluments will thereby be diminish'd or made to cease and the compensations which in his Lordship's judgement they will be severally justly entitled, taking care that in those offices which not being necessary may be altogether abolish'd, the charge should cease after the death of the incumbent.

And Lord B. trusts that he may be authorised to accompany the order to the naval officers in question not in future to receive the accustom'd fees, with an assurance that their Lordships are prepared to recommend to the liberality and justice of Parliament a due compensation for the loss of those fees which the Legislature has thus abolish'd.[2]

In his opinion, which was as much a declaration of policy as of law, James Stephen expressed a disagreement with Wilmot Horton's proposals almost as pronounced as that of Lord Bathurst:

... You argue that the declaratory Act of 1778 having authorized the deduction from Parliamentary duties payable in the Colonies of 'the necessary charges of Management' the Salaries thus to be

[1] C.O. 323/203 Bathurst to Wilmot Horton, Sept. 2, 1825, ff. 113-4.
[2] C.O. 323/203, f. 115.

granted must be considered as such 'necessary charges'. I do not venture to maintain the contrary doctrine with absolute confidence; although, upon the whole, I think it the more reasonable view of the subject. I proceed to state the grounds of my opinion; premising however that this is rather a subject for Statesmen than for Lawyers. The promises given by the Mother Country to its Dependencies, are not to be interpreted by the narrow rules which apply to the contracts of private persons. . . .

These fees then you propose to commute for a Salary, taking the amount of that Salary from the produce of the duties. In other words you would relieve the Merchant from his fees, at the expence of the Colonial Treasury.

I have further to observe that this commutation of fees for Salary cannot be said to have been contemplated by Parliament. On the contrary, Parliament expressly assumes that in every part of His Majesty's Dominions fees will be payable to the Officers of Customs under an order or on permission from the Commissioners of the Treasury. That is—Parliament contemplated the continuance of this charge on the Merchant. Can the Government then relieve the Merchant, and throw the burden on the Revenue of the Colony?

I may further remark that between the declaratory Act of 1778 and Mr. Huskisson's Bill of 1825, there is one remarkable variance. Forty seven years ago Parliament pledged itself that the *net* produce of all these duties should be paid to the Colonial Treasury. In the present year, Parliament has provided that 'the produce' of the duties shall be so paid; omitting the qualifying word '*net*'. I do not attach much importance to this observation. The word 'produce' taken simply and absolutely, may be well enough understood to mean net produce; although I should rather incline to think that this variation of language might be construed as implying some corresponding variation of purpose; and the rather because the section in which this expression occurs, is avowedly framed in reference to the declaratory Act. I am aware however that this argument has two edges, and may be made to apply either way. If Parliament legislated in reference to the declaratory Act, then, it may be said that the generality of its language must be qualified by the more precise expressions of the promise which it was intended to fulfill. Upon the whole I should reject all verbal criticisms of this kind from the argument, as too minute for so considerable an occasion, were it not for the circumstance which I have next to notice.—

You will observe that this question must be brought to trial before Colonial Tribunals[1] with what prejudices and prepossessions I need hardly mention. If the Collector of Customs deducts his own Salary he will be treated with an Action of Information, grounded upon the assertion that he has not paid over his receipts in full. That action can be brought only in the colony where the Collector resides. It will be tried before a Colonial Judge, assisted by a Colonial Jury. I conceive that such a Tribunal would be apt to make much of the argument built upon the distinction between the Words 'produce' and 'net produce'.

If there is sufficient reason to deny the right of the Crown to charge upon the produce of these duties the Salaries of Continuing Officers then a multo fortiori must the right be denied of deducting Salaries granted as an indemnity for loss of office.

Why is the Office abolished? Plainly because it was unnecessary. And why is the compensation granted? To satisfy a moral obligation, and not in consequence of any strict legal right. Can you then, as a matter of right, require the Colony to pay that which the Claimant does not demand as a matter of right from you?— Or can you reasonably call upon them to pay an indemnity for the abolition of that which, ex-hypothesi was an unreasonable burden on their trade.

With respect to Governors, Secretaries, Receivers General, and other Officers of that class, I must observe that as these are not Officers of Customs they do not come within the reach of Mr. Huskisson's Acts. Parliament of course might have abolished these fees also. The Government cannot; for they are claimed not by virtue of any Government Regulation, but under Statutes passed by the Colonial Assemblies. You must persuade the Assemblies to repeal these Laws, or you must repeal them by Act of Parliament a strong measure indeed; but one which Mr. Huskisson was not afraid to take in reference to Custom House fees in his Acts of the last Session.[2]

Wilmot Horton, after conversations with Stephen, had already anticipated Stephen's written opinion in a long letter to Lord Bathurst. His almost complete disagreement with Stephen is revealed in his advocacy of strong action on the most questionable legal point, the payment of pensions to naval officers as a charge on colonial duties.[3] As the spokesman for the Colonial

---

[1] For a reference to a case that was brought before a colonial court and terminated as Stephen had foreseen, see C.O. 407-3 Murray to Maxwell, confidential, Feb. 17, 1829, pp. 62-3.

[2] C.O. 323/202 Stephen to Horton, private, Sept. 15, 1825, ff. 191-5.

[3] C.O. 323/203 Horton to Bathurst, Sept. 13, 1825, f. 152.

Office in the House of Commons, he was more concerned with the opposition of that body to new colonial expenditures than he was with the protests of the colonial assemblies. He foresaw not only the objections of the economists to the payment of the salaries by the Mother Country, but also anti-slavery protests against aid to the planters and a refusal by East Indian interests to support a charge that would benefit West Indian shipping. He forcefully opposed Lord Bathurst's proposal for an appeal to Parliament.[1]

Lord Bathurst, however, continued to reject Wilmot Horton's suggestions and reiterated his previous stand 'that the only way of getting out of the scrape in this business, is by manfully meeting the whole by a vote in Parliament.'[2] On the legal aspect of Wilmot Horton's proposals he agreed with Stephen that the assemblies should be consulted, maintaining that where salaries were to be taken from revenue previously at the disposal of the assemblies 'the spirit of the law will require that such charge should be approv'd by the several legislative Assemblies before it can be adopted.'[3]

There is an air of resignation in Lord Bathurst's handling of this issue. In part this was consistent with his personality and business habits. He seldom took an intractable stand on an issue. He avoided conflict with associates except on a few occasions in the factional disputes within the Cabinet, and even then his actions were interpreted as being in support of his friends rather than in opposition to his opponents. When the talks with the Treasury began he was in the country, and not well informed when the critical decisions were being made. It seems doubtful that he knew of Huskisson's disagreement with Wilmot Horton and there is no record of his being in direct touch with Lord Liverpool, who had been under severe strain in May during a Cabinet crisis over the question of Catholic emancipation. Lord Bathurst shared the lack of energy that afflicted several members of Liverpool's ministry in its later years. His policy of an appeal to Parliament for money would not have involved the Colonial Office in a struggle with the colonies. Any other policy would. And a struggle he wished to avoid. He was willing that the

[1] C.O. 323/203 Horton to Bathurst, Sept. 18, 1825, ff. 155–6.
[2] *Ibid.* Lord Bathurst's minute on Horton's note of Sept. 18, f. 157.
[3] *Ibid.*

question of the legality of the procedure suggested by Wilmot Horton be referred to the law officers of the Crown for an opinion, but he categorically refused to accept any responsibility for the implementation of a policy that by-passed the assemblies.

> I am afraid [he wrote] the Naval Officers stand in a more critical Situation than the Custom House Officers—But I have no objection to the Treasury giving directions both on this, and on the Question respecting the Custom House Officers, provided I am neither called upon to give the Instructions, or by communicating them, appear to support them.[1]

Huskisson, too, continued to insist that the assemblies be consulted and had no doubts about the efficacy of an appeal to their reason and gratitude, backed by a threat of penalties against any colony that refused to conform. A letter written to Wilmot Horton on 26 September is pure Huskisson, vigorous, forthright, clear, concise:

> Send them instructions to pay the necessary charge of collection either out of the gross proceeds of the Revenue collected, or to make the Salaries of the Officers payable by the Colonial Treasury, as they may think most convenient; and let them understand that the trade permitted by Robinson's Acts and mine is only conditional to an arrangement of this nature, and that it will be put a stop to in respect to any Colony that does not make this necessary provision for the Officers, after the Fees shall be abolished. Of course this information would be conveyed to them in the mildest form, and not in the shape of a threat.[2]

Despite the opposition of Lord Bathurst, Stephen, and Huskisson, Wilmot Horton pressed on with the policy that he had decided on in consultation with the Customs and Treasury officials. At the end of September the Treasury secretary had some doubts about the practicability of making the required deductions from the revenues collected by the Customs officers, not from a concern for the propriety of using funds claimed by the colonial assemblies but because the expense of the salaries might exceed the duties collected.[3] By mid-November, however,

[1] C.O. 323/203 Lord Bathurst's minute on Wilmot Horton's letter of Sept. 18, 1825, f. 157.
[2] C.O. 323/202 Huskisson to Horton, private, received Sept. 26, 1825.
[3] C.O. 323/203, f. 218.

the Commissioners of Customs announced that they were ready to open 'a correspondence with your Department through the proper official channel of the Treasury'[1] and on the ninth of December a Treasury minute was issued setting the scale of the salaries on a temporary basis and authorizing their deduction from the produce of the parliamentary duties. In keeping with Lord Bathurst's wishes the instructions were to be sent to the colonies by the Commissioners of Customs, not by the Colonial Office.[2]

Included in the minute, however, was a clause providing that in the event the duties should prove insufficient to meet the salaries bill, the officers were to draw on the Commissioners of Customs in the United Kingdom to meet the deficiency, 'unless such deficiency be made good out of duties collected by Officers of the Colony, or out of any Colonial funds in pursuance of directions which may be given by the Secretary of State.'[3] In a letter that accompanied the minute when it was sent officially to the Colonial Office the Secretary to the Treasury made it clear that Lord Bathurst would be expected to bring pressure to bear on the assemblies to ensure that the salaries would not have to be paid out of the revenue of the United Kingdom.[4]

The Treasury's anxiety arose out of a misconception that can be explained only by assuming that Wilmot Horton and the officials of the Customs and Treasury were not familiar with the legislation they were administering. Though the reason for the Secretary to the Treasury's doubts about the practicability of deducting the salaries from the duties was not explicitly stated in his September letter, it is clear from information supplied in an enclosure[5] that he believed that the duties levied under the new consolidated law of customs could, under certain circumstances, be collected by officials appointed by the colonial assemblies. A provision had been introduced into the trade legislation of 1822 inviting the colonial legislatures to replace British acts by colonial acts providing equal or higher rates of duty. A similar provision was introduced into one of the 1825 acts[6] and it was apparently taken for granted that the assem-

[1] C.O. 323/203, f. 432.   [2] *Ibid.*, f. 249.
[3] *Ibid.*   [4] *Ibid.*, f. 247.   [5] *Ibid.*, ff. 414–424.
[6] 6 Geo. IV., Cap. 73, Sect. 5.

blies would take advantage of that provision and have the duties collected by their own officials. The duties left to be collected by the imperial officers, mainly those levied under pre-1778 acts, would then not be sufficient to pay their salaries. It was, therefore, not to the small colonies, whose trade was so insignificant that they were unable to afford the salaries charged to their revenue, but to the large colonies, whose assemblies were expected to control the collection of the duties, that the Treasury referred on 13 December, 'trusting'

> that Lord Bathurst will be enabled to make such arrangements with the several Colonies as may ensure the application of any Customs Duties collected or received by Colonial Officers (as the first charge upon them) towards making good the deficiency in all cases in which the Fund at the disposal of the Officers of the Crown may prove inadequate to the payment of these Salaries.[1]

The Colonial Office shared the view that the assemblies could make arrangements to have the duties collected by their own officers. An undated memorandum, commenting on the Treasury letter of 13 December 1825, suggested that, since colonial acts superseding British acts were passed annually, the remedy would be to disallow any future act that did not make provision for the payment of the salaries out of the proceeds of the duties. This memorandum also carefully pointed out that 'the King's Officer' had nothing whatever to do with the proceeds received under such colonial acts.[2] Although this document is unsigned and not in Wilmot Horton's handwriting, the style is his and very likely it was dictated to an amanuensis. His shocking weakness for devious and impractical measures could scarcely have led him to make a more foolhardy suggestion; no surer way could have been found to undermine the position of a colonial governor than by sending him instructions to disallow the annual revenue bill.

By September 1826 Wilmot Horton was writing that 'Mr. Huskisson's Act' had distinctly repealed the permission granted in the 1822 Act permitting colonial legislatures to supersede a British act and had provided that 'in all cases the duties should be levied under the British Act by the King's Collector, & by him paid over to the local Treasurer. . . .'[3] By May 1827 he was

[1] C.O. 323/203, f. 247.   [2] C.O. 323/203, f. 159.
[3] C.O. 137/168 Horton to Hibbert, Sept. 7, 1826, enclosed under 'Agents'.

writing that a colonial legislature could not levy its own duties unless Mr. Huskisson's Act was repealed 'inasmuch as that Act is peremptory with respect to the supersession of local acts, and equally so as to the levying of the Revenue by the King's Custom House Officers.'[1] A year later R. W. Hay stated officially in a letter to the Treasury that the reason for enacting that the duties had to be received by the 'King's Collector' was to enable the Government to retain sufficient funds for the payment of adequate salaries.[2] Time and the administrator's assumption of official infallibility had turned accident into conscious design. This foresight of the legislators was not apparent to those administering the law during the first few months that it was on the statute book.

The explanation of the fact that the Treasury officials and Wilmot Horton misinterpreted the law in a manner unfavourable to their own declared policy undoubtedly lies in the existence of two contradictory and opposed clauses in the legislation. A clause in one act specifically followed the 1822 precedent of allowing colonial duties to supersede the duties raised under British acts;[3] a clause in a later act required all the duties to be levied by Custom House officers.[4] The clause that was overlooked at first must have been framed with another purpose in mind and its meaning in the context in which it was later interpreted must also have been entirely unforeseen. James Hume, the draftsman of the legislation, whose skill was admired even by James Stephen,[5] was certainly unaware of it. In a memorandum, dated 16 March 1826, he wrote:

> But to show the inutility of any attempt to absorb their duties in such charges, against the will of the colonial legislatures, it is only necessary to examine the existing law a little further, when it will be seen, that power is expressly given to those Bodies to put an end to any such struggle by levying colonial duties of equal amount to the Parliamentary.[6]

Huskisson also was obviously unaware of it, for he continued to

[1] C.O. 138/50 Horton to Hibbert, private, May 21, 1827.
[2] C.O. 138/50 Hay to Hill, May 24, 1828, pp. 392–3; see also C.O. 407/3 Murray to Maxwell, Feb. 17, 1829, pp. 42 and 44.
[3] 6 Geo. IV, Cap. 73, Sect. 5.
[4] 6 Geo. IV, Cap. 114, Sect. 11.
[5] See Fay, C. R., *Huskisson and His Age*, p. 280.
[6] *Ibid.*, pp. 284–5.

regard the imposition by the assemblies of duties equal to those found in the British acts as 'the most regular and *constitutional* mode of collecting those duties.'[1] The legislation had been prepared and rushed through Parliament with such urgency that omissions and contradictions could not be avoided. In fact the precaution was taken of having the laws come into force gradually over a period of several months so that the deficiencies could be noted and remedied.

It was not inaccurate drafting but lack of foresight that led to the inclusion of some impractical instructions in the Treasury minute of 9 December 1825. In several of the smaller colonies, for example, the authorized salaries exceeded the total customs revenue.[2] Moreover, most of the existing revenue had, as Lord Bathurst had already pointed out, been committed to the payment of essential services. The expectation of more profitable trade and increased revenues, which the Treasury emphasized in its instructions, would not meet the immediate expenses of their government. In response to the intercession of Lord Bathurst, the Treasury issued a further minute on 25 April 1826 designed to afford them some relief.[3] It decreed that an amount equal to three-quarters of the average of all the customs duties 'existing' in a colony in the three years previous to January 1826 was to be paid over to the financial officer of the colony; the other quarter was to be retained for the payment of salaries. All excess customs revenue beyond the average for those three years was to be liable in the first instance to the charge of the salaries, the surplus, if any, to be made over to the colony. While this arrangement was advantageous to the smaller colonies, the larger colonies, where the one quarter retained was more than enough to meet the salaries, were to be required to subsidize the others, the quarter set aside for salaries being regarded as part of a general fund available for the payment of customs officers anywhere in the colonial empire. That, at least, was the initial interpretation of Lord Dalhousie in Lower Canada who protested against the proposed deduction of £24,000 in order to pay a bill of £6,000.[4] 'The legislature will say,' he continued, 'if

---

[1] C.O. 323/202 Huskisson to Horton, private, received Sept. 26, 1825, ff. 124–5.

[2] C.O. 323/207, f. 135.　　　　　　　　[3] *Ibid.*

[4] P.A.C., L.C. 'Q' Series, Dalhousie to Bathurst, Sept. 4, 1826, Vol. 176–3, pp. 717 and 720, also Herries to Horton, Apr. 11, 1827, Vol. 180, p. 179.

Government can by a Minute, take one fourth of our Revenue, it can with the same propriety seize a larger proportion.'

In issuing this second order the Treasury violated one of the conditions which Lord Bathurst had stated earlier that he would insist upon, namely, that the colonies without legislatures should receive the same treatment as the legislative colonies. Under the new instruction they were required to bear '. . . the whole or a much larger proportion of the Expense of the Custom House Establishment' than was to be borne by the colonies with legislatures. What this meant in terms of revenue available for colonial purposes is indicated by the situation in Demerara and Berbice in 1831 where, out of a total customs revenue of £6,845, the net receipts were only £145, all the rest being absorbed in the expenses of collection.[1]

If the formal, matter-of-fact statements in Treasury minutes ever permit of any deduction beyond their outward and obvious meaning, the care with which the Treasury pointed out to Lord Bathurst that the new arrangement was to apply only to the legislative colonies almost certainly indicates that the policy was not all to his liking. However, to one new decision announced at this time he must have given a positive welcome. On the question of naval officers' pensions the Lords of the Treasury announced that:

Although the Fees taken by those officers were a charge upon the Colonies yet as their Duties were not immediately connected with the Collection of the Revenue my Lords conceive that under all the circumstances of the case it may be proper to give to the Colonies the full benefit of the abolition of the offices and to defray the charge of these retired allowances out of the Gross produce of the Customs at Home.[2]

Beware of the Treasury's making gifts is always a safe maxim. In this instance the bland generosity was engendered by an opinion of the law officers of the Crown that, although the expenses of collecting the colonial revenues could legally be deducted from the gross revenues, the compensation for offices abolished could not.[3] It was a very reluctant Treasury that was forced to draw on funds raised in Britain to meet the cost of the

[1] C.O. 324/146 Hay to J. K. Stewart, May 16, 1831, p. 292.
[2] C.O. 323/207, f. 136.
[3] C.O. 323/205, f. 295 and C.O. 323/208, ff. 157–62.

pensions. Privately, in the months that followed, Treasury officials continued to express a hope that the assemblies could be persuaded to pay the compensation.[1]

To the man on the spot on the periphery of the empire, trying to find a negotiable route between the peremptory order from on high and the stratagems of a recalcitrant assembly, it was urgent that some middle way exist or government business might be brought to a standstill. In private letters to the Secretary of State and to the Under-Secretary the governors put forward suggestions for adapting the legislation to their local situations. Sir James Kempt, in Nova Scotia, was able to prevent the assembly from passing strong resolutions critical of British policy in 1826, but privately the leading members maintained that the colonial legislature had the sole right to control the duties and to make such allowances as it saw fit to the officers of customs. Yet, in his opinion, '. . . a more unsatisfactory course could not be taken . . . than to leave to the discretion of the Assembly the fixing the Amount of those Salaries and the voting of them periodically.'[2] Kempt's middle way between the existing situation, which was intolerable to the assembly, and the assembly's proposed solution, which was intolerable to the Treasury, strongly favoured the Treasury. He proposed the setting up of a fund made up of handsome permanent contributions from the colonial legislatures, a tonnage duty, and the Crown duties levied under acts passed prior to 1778.[3] On the other hand, the first reaction of Sir Howard Douglas in neighbouring New Brunswick was to suggest that the new charges for salaries be determined in proportion to the relief afforded to the colonies and to the merchants. According to his reckoning one-third would be paid by the colony and two-thirds by the United Kingdom.[4] But being more concerned to head off an awkward political question than to obtain abstract justice, Douglas, a few weeks later, twice asked permission to approach the colonial legislature for funds to pay the salaries.[5] He had

[1] C.O. 323/205 Hill to Horton, private, Aug. 19, 1826.
[2] P.A.C., N.S. 'A' Series, Kempt to Horton, secret and confidential, Apr. 17, 1826, Vol. 168, p. 62.　　　　　　[3] *Ibid.*
[4] P.A.C., N.B. 'A' Series, Douglas to Bathurst, Mar. 16, 1826, Vol. 36–1, p. 74.
[5] *Ibid.* Douglas to Bathurst, private and confidential, June 4, 1826, p. 118; and, private, June 12, 1826, p. 126.

to wait nearly three years for authorization to do so. In New Brunswick the economy practised by the assembly in rewarding its servants provided a striking contrast to the open-handed generosity of the Treasury in setting the new salaries. The treasurer of New Brunswick received £550 a year for collecting the colonial revenues, arranging for the banking of funds on hand, paying out all authorized sums under the direction of the governor, and for supervising the provincial revenue officers. In addition, he served on the governor's council and was his chief lieutenant in dealing with the assembly. The total cost of collecting and paying out the duties levied under acts of the colonial legislature was less than £2,000.[1] In its order of 9 December 1825, the Treasury authorized salaries, pensions and expenses of over £10,000 to be deducted from the much smaller revenues collected by the King's officers, revenues which Parliament had, except for a small portion, handed over to the colony.[2]

In Lower Canada the Treasury order added another strand to the inextricable confusion of that colony's financial system, if such chaos can be described as a system. Common sense should have dictated that Lower Canada not be included in any general order applied to the legislative colonies. It had always been treated as a colony apart. Under the constitution of 1791 the governor had been assured a considerable measure of independence of the assembly in financial affairs. The assembly differed from most other assemblies in having no financial officers of its own, the colonial revenue being collected and dispensed by officers appointed by the British Treasury. In addition the bitter quarrel that was racking the colony had become centred on financial questions. The Treasury orders not only added, needlessly, to the assembly's suspicions of the British Government but also, by their very nature, were bound to give rise to a series of petty administrative decisions that would act as further pinpricks to keep the hostility alive. The complete absence of planning by the Treasury and the Colonial Office for the implementation of the new customs legislation is nowhere better illustrated. Simple and obvious questions with a direct bearing on the payment of the customs officers were left unanswered.

[1] P.A.C., N.B. 'A' Series, Douglas to Bathurst, March 19, 1827, Vol. 38–1, pp. 56–7.
[2] *Ibid.* Douglas to Bathurst, March 16, 1826, Vol. 36–1, p. 66; also C.O. 323/208, ff. 163–4.

There was, for example, a long-standing feud between the assembly and the Treasury over the right of the customs officers to deduct a percentage from the provincial duties as a payment for their collection. The absence of precise instructions from the Treasury led to attempts to continue the collection of these percentage fees for years after adequate salaries were awarded.[1]

While the Custom House salaries question was overshadowed by other issues in Lower Canada, there was a series of petty annoyances associated with it that pointed up the basic problems. The situation had become intolerable. The assembly was being called upon to pay officials and to depend upon them for the management of its revenue and yet was not to be allowed to control them. For the regulation of the trade of the Empire the Treasury had to depend on officers whose right to their incomes was challenged by the authority on which those incomes ultimately depended. And the revenue officers were in continual uncertainty about the future. Goodwill alone, and there was little of it, could not have prevented disputes. The problem could be resolved only by a new definition of the colonial relationship, a definition that would place constitutional and financial power in the same hands.

The two extremes in their reactions to the Treasury orders were Jamaica and Prince Edward Island. In Prince Edward Island the duties collected by the customs officers were so small in amount that most of the charge of £525 that the colony was assessed for the payment of the salaries and expenses of the customs establishment had to be met from sources outside the colony. A dispute between the council and the assembly over appropriations took priority over all other issues on the political scene, temporarily driving into eclipse even such perennial favourites as the non-residence of the chief justice and quit rents.[2] In Jamaica, on the other hand, the instruction to the customs officers added explosive fuel to the already blazing fire. Asserting that they had been 'visited with a fiscal Regulation too oppressive to be borne and calculated to destroy those chartered rights most solemnly conceded' to them, the assembly

[1] See P.A.C., L.C. 'Q' Series, Dawson to Hay, Nov. 17, 1829, Vol. 191–2, pp. 206–26.
[2] P.A.C., P.E.I. 'A' Series, Wright to Horton, private, June 15, 1826, vol. 43, p. 229, and Ready to Huskisson, private and confidential, Oct. 13, 1827, vol. 44, p. 209. See also C.O. 323/208, ff. 163–4.

forced the governor to order the customs officers to give up to the receiver-general of the colony the collecting of all duties on imports into the colony, those authorized under acts of the British Parliament passed before 1778 as well as those received under the new legislation. The legislature then proceeded to pass a tonnage duty on shipping entering the ports of the colony, the proceeds of which were to be used for the payment of the salaries.

To all this the governor agreed, even to ordering the customs officers to surrender to the receiver-general all duties collected after the date of the Treasury minute, defending himself thus to Lord Bathurst:

> . . . when I reflected that the great object your Lordship had in view of improving the Condition of the Slaves would have been lost; that the Supplies would have been immediately stopped and that . . . the Duty on Tonnage was not of a new or unusual nature and of far less amount than the fees which had previously . . . been taken on the Entry and Clearance of ships—that it was in the power of His Majesty's Government to put a stop to this arrangement whenever it may be deemed expedient; that in the mean time the object of the Treasury Minute by providing for the salaries of the Custom House Department is accomplished, I hope I may be excused for having exercised a discretion which under any other less difficult circumstances could not be justified.[1]

Any colonial assembly could make things awkward for a colonial governor and tire the Secretary of State with its protests but only Jamaica could bring direct pressure to bear on the Treasury. This it could do because of its agreement with the Government to meet a large part of the cost of the basic subsistence of the troops stationed on the island. Barracks and furnishings were provided, and the cost of supplies was met by an annual vote of the legislature. By refusing to supply the troops the Jamaicans could force the British government to apply to Parliament for an increased grant for the Army, never a very popular step. Of course the British government could hold an axe over the legislature by threatening to withdraw the troops which were the island's chief protection against a large-scale slave rebellion, but that would entail a reduction in the Army which would be unpopular with the military, as well as with

[1] C.O. 137/163 Manchester to Bathurst, Dec. 23, 1826, No. 72.

the West Indian merchants and planters, mostly government supporters, in the House of Commons.

It was Jamaica, therefore, that made the most effective protest against the Government's policy. In September 1826, in an effort to head off precipitate action by the Jamaican legislature, Wilmot Horton sent an unsolicited, unofficial letter (Lord Bathurst was at Cirencester and could not be consulted before the mail packet was due to sail) to George Hibbert, the agent for Jamaica, for transmission to the speaker of the assembly. In his haste, he maintained that the British Government had agreed, in the Treasury minute of 9 April, to assume two-thirds of the burden of the salaries, thus getting both his facts and his figures wrong and revealing an unforgivable lack of familiarity with the details of the question.[1] Hibbert had already had a letter from Herries, the Secretary to the Treasury, declaring that the Treasury could not reconsider the question until it was officially brought to their attention.[2] Hibbert continued to press for ministerial action to anticipate the demands of the Jamaican assembly,[3] and in November Herries promised to arrange an appointment for him 'to *talk over* the subject of the Duties' with Lord Liverpool and Huskisson.[4]

With the arrival of the Duke of Manchester's despatch[5] announcing the assembly's insistence on receiving the gross proceeds of the duties and on the imposition of a tonnage duty, ministerial action could no longer be deferred.[6] On 6 February 1827, Lord Bathurst reluctantly attended a meeting at the Treasury called by Robinson, the Chancellor of the Exchequer. Wilmot Horton, Charles Grant, the Vice-President of the Board of Trade, Herries, the Treasury secretary, and Hibbert were

[1] C.O. 137/168 Horton to Hibbert, private, Sept. 7, 1826, copy enclosed in 1828 correspondence under 'Agents'. See also C.O. 137/164 Hibbert to Horton, Sept. 4, Sept. 7 and Sept. 8, 1826.

[2] C.O. 137/164 Hibbert to Horton, Sept. 7, 1826.

[3] C.O. 137/164 Hibbert to Horton, Sept. 16, Oct. 1 and Nov. 9, 1826.

[4] *Ibid.* Nov. 12, 1826.

[5] See above; see also C.O. 324/75 Lord Bathurst's Minutes, 'W. Indies Generally', Feb. 1, 1827.

[6] There had evidently already been a conference between Lord Bathurst and Huskisson on the question of tonnage duties, for early in January Lord Bathurst intimated to the governors of the North American colonies that a moderate tonnage duty imposed by the assembly would meet no objection from the government. See P.A.C. New Brunswick Despatches Received, Bathurst to Douglas, private, Jan. 6, 1827, vol. VIII.

also present.[1] At this meeting it was agreed that the Custom House officers would collect the revenue and hand it over immediately to the receiver-general of the colony. The tonnage act was to be left to its own operation for the year.[2] There the question rested during the next three months, the collapse of Lord Liverpool in February having caused such a deep rift in the ministry that controversial issues could not be discussed until the leadership of the Government was settled.

It was not until the 21st of May that a firm policy decision was taken. On that day Robinson, the former Chancellor of the Exchequer, who had become Lord Goderich and Secretary of State for the Colonies, informed Hibbert that the course adopted by the Duke of Manchester, in authorizing a tonnage duty and handing over customs duties to the assembly,[3] was to be sanctioned until the next session of Parliament. No permanent arrangement had been decided on but it was intended that the legislation of 1825 should be amended to allow the supersession of parliamentary duties by local duties and to permit the levying of the revenue by colonial officers. Directions were to be sent for paying over the receipts from Huskisson's acts in gross to the receiver-general.[4]

A memorandum drawn up in the Colonial Office[5] on 11 July outlined a proposal for a general settlement with all the colonies that accepted the constitutional arguments of the assemblies. It was in fact more favourable to colonial opinion than the original proposals by Huskisson and James Deacon Hume in 1825. The principle to be adopted was that:

> . . . in each Colony where there is a local Legislature, the Governor, on the part of the Crown, should negotiate with the Assembly the amount of Salary to be paid to each officer, and the number of Officers whom, for revenue purposes, it may be expedient to appoint—and that a permanent Bill should be brought in, fixing these places and salaries according to the mutual agreement between the Governor and the Legislature.[6]

[1] See C.O. 137/166 Hibbert to Bathurst, Feb. 1, 1827 and Hibbert to Horton, May 20, 1827.
[2] *Ibid.* Also Hibbert to Horton, April 2, 1827.
[3] See above, p. 229.
[4] C.O. 138/50 Horton to Hibbert, private, May 21, 1827. See also Hibbert to Horton, May 16, May 20 and May 22, 1827.
[5] C.O. 323/207 July 11, 1827, ff. 137–8.   [6] *Ibid.*

Although this memorandum is unsigned it appears to have been corrected by Wilmot Horton; it was addressed to Lord Goderich. The time was propitious for a settlement for, although almost every governor had been prophesying a second American revolution, the protests of the assemblies were still entirely verbal, and the Jamaica assembly had not yet carried out its threat to cut off the supplies to the troops. Moreover, Canning was Prime Minister and to his decisiveness was added that of his chief adviser on economic affairs, William Huskisson.

A month later Canning was dead and Lord Goderich became Prime Minister. Huskisson became Secretary of State for the Colonies in September, and Herries, who had handled the question for the Treasury from the beginning, became Chancellor of the Exchequer. Had these three men remained at the head of affairs it is likely that a new policy favourable to the assemblies would have been adopted early in the following year. On 21 September Huskisson informed the administrator in Jamaica that no objection was entertained to the restoration of the law to the condition in which it was left by the 1822 Acts.[1] His specific proposals for a settlement were sent to the Treasury on 17 January 1828 just a few days before the government of Lord Goderich collapsed.[2] The succeeding government, with the Duke of Wellington as Prime Minister and Henry Goulburn as Chancellor of the Exchequer, did not adopt a new policy until December.

In February 1828 the assembly of Jamaica informed the Secretary of State, through its agent, of the conditions it considered necessary for a settlement[3] stating, among other things, what salaries it would be willing to pay. Another instance of administrative oversight came to light as a result of the assembly's presentation of its case. The assembly's request that the fees received by the naval officer be abolished[4] led the Colonial Office to make enquiries and to discover that, two years after its supposed abolition, the office was still in existence and collecting fees on shipping. In an interview with Huskisson the assembly's agent received assurance of the Government's conciliatory attitude but the assembly was severely rapped for its refusal to pay

[1] C.O. 138/51, pp. 233–5.
[2] This letter addressed from R. W. Hay to Frankland Lewis has not been located. It is discussed in C.O. 138/50 Hay to Hill, May 24, 1828, p. 397.
[3] C.O. 137/168 Hibbert to Hay, Feb. 5, 1828.   [4] *Ibid.*

accommodations of the first necessity for the garrison and for taking action towards 'establishing a concert with the Legislature of Lower Canada upon matters of difference wholly foreign to the Island of Jamaica.'[1] While agreeing that the assembly's report on salaries would be taken into consideration, Huskisson insisted that the Government would only surrender the duties in return for a permanent provision for the salaries. In May, shortly before Huskisson's resignation of his office, the Colonial Office sent a long letter to the Treasury recapitulating the details of the dispute with the Jamaica legislature, 'for the purpose of placing upon record . . . the course of these proceedings which have not hitherto been the subject of written communications between this Department and the Treasury.'[2]

Finally, on 2 December 1828, the Treasury made its decision. Its only major concession was an acknowledgement of the constitutional right of the colonial legislatures to make provision for the salaries. Some reductions were made in the salaries bill but 'the just and acknowledged right of the Crown to appoint the officers of the Customs, and to assign to them a reasonable and proper remuneration' was reasserted. And the governors were especially cautioned not to give their assent to any bill which would leave the colonial legislatures the power, at a future date, of withholding the salaries or of regulating them according to local views.[3]

Early in 1829 the assembly of Jamaica had two complaints. First, that despite an assurance given by the Secretary of State, the Custom House had not paid over certain funds to the receiver-general of the colony and, when enquiry was made, it had been informed that the money had been expended by order of the Government. Second, that although the tonnage bill for 1829 was continued as originally passed in 1825, an annual bill, the governor had without previous warning refused his assent. In turn, the assembly refused to provide supplies for the troops and claimed that the duties received under acts of Parliament passed before 1778 should be appropriated for the payment of the salaries.[4]

[1] C.O. 137/168 George Hibbert's memorandum (copy) on his interview with Huskisson, Feb. 16, 1828.
[2] C.O. 138/50, pp. 389–399.
[3] C.O. 323/208 Treasury Minute 1229, ff. 157–161.
[4] C.O. 137/170 Hibbert to Murray, Jan. 31 and Mar. 17, 1829.

Finally, in October 1829, Henry Goulburn, the Chancellor of the Exchequer, promised that the money would be handed over if the assembly would make provision for the salaries for the year 1826 and would vote fixed salaries for a period of not less than seven years.[1] The despatch to the governor was written by Henry Taylor and approved by Goulburn and Sir George Murray.[2] Taylor disapproved of the proposal but was consoled by the thought that it was unlikely to be accepted. His prophecy proved wrong, however, and though the assembly altered somewhat the apportionment of the salaries laid down by the Treasury, its terms were accepted by the Treasury as reasonable.[3] The legal difficulty imposed by the requirement that the duties be levied by the Custom House was circumvented by having the officers of customs raise the charge and the receiver-general and his deputies receive the money.[4]

In North America the belated recognition of their constitutional claims was appreciated by the assemblies. In Lower Canada a special committee of the assembly, chaired by John Neilson, one of the most prominent radicals in the colony, produced a statesmanlike report setting forth the difficulties involved in the dual responsibilities of the customs officers.[5] The Treasury minute arrived too late in the session, however, for the goodwill it engendered to be translated into action. A year later the temper of the assembly was such that the governor reported that he was sitting on a barrel of gunpowder, not knowing how soon an explosion would take place.[6] The issue then became lost in the general confusion leading up to the rebellion of 1837. A suggestion by Stephen in 1831 that the fees be re-established drew an emphatic negative from the Treasury.[7]

An interesting sidelight on the Treasury's attitude throughout the whole affair is provided by a minor incident. When the

---

[1] C.O. 137/170 J. Stewart to Murray, immediate, Oct. 6, 1829. The letter was signed by Stewart but Henry Taylor, in a letter written three days later, said that it was written by Goulburn.

[2] C.O. 137/170 Draft of a letter, presumably to Hibbert, signed by Taylor, Oct. 9, 1829, under 'Treasury'.

[3] C.O. 137/178 Stewart to Twiss, Aug. 23, 1830. See also Goulburn to Murray, private, Aug. 19, 1830.

[4] H.C. 1837 VII (516) 374.

[5] P.A.C., L.C. 'Q' Series, vol. 187-3, pp. 624-630.

[6] Ibid. Kempt to Hay, private and confidential, Mar. 2, 1830, vol. 193-3, p. 377.

[7] Ibid. J. Stewart to Howick, private, Sept. 9, 1831, vol. 199, p. 146.

governor of Lower Canada, Sir James Kempt, was dealing with the assembly in 1829, he sent to the special committee a copy of a schedule transmitted with the Treasury minute of the second of December setting out the amount of the salaries to be paid by the colony. A few weeks later, he discovered that the Commissioners of Customs in London had authorized the addition of two minor officers to the customs establishment of the province and had ordered their salaries paid from the duties collected. On 2 October 1829, when he was still hopeful that an arrangement would be made with the assembly, he wrote to the Secretary of State pointing to the impropriety of this action, which was based on the principle that new salaries could be charged on provincial funds to the extent of the amount of fees formerly paid in the colony.[1] Kempt knew that the assembly would never accept this principle and he asked that the insignificant salaries of the new officers be paid from the Crown revenues. His request, that his negotiations with the assembly be not jeopardized for the sake of this small amount of money, met with a curt refusal from the Treasury.[2]

In response to the recognition of its constitutional rights, Nova Scotia, taking pride in its self-appointed role of 'Pattern to Other Colonies for Moderation and Harmony in its Legislative Proceedings',[3] and hoping to gain some reduction of the salaries by a show of moderation, formally made a grant to His Majesty of an annuity of £6,430/9/0 sterling, and further decreed that the sum of £23,857/1/11¼, not paid to the provincial treasury by the officers of the customs at Halifax from the duties collected in 1826, 1827, and 1828, 'is hereby humbly, absolutely and freely given, and granted to His Majesty.'[4] Even the very loyal Nova Scotia assembly could not, however, resist one parting shot. The grant was made payable in Nova Scotia where foreign coins were usually assigned a higher sterling value than in London,[5] making a difference of from two to five hundred pounds in its annual value.

---

[1] P.A.C., L.C. 'Q' Series, vol. 189–2, p. 278.
[2] *Ibid.* Dawson to Hay, Jan. 30, 1830, vol. 196–1, p. 31.
[3] Martin, C., *Empire and Commonwealth*, Oxford (1929), pp. 160–1.
[4] N.S. Act 10 Geo. IV. Cap. 31.
[5] £3/7/2 stg. in London, £3/12/0 in Nova Scotia. See P.A.C., N.S. 'A' Series, Maitland to Murray, No. 9, May 8, 1829, vol. 171, pp. 48–50, also Stewart (Treasury) to Hay, Aug. 17, 1829, p. 153.

When the Whigs came into office in November 1830 most colonial legislatures were still unwilling to accept the Government's terms. The prospect of coming to terms with the assemblies was greatly improved, however, by the new Government's support for the principle of reducing expenditure in government, symbolized by the ministers' action in reducing their own salaries on taking office. The incomes of the Tory appointees in the colonies were no longer sacrosanct and, in May 1831, the Colonial Office officially urged the Treasury to facilitate a settlement 'by a diminution of the object in dispute'.[1] The Treasury moved cautiously to effect a reduction in the following years. Though the principle of not reducing the salary attached to an office except in a vacancy was retained, considerable savings were effected by a judicious transfer of officers. Thus, an opening in the post office in Jamaica in January 1833 led to the transfer of the collector of customs of Barbados to that post, but what would normally have been a promotion was not accompanied by any increase of salary. The collector at Antigua was, in turn, moved to Barbados, but at a lower salary as a manifestation of displeasure at his conduct. The salary of the collector's office at Antigua was in turn reduced and the comptroller at Quebec was transferred to fill the office. As a result of one opening a reduction of £1,350 was effected in the customs service[2] and of £500 in the Post Office.

The salaries question continued, nevertheless, to arouse bitterness in some colonies. In 1832, for example, the assembly of St. Kitts refused to pay the governor any salary on grounds of economy, the expense of the Custom House salaries being too great a burden on local revenues.[3] On the other hand, an offer of the assembly of New Brunswick, in 1831, to make a permanent annual grant equal to about two-thirds of the amount requested by the Treasury was accepted.[4] The assembly, some of whose members had in 1828 been in correspondence with members of neighbouring assemblies and had tried to co-ordinate the opposition to the British Government's policy,[5] did not pass the

---

[1] C.O. 324/146, p. 292.
[2] T.29/337 Treasury Minute 302, Jan. 4, 1833, pp. 133-4.
[3] C.O. 407/3 Goderich to Nicolay, May 7, 1832, p. 368.
[4] Hannay, R., *History of New Brunswick*, vol. I., pp. 416-7.
[5] P.A.C., N.B. 'A' Series, Douglas to Murray, May 18, 1829, vol. 42-1, p. 54.

necessary legislation to implement the agreement until 1835.[1] The salaries in Lower Canada came under colonial control in 1838 when the Canada Act of 1791 was suspended and the governor was placed in control of the colony's revenues.[2] In the same year the four and one-half per cent duties in the West Indies were finally abolished,[3] thus contributing to the final settlement in the colonies in which they were levied. In 1837, according to evidence given before the Select Committee on the Preparation of Colonial Accounts, over £14,000 a year was being paid out of general customs revenue for the support of colonial establishments, there being still several colonies in which the expenses of collection were in excess of receipts.[4]

> If a community, forming part of a larger political entity, is subject to a local and central government, the sphere of each must be marked out, in practice if not in law, if constant friction between the two governments is to be avoided.[5]

The distinction between law and practice, between legal power and constitutional right, has long been a feature of British government. Thirty years ago R. L. Schuyler drew attention to the existence of this distinction in Burke's thought[6] and it appears constantly in James Stephen's legal opinions, notably summed up in a sentence from an opinion already quoted in this chapter: 'The promises given by the Mother Country to its Dependencies, are not to be interpreted by the narrow rules which apply to the contracts of private persons.' Both Stephen and Lord Bathurst placed emphasis on the 'spirit of the law' governing relations between Britain and the colonies. In part this attitude may have been dictated by administrative convenience, but it also rested on a recognition that there are legal powers of government which, 'being contrary to the opinions and feelings of the people', can in fact be exercised no more than if they had been legally abolished.

[1] Hannay, R., *History of New Brunswick*, I, p. 417.
[2] I am indebted to Prof. Gordon Blake for drawing this to my attention.
[3] Ragatz, L. J., *Fall of the Planter Class in the British Caribbean 1763–1833*, New York, 1928, p. 101.
[4] H.C. 1837 VII (516) 325 and 372.
[5] Schuyler, R. L., *Parliament and the British Empire*, pp. 204–5.
[6] *Ibid.*, p. 198.

The Treasury concept of the colonial relationships placed much more emphasis on the validity of legal forms. In a brief debate in the House of Lords when Huskisson's bills were introduced on 14 June 1825, Lord Liverpool gave expression to the viewpoint that seems to have guided the later Treasury decisions in implementing the legislation:

> South America [he said] had nearly effected its independence; and when that was once established our colonies would cease to exist as such, and must be considered as integral parts of Great Britain, as much as London, or Liverpool.[1]

Wilmot Horton shared this concept of the colonies as 'overseas extensions' of the United Kingdom and this may help to explain his disagreement with his colleagues in the Colonial Office. The Treasury insisted throughout on its right to appoint and direct the Custom House officers and to decide how much they should be paid. This insistence was accompanied by certain inconsistencies. Thus, the Treasury would not approach Parliament for the salaries, although it relied on a parliamentary act for its authority to deduct them from colonial revenues. And again, in setting the salaries of its colonial officers, although relying on parliamentary authority, it did not apply the principles of economy that Parliament forced it to apply to its servants in the United Kingdom. In the end salaries in the colonies had to be brought into line with what the colonies regarded as fair remuneration for the work performed, just as salaries in the United Kingdom could not greatly exceed what Parliament considered to be adequate.

The Treasury ideal of a unified revenue service for the whole Empire was impractical. Contradictions arose whenever it met the awkward fact of the existence of the constitutional rights of the legislative colonies. The Canada Committee of the House of Commons sensed the contradiction involved in the situation in 1828 and recommended that the Crown revenues in the Canadas be turned over to the assemblies. On the other hand, the Treasury commission appointed in 1830 to enquire into the receipt and expenditure of colonial revenue was unaware of this contradiction and asserted, quite simply, that the Treasury 'should exercise a strict efficient control over every branch &

---

[1] *Parliamentary Debates, New Series*, vol. XIII, col. 1134.

every article of Colonial Expenditure.'[1] Such a concept of the role of the Treasury was never entertained in the colonial assemblies nor by men, such as Lord Bathurst and James Stephen, who were familiar with the colonies.

The difficulties that arose out of the incompatibility of the Treasury outlook with the established constitutional position of the legislative colonies served to emphasize the inadequacy of the means available for arriving at and implementing decisions on colonial affairs. Neither the Colonial Office nor the Treasury was in a position to undertake the planning necessary as a prelude to executing a major piece of reform legislation, such as that embraced in Huskisson's acts. In being forced to work together the problem was several times compounded, for although the informal consultations between members of the departments that sufficed for routine day-to-day business served well enough when their purpose was the exchange of information or points of view, or even the formulation of questions, it was not designed for the hammering out of involved policy decisions. The drafting of the legislation and its passage through Parliament was not a triumph of the administrative machinery of the Board of Trade and Customs but a *tour de force* by William Huskisson, made possible by the industry and perspicacity of James Deacon Hume and by Huskisson's influence with the Prime Minister and the leader of the House of Commons. Only a similar display of political ingenuity could have resolved the differences between the Treasury and the colonial assemblies of Lower Canada and Jamaica. This would have involved either adopting Lord Bathurst's policy of appealing to Parliament for imperial funds or the forestalling of Lord Durham by trusting the assemblies. For obvious reasons neither was practicable.

In the absence of other leadership Wilmot Horton assumed the lead by default, and his carelessness, deficiencies of judgement, and inexperience soon led to hopeless confusion. It is probable, however, that the failure of his original policy would not have led to the interminable recriminations and threats had the machinery of government not moved with such unconscionable slowness in formulating an alternative.

One interesting sidelight of the question was the almost com-

[1] C.O. 323/212 Report of the Commissioners of Colonial Enquiry, Dec. 13, 1830, ff. 177–183.

plete absence of comment in Parliament. The members who spoke in defence of colonial interests on other occasions were conspicuous by their silence.[1] A show of interest by the House of Commons might have done wonders to hasten the Treasury's deliberations.

[1] See C.O. 137/166 Hibbert to Horton, Feb. 20, 1827.

THE COLONIAL OFFICE AND
THE CIVIL SERVICE

'And business thou wouldst find and wouldst create.'
COWLEY—'The Complaint'

In *Huskisson and His Age*, a fascinating impressionistic study of
Britain in the early nineteenth century, C. R. Fay has distinguished two motives for administrative reform. The one, represented by John Charles Herries and Peel, emphasized financial
administration and would reduce government business within
a small compass so that it could be more efficiently handled.
The other, represented by Huskisson and Wilmot Horton,
pressed for great measures of imperial, economic, and social
development. Fay suggests that Peel's decision to adopt a free
trade policy was determined fundamentally by his desire to
reduce the administrative burden of the Treasury and thus leave
it free to concentrate on its main function, the supervision of
expenditure[1]—the logic of the decision will be apparent to those
who are familiar with the numerous petty details of customs
business that were daily referred to the Treasury for decision.
The conviction that the Government was capable of undertaking
additional tasks and of discharging its admitted responsibilities
more competently became part of the tradition of the Colonial
Office. Henry Taylor expressed it very succinctly in 1836:

> . . . it is one business to do what must be done, another to devise
> what ought to be done. It is in the spirit of the British government,
> as hitherto existing, to transact only the former business; and the
> reform which it requires is to enlarge that spirit so as to include
> the latter.[2]

It can scarcely be coincidental that one Colonial Office clerk,
Henry Taylor (*The Statesman*, 1836), attempted the first serious

---

[1] Fay, C. R., *Huskisson and his Age*, p. 123.
[2] *The Statesman*, p. 103.

analysis of the role of the civil servant in the central offices of the British Government and another, Sidney Webb, became the great champion in Great Britain of the idea that pigeon-holes and statistics could serve to enrich the life of the community.

The significance of the role of the civil servants in the central departments of government was not generally recognized until the third quarter of the nineteenth century. The man primarily responsible for bringing about this recognition was Sir Charles Trevelyan, who was appointed Assistant Secretary to the Treasury in 1840. He was joint-author, with Sir Stafford Northcote, of the famous 1854 'Report on the Organization of the Permanent Civil Service . . .'.[1] This was the central document in his campaign to bring about reform in recruitment and to combat what the Report referred to as 'the fragmentary character of the Service', there being no civil service as such but only congeries of departmental services.

One of the major defects that Trevelyan noted was the need to bring in 'outside' men to fill the highest posts because not enough of the regular men in the departments were considered capable of undertaking the most responsible duties. Trevelyan himself had spent twelve years in the East India Company's service. Many of his idea on administration had been developed in that great laboratory where Britons had an opportunity to experiment with bureaucratic government. He found support among men who had arrived at similar conclusions while serving in the civil service at home. Henry Taylor had written in 1836:

> Till a wise and constant instrumentality at work upon administrative measures . . . shall be understood to be essential to the government of a country, that country can be considered to enjoy nothing more than the embryo of a government—a means towards producing, through changes in its own structure and constitution and in the political elements acting upon it, something worthy to be called a government at some future time.[2]

In the late eighteenth century contemplation on the responsibilities of permanent civil servants had been overshadowed by, and incidental to, the need to define the relationship between

---

[1] The Report was dated November 23, 1853 and presented to Parliament in February 1854.
[2] *The Statesman*, pp. 106–7.

King and Parliament. As Sir Lewis Namier has pointed out, not until the Crown had become unpolitical did it become possible to draw a firm distinction between civil servants and parliament men.[1] The Crown and the civil service 'not by chance together left the political arena.'[2] But this not ungracious *pas de deux* cannot be given a precise date. Its beginning was in the eighteenth-century effort to prevent the King from using dependent office holders to control Parliament; its ending came when 'strongly organized, disciplined parliamentary parties came into existence'.[3]

At no time was the public service without prominent permanent career men. They supplied the expertise and the continuity without which government could not have operated. In the postal service, the revenue departments, and the military and naval offices there were men who spent their working lives supervising large organizations and performing responsible and extensive duties. But they were looked upon as mere agents of policy to whom specific functions were assigned. Even so, there were not many of them and the task of directing them and co-ordinating their efforts did not require any extraordinary capacity in the central departments of government. Administration was almost entirely confined to functions that were essential for the existence of the state—defence, taxation, and foreign affairs. Most affairs directly affecting the individual citizen were left to private initiative or to local government. Local authorities even assumed most of the responsibility for maintaining the internal security of the country.[4]

Professor Parkinson's observation that 'Work expands so as to fill the time available for its completion' has received deservedly popular recognition as a characteristic feature of bureaucracy. That business will expand to the capacity of the administrative structure seems obvious from any statistical analysis of government business over the past hundred and fifty years. That it always exceeds the capacity of the administrative structure at

[1] 'Monarchy and the Party System' (Romanes Lecture 1952), *Personalities and Powers*, pp. 13–24.
[2] *Ibid.*, p. 14.
[3] *Ibid.*
[4] See Darvall, F. O., *Popular Disturbances and Public Order in Regency England*, pp. 218–249.

any given moment is also apparent to any person who has read the appeals of departments to the Treasury for additional staff. Professor Parkinson was not the first person to detect the working of his 'law'.

> Thou wouldst, forsooth, be something in a State,
> And business thou wouldst find, and wouldst create.

sang the poet Cowley in 'The Complaint', not appreciating that a later age would demand scientific precision. The Parkinson or Cowley effect cannot easily be assessed. It undoubtedly was a factor in the increase of business in the Colonial Office in the early nineteenth century, but the increase of work was associated with genuine demands of the Colonial territories.

In evidence given before a committee of the House of Commons in 1839 George Mayer, the Colonial Office librarian, asserted that business had increased a hundredfold since 1824.[1] He stated that the yearly number of letters sent by the office had jumped from five thousand to twelve thousand. There were twelve volumes of parliamentary papers in 1839;[2] there had been 780 pages in 1824.[3] Mayer's assertion that business had increased a hundredfold appears to have been hyperbolical yet it should not be lightly dismissed. He was a responsible official who had at that time served in the office for almost thirty years. The apparent discrepancy in his evidence may serve as a useful warning against any facile attempt to base an analysis of government business or of a department's capacity for business on a simple statistical study of the output of paperwork.

Even within the Colonial Office there was a vast difference in the amount of consideration given, for example, to the average despatch sent to the West Indies and the average despatch sent to New South Wales. In the modern Civil Service, though not in the Colonial Office, a distinction is made between 'executive' and 'administrative' functions. The term 'executive' 'includes almost everything above routine and below the formulation of policy.'[4] The term 'administrative' is reserved for decisions made at the highest level. Applying this terminology

---

[1] H.C. 1839 XIII, pp. 252–9. See Williams, T., 'The Colonial Office in the Thirties', p. 142.
[2] *Ibid.*
[3] C.O. 324/146 Horton to Herries, Dec. 15, 1826.
[4] Griffith, Wyn, *The British Civil Service 1854–1954*, p. 24.

to colonial affairs in the early nineteenth century, West Indian business required a much higher proportion of administrative decisions than did the business of New South Wales.

Despite the limitations on the usefulness of a mere count of pages in the letter books the output of paperwork does provide a rough indication of the increase in the business and of the distribution of that business. No attempt will be made, however, to estimate what proportion of Colonial Office business arose as a result of increased activity in the colonial communities, how much was due to Westminster's concern for the Empire, or exactly how much should be ascribed to the adoption of an authoritarian system of government in the colonies acquired after the American Revolution.

In 1806, 1,653 letters on colonial affairs were received in the office and 902 despatched; in 1816, 4,487 letters were received and 3,161 despatched; in 1824, 7,491 letters were received and 4,959 sent out.[1] In the mid-twenties the increase from year to year was phenomenal—61,608 folio pages were received in 1825 compared to 35,836 in 1824.[2] The increase was in much the same proportion between 1825 and 1826.[3] The office was also very busy in 1827 but there was a marked decline in the 'years of torpor', 1828 to 1830. Parliament's demands on the Colonial Office became intensified about the mid-twenties. Only 14 printed folio pages were laid before the House of Commons by the colonial department in 1806.[4] In 1816 there were 246 pages; in 1824, 780 pages; in 1825, 2,200 pages, and in 1826, 2,694 printed folio pages.[5] From 1803 to 1812 the average number of colonial legislative acts sent to the legal counsel of the office for review was 137; from 1817 to 1822 it was 227. In 1826, James Stephen reviewed 480 colonial acts.[6]

Many of these figures have been extracted from a statistical table—probably more accurate than any that could be readily compiled from the records—that was drawn up in 1825. It is given, in full, as Appendix VIII of this study. The number and

---

[1] See Appendix VIII.
[2] C.O. 324/146 Horton to Herries, Dec. 15, 1826, pp. 69–70.
[3] *Ibid.*
[4] See Appendix VIII.
[5] C.O. 324/146 Horton to Herries, Dec. 15, 1826, pp. 69–70.
[6] *Ibid.* See also C.O. 323/192 Table enclosed with James Stephen's letter to Goulburn of July 20, 1820.

volume of incoming and outgoing letters were compared for the three years 1806, 1816, and 1824, with the totals for each colony being given. The choice of these three years was not entirely arbitrary, the first being the year of the original appointment of a second under-secretary in the office, the second the year in which the second under-secretaryship was abolished at the end of the war, and the third the year previous to its restoration.

The random choice of almost any year for the purpose of noting each colony's share of the total business is subject to local factors that may momentarily focus attention on a particular colony or group of colonies. Thus, in 1816, particular attention to Canada, as an aftermath of the American war, is clearly indicated by the number of letters sent and received. In 1824, as a result of the report of the Bigge commission of enquiry,[1] New South Wales was receiving an even larger share of attention than it had hitherto enjoyed and the presence of a commission of enquiry at the Cape of Good Hope[2] increased the correspondence with that colony. These local variations, while significant, are not large enough to conceal or to emphasize unduly the principal trends.

The word colony is itself not used in the precise sense of an overseas settlement, or even in the larger sense that would include plantations and military stations. It is rather a convenient administrative distinction, which usually, but not always, indicates a territory administered by an official responsible to the Secretary of State for the Colonies. Thus, it includes true colonies such as Upper Canada, plantations such as Jamaica, military stations such as Gibraltar, and in New South Wales a penal settlement containing a large number of free settlers. But it also includes the Barbary States or, more truly, the consuls to Algiers, Tunis, Morocco, and Tripoli.[3] These consulates came under the War Office because of the extensive supplies drawn from North Africa for Gibraltar, Malta, and the Mediterranean fleet; the transformation of the War Office into Colonial Office had made of them a unique 'colony', noted for its valuable patronage[4] and interesting because of its connection with the missions sent to

---

[1] See above, pp. 36–7.
[2] *Ibid.*, pp. 72 and 189.
[3] See Anderson, M. S., 'Great Britain and the Barbary States in the Eighteenth Century', *Bull. Inst. Hist. Res.*, XXIX, pp. 87–107.
[4] See H.C. 1830 XVIII, p. 496.

explore the interior of Africa. In 1815 another unique 'colony' was added to the British Empire in the Mediterranean when the states of the Ionian Islands were placed under British protection. In the West Indies the islands of St. Christopher, Nevis, Tortola, Antigua, and Montserrat, while having a separate existence to the extent of having lieutenant-governors, were at first one and later two 'colonies'. Again in the West Indian complex of colonies, Honduras, under a superintendent, was a colony with no parallel in the empire.[1] The total number of colonies varied through the years. The table distinguishes twenty-nine in 1806, of which three were conquered colonies later given up; for 1816 thirty-three colonies are listed, of which one, Cape Breton, was in 1820 merged into Nova Scotia. In 1825 Van Diemen's Land was separated from New South Wales and in 1828 a third Australian colony formed by a settlement at Swan River.

For administrative purposes it was found convenient in the twenties to divide the colonies geographically into four divisions 'North America', 'West Indies', 'Mediterranean and Africa' and 'Eastern'. A more revealing breakdown for the purpose of analysing the distribution of paperwork can beo btained by dividing the North American, West Indian and Eastern divisions according to the form of government in the individual colonies; 'legislative colonies', the remnants of the old empire, in North America and the West Indies, and 'non-legislative colonies', New South Wales and the colonies newly taken from continental powers—Trinidad, Berbice, Demerara and Essequibo, Cape of Good Hope, Mauritius, and Ceylon.[2] The Mediterranean and Africa administrative division can be conveniently broken down into its two elements, the Mediterranean colonies, new and old, forming one with the other being West Africa. A few 'colonies' remain outside these divisions: the East Indies where, with the Admiralty and the East India Company, the Secretary of State kept a watching brief on British interests; Newfoundland, in the North American complex but not of it;

[1] In 1846 James Stephen described the legislature of Honduras as 'a voluntary compact of certain English people inhabiting SpanishTerritory to make Laws for their own Government....' Knaplund, P., *James Stephen...*, p. 257.
[2] For the government of the conquered colonies, see Manning, H. T., *British Colonial Government after the American Revolution*, pp. 293, 345 and 362.

and Heligoland, which, although a conquest of war, would have fitted more conveniently under the Home Office, which had responsibility for the Channel Islands and the Isle of Man.

Of the 902 colonial letters sent from the Secretary of State's office in 1806, only 290 were sent to the colonies, of which 72 were sent to Malta, Gibraltar, and the Barbary States. Many of these letters could be classed as 'military', but since 'colonial' and 'military' are not always separable categories, it is convenient to consider these as colonial for purposes of comparison with later years, using not subject matter but destination as the criterion for separating the one from the other. The number sent to the colonies in 1816 was more than six times as great as in 1806 and the 1816 total had more than doubled by 1824 when 3,460 letters were despatched—this was in addition to the over fourteen hundred letters sent to other departments and persons in Britain in each of those years. In 1806, two colonies, Surinam and St. Lucia, received only two despatches each; two others, Cape Breton and New Brunswick, received only three each. No colony outside of the Mediterranean area had more than twenty despatches sent to it but nineteen each were sent to the Cape of Good Hope and the Windward and Leeward Islands. The nine despatches sent to lower Canada and sixteen to Jamaica compare favourably with the numbers sent to their non-legislative rivals, twelve to Trinidad, fifteen to New South Wales, and eleven to Ceylon. By 1816 even the increased interest in North America as a result of the American war and the endeavours to strengthen the North American colonies through emigration serve only to illustrate the increased attention paid to the non-legislative colonies. Beside the 114 despatches to Lower Canada and the 31 to Jamaica there were 349 for New South Wales, 135 for Ceylon, 173 for Mauritius, 86 for the Cape of Good Hope, and 59 for Trinidad. In 1824 only seven out of the thirty-three colonies received fewer than twenty despatches, and in one of those, Nova Scotia, the governor was on leave of absence in England and thus in frequent contact with the Colonial Office. In that year 48 despatches were sent to Lower Canada and 52 to Jamaica; 1,104 were sent to New South Wales, 224 to Ceylon, 240 to the Cape of Good Hope, 354 to Mauritius, and 53 very lengthy despatches to Trinidad. Attention to the affairs of the Mediterranean area increased at about the same rate as the overall increase in colonial business. Malta received a steady five to seven per cent share of the outgoing letters. By 1824 the Ionian Islands were receiving a larger number of despatches than Malta.

The slavery question brought West Africa forward in this era as a significant factor in colonial administration. In 1806 correspondence to West Africa consisted of four letters sent to the conquered French colony of Gorée, which was later returned to France. New responsibilities were undertaken in 1807 when the Sierra Leone Company turned over its settlement for freed slaves to the government; in 1816 thirty-five letters were sent to West Africa. The winding up in 1821 of the affairs of the old companies, successors to those which in Charles II's day had held trading rights on the African coast, brought certain African forts under the control of the Colonial Office; 324 letters were sent to Sierra Leone and the African Forts in 1824. Of these colonies only the Gambia was considered worth keeping for its trade.[1]

The most striking increase in correspondence was with New South Wales. Fifteen letters were sent in 1806; in 1824 there were 1,104, almost a third of the despatches sent overseas that year. Most of these letters were very short, concerning individual convicts or recommending new settlers for land grants, and in volume the 1,104 letters occupy only 729 pages in the entry books. The population, in the eighteen-twenties was less than 40,000, more than half of whom were free.[2] New South Wales was an example of long-range administration carried to its utmost extreme. The Colonial Office had political control, the Home Office was responsible for the convicts, the Transport Office of the Admiralty arranged transports, the Treasury kept an eye on finances, the Audit Office audited parliamentary moneys expended in the colony, the Colonial Audit Office audited internal accounts, the Commander-in-Chief's Office, the Secretary at War's Office and the Commissariat were responsible for troops stationed there and for pensioners settled there, the Ordnance Office was responsible for military buildings, the

[1] See C.O. 537/155 Unsigned Memorandum on West Africa, military confidential, Dec. 6, 1827 (Copy).

[2] Total population in 1819 was 26,026 of whom 17,040 were free. By 1828 the population had increased to 36,598 of whom 20,930 were free. H.C. 1830–31 IV (64) 85.

Post Office looked after the mails, the Mint issued currency, the Ecclesiastical Commissioners were consulted on religious matters and, beginning in the twenties, the Board of Customs supervised the collection of customs revenue.

Incoming correspondence, unlike the outgoing, gives little indication of a shift in the attention of the Colonial Office. Incoming mails from the legislative colonies had always brought their tide of tribulation from unhappy governors and furious assemblies; even in 1806 almost a thousand letters came to the office from the colonies with representative institutions. In 1816, 1,676 letters were received from them and in 1824 over two thousand. While thus doubling the burden of their tales their proportion of the total correspondence received from all the colonies declined, from over sixty per cent in 1806, to around forty per cent in 1824. In the same period, the people of New South Wales had increased their representations to the Colonial Office eleven and a half times, from 83 in 1806 to 964 in 1824. Apart from New South Wales, non-legislative colonies showed proportionately very little more increase than the old colonies.

However, the number of letters sent is surely more indicative of Colonial Office preoccupation than the number received. In 1806 almost half of all the letters despatched went to the old legislative colonies, in 1816 the proportion was only a quarter, and by 1824 it had declined to an eighth. Despite internal quarrels, civil lists, immigrants and clergy reserves, the number of letters sent to all the North American colonies, including Bermuda, in 1824 was about equal to the number sent to Malta. And despite the troubles over slaves and sugar, almost as many letters were sent to the Cape of Good Hope as to all the old West Indian colonies put together. These figures, of course, bear little relation to the extent of the Secretary of State's preoccupation with them. Delegations of merchants, planters, and shipowners regularly appeared before him, colonial agents pressed the desires of the assemblies, Parliament was ever concerned for their slaves and, above all, there was that tremendous pile of correspondence to be read.

Some idea of the difference in the scale of operations between the nineteenth century and the twentieth can be obtained by comparing the output of paperwork. In 1824 a total of 12,450 letters and despatches were sent out and received.[1] In 1939 the total was 300,841.[2] As noted earlier in this chapter the tally of letters outward was almost two and a half times as great in 1839 as it had been in 1824; in the seventy years between 1839 and 1909 the output of paperwork increased about four times and 1939 was three times as busy as 1909 in the number of letters registered and indexed.[3] These figures do not, of course, make allowance for such developments as the advent of the telegraph. There was a provision of £7,000 for outward telegrams from the Colonial Office in 1909; in 1939 the expenditure was £51,484 and in 1945-6 the provision for colonial telegrams was £140,000.[4]

Technological innovation played a large part in increasing the capacity of the administrative machine. Carbon paper and the typewriter reduced the amount of hackwork and greatly speeded up the reproduction of documents, making possible, among other things, a great increase in the efficiency of committees—in the early nineteenth century copying services were so inadequate that even the members of the Cabinet could not be provided with individual copies of the Foreign Office despatches and papers pertaining to matters under discussion.[5] Filing systems also improved beyond all recognition in the century after 1824 and though the official memory did not become infallible, it became relatively efficient. In the two decades since 1939 the machine age has caught up with administrators though the author does not know to what extent new machines have been introduced in the Colonial Office. Equipment that can reproduce documents extremely rapidly is now available, the application of electronics is revolutionizing the process of consulting records, and microphotography is preventing the problem of their storage from becoming insurmountable. The evolution of the administrative building in the past century and a half has in itself been remarkable; from the gentleman's house, where his retainers met daily to perform the tasks that he required of them, to the elaborately contrived 'pentagons' of the present day. The introduction of the telephone, too, should be noted;

[1] See Appendix VIII.
[2] Parkinson, Sir Cosmo, *The Colonial Office from Within, 1909-1945*, p. 53.
[3] *Ibid.*
[4] *Ibid.*
[5] Aspinall, A., 'The Cabinet Council 1783-1835', pp. 171-3.

for when the official machinery was threatening to become completely paper bound, emphasis on the use of the telephone restored some of the flexibility and, when the occasion demanded, the speedy despatch of business, which had been admirable features of the oral tradition that prevailed in the early nineteenth century.

The new gadgetry has been indispensable but the vital change has taken place in the organization of men. Methods had to be evolved for bringing to bear on a question not only extensive information from the official records but also the experience and specialized knowledge of a great many individuals. Techniques had to be perfected for co-ordinating the work of many persons yet there had to be sufficient flexibility to permit individuals to make their specialized talents available in several fields at the same time. An *esprit de corps* had to be created so that civil servants would give sustained and effective service with little public recognition of their efforts;[1] their reward coming from their standing with others in the same position as themselves, their petty authority within the larger structure of authority, their consciousness of serving the State, and the prestige and satisfaction of being at the centre of affairs. As the tasks of government increased a higher level of individual efficiency had to be achieved. Stability in the government service and security of tenure were basic requirements in attracting and holding the men that were needed.

No significant technological developments accompanied the administrative changes of the early nineteenth century. Steamboats were on the rivers but not on the high seas; on land the age of steam transportation was marked by Huskisson's tragic death in 1830. Improvement in the condition of the roads may have speeded up the mail coaches on their way to catch the sailing packets at Falmouth but, in general, it was as true in 1830 as it had been over half a century earlier that 'Seas roll and months pass between the order and the execution'. Within the Colonial Office in 1830 the basic tool was still the quill pen, and the major technical problem was the copying and sending off of letters and despatches. James Stephen drew attention

[1] For a more recent phase in the relations between the public and the civil service see Bridges, Sir Edward. 'The Reforms of 1854 in Retrospect', in *The Civil Service in Britain and France*, W. A. Robson, ed. (1956), pp. 32–3.

to this whenever he had occasion to comment on the structure of the office.[1]

Stephen in 1832 and Henry Taylor in 1836 anticipated the recommendations of the Northcote-Trevelyan Report by pointing to the need for a distinction between 'intellectual' and 'mechanical' or, as Stephen called them, 'manual' workers. At India House, which was not subject to the restrictions of the government service, a separate establishment of superior clerks was set up in 1831,[2] just twelve years after the reorganization of 1819 when the emphasis had been on the hiring of 'intellectual' workers; in addition, copyists were employed for routine copying. Both Stephen and Taylor drew attention to the traditional division of labour on class lines in British society. 'Gentlemen' —there is frequently an ironical note in Stephen's use of the term—could not be expected to perform manual duties efficiently. The copyists, said Taylor, should be 'persons in the rank of life of law-stationers and their hired writers.'[3] Men of that rank in society were accustomed to taking orders; men of the class employed as clerks in the Colonial Office were not— 'control . . . can hardly be exercised with success by persons of a certain class in life over each other.'[4] Control over lower-class persons employed as copyists could be made even more effective by paying them on a piecework basis—'Upon the system of salaries, every person who is employed as a copyist is desirous to do as little as he can; upon the other there is a daily appetite and eagerness for work. . . .' In earlier decades extra clerks attached to the office had been paid a daily wage; in the early thirties, before the time when Taylor was writing, a copying pool had been established in which payment was made according to the amount of work done. Taylor regarded the copying pool as so efficient that he advocated the retention of salaried copying clerks only for business that required secrecy.[5]

The clerks who worked in 'the commonplace brick house at the end of Downing Street', with an occasional exception, 'had the education, the manners, the feelings and the characteristic principles of gentlemen',[6] though a few of them may have been

[1] See above, Chapter III.
[2] H.C. 1854 XXVII (1715) 86.
[3] *The Statesman*, p. 110.
[4] *Ibid.*.   [5] *Ibid.*
[6] H.C. 1854-5 XX (1870) 74. The words are James Stephen's.

recruited from that fringe of gentility whose female members were sometimes referred to as 'needy gentlewomen'. Disraeli, in *Endymion,* pictured a middle-class youth appointed to a government office in the thirties whose accent, manners, and attitude to work were not in keeping with the upper-class atmosphere of the place. Although he was writing almost fifty years after the events that he was describing, Disraeli was almost certainly correct in regarding the appointment of a lower middle-class man to a clerkship in one of the government offices in Westminster as exceptional even in the decade after 1832. The event must have been very rare, for one of the chief criticisms made of the Northcote-Trevelyan report when it was issued in 1854 was that a system of entry into the Civil Service dependent on written examinations in assessing the worth of the candidates might lead to the dilution of the Civil Service with individuals who did not have the manners of gentlemen.[1]

Though the men at work in Downing Street and Whitehall in 1831 were still Anglicans and Church of Scotland Presbyterians such as would have been found there a generation earlier, greater demands were being made upon them—'upper class men and middle class measures', to paraphrase Disraeli. The extension of the working day is indicative of a notable change in conditions of work. In 1831 clerks were expected to remain at their desks in the Colonial Office until six o'clock in the evening, two hours later than what had been regarded as normal a generation earlier. This longer working day is the most obvious, but not the only sign that a utilitarian and mechanical yardstick of efficiency was being applied to the public service; the hiring of copyists on a piecework basis is another. In 1828 a parliamentary committee even subscribed to the notion that civil servants should devote the same attention to government affairs as clerks in banks and business establishments devoted to the affairs of their masters.[2]

The parliamentary committee of 1828, in declaring the doctrine of work to be official gospel, was under no illusion that the ideal could be immediately realized. Side by side in the Colonial Office in the thirties were James Stephen, with his slavish devotion to his desk, and those clerks whom he described, who

---

[1] For comments on the report see H.C. 1854–5 XX (1870) 1–477.
[2] H.C. 1828 V (420) 20.

found it difficult to fit in their official employment between their morning rides and their afternoon dinner parties.[1] The dedicated Stephen was very human in his resentment of the presence in the office of men who looked upon their official duties as incidental to their living a gracious life. Reform in the government services was never clearcut, thorough-going or logically developed. Changes were made in response to immediate needs, though they might be influenced by abstract considerations. Old traditions and attitudes were reluctantly modified, never suddenly abandoned.

The major new element introduced into the administrative structure of the Colonial Office in the early eighteen-twenties was the assigning of intellectual duties to the senior clerks. This device was resorted to at a time when Parliament's insistence on economy made it impossible for the department to add new men at a higher level. Even in that brief Indian summer, in 1824 and 1825, between the 'economy' of the post-war years and the permanent liberal 'economy' that was ushered in by the crisis of 1826, the Prime Minister was unwilling for a long time to sanction the appointment of a second under-secretary.[2] But because they were prepared to strike hard in that brief moment of prosperity, and because Parliament was sympathetic to a department that the questions of slavery and emigration were keeping in the public eye, the leaders of the Colonial Office obtained authorization for a great increase in the strength of the establishment in 1824 and 1825. That the need for differentiation of clerks into superior and inferior grades was not appreciated is understandable. The need had not then been recognized even at India House. Moreover, the only precedent for differentiation that existed in the government offices was beset with pitfalls. Most offices had long been in the habit of hiring extra clerks on a part-time basis whenever there was extra copying to be done. These clerks were paid from the contingency funds of the offices. In the three years from 1820 to 1822 the contingency funds came under such close scrutiny by Parliament that the Treasury refused all requests for the employment of copyists. If such a situation should recur it would obviously be very much to the advantage of a department to

---

[1] C.O. 537/22, No. I.
[2] See above, pp. 78–9.

have an establishment of permanent clerks large enough not only to handle day-to-day business but to meet unforeseen emergencies. However, the gentlemen who received the appointments to the swollen Colonial Office establishment proved to be indifferent copyists and they were far too numerous for all to be employed on intellectual duties. Moreover, the establishment was out of balance not only functionally but also in its age structure.

In 1836 only two of the clerks on the staff had more than twelve years' service. The others had all been recruited in the five-year period between 1824 and 1828. They were in their teens or early twenties when they entered the office, and they grew old together forming a solid incubus in the middle ranks, secure in their tenure but with little hope of promotion since the men above them were of the same age as themselves. The rapid advancement through the ranks of the two most able juniors among those recruited in the twenties[1] caused so much resentment that the experiment of advancing able men over worthy men of mediocre talents was not repeated. 'My own experience teaches me that a Secretary of State who should promote any one of his clerks over the heads of his seniors must arm himself with the fortitude of a martyr,' wrote James Stephen many years later.[2] One or two able youngsters who entered the office as probationers in the thirties did not stay long, for they soon became aware of the complete bar to advancement that would continue to exist until the men of the twenties reached the age of retirement; one of them was offered the post of Permanent Under-Secretary in 1847 and refused it.[3] A few of the men of the twenties were completely incompetent. Speaking of clerks in the Colonial Office in 1855, Herman Merivale, then Permanent Under-Secretary, said that a few of them were very inefficient, 'not many, but some.'[4]

Stephen's strictures on Colonial Office clerks contained in his published comments on the Northcote-Trevelyan report have been widely quoted. The 'majority of the members of the Colonial Department in my time,' he wrote,

[1] See Chapter III, also Appendix III.
[2] H.C. 1854–5 XX (1870) 79.
[3] Taylor, H., *Autobiography*, vol. II, p. 27.
[4] H.C. 1860 IX (440) 310.

possessed only in a low degree, and some of them in a degree almost incredibly low, either the talents or the habits of men of business, or the industry, the zeal, or the knowledge required for the effective performance of their appropriate functions.[1]

He did, of course, make an exception of the half dozen men 'who must have risen to eminence in any field of open competition[2] —and at least four of those six received their appointments in the twenties. He also made an exception of another group,

> men who performed diligently, faithfully, and judiciously the duties to which they were called; and those duties were, not rarely, such as belonged rather to ministers of state, than to the clerks in the office of such a minister.[3]

It is surely remarkable that so many men of high calibre received appointments and had an opportunity to develop their abilities. This is the other aspect of the unbalance that resulted from the excessively large number of appointments made in the mid-twenties. It was the outstanding abilities of so many of the Colonial Office clerks that impressed outsiders who became familiar with their work. The commissioners who enquired into the state of the office in 1849 reported:

> The functions of the Colonial Office are remarkable for their variety, importance and difficulty, and experience and ability of a high order are necessary for their proper performance...[4]
> ... we are of the opinion that the duties at the Colonial Office require qualifications of a higher kind than the greater part even of those at the India House....[5]

Herman Merivale, Stephen's successor as Permanent Under-Secretary, was even more emphatic:

> In my own department the duties imposed on clerks involve more intellectual exertion than in almost any other of that service. It is, in fact, difficult to over-rate the ability and knowledge required to perform a portion of the functions of its first-class clerks with complete effectiveness. No amount of talent, which the system of competition or any other could bring into the arena, would be thrown away.[6]

[1] H.C. 1854–5 XX (1870) 75.   [2] *Ibid.*, p. 74.
[3] *Ibid.*, p. 75.
[4] H.C. 1854 XXVII (1715) 82.   [5] *Ibid.*, p. 87.
[6] H.C. 1854–5 XX (1870) 314–5.

The reform of the Civil Service came at a time when replacements had to be found for the men of the twenties. Seven new appointments were made between December 1855 and May 1860. There were still only twenty-two clerks in the office at the latter date.[1] Several of the new appointees advanced rapidly from junior posts to senior positions that had been occupied by men who had learned their trade from James Stephen and had sought to satisfy his standards. Whereas the men of the twenties had had their work thrown at them and had gradually built up their own positions, their successors took over roles that had become institutionalized. There were definite duties and responsibilities attached to their posts and an established pattern of relations with the other posts on the establishment. The new system of recruitment that was adopted required that the best men available should be chosen, mature men of broad general education drawn from all ranks of society and owing their appointments to merit alone.

Few observers of the British government in the eighteen-twenties noted the increasingly important part being played by the permanent officials in the making of decisions. One of the few was Charles Greville, who observed in 1829 that 'a few obscure men of energy and ability' were doing the business and supplying the required knowledge in all departments of government.[2] He gave specific references, however, only to the Board of Trade and the Colonial Office, and at the Board of Trade to only a single individual. There is no evidence in the literature of the twenties of any concern of the public with bureaucracy. In 1820 Byron, in penning his *The Vision of Judgment*, allowed his imagination free rein in describing the bureaucracy of Heaven —'the recording angel's black bureau'—it is unlikely that he could have resisted a few asides on the bureaucracy of Whitehall had there been any popular preoccupation with it. It was not until two decades later that Carlyle penned his attacks on Downing Street. In the fifties Dickens portrayed the Circumlocution Office and made the fumbling laxity of public servants

---

[1] H.C. 1860 IX (440) 310.

[2] *Greville Memoirs*, I, p. 306. Entry of Aug. 8, 1829. A Treasury commissioner wrote to Huskisson in 1827: 'The great mass of [Treasury] business is now in the hands of its clerks. Over these the Lords have a nominal control.' Fay, C. R., *Huskisson and His Age*, p. 71.

an object of satire. It is notable that the outstanding literary attack on the Colonial Office in the forties, Charles Buller's *Mr. Mother Country*, did not attack inefficiency but the misapplied efficiency of 'Mr. Over-Secretary Stephen', who was pictured as managing the Colonial Secretary as well as the colonial empire.

In the twenties and early thirties there were a few articles in newspapers and periodicals that made suggestions for the improvement of the office. Mr. Henry F. G. Tucker in his comprehensive M.A. thesis, 'The Press and the Colonies 1802–1833', has noted one such suggestion that was made in 1823. The emphasis on that occasion was on the need for proper provision for the transaction of colonial business 'and especially for a confidential intercourse between those responsible for ecclesiastical affairs.'[1] This may be the germ of the idea that led in the following year to the establishment of the office of Chaplain-General for the Colonies.[2] A more detailed suggestion made in 1830 proposed the attachment to the Colonial Office of a council of three or more commissioners whose duty it would be to develop the resources of the empire. The members of the council would have referred to them all questions concerning emigration, colonial constitutions, laws, and appointments. An interesting constitutional innovation was proposed, namely, that the commissioners be both permanent officials and members of the Privy Council.[3] They would be required to attend the Privy Council whenever appeals from the colonies were to be heard. The idea of a council without executive responsibilities equipped to give expert advice on colonial matters was an old one. The Board of Trade, in theory at least, was such a council in the old empire and the restored Board of Trade, when put on a permanent basis in 1786, was supposed to exercise the same function. It did not do so after 1800 and an attempt made in 1848 to revive its consultative functions[4] in colonial questions met with little success. In foreign and home affairs the conciliar role was filled by the Cabinet, but the Cabinet seldom had the time or the inclination to discuss the internal affairs of the colonies. In the absence of a council conversant with colonial

---

[1] p. 55.   [2] See above, pp. 76–7.
[3] Tucker, H. F. G., 'The Press and the Colonies 1802–1833', p. 55.
[4] Pugh, R. B., 'The Colonial Office', p. 725.

matters, the Secretary of State for the Colonies was forced to find the answers to problems within his own office.

The Colonial Office was left to its own devices at a time when its duties were increasing both in extent and in variety. Though, in 1830, the office used less paper than the Admiralty, the Foreign Office, or the Treasury,[1] the range of its responsibilities encompassed virtually the whole spectrum of government and it exercised many functions not performed by the central government in the United Kingdom. The decision to maintain authoritarian institutions in several colonies required the assumption by the state of many tasks for continuous management that, under the traditional British system, were discharged by local authorities.

There was no limit to the variety of issues on which the Secretary of State made decisions. He was consulted on the building and administration of jails, schools, churches, universities, hospitals, roads, canals, botanical gardens, defence works and barracks. He was responsible for regulations governing health, marriage, missionaries, race relations, slavery, land alienation, land use, newspapers, ship-building, and shipping. He encouraged exploration and assessed the significance of geographical discoveries. He watched over currency and banking. He had to keep in mind the interests and susceptibilities of Christians, Moslems, Jews, and animists. Law codes derived from British, Italian, Greek, French, Spanish, Portuguese, and Dutch systems, and in many cases influenced by indigenous customary law, had to be amended. Moreover, general policy applicable to a number of colonies had to be fitted into the context of each individual social and legal system. And overriding all else was the golden calf of revenue and expenditure before which all administration bowed down.

At the beginning of the century colonial policy was, as was said of American foreign policy in the inter-war years, 'largely a product of cables received from abroad.' The management of affairs was left in the hands of the men on the spot. Gradually, however, the office equipped itself with a body of information and of principles, prejudices, and practices that guided its decisions. Colonies were to be imbued with the principles of the Mother Country but were not to be saddled with the Mother

[1] See above, p. 156.

Country's institutions—unless they were demanded by the colonials themselves. Colonial legal systems should be allowed to develop independently of the legal system in England and should be amended in response to the needs of the colonial community. The protection of the rights of native peoples in the colonies were to be looked upon as a special responsibility. The basic traditions of the office owe a great deal to James Stephen, who established an enormous body of precedents for his successors to follow.

In the British system of government as it existed at the beginning of the nineteenth century it was still easy for the administrative structure to be altered in response to new needs. The distinction between practice and theory, between constitutional and legal, was a manifestation of the flexibility that underlay and underpinned the rigid superstructure of ancient custom. Circumvention, rather than reform, was, however, the accepted method of dealing with restrictive conventions. It is, therefore, only by studying the actual day-to-day operations of government departments that it is possible to discover how decisions were reached. Between 1820 and 1850 great changes took place in the relationship between the permanent officials and the political heads in almost all the central departments, perhaps most notably in the Treasury and the Colonial Office. It is unfortunate that so little is known about the process of change in the Treasury, for its decisions affected the day-to-day working of all other departments.

Several worth-while features of the early nineteenth-century government service were inherited by the Civil Service as it emerged in the last half of the century. The informality and sense of social equality, which, James Stephen complained, made office discipline impossible, acted as a bar to the emergence of a rigidly hierarchical administrative structure. This informality arose out of the association between government and gentility which also gave to employment in the government service a social prestige that may have helped to attract able men who would not otherwise have been tempted by the prospects that such employment offered. Security of tenure, pensions on retirement, and adequate, though not handsome, salaries were also valuable legacies from the earlier period. So was the tradition of regulating conditions in the service by order in council rather than by parliamentary statute. The most important inheritance of all, however, was the eighteenth-century practice of placing a Parliament man at the head of every efficient office and assigning him responsibility for policy. In the co-ordination of government policies he represented the office in the Cabinet and in dealing with the Prime Minister. The policies for which he accepted the praise and took the blame from Parliament were looked upon as his own policies, framed by himself and not merely selected from alternative proposals by his subordinates. All transactions of the department were conducted by him or in his name, and the use of the name of a Secretary of State by an Under-Secretary was not, and did not become, the mere ritual that was involved in the use of the King's name by the Secretary of State.

APPENDIX I

OFFICE OF THE THIRD SECRETARY OF STATE 1794 – 1830

SECRETARIES OF STATE		UNDER-SECRETARIES	
(Henry Dundas)		(Evan Nepean)	
July 11, 1794–Mar. 17, 1801		July 11, 1794–Mar. 1, 1795	
		(Wm. Huskisson)	–May 18, 1801
Lord Hobart	–May 14, 1804	John Sullivan	–May 14, 1804
Lord Camden	–July 10, 1805	Edward Cooke[1]	–Feb. 16, 1806
Lord Castlereagh	–Feb. 4, 1806		
Wm. Windham	–Mar. 25, 1807	Sir George Shee	–Mar. 25, 1807
		(Sir Jas. Cockburn)–	
		No. 26, 1806–Mar. 25, 1807	
Lord Castlereagh	–Oct. 31, 1809	Edward Cooke	–Oct. 31, 1809
		(Hon. Charles	
		Stewart)	–Apr. 30, 1809
		(Hon. Frederick	
		Robinson)	–Oct. 31, 1809
		(Henry E.	
Lord Liverpool	–June 10, 1812	Bunbury)[2]	–July 5, 1816
		Hon. Cecil	
		Jenkinson	–June 10, 1810
		Robert Peel	–Aug. 4, 1812
Lord Bathurst	–Apr. 30, 1827	Henry Goulburn	–Dec. 11, 1821
		R. J. Wilmot	
Lord Goderich	–Sept. 3, 1827	Horton	–Jan. 5, 1828
		Robert Wm. Hay[3]	
		July 5, 1825–	1836
		Hon. E. G. Stanley	
Wm. Huskisson	–May 30, 1828	Oct. 15, 1827[4]–Feb. 5, 1828	
		Lord Francis	
		Leveson Gower	–May 30, 1828
Sir Geo. Murray	–Nov. 22, 1830	Horace Twiss	–Nov. 22, 1830

The round brackets indicate War Department.

[1] On pension of £600: Feb. 17, 1806–March 25, 1807: Nov. 1, 1809–Feb. 27, 1812.

[2] Pension July 6, 1816–£650 a year, forfeited in 1821.

[3] Permanent under-secretary.

[4] Did not draw official salary until Jan. 6, 1828.

APPENDIX II

Name	Dates
Wm. Garthshore	on original Est^t – July 5, 1797
Wm. Budge	
Fred^k Colquhoun	shared salary
Arch^d Hepburn Mitchelson	July 5, 1797 – July 5, 1799
Wm. Budge	
Hugh Stuart	July 5, 1799 – March 17, 1801
James Colquhoun	(Hugh Stuart to Feb. 20, 1801)
R. B. Adderley	Feb. 17, 1801 – Sept. 18, 1801
Granville Penn	Sept. 18, 1801 – Jany 19, 1802
Honble Wm. Eden	Jany 19, 1802 – May 14, 1804
George Watson	May 15, 1804 – July 10, 1805
Robt Wood	July 10, 1803 – Feby 4, 1806
Thomas Amyot	Feby 5, 1806 – March 25, 1807
Robt Wood	March 26, 1807 – Oct. 31, 1809
Robt Willimot	Nov. 1, 1809 – June 10, 1812
Charles Greville	June 11, 1812 – June 13, 1821
Honble Charles Percy	June 14, 1821 – Jany 5, 1826
Henry Greville	Jany 5, 1826 – April 30, 1827
B. Balfour	May 1, 1827 – Sept. 3, 1827
Edward Leeves	Sept. 4, 1827 – May 30, 1828
Lt.-Col. Wedderburn	June 21, 1828 – Nov. 22, 1830
B. Balfour	Nov. 23, 1830 –

A minister's Private secretary has the care and management, under his principal's direction, of all affairs relating to the disposal of offices and employments. Henry Taylor, *The Statesman* (1836), p. 109.

Private secretaries formed part of the political element of the Colonial Office from the time of its creation, entering and leaving office with their patrons. Because of Lord Bathurst's personal idiosyncrasies his private secretaries performed little official business. Charles Greville, who was paid the salary of the office from 1812 to 1821,[1] led an official life very different from that of his opposite number at the Foreign Office, Joseph Planta, Castlereagh's able assistant. At the time of Lord Bathurst's death Greville declared:

[1] The editors of the definitive edition of his diary give the starting date as 1814. His duties from 1812 to 1814 evidently did not prevent his keeping terms at Oxford. *The Greville Memoirs*, eds. L. Strachey and R. Fulford, vol. I, p. xiii.

I was Lord Bathurst's private secretary for several years, but so far from feeling any obligation to him, I always consider his mistaken kindness in giving me that post as the source of all my misfortunes and the cause of my present condition. He never thought fit to employ me, never associated me with the interests and the business of his office, and consequently abandoned me at the age of eighteen to that life of idleness and dissipation from which I might have been saved had he felt that my future prospects in life, my character and talents, depended in great measure upon the direction which was at that moment given to my mind.[1]

Whereas all three of Bathurst's private secretaries in his fifteen years as Secretary of State were selected from his circle of family friends, Huskisson's Edward Leeves and Murray's Lt.-Col. Wedderburn were working secretaries of the type described by Taylor, responsible for social correspondence and to some extent for patronage. Wedderburn also took an interest in the military business of the office.

[1] *The Greville Memoirs 1814–1860*, Aug. 5, 1834, vol. III, pp. 65–6.

CLERKS IN THE OFFICE OF THE SECRETARY OF STATE FOR WAR
(and the colonies after 1801) 1794 – 1830

Name	Dates of Entry and End of Service	Remarks (beginning with rank on entry) (figures in brackets refer to age on appointment)
William Huskisson	Jan. 1795 Mar. 1, 1795	Chief Clerk. Promoted Under-Secretary. Needs no further introduction.
James Chapman	Jan. 1795 Apr. 5, 1824	2nd Clerk. Original appointment Home Office 1784. Chief Clerk Mar. 1, 1795. Retired at age of 57. Held sinecure post of secretary Trinidad. Pension £1,100.
Adam Gordon	Jan. 1795 Mar. 31, 1833	3rd Clerk. Original appointment Home Office 1791. 2nd Clerk Mar. 1, 1795. Senior clerk in the colonial department. Chief Clerk Apr. 5, 1824. Naval officer Trinidad, 1801. Agent for Demerara 1804. Agent for Lower Canada, 1814. Son of an American Loyalist.
William Budge	Jan. 1795 Apr. 9, 1805	4th Clerk.
Frederick Colquhoun	Jan. 1795 Feb. 20, 1801	5th Clerk. Pension £300.
Henry Manningham	Jan. 1795 Oct. 10, 1798	6th Clerk.
Anthony Benn	Mar. 1, 1795 Aug. 2, 1812	6th Clerk. Pension £220 paid to his widow Francis Maria Benn until her death Apr. 5, 1821.
Edm^d Faunce Chapman	Oct. 10, 1798 Oct. 10, 1801	6th Clerk. Listed as absent-on-leave until Jan. 5, 1804.
Francis Kelsey	Jan. 1798 Apr. 5, 1816	Extra Clerk. Sometimes appears after 1816 as a copying clerk. Was 58 in 1816. Pension £239/10.

Name	Dates of Entry and End of Service	Remarks (beginning with rank on entry) (figures in brackets refer to age on appointment)
W. R. Wulbier	Jan. 1798 Apr. 5, 1816	Extra Clerk. Appointment at Exchequer Nov. 16, 1815–1829. His cash book of fees listed in Audit Office papers, A.O. 3, vol. 321. Appears occasionally as a copying clerk after 1816.
John Wilder	Oct. 10, 1799 Apr. 5, 1816	Précis Writer. Retired at age of 50. Pension £450.
Hugh Stuart	Feb. 20, 1801 Apr. 5, 1816	6th Clerk. 3rd Clerk Aug., 1812. Retired at age of 50. Private secretary July 5, 1799, Secretary and registrar, St. Lucia 1813. Spent several years of retirement in debtors' prison. Pension £562/10.
Richard Plasket	Sept. 23, 1801 Mar. 5, 1802	7th Clerk. Later as Sir Richard Plasket, colonial secretary at Malta and the Cape of Good Hope.
Granville Penn	Aug. 12, 1801 Feb. 20, 1806	Extra Clerk. Assistant Chief Clerk in war department. Private Secretary to Lord Hobart Sept. 18, 1801 to Jan. 19, 1802. Retired at age of 44. Employed in the public service for a time in 1816 but his pension was repaid him. Classical scholar and author. D.N.B. Pension £550.
George Lud. Wilder	Oct. 1, 1801	Extra Clerk. 8th Clerk Jan 5, 1804. Senior (Supernumerary) Jan. 5, 1822. 2nd. Clerk (Senior); Acting as Registrar Jan. 5, 1824.
Richard Penn	Nov. 27, 1801 Jan. 5, 1825	7th Clerk. Librarian March 15, 1807–Jan. 5, 1814. Senior clerk in war department. 3rd Clerk Apr. 5, 1816. Retired at age of 40. Agent for Ceylon 1824. Wrote humorous books. D.N.B. Pension £750.

Name	Dates of Entry and End of Service	Remarks (beginning with rank on entry) (figures in brackets refer to age on appointment)
John Forbes	Mar. 5, 1802 Jan. 5, 1824	7th Clerk. 4th Clerk Apr. 5, 1816. Senior Clerk 1822. Retired at age of 38. Died 1830. Pension £650.
Edward Barnard	Jan. 5, 1805	9th Clerk. 2nd Class Clerk Jan. 5, 1822. Retired at age of 36. Agent for N.S.W. 1822. General agent for the colonies 1833. Pension £200.
John Strachan	Apr. 10 1805 Apr. 5, 1816	9th Clerk. 8th Clerk Aug. 3, 1812. Retired at age of 37. Pension £220.
Charles Shee	Sept. 1, 1806 Sept. 13, 1807	10th Clerk. Son of Sir George Shee the Under-Secretary.
Henry Cutler	Sept. 1, 1806 Apr. 5, 1816	11th Clerk. 9th Clerk Aug. 3, 1812. Retired at age of 32. Agent for Trinidad 1816. Defaulted for £3,000, 1828. Pension £213/6/8.
Thomas Amyot	Sept. 1, 1806 July 31, 1819	12th Clerk. Norfolk attorney. Private Secretary Feb. 5, 1806. 7th Clerk 1816. Registrar of colonial slaves 1819. Wm. Windham's literary executor. Agent for Curaçao 1807. Secretary Lower Canada 1807. 'Expert in Archaeology and historical research.' D.N.B.
John M. Marsh	Sept. 14, 1807 Mar. 31. 1809	12th Clerk.
W. R. Bankhead	Jan. 22, 1808 Jan. 22, 1810	13th Clerk.
Henry Trevor Short	Mar. 31, 1809 Jan. 19, 1836	13th Clerk. 2nd Class Jan. 5, 1822: Senior Jan. 5, 1824, Head of Eastern department.
Charles de la Garde	Sep. 16, 1809 Apr. 5, 1816	Arabick Interpreter. Son-in-law of former Russian governor of Kamchatka. Lost Polish lands as result of French Revolution. Post was a sinecure. Pension on secret service funds, 1825.

Name	Dates of Entry and End of Service	Remarks (beginning with rank on entry) (figures in brackets refer to age on appointment)
George Baillie	Jan. 23, 1810 Mar. 31, 1833	13th Clerk. 2nd Class (Supernumerary) Jan. 5, 1822; Senior Jan. 5, 1824. Head of North America Department. Agent Berbice 1812. Agent Sierra Leone 1822. Acting Agent for African Corps. General Agent for the Colonies 1833. Died May 17, 1855. (18).
Peter Smith	Aug. 20, 1810	Extra Clerk. Translator of foreign languages 1814. 10th Clerk July 6, 1819. 2nd Class (Supernumerary) Jan. 5, 1822. Senior Jan. 5, 1824. Head of Mediterranean and Africa department. Agent Mauritius 1824. Remained in office for many years.
George Mayer	Dec. 17, 1810	Extra Clerk. Librarian Jan. 5, 1814. Senior status 1824.
R. W. St. John	Aug. 3, 1812 Apr. 5, 1816	13th Clerk. Later became Consul-General at Algiers.
Thomas Baillie	Aug. 1, 1819 Feb. 5, 1824	10th Clerk. Commissioner of Crown Lands, New Brunswick, 1824. (19).
Hyde Villiers	Oct. 10, 1822 July 5, 1825	3rd Class (3rd Clerk). Senior Jan. 5, 1824. Benthamite, friend of J. S. Mill. At Cambridge. Brother became Earl of Clarendon. In charge of West Indies department. Resigned to enter on a political career. (22).
Abraham Salamé	Jan. 5, 1823	Arabick Interpreter. Born Alexandria, Egypt. Came to England via British Embassy at Ankara. Also employed by Foreign Office.

Name	Dates of Entry and End of Service	Remarks (beginning with rank on entry) (figures in brackets refer to age on appointment)
Henry Taylor	Jan. 22, 1824 1872.	2nd Class (1st Clerk). Senior Jan. 5, 1825. Minor poet. Student of political theory. *Autobiography* (1885). Head of West Indies Department. (23.)
Thomas Hay	Jan. 22, 1824 July 5, 1826	2nd Class (2nd Clerk). Had been a copying clerk for a few months.
Samuel J. Blunt	Jan. 22, 1824	2nd Class (3rd Clerk). Senior Feb. 6, 1839. Trained by Stephen to review colonial laws.
William G. Chapman	Jan. 5, 1824	2nd Class (4th Clerk). Enrolled at Eton. Was never promoted to the higher class. (25).
Gordon Gairdner	Jan. 5, 1824	3rd Class (1st Clerk). 2nd Class Jan. 5, 1825. Senior Apr. 20, 1837. Chief Clerk Jan. 1, 1860. (16).
W. L. Patterson	Jan. 5, 1824	Assistant Librarian. (19).
Edmund T. Harrison	Jan. 26, 1824	3rd Class (2nd Clerk). 2nd Class July 5, 1826. Serious, hard working. Expert on constitutional questions. Senior Clerk North America department 1839. Died 1840. (21).
Hugh Drummond	Apr. 5, 1824 Jan. 27, 1829	3rd Class (3rd Clerk). 2nd Class July 5, 1826. Died 1829.
Arthur Blackwood	Apr. 5, 1824	3rd Class (4th Clerk). 2nd Class Jan. 28, 1829. Senior Aug. 30, 1840. (16).
Hon. Robert Stopford	Jan. 5, 1825 Aug. 24, 1828	3rd Class (4th Clerk). Private Secretary to Mr. Twiss (June to August 1828). Died 1828 at age of 26. Youngest brother of Earl of Courtown. Eton.

Name	Dates of Entry and End of Service	Remarks (beginning with rank on entry) (figures in brackets refer to age on appointment)
Thomas Fred^k Elliott	July 5, 1825	3rd Class (4th Clerk). Précis Writer July 5, 1827. Senior Clerk Apr. 1, 1833 in North America department. In Canada 1835. Later became one of the top officials in the office. (17).
George Barrow	July 5, 1825	3rd Class (5th Clerk). 2nd Class Jan. 20, 1836. Senior July 1, 1843. Private Secretary to Mr. Hay 1825. Son of Sir John Barrow, Secretary to the Admiralty. (18).
William Unwin	July 5, 1825	4th Class (1st Clerk). 3rd Class July 5, 1826. Second Class Aug. 28, 1839. Was still in 2nd Class in 1860s. (20).
F. Munday	July 5, 1825	4th Class (2nd Clerk). Copying clerk before his appointment. Private Secretary to Mr. Horton July 1825. Assistant Registrar June 8, 1828. (18).
Hugh Stuart Kelsey	July 5, 1825	4th Class (3rd Clerk). Extra Clerk Mar. 4, 1823. Third Class June 9, 1828. His name suggests a hereditary connection with the office. (17).
Edward Winslow	July 5, 1825 July 5, 1827	Précis Writer. Copying Clerk before his appointment.
W. Matheson	July 5, 1825 June 8, 1828	Assistant Registrar. Drew an allowance of £200 p.a. as Extra Clerk from beginning of 1824— in addition to his salary as Assistant Registrar after July 5, 1825. 'W. Matheson' was appointed secretary and Clerk of the Crown in Nevis, Oct. 10, 1828.

Name	Dates of Entry and End of Service	Remarks (beginning with rank on entry) (figures in brackets refer to age on appointment)
Clere Talbot	July 5, 1826	4th Class (3rd Clerk). Private Secretary to Mr. Twiss, Lord Howick and later Parl. Under-Secretaries. 3rd Class Aug. 25, 1828. (19).
Vane Jadis	Aug. 6, 1827	4th Class (3rd Clerk). 3rd Class Jan. 28, 1829. 2nd Class Apr. 1, 1846. Still in 2nd Class in 1860s. (19).
James Walker	June 9, 1828 Jan. 25, 1837 (resigned).	4th Class (3rd Clerk). Supernumerary 1825. 3rd Class Jan. 20, 1836. (19).
W. H. C. Murdoch	Aug. 25, 1828	4th Class (3rd Clerk). Supernumerary 1826. 2nd Class 1836. Very brilliant clerk. Became one of the leading officials in the office. In Canada in the forties. (19).
J. S. Martin	Apr. 5, 1829	4th Class (3rd Clerk). Supernumerary 1828. 3rd Class 1836. Private Secretary to Earl of Aberdeen Dec. 1834–July 1835; to Mr. Stephen 1836. Died 1839.
Charles Cox	Jan. 20, 1836	4th Class. Supernumerary 1829. 3rd Class 1839. 2nd Class 1847. Senior 1860. Son of the army agent. Eton.
J. Walpole	Jan. 26, 1837	4th Class. Supernumerary 1830. Eton.

Other individuals who appear as supernumeraries (paid) are E. Lamb (1829); – Stewart (1829 to March 9, 1830) and G. Armstrong.

Lamb and Stewart were accepted as supernumeraries in Letters dated Sept. 6, 1828.

APPENDIX IV

An Account of the Salaries, Allowances, New Year's Gifts, and Perquisites, received in the Office of The SECRETARIES OF STATE for The Home, Foreign, and War Departments, in the Years ended the 5th January 1815, and the 5th January 1816; distinguishing each year, and the different Departments, and the Persons by whom the Salaries have been received.

So far as the same regards the Office of the Secretary of State for the COLONIAL and WAR Departments, for the Year ended 5th January 1815.

Employment	Salary £ s. d.	Remuneration for Length of Service £ s. d.	Allowances £ s. d.	New Year's Gifts	Perquisites	Names of Persons Employed
Secretary of State	6000 0 0	None	None	None	None	The Earl Bathurst
Private Secretary	300 0 0	None	None	None	None	Charles Cavendish Greville
Chief Clerk	1000 0 0	B.250 0 0	75 8 4	None	£42 Agency on Passing Commissions under the Great Seal	James Chapman
Précis Writer	300 0 0	C.300 0 0	None	None	None	John Wilder. Employment ceases on 5th April 1816
Keeper of the Papers and Librarian	200 0 0	None	None	None	None	George Mayer
Translator	200 0 0	None	None	None	None	Peter Smith
Office-Keeper	44 4 7	None	None	£20 0 0	£60 with Coals and Candles	Ths. Camis to 14th June 1814 (Deceased)
	24 7 4	None	None			Ths. Allsop from 13th Oct. to 5th January 1815
Second Office-keeper	78 3 3	None	None	£20 0 0	£60 with Coals and Candles	John Smith to 21st Oct. 1814 (Deceased)
	18 7 9	None	None			John Littlewood from 2nd Nov. to 5th Jan. 1815
Porter	136 17 6	None	None	None	None	Arnauld Le Sage
	106 7 6	None	None			
Second Porter	7 17 6	None	None	None	None	Thos. Robinson from 3rd Nov. to 31st Dec. 1814
	22 2 6	None	None			Mrs. Pillochody
Housekeeper	100 0 0	None	None	None	£50 out of which two servants are	

274

WAR DEPARTMENT

To this Department belonged the transaction of all Business connected with Military Operations; the Garrisons and Governments of Gibraltar, Malta, the Ionian Islands, and Heligoland; and the Consulates on the Coast of Barbary.

Employment	Salary £ s. d.	Remuneration for Length of Service £ s. d.	Allowances £ s. d.	Names of Persons Employed	Remarks
U'Sec'y of State	2000 0 0	A 500 0 0	None	Sir Hy E'd Bunbury	Employment ceases 5 July 1816
Clerk	300 0 0	C 200 0 0	E 200 0 0		
Do.	200 0 0	C 200 0 0	75 8 4	Richard Penn	
Do.	100 0 0	C 61 6 8	75 8 4	John Forbes	
Extra Clerk	136 17 6	None	75 8 4	Henry Short	
	136 17 6	None	None	Peter Smith	Employment ceases 5 April 1816
Do.	136 17 6	None	None	George Mayer	Do.
Do.	121 15 0	None	None	Wm. S. Mesban. To March 4, 1814	
Do.	101 5 0	None	None	Edd Phillips. From 11 Apr. 1814	Do.
Arabick Interpreter	80 0 0	None	None	Charles de la Garde	Do.

continued overleaf

COLONIAL DEPARTMENT

This Department transacted the Business of all His Majesty's Colonies in North and South America, and the West Indies; the Settlements on the Coast of Africa, the Cape of Good Hope, the Isle of France, Ceylon and New South Wales.

Employment	Salary			Remuneration for Length of Service			Allowances			Names of Persons Employed	Remarks
	£	s.	d.	£	s.	d.	£	s.	d.		
U'sec'y of State	2000	0	0	A 500	0	0	None			Henry Goulburn, Esq	
Clerk	650	0	0	C 400	0	0	D 250	0	0		
Do.	450	0	0	C 300	0	0	75	8	4	Adam Gordon	Employment ceases
							75	8	4	Hugh Stuart	5 April 1816
Do.	150	0	0	C 200	0	0	75	8	4	Geo L. Wilder	Employment ceases
Do.	140	0	0	C 80	0	0	75	8	4	Edwd Barnard	5 April 1816
Do.	130	0	0	C 80	0	0	75	8	4	John Strachan	Do.
Do.	120	0	0	C 80	0	0	75	8	4	Henry Cutler	
Do.	110	0	0	C 80	0	0	75	8	4	Thomas Amyot	Employment ceases
Do.	80	0	0	None			75	8	4	George Baillie	5 April 1816
Do.	80	0	0	None			75	8	4	Robt W. St. John	
Extra Clerk	136	17	6	F 182	10	0	None			Fras Kelsey	Employment ceases
Extra Clerk	103	15	0	F 45	12	6	None			Wm. Rose Walbier	5 April 1816
											Do.
											Do.

A Paid under an Order of His Majesty in Council, dated 23rd January 1799.

B Paid under an Order of His Majesty in Council, dated 18th February 1801.

C The Remuneration for Length of Service is paid under an OiC, 28th Jan. 1809 for the following scale: after 5 years service £80; after 10 years service £200; after 15 years service £300; after 20 years service £400.

D Paid under OiC, 20th January 1804.

E Paid under an Order of His Royal Highness the Prince Regent in Council.

F Paid by Order of the Secretary of State, as a Remuneration for long Service. Every clerk on the Establishment receives an Allowance of £75/8/4 in lieu of Gazettes, as above.

COMPARATIVE STATEMENT OF ESTABLISHMENT OF COLONIAL OFFICE FOR THE YEARS 1821 AND 1822

Salaries 1821 £ s. d.	Establishment 1821	Establishment 1822	Scale of Salaries 1822 Minimum £ s. d.	Scale of Salaries 1822 Maximum £ s. d.	Salaries and Emoluments 1822 £ s. d.	Excess over scale £ s. d.	Assessments of 5% and 10% £ s. d.	Net Salaries 1822 £ s. d.
6000 0 0	Secretary of State	Secretary of State	6000 0 0	6000 0 0	6000 0 0	None	None	6000 0 0
2500 0 0	Under Secretary of State	Under Secretary of State	2000 0 0	2000 0 0	2000 0 0	None	None	2000 0 0
1325 8 4	Chief Clerk	Chief Clerk	1000 0 0	1250 0 0	1325 8 4	75 8 4	70 10 10	1254 16 6
1375 8 4	2nd Clerk	1st Senior Clerk	700 0 0	900 0 0	1375 8 4	475 8 4	92 10 10	1282 17 6
1125 4 4	3rd Do.	2nd Do.	600 0 0	800 0 0	1125 8 4	325 8 4	72 10 10	1052 17 6
758 15 0	4th Do.	3rd Do.	600 0 0	800 0 0	758 15 0	38 15 0	39 17 6	718 17 6
675 8 4	5th Do.	1st Assistant Clerk	350 0 0	545 0 0	720 0 0[a]	None	36 0 0	684 0 0
525 8 4	6th Do.	2nd Do.	350 0 0	545 0 0	525 8 4	25 8 4	27 10 10	497 17 6
415 8 4	7th Do.	3rd Do.	350 0 0	545 0 0	440 0 0[b]	None	22 0 0	418 0 0
405 8 4	8th Do.	1st junior Clerk	150 0 0	300 0 0	440 0 0	None	22 0 0	418 0 0
395 8 4	9th Do.	2nd Do.	150 0 0	300 0 0	395 8 4	95 8 4	19 15 9	375 12 7
185 8 4	10th Do.	3rd Do.	150 0 0	300 0 0	185 8 4	5 8 4	5 5 4¼	180 2 11¼
300 0 0	Private Secretary	Private Secretary	300 0 0	300 0 0	300 0 0	None	None	300 0 0
400 0 0	Librarian	Librarian	350 0 0	545 0 0	480 0 0	None	24 0 0	456 0 0
100 0 0	Housekeeper	Housekeeper	100 0 0	100 0 0	100 0 0	None	2 10 0[d]	97 10 0
100 0 0	Office Keeper	Office Keeper	100 0 0	100 0 0	180 0 0[f]	None	4 10 0[d]	175 10 0
100 0 0	2nd Do.	2nd Do.	100 0 0	100 0 0	180 0 0[f]	None	4 10 0[d]	175 10 0
136 17 6[e]	Office Porter[c]	Office Porter	136 17 6	136 17 6	160 0 0[f]	None	4 0 0[d]	156 0 0
136 17 6[e]	2nd Do.	2nd Do.	136 17 6	136 17 6	160 0 0[f]	None	4 0 0[d]	156 0 0

* Based in a draft in CO 323/194 under 'Treasury'.

a The 5th clerk, George Wilder, was classed as a supernumerary senior clerk.

b The 8th, George Baillie, and the 9th clerk, Peter Smith, were classed as supernumerary assistant clerks.

c Placed on establishment in 1822: previously paid from contingency fund.

d On salaries between £100 and £200 the assessment was 2½% (3 Geo. IV. C. 113).

e These figures appear in the original draft table as £137/5/0, but in other places as £136/17/6. They had been paid up to this time at the rate of 7/6d per day, so the figure £137/5/0 must have been taken from 1820 which was a leap year.

f Salaries, plus New Year's Gifts and Perquisites.

APPENDIX VI

ESTABLISHMENT OF THE COLONIAL OFFICE 1831*

Office	Date of Appointment		Salary		
			£	s.	d.
Secretary of State	23 Nov^r	1830	6000	0	0
U. Sec'y of State	5 July	1825	2000	0	0
Do.	23 Nov^r	1830	2000	0	0
Chief Clerk	17 May	1791	1500	0	0
2nd Clerk (Acting as Registrar)	1 Oct^r	1801	900	0	0
1st Senior Clerk (a)	31 March	1809	875	6	8
2nd Do. (b)	23 Jan^y	1810	759	1	4
3rd Do. (c)	20 Aug^t	1810	747	12	4
4th Do.	22 Jan^y	1824	700	0	0
1st Assistant Clerk	22 Jan^y	1824	440	0	0
2nd Do.	5 Jan^y	1824	440	0	0
3rd Do.	5 Jan^y	1824	425	0	0
4th Do.	26 Jan^y	1824	417	10	0
5th Do.	5 April	1824	364	1	8
1st Junior Clerk	5 July	1825	195	0	0
2nd Do.	5 July	1825	185	0	0
3rd Do.	5 July	1825	165	14	10
4th Do.	5 July	1826	163	14	2
5th Do.	6 Aug^t	1827	159	7	9
1st Assist^t Junior Clerk	9 June	1828	115	14	10
2nd Do.	25 Aug^t	1828	113	14	2
3rd Do.	5 April	1829	107	10	0
Private Sec'y to Sec'y of State	23 Nov^r	1830	300	0	0
Librarian	17 Dec^r	1810	741	2	0
Assist^t Do.	5 Jan^y	1824	260	9	0
Assist^t Registrar	5 July	1825	175	14	10
Precis Writer	5 July	1825	337	10	0
Private Sec'y to Un. Sec'y[1]			150	0	0
Do.[1]			150	0	0
Office Keeper	22 May	1810	100	0	0
Do.	7 April	1819	100	0	0
Office Porter	20 Jan^y	1823	136	17	6
Do.	5 Jan^y	1829	136	17	6
Housekeeper	5 Jan^y	1795	100	0	0
Colonial Counsel[2]		1813	1000	0	0

Emoluments from other Appointments

Chief Clerk [Adam Gordon]

Agent for Demerara appointed in 1804 by the Governor and Court of Policy. Salary £400 per Annum paid by the Colony.

Upon the abolition in 1826 of the Naval Offices in all the Colonies the compensation for the loss of the appointment of Naval Officer at Trinidad was fixed as £572/11 per Annum payable from the Colonial Funds. A saving was thereby immediately effected; the whole to fall in at the death of the present holder to whom the appointment was granted on the capture of the Island in 1801.

(a) [Henry Short]

Agent for Trinidad appointed by Governor and Council August 1828 £344 per Annum from Colonial Funds.

(b) [George Baillie]

Agent for Sierra Leone and other settlements on the West Coast of Africa. Appointed 1 April 1822 by Act of Colonial Legislature £500 payable from Colonial Funds and as Acting Agent for the African Corps £55/9/5 on Army Estimates.

(c) [Peter Smith]

Agent for Mauritius appointed in 1824 by the Governor and Council—Salary £500 per Annum for [*sic*] Colonial Funds.

*C.O. 324/146   Hay to Spring Rice (Treasury), July 22, 1831.

1. Clere Talbot,
fifth junior clerk was private secretary to the political under-secretary Lord Howick: George Barrow, the first junior clerk was private secretary to the permanent under-secretary, Robert W. Hay.

2. James Stephen's salary of £500 from the Board of Trade has been omitted from the original.

C.O. 324/75, ff. 193-5.

AN OFFER OF AN APPOINTMENT IN THE COLONIAL OFFICE

S. T. Wilde to Robert William [*sic*] Horton, private, (January 1824)

With reference to the communication you have done me the honor to make to me this morning respecting the situation in the Colonial Department which Lord Bathurst has been so kind as to offer to my acceptance I request you will have the goodness to present to his Lordship my warmest thanks, for the interest he has taken in my affairs and to assure him that I will endeavour by my exertion to merit the patronage which he has thus shewn himself willing to extend to me.—As you have expressed a wish that I should detail to you the conversation that has taken place between us this morning, I beg leave to state that upon my introduction to you after promising that the communication was strictly confidential, you were kind enough to offer to my acceptance a situation in the Colonial Office of 350£ per annum holding out the prospect of succeeding at the next vacancy to one of 600 and ultimately to one of 900£. You mentioned at the same time that the duties to be fulfilled were of the most important nature and required the strictest attention and great ability in the person appointed to perform them. I represented to you that my present income was about 750£—my assured income being 250 and my professional one averaging 500—and increasing. You then asked me whether if my income could be made up to 600£ I would accept the situation. I requested to be permitted to leave it to yourself whether under such circumstances I ought to do so or not. You then enquired whether I knew any person capable of fulfilling the duties required. I immediately mentioned the name of my brother-in-law Mr. Sam[l] Howlett, a gentleman whose knowledge of the French Language and whose former commercial pursuit added to his general habits of business rendered him in my humble opinion fully capable of performing all that might be required of him. In compliance with your request that I would refrain from making any communication to him of what has passed this morning as you were fearful that his age being about 43 might be an objection I will certainly not do so until I have your permission. I have once more to request that you will present to Lord Bathurst my best thanks for his condescension requesting that you will attribute any misunderstanding of what has passed between us to the agitation which your communication has caused.

Minute by Wilmot Horton:

This is the result of my conference with Mr. Wilde, which I desired him to put in writing. He has not reported it *quite* correctly, but sufficiently so for your Lordship to perceive that it could not answer *to him* to accept it.

With respect to his Brother-in-Law it would appear that his appointment would almost be an equal favour to Mr. Wildeand I laid *a ship* (skip?) on the objection *of age*, not as really considering it an impediment, but that if your Lordship did not approve any experiment being made of him, I could slide out of the proposal upon grounds not hurting the amour propre of *any* party.

I explained that in either case, vizt of Mr. Wilde's or of his Beau-frere's appointment, if at the expiration of an adequate period of probation they were not found to be competent to the arduous duties etc. etc., they would have to retire—to that condition he *willingly* assented both with respect to his Brother in Law as well as to himself *could* he have taken the situation.

Minute by Lord Bathurst:

You had better *slide out* of the proposal for the Brother-in-Law as I am sure as good may be found, for he seems not to be in official habits.

CO 854/1

APPENDIX VIII

See above, pp. 244–51.

COMPARATIVE STATEMENT OF THE INCREASE OF BUSINESS IN THE SECRETARY OF STATE'S OFFICE WAR AND COLONIAL DEPARTMENT, FOR THE YEARS 1806, 1816, AND 1824

Colonies	1806 Second Under Secretary appointed by Mr. Wyndham [sic]				1816 Office of Under Secretary abolished				1824 Year previous to re-appointment of Second Under Secretary			
	Received		Dispatched		Received		Dispatched		Received		Dispatched	
	Letters	Pages	Letters	Pages	Letters	Pages	Letters	Pages	Letters	Pages	Letters	Pages
Lower Canada	70	222	9	10	550	2476	114	144	223	1338	48	72
Upper Canada	72	245	10	9	111	657	43	47	201	1545	36	39
Nova Scotia	33	168	6	10	115	355	32	41	90	458	12	11
Cape Breton	45	158	3	4	40	151	4	4				
New Brunswick	35	102	3	7	32	121	11	10	86	368	31	64
Prince Edward Island	50	184	5	5	60	327	11	8	105	1156	19	32
Newfoundland	39	340	4	6	105	386	10	10	162	1233	20	17
Bermuda	73	186	9	11	71	193	16	19	103	667	11	16
Barbados	30	120	7	10	56	257	27	34	165	516	37	64
Berbice	19	210	5	4	67	1006	18	35	74	404	36	37
Demerara and Essequibo	25	82	8	17	102	629	29	44	173	1236	70	145
Grenada	85	249	11	12	42	154	14	12	48	138	17	19
St. Kitts, Nevis & Tortola					57	217	24	26	132	288	37	58
Antigua and Montserrat	53	278	13	16	50	180	21	19	100	473	31	45
St. Lucia	21	65	2	2	34	216	13	7	79	514	25	20
St. Vincent	59	271	5	13	45	114	16	14	35	155	16	22
Trinidad	104	550	12	13	206	1296	59	54	140	543	53	210
Tobago	33	106	5	8	37	86	12	7	53	128	14	27
Dominica	44	103	8	10	87	335	14	19	129	550	30	37

Column group descriptions:
- **1806** — Second Under Secretary appointed by Mr. Wyndham [sic]
- **1816** — Office of Under Secretary abolished
- **1824** — Year previous to re-appointment of Second Under Secretary

Colonies	1806 Received Letters	1806 Received Pages	1806 Dispatched Letters	1806 Dispatched Pages	1816 Received Letters	1816 Received Pages	1816 Dispatched Letters	1816 Dispatched Pages	1824 Received Letters	1824 Received Pages	1824 Dispatched Letters	1824 Dispatched Pages
Bahamas	83	166	7	13	76	535	19	20	51	168	24	34
Jamaica	109	393	16	26	156	530	31	47	233	875	52	66
Honduras	15	71	—	—	52	258	9	12	55	143	9	9
Surinam	38	225	2	6	Surinam ceded to the Netherlands							
Malta	41	263	21	24	97	398	97	75	254	486	170	261
Gibraltar	54	295	25	23	128	864	79	69	88	290	66	64
Barbary States and Missions to Interior of Africa	50	328	26	24	76	260	63	52	225	1336	128	169
Cape of Good Hope	40	460	19	28	135	570	86	95	182	2074	240	270
Ceylon	130	920	11	15	228	2373	135	140	216	662	224	234
New South Wales and Van Diemen's Land	83	680	15	29	374	1355	349	320	964	2265	1104	729
Windward and Leeward Islands	56	340	19	32	Included in Barbados Correspondence							
East India	—	—	—	—	45	152	27	25	8	15	15	138
Goree	6	104	4	7	Goree ceded to France							
Sierra Leone and African Forts	New Possessions				247	812	35	96	240	1776	324	289
Mauritius					286	1228	173	138	289	2213	354	330
Ionian Islands					142	1016	63	74	225	2160	193	300
Heligoland					51	164	30	23	26	35	14	16
Miscellaneous Correspondence with various Departments and Private Individuals on Colonial Affairs.[1]	58	170	612	528	527	2598	1477	1207	2153	9351	1416	1313
Total Colonial Correspondence..	1653	8054	902	922	4487	22269	3161	2957	7491[2]	35836[2]	4959[2]	5257[2]

continued overleaf

The War Department's correspondence for 1806 was about two-thirds that of the Colonial Department; 1,078 letters received containing 4,621 folio pages; 645 letters despatched occupying 727 pages in the entry books. The total correspondence of the Secretary of State's office for 1806 was, therefore, 2,731 letters received filling 12,675 folio pages; 1,547 letters despatched filling 1,649 pages in the entry books.

Papers laid before the House of Commons.

1806	2 papers filling		14 printed folio pages		
1816	14 ,,	,,	246 ,,	,,	,,
1824	22 ,,	,,	780 ,,	,,	,,
1825	36 ,,	,,	2,200 ,,	,,	,,

Number of Clerks in Office of Secretary of State for War and the Colonies.

1806	1816	1824
1 Chief Clerk	1 Chief Clerk	1 Chief Clerk
11 Clerks	9 Clerks	13 Clerks
1 Précis Writer	1 Librarian	1 Librarian
		1 assistant librarian
2 extra Clerks		1 extra clerk
—	—	—
15	11	17[3]

Increase in Business in the Admiralty (from 8th Report Select Committee Finance)[4]

	1791	1799	1812	1816	1817
Pages of Entry	998	2447	8068	4727	4969
Number of Clerks	16	26	56	30	30

Number of Clerks Employed in Each of the Six Principal Banking Establishments in the Metropolis

Barclay & Co.	56	Pole & Co.	40	Esdaile & Co.	37
Coutts & Co.	32	Masterman & Co.	36	Glyn & Co.	40

[1] Before 1817 the incoming letters later classified under this heading were not filed separately: the figures given for 1806 and 1816 appear to be a count of letters in the general correspondence, the total for 1824 includes both general correspondence and miscellaneous and inter-departmental letters referring to particular colonies.

[2] These totals include letters from and to the commissions of enquiry overseas: viz., 26 letters of 157 pages from the Commission on Apprenticed Africans with 27 letters of 27 pages sent to these commissions: 50 letters of 120 pages from the Commission on Criminal Justice in the West Indies, 56 letters of 72 pages in the entry books sent to the commissioners.

[3] A home secretary and clerk to the overseas commissions of enquiry were also employed during most of 1824.

[4] These figures appear as a note on the original printed document.

APPENDIX IX

See above, p. 137.

Regulations for Numbering and Docketing Despatches and Papers Sent to the Colonial Office.

1. To be written in large legible hand on folio paper ¼ of page being left on inner side as a margin.

2. Despatches to be numbered, beginning at the commencement of each year with number I.

3. Despatches on subjects not immediately connected with the series of official correspondence, or on private matters, not to be numbered, but they should be marked 'Separate' or 'Private'.

4. Each despatch is to be confined to one subject.

5. Contents of the enclosures are to be briefly stated in the body of the despatch, attention is to be paid to points particularly deserving of notice. Translations are to be provided of enclosures in a foreign language. Wherever an enclosure is referred to in the body of a despatch a line is to be drawn in the margin with the number of the enclosure affixed to the line. Each series of enclosures is to be numbered in each despatch commencing with number 1.

6. Docketing.

1st line	Writer.
2nd line	Number.
3rd line	Number of its enclosures, if any.
4th line	the word 'Received'.
5th line	Blank for the date of the day on which the Despatch shall be received.
6th line	Short precis or abstract of its contents. Docket of Enclosure will state what the enclosure is, also the date and number, the reference to the despatch in which it is transmitted.

7. 'All Dispatches are to be made up and sealed in the manner used for the letter which accompanies this memorandum.'

8. 'The receipt of Dispatches from this Office is to be acknowledged by the first opportunity.'

9. On the thirty-first of December each year a letter is to be addressed to the Colonial Office stating the number of despatches and letters which the writer may have addressed to the office during the year.

10. Despatches are to be sent direct to the secretary of state or

under-secretary and not under cover to any other person. Private correspondence is not to be sent in the same cover with official letters.

C.O. 854/1
Circular
January, 1818

APPENDIX X

See above, p. 50.

THE GOVERNMENT AND JOSEPH HUME

C.O. 324/142 Goulburn to W. Lawrence, Sept. 11, 1820.

... Grants of Land to the Extent of that solicited by you have been found so prejudicial to the Interests of the Colony and so entirely at variance with all the regulations to which his Lordship has thought it his duty to adhere, that he cannot hold out the slightest expectation of a compliance with your request.

C.O. 324/143 Goulburn to Hume, Feb. 28, 1821, refusing Hume's request of a grant of 10,000 acres in New South Wales to each of the Lawrence brothers.

... considering the great evils which have resulted to the Colonies from making large Grants of Land in the first instance, His Lordship cannot consider himself justified in departing from the established Rule. ...

C.O. 324/143 Goulburn to Lord Liverpool, Aug. 4, 1821, giving information on action taken on Hume's letter of May 21. The governor had been instructed to give grants contiguous to each other. A further portion of land was to be reserved for each of the brothers for five years, to be granted if the first portion had been cultivated.

C.O. 324/143 Goulburn to Hume, Aug. 31, 1821 informing him that a despatch, under a 'flying seal', had been sent from Lord Bathurst to the governor of New South Wales regarding land grants to the brothers Lawrence.

BIBLIOGRAPHY

Manuscript Sources

This study has been based mainly on general and miscellaneous correspondence of the Colonial Office preserved in the Public Record Office in London. The original correspondence from the public offices and from individuals, and the copies of out-letters preserved in the entry books, have provided both details of the establishment and an opportunity to observe the methods of conducting business. The correspondence of one colony, New Brunswick, has been examined in complete detail for the whole period, and the correspondence of several North American and West Indian colonies looked into (as have also the published records of Cape Colony and New South Wales). From 1823 to 1830 the registers of correspondence received were quite competently kept, and provide a useful guide to the business of the various colonies. No very significant results were obtained from efforts to delve into the papers of other departments, but Treasury Minute books (Series T.29) and Treasury indexes of letters received from the Colonial Office and from governors, commanders-in-chief, and colonial agents give a useful indication of the arrangement of business between the two departments.

Of the manuscripts in the British Museum, the Windham papers are of particular interest for Windham's period as Secretary of State and for his relations with Thomas Amyot; the Huskisson papers, already extensively used in secondary works, have been consulted, and there is much of interest in the papers of Lord Liverpool and those of Frederick Robinson, first Earl Ripon. The Sir George Murray papers in the National Library of Scotland in Edinburgh have been very helpful for the years 1828 to 1830; the Sir Thomas Cochrane papers and the Melville papers preserved there contain little material of interest for this study. At the Public Archives of Canada in Ottawa a few very interesting private letters on official matters exchanged between George Baillie, senior clerk in the North America department, and Sir Howard Douglas, the lieutenant-governor of New Brunswick, are contained in the Douglas papers.

Public Record Office

C.O. 137/	Jamaica, governors' despatches.
C.O. 138/	Jamaica, entry books of out-letters.
C.O. 188/	New Brunswick, lieutenant-governors' despatches.

C.O. 189/   New Brunswick entry books of out-letters.

C.O. 323/

     94 and 95   Law Officers' opinions on cases 1810–15, 1827–31.

     /117–139   Applications for colonial appointments, 1819–30.

     /142–3   Private letters to Earl Bathurst from the West Indies, 1824–25.

     /176–212   Original correspondence received by the Colonial Office, 'Miscellaneous and Colonies General', 1801–30.

C.O. 324/   Entry books of out-letters.

     73–4   Private letters from Earl Bathurst, 1821–27.

     /75   Minutes by Earl Bathurst, 1823–27. A miscellaneous collection, many undated, of considerable interest.

     /76–94   Private letters of R. W. Hay, 1825–36.

     /95–100   Private letters from Wilmot Horton, 1825–27.

     /101–2   Private letters from Lord Goderich and Huskisson, 1827–28.

     /103   Circulars to governors (colonial), 1794–1815.

     /104   Circular to governors, consuls and others (military), 1811–1820.

     /105–6   Circulars to governors, 1825–41.

     /133   Letters on the establishment of the office—listed as 'Letters from Chief Clerk', 1810–47.

     /134–146   Letters from Colonial Office (domestic), 1811–1832.

C.O. 325/13–19   Returns of colonial appointments, mostly replies to the enquiry in 1817.

C.O. 537/

     22   Colonial Office establishment 1832–72. Minutes, letters and memoranda.

     /25   Defence papers (Miscellaneous), 1827–46.

     /40   Personal cases (Miscellaneous), 1821–85.

     /43   Secret Service pensions.

     /89   Miscellaneous unregistered correspondence, 1792–1844.

     /155   Miscellaneous military correspondence, 1827–61.

C.O. 701/

    1–2   Contingent fund accounts of the Colonial Office, 1795–1834.

    /6   Applications to the Treasury for money, 1794–1840.

    /8, 9 and 10 Fee fund accounts, 1795–1836.

    /13   Fee book (Home Office, Foreign Office and War Office), 1795–1799.

    /14   Colonial Office estimates, 1794–1833.
    /16

C.O. 854/1   Circular despatches, mostly printed, 1808–36.

C.O. 325/21 and 22 Registers of applications for colonial appointments. The applications for 1819 to 1830, which have seldom been referred to in this study, are in C.O. 323/117 to 139.

C.O. 714/   Indexes of governors' despatches for various colonies. With the exception of Ceylon, Mauritius, New South Wales, and Trinidad, these begin in 1815 or later.

P.R.O. Indexes (C.O. 326).

8300   Notes and abstracts of Law Officers' opinions, arranged both geographically and topically, mainly 1816 to 1828 but covering the years 1811–1856.

8377–8382   Letters received and despatched in the war department, 1810–1816.

8383   Letters despatched: Malta, Barbary States, Heligoland, Cape of Good Hope, India, and Mauritius, 1816–17.

8384   Letters received from commissions of enquiry in the colonies, 1821–31.

8385–8466   Letters and despatches received by Colonial Office 1822–30. From 1825 onwards these registers follow the departmental pattern of the office—four registers of colonial despatches, one for each of the geographical departments; two of correspondence from public offices and miscellaneous persons, one for each of the under-secretaries. Additional registers of colonial despatches marked 'Letters to Mr. Wilmot Horton' and 'Letters to Mr. Hay' appear to be copies of departmental registers and are not always complete; they do, however, occasionally contain references to parliamentary questions not included in the other registers. Index 8390 (1823) and Index 8394 (1824), appearing in the P.R.O. lists as 'Letters to Mr. Hay', should be listed as 'Letters to Mr. Wilmot Horton'.

18768   Letters patent, commissions, royal instructions, warrants, etc., 1787–1842.

Manuscripts in the British Museum

Egerton Mss.	2660
Br. Mus. Add. Mss.	Chalmers papers, containing two letters
18,902	from Adam Gordon to Chalmers on West Indian trade.
37,906	Windham papers. Correspondence of Windham with Thomas Amyot.
38,290–38,302	Liverpool papers.
38,745–38,762	Huskisson papers.
40,862	Ripon papers.

National Library of Scotland

Sir George Murray papers — vols. 119 and 120 deal with the Canadian phase of Murray's career.

vols. 168–172 inclusive cover his years as Secretary of State, and also contain material on military matters not connected with his office.

vol. 203 contains a memorandum on the events of his career in his own handwriting; also a long memorandum on New South Wales by one of his protégés.

Public Archives of Canada

Sir Howard Douglas papers — Miscellaneous papers containing the Baillie letters.

New Brunswick Civil Government Letter Books, two volumes, 1824–31, containing Douglas's letters to Baillie.

Lower Canada	'Q' Series.
New Brunswick	'A' Series.
New Brunswick	Despatches Received.

Nova Scotia   'A' Series.
Prince Edward Island   'A' Series.
Calendar of Prince Edward Island State Papers—(typescript):
  vol. I   1802–27.
  vol. II 1828–40.

Printed Sources

Although this study has been based primarily on manuscript material, much use has been made of printed documents and special works. Of the monographs Mrs. Helen Taft Manning's *British Colonial Government after the Anerican Revolution* has been invaluable, and extensive use has been made of an unpublished biography of Sir Robert Wilmot Horton by E. G. Jones, presented as a thesis for the degree of M.A. at the University of Bristol in 1936. Of contemporary works, Henry Taylor's *The Statesman* is the most acute in its comments on the administrative structure. Of the printed documents the manuscripts of Henry, third Earl Bathurst, published by the Historical Manuscripts Commission, and the parliamentary papers have been most important. *The Cambridge History of the British Empire*, vol. II (1940), provides a comprehensive bibliography of colonial materials for this era (pp. 885–1004); Mr. R. B. Pugh's study, 'The Colonial Office', Chap. XIX, vol. III (1959) provides an excellent survey of the development of the office down to recent times.

Various contemporary almanacs provide lists of persons employed in public offices which are sometimes useful. They are not listed below, nor is a much more important reference work, *The Dictionary of National Biography*, which has been frequently consulted. Various school lists, lists of graduates of the universities and of members of the legal fraternity have been consulted. Always in the background of one's mind in this type of study are the works of fiction in which government offices form a background; Dickens' *Little Dorrit* with its 'Circumlocution Office', Trollope's *The Three Clerks*, and Disraeli's *Endymion* are three outstanding examples.

Parliamentary Papers

The reports of the commission appointed in 1780 to enquire into public accounts (see Keir, D. L., 'Economical Reform 1779–1787' in the *Law Quarterly Review*, July 1934) provide a wealth of information on the civil service of the late eighteenth century. Later, parliamentary committees on finance, notably those of 1797 and 1828, carried on this tradition of intensive enquiry into the departments of government. The 'Report of the Select Committee on Public Offices, Downing Street' in 1839 gives a clear picture of the nature of the accommodation provided for the Colonial Office (H.C. 1839 XIII (466) 241–54). For an insight into the complicated structure of colonial finances an excellent document is the 'Report of the Select Committee on the Preparation of Colonial Accounts' (H.C. 1837 VII (516) 305–543). Statements were published annually in the parliamentary papers giving the increase and diminution of salaries, pensions and departmental expenses; they record the changes in the establishment from year to year. They can be readily consulted in their manuscript form in C.O. 701/14 in the Public Record Office. A list of parliamentary papers on colonial policy and administration for this period is available in the *Cambridge History of the British Empire*, vol. II (1940), pp. 898–9. Most of the parliamentary debates that have been helpful have already been quoted in other works.

The most useful of the parliamentary papers for the immediate purposes of this study were:

H.C. 1814–15 VII (353) 399–405.	Salaries and emoluments of governors and military officers in the colonies.
H.C. 1816 XIII (196 and 197) 128–33.	Salaries and emoluments in the Colonial Office in 1814 and 1815.
H.C. 1817 XVII (129) 231–242.	Accounts relating to officers in the colonies.
H.C. 1821 XIV (602) 135–7.	Return of all persons in civil, military and naval establishments in Great Britain and Ireland who hold two or more commissions, retired allowances or pensions.
H.C. 1825 XV (157) 233–310.	First Report of the Commission of Criminal Justice in the West Indies.
H.C. 1825 XIX (314) 17–18.	Increase and diminution of salaries and pensions in the Colonial Office for 1824.
H.C. 1826 XXII (220) 501–31.	Superannuation allowances granted subsequently to 5 July 1822.
H.C. 1826–27 XX (301) 499–507	Account of the expense of commissions of enquiry in the last twenty years.
H.C. 1828 V (420) 3–475.	Second Report from the Select Committee on Public Income and Expenditure, Ordnance Estimates.
H.C. 1828 V (480) 479–539	Third Report from the Select Committee on Public Income and Expenditure, Superannuations.
H.C. 1828 V (519) 543–665	Fourth Report from the Select Committee on Public Income and Expenditure, Revenue, Expenditure, Debt.

H.C. 1828 VII (569) 375–733	Report from the Select Committee on the Civil Government of Canada.
H.C. 1829 VI (290 and 325).	Reports of Commissioners appointed to inquire into the mode of keeping Official Accounts, etc.
H.C. 1829 XXI (212) 63.	Account of expenses incurred and of reports of commissions of enquiry 1827–8.
H.C. 1830 XVIII (88 and 89) 485–505.	Estimates, etc. Miscellaneous services 1830.
H.C. 1830 XVIII (127) 546–551.	Sum expended for civil contingencies 1829.
H.C. 1830–31 IV (64 and 194) 1–179.	Reports of the Commissioners appointed to enquire into the Receipt and Expenditure of the Revenue in the Colonies and Foreign Possessions.
H.C. 1830–31 VII (23) 227–283.	Persons receiving emoluments of more than £1,000 from posts under government 1829–30.
H.C. 1830–31 VII (92) 299–415.	Returns of the number and pay or salaries of all persons employed in public departments: 1797–1827.
H.C. 1831–32 XXVI (194) 566.	Return of all houses the property of the public, and how occupied.
H.C. 1831–32 XXVI (512) 501.	Account of expenses incurred and of reports of commissions of enquiry 1829–30.
H.C. 1833 VII (650) 1–354	Report of the Select Committee on Army and Navy Appointments.
H.C. 1833 XII (717) 126	Treasury Minute (1831) on the Expenditure and Revenues of the Colonies.
H.C. 1837 VII (516) 305–543.	Report of the Select Committee on the Preparation of Colonial Accounts.
H.C. 1839 XIII (466) 235–59.	Minutes of Evidence before the Select Committee on Public Offices, Downing Street.
H.C. 1845 VIII (520) 1 et seq.	Report of the Select Committee on the Preparation of Colonial Accounts.
H.C. 1854 XXVII (1715) 79–97.	Report of the Committee of Enquiry into the Colonial Office, dated Dec. 15, 1849.
H.C. 1854–55 XX (1870) 1–477.	Papers relating to the reorganization of the Civil Service.

Collections, Publications of Documents, Personal Correspondence, Contemporary Historical Works and Memoirs

Arbuthnot, Charles   *The Correspondence of Charles Arbuthnot,* ed. A. Aspinall, Camden Third Series, LXV, 1941.

Arbuthnot   *The Journal of Mrs. Arbuthnot 1820–1832,* eds. Francis Bamford and the 7th Duke of Wellington, 2 vols., 1950.

Aspinall, Arthur, ed.   *Three Early Nineteenth Century Diaries,* 1952.

Australia, Historical Records of, introduction by Frederick Watson, Series I, 26 vols., Series IV, 1 vol., Sydney, 1914–25.

Baillie, Thomas   *Summary of the Case of Mr. Thomas Baillie, Late Chief Commissioner of Crown Lands and Forests and Surveyor General of New Brunswick,* 1858.

Banks, Joseph   *The Banks Letters, a Calendar of the Manuscript Correspondence of Sir Joseph Banks preserved in the British Museum, the British Museum (Natural History) and other collections in Great Britain.* ed. Warren R. Dawson, 1958.

Barrow, Sir George   *Ceylon: Past and Present,* 1857.

Barrow, Sir John   *Autobiographical Memoir,* 1847.

Bathurst Papers   *Report on the Manuscripts of Earl Bathurst, preserved at Cirencester Park,* ed. Francis Bickley, Hist. Mss. Comm. No. 76, 1923.

Bell, K. N. and Morrell, W. P.   *Select Documents on British Colonial Policy 1830–1860,* Oxford, 1928.

Bunbury, Sir H. E., Bart.   *Memoir and Literary Remains of Lieutenant-General Sir Henry Edward Bunbury, Bart.,* ed. by his son Sir C. J. F. Bunbury, 1868.

Canadian Archives Reports, Ottawa. Those for 1897, 1898, 1930, 1933, 1935, 1938, 1946 and 1948 have calendars of state papers for the colonies of Lower Canada, Upper Canada and Nova Scotia in the years 1812 to 1830.

Castlereagh   *Memoirs and Correspondence of Viscount Castlereagh,* ed. by his brother, 12 vols., 1848–53.

Clark, C. M. H., ed.   *Select Documents in Australian History, 1788–1850,* Sydney, 1950.

Colquhoun, P.   *A Treatise on the Population, Wealth, Power and Resources of the British Empire in Every Part of the World,* 1814.

Costin, W. C. and   *The Law and Working of the Constitution*:
Watson, J. S.   *Documents 1660–1914.* Vol. II, 1952.

Croker, J. W.   *The Croker Papers. The Correspondence and Diaries of the Late Right Honourable John Wilson Croker, . . . Secretary to the Admiralty from 1809 to 1830.* ed. L. J. Jennings, 3 vols., 1884.

Doughty, A. G. and   *Documents relating to the Constitutional History of*
McArthur, D. A. eds.   *Canada 1791–1850.* Ottawa, 1941.

Dropmore Papers   Official Mss. of J. B. Fortescue preserved at Dropmore, Hist. Mss. Comm., 10 vols., Vols. VIII and IX, 1894. These contain correspondence of Lord Grenville when he was Prime Minister 1806–7.

George IV.   *The Letters of King George IV, 1812–1830,* ed. A. Aspinall, 3 vols., 1938.

Gourlay, R. F.   *General Introduction to a Statistical Account of Upper Canada,* 3 vols., 1822.

Greville, C. C. F.   *Journal of the Reigns of George IV and William IV.,* ed. Henry Reeve, 3 vols., 1874.
   The Greville Memoirs, 1814–1860. eds. Lytton Strachey and R. Fulford, 7 vols. (vol. I, 1814–1830), 1938.

[Grillon]   *Portraits of the Members of Grillion's Club,* vol. I, 1829, new edition 1864.

Harlow, V. and   *British Colonial Developments 1774–1834,* Ox-
Madden, A. F., eds.   ford, 1935.

Herries, E.   *Memoir of the Public Life of the Rt. Hon. J. C. Herries.* 2 vols., 1880.

Hobhouse, Henry   *The Diary of Henry Hobhouse 1820–1827,* ed. A. Aspinall, 1947. Hobhouse was Under-Secretary at the Home Office.

Horton, R. J. W.,   *Exposition and Defence of Earl Bathurst's Administration of the Affairs of Canada during the years 1822 to 1827 inclusive,* 1839.
   Letters (signed Philalethes) containing observations on Colonial Policy originally printed in Ceylon in 1832, 1839.

Huskisson, William   *The Huskisson Papers 1797–1830,* ed. Lewis Melville, 2 vols., 1931.
   The Speeches of the Rt. Hon. William Huskisson, 3 vols., 1831.

Keith, A. B.   *Selected Speeches and Documents on British Colonial Policy 1763–1917.* 2 vols., Oxford, 1918.

Kennedy, W. P. M., ed.   *Statutes, Treaties and Documents of the Canadian Constitution 1763–1929*, 2 vols., Oxford 1930.

Peel, Sir Robert   *Sir Robert Peel from his Private Papers*, ed. G. S. Parker, 3 vols., 1891.

Private Letters of Sir Robert Peel, ed. G. Peel, 1920.

Pellew, G. P.   *The Life and Correspondence of the Right Honble Henry Addington, First Viscount Sidmouth*, 3 vols., 1847.

Shortt, A. and Doughty, A. G., eds.   *Documents relating to the Constitutional History of Canada, 1759–1791*, Ottawa, 1918.

Taylor, Sir Henry   *Autobiography 1800–1875*. 2 vols., 1885.

Correspondence of Sir Henry Taylor. ed. E. Dowden. 1888.

The Statesman. (1836), New York, 1958.

Taylor, Sir Herbert   *The Taylor Papers*, ed. Ernest Taylor, 1913.

Theal, G. M.,   *Records of the Cape Colony*, 36 vols., 1905.

Wade, John   *The Black Book or Corruption Unmasked.* 1820.

The Extraordinary Black Book . . . 1832.

Wellesley, Arthur, Duke of Wellington   *Despatches, Correspondence and Memoranda* ed. by his son. These cover the years in which Wellington held civil office. 8 vols., 1867–78.

Wentworth, W. C.   *A Statistical, Historical and Political Description of the Colony of New South Wales . . .* 1819.

Windham, William   *The Windham Papers*, ed. Thomas Amyot, introduction by the Earl of Rosebery, 2 vols., 1913.

Yonge, C. D.   *The Life and Administration of Robert Banks, second Earl of Liverpool.* 3 vols., 1868.

Monographs and Special Works

Adams, W. F.   *Ireland and Irish Emigration to the New World from 1815 to the Famine*, 1932.

Anderson, M. S.   'Great Britain and the Barbary States in the Eighteenth Century', *Bull. Inst. Hist. Res.*, XXIX (1956), pp. 87–107.

Aspinall, Arthur   *Politics and the Press, c. 1780–1830*, 1949.

The Formation of Canning's Ministry, February to August 1827, Camden Third Series, LIX, 1937.

'The Cabinet Council, 1783–1835', The Raleigh Lecture on History, *The Proceedings of the British Academy*, XXXVIII (1952), pp. 145–252, and appendices.

Auchmuty, J. J.   'The Background to the Early Australian Governors', *H.S.A.N.Z.*, VI (1954), pp. 301–314.

Bagot, J.   *George Canning and His Friends.* 2 vols., 1909.

Beaglehole, J. C.   'The Colonial Office 1782–1854', *H.S.A.N.Z.*, I. (1941).
                       'The Royal Instructions to Colonial Governors, 1783–1854: a Study in British Colonial Policy', unpublished Ph.D. thesis, London, 1929.
                       Summary of Ph.D. thesis, *Bull. Inst. Hist. Res.*, VII, pp. 184–7.

Bertram, Sir A.   *The Colonial Service*, 1930.

Brady, A.   *William Huskisson and Liberal Reform*, 1928.

Brock, W. R.   *Lord Liverpool and Liberal Toryism 1820–1827.* Cambridge, 1941.

Bulwer, H. L.   *The Life of Henry John Temple, Viscount Palmerston.* 2 vols., 1870.

Burn, W. L.   *Emancipation and Apprenticeship in the British West Indies*, 1937.

Cambridge History of the British Empire, vol. II. Cambridge, 1940.

Christie, Robert,   *A History of the Late Province of Lower Canada*, 6 vols., Quebec, 1848–55.

Clark, Dora M.   'The Office of Secretary to the Treasury in the Eighteenth Century', *A.H.R.*, XLII, pp. 22–45.

Cockroft, Grace A.   *The Public Life of George Chalmers, Chief Clerk to the Board of Trade 1786–1825*, New York, 1939.

Cohen, Emmeline W.   *The Growth of the British Civil Service 1780–1939*, 1941.

Cowan, Helen I.   *British Emigration to British North America 1783–1837*, Toronto, 1928.

Creighton, D. G.   'The Struggle for Financial Control in Lower Canada, 1818–1831', *C.H.R.*, XII (1931) pp. 120–144.

Darvall, F. O.   *Popular Disturbances and Public Order in Regency England*. . . . 1934.

Dibben, Miss L. B.   'Secretaries in the Thirteenth and Fourteenth Centuries', *E.H.R.*, XXV (1910), pp. 430–444.

Dicey, A. V.   *Lectures on the Relation between Law and Public Opinion in England during the Nineteenth Century*, 1914.

Dixon, C. Willis — *The Colonial Administrations of Sir Thomas Maitland*, 1939.

Dunham, Aileen — *Political Unrest in Upper Canada 1815–1836*, 1927.

Edwards, Isobel E. — *The 1820 Settlers in South Africa*, 1934.

Ellenborough, Lord — *A Political Diary 1828–1830*, ed. Lord Colchester, 2 vols., 1881.

Evans, F. G. — *The Principal Secretary of State: a Survey of the Office from 1558–1680*, Manchester, 1924.

Eybers, G. W., ed. — *Select Constitutional Documents illustrating South Africa's History 1795–1910*, 1918.

Fay, C. R. — *Huskisson and His Age*, 1951.

Fiddes, Sir George — *The Dominions and Colonial Offices*, 1926.

Foord, A. S. — 'The Waning of "The Influence of the Crown" ', *E.H.R*, LXII (1947), pp. 484–507.

Fortescue, Sir John — *British Statesmen of the Great War*, Oxford, 1911.

Foster, Sir William — *The East India House its History and Associations*, 1924.
'The India Board (1784–1858)', *Trans. Roy. Hist. Soc.*, 1917, pp. 61–86.

Furber, Holden — *Henry Dundas, First Viscount Melville*, 1931.

Gash, Norman — *Politics in the Age of Peel*, 1953.

Gilroy, Marion — 'Customs Fees in Nova Scotia', *C.H.R.*, XVII (1936), pp. 9–22.

Graham, Gerald — *Empire of the North Atlantic*, Toronto, 1950.
'The Maritime Foundations of Imperial History', *C.H.R.*, XXXI (1950), pp. 113–124.
'The Origin of Free Ports in British North America', *C.H.R.*, XXVI (1941), pp. 25–34.
Sea Power and British North America 1783–1820, Harvard, 1941.
'Views of General Murray on the Defence of Upper Canada, 1815', *C.H.R.*, XXXIV (1953), pp. 158–165.
Peculiar Interlude the Expansion of England in a Period of Peace 1815–1850. The Fourth George Arnold Wood Memorial Lecture, University of Sydney, 1959.

Greaves, H. R. G. — *The Civil Service in the Changing State*, 1947.

Grillion's Club from its Origin in 1812 to its Fiftieth Anniversary—by P.G.E. 1880.

Gulland, J. A.   'The history of the criminal law reforms of the period of Peel's home secretaryship, 1822–1827'. Summary of thesis, *Bull. Inst. Hist. Res.*, VIII, pp. 182–4.

Gwynne-Timothy, J. R. W.   'The Role of the Overseas Colonies in the European Power Balance 1793–1815', *Can. Hist. Assoc. Ann. Rep.*, 1953, pp. 77–83.

Halévy, Elie   *A History of the English People*, translated by E. I. Watkin and D. A. Barker, vols. I and II, 1924.

Hall, H. L.   *The Colonial Office, A History*, 1937.

Hampden, Gordon C.   *The War Office*, 1935.

Hannay, Richard   *History of New Brunswick*, 2 vols., Saint John, 1909.

Hardy, S. M.   'William Huskisson 1770–1830: imperial statesman and economist,' unpublished Ph.D. thesis, London, 1943.

Harrington, Elsie I.   'British Measures for the Suppression of the Slave Trade upon the West Coast of Africa, 1807–1833'. Summary of M.A. thesis, *Bull. Inst. Hist. Res.* II, pp. 54–6.

Harvey, D. C.   'The Civil List and Responsible Government in Nova Scotia', *C.H.R.*, XXVIII (1947), p. 365.

Hertslet, Sir Edward   *Recollections of the Old Foreign Office*, 1901.

Howard, Dora   'English activities on the north east coast of Australia during the first half of the Nineteenth Century'. Summary of M.A. thesis, 1925, *Bull. Inst. Hist. Res.* II, pp. 60–2.

Howse, E. M.   *Saints in Politics the 'Clapham Sect' and the Growth of Freedom*, Toronto, 1952.

Hughes, Edward   'Sir Charles Trevelyan and Civil Service Reform, 1853–5', *E.H.R.*, LXIV (1949), pp. 53–88, 206–234.

Jeffries, Sir Charles   *The Colonial Empire and its Civil Service*, 1935.

Jones, E. G.   'Sir R. J. Wilmot Horton, Bart., Politician and Pamphleteer', unpublished M.A. thesis, Bristol, 1936.

Keir, D. L.   'Economical Reform 1779–1787', *Law Quarterly Review*, L (1934), pp. 368–385.

Kennedy, W. P. M.   *The Constitution of Canada: An Introduction to its Development and Law*, 1922.

Klingberg, Frank J.   *The Anti-Slavery Movement in England*, New Haven, 1926.

Knaplund, Paul   *James Stephen and the Colonial Office 1813–1846*, Madison, 1953.

Knorr, Klaus E.   *British Colonial Theories, 1570-1850*, Toronto, 1944.

Labaree, L. W.   *Royal Government in America*. New Haven, 1930.

Laing, L. H.   'Nova Scotia's Admiralty Court as a Problem of Colonial Administration', *C.H.R.*, XVI (1935), p. 151.

Lewis, Sir G. C.   *Essays on the Administration of Great Britain from 1783 to 1830*, ed. Sir E. Head, 1864.

Lingelbach, Anna L.,   'The Inception of the British Board of Trade', *A.H.R.*, XXX (1925), pp. 701–27.
'William Huskisson as President of the Board of Trade', *A.H.R.*, XLIII (1938), pp. 759–774.

Long, Dorothy E. T.   'The Elusive Mr. Ellice', *C.H.R.*, XXIII (1942), p. 42.

Lower, A. R. M.   'Immigration and Settlement in Canada 1812–1820', *C.H.R.*, III (1922), pp. 37–47.

MacKinnon, Frank   *The Government of Prince Edward Island*, Toronto, 1951.

McLintock, A. H.   *The Establishment of Constitutional Government in Newfoundland, 1783–1832*, 1941.

MacNutt, W. S.   'The Politics of the Timber Trade in Colonial New Brunswick 1825–1840', *C.H.R*, XXX (1949), pp. 47–65.

Manning,
  Helen Taft   *British Colonial Government after the American Revolution*, New Haven, 1933.
'The Civil List of Lower Canada', *C.H.R.*, XXIV (1943), pp. 24–47.
'The Colonial Policy of the Whig Ministers 1830–1837', *C.H.R.*, XXXIII (1952), pp. 203–37, 341—68.
'Colonial Crises Before the Cabinet, 1829–1835', *Bull. Inst. Hist. Res.*, XXX (1957), pp. 41–61.

Martin, Chester   *Empire and Commonwealth, Studies in Governance and Self-Government in Canada*, Oxford, 1929.

Martin, Eveline C.   *The British West African Settlements, 1750–1821*, 1927.

Matheson, Cyril   *The Life of Henry Dundas, First Viscount Melville, 1742–1811*, 1933.

Mathieson, W. L.   *England in Transition 1789–1832*, 1920.
British Slavery and its Abolition 1823–1838, 1926.

Mellor, G. R.   *British Imperial Trusteeship 1783–1850*, 1951.

Merivale, H.   *Lectures on Colonization and Colonies Delivered Before the University of Oxford in 1839, 1840 and 1841 and Reprinted in 1861*, 1928.

Mills, Col. Dudley, R.E.   'The Duke of Wellington and the Peace Negotiations at Ghent in 1814', *C.H.R.*, II (1921), pp. 19–32.

Mills, Lennox A.   *Ceylon under British Rule 1795–1932*, 1933.

Milne, A. T.   'The Slave Trade and Anglo-American Relations, 1807–1862', M.A. thesis summary *Bull. Inst. Hist. Res.* IX, pp. 126–9.

Minty, L. A. M.   *The Constitutional Laws of the British Empire*, 1928.

Morrell, W. P.   *British Colonial Policy in the Age of Peel and Russell*, Oxford, 1930.

Morton, W. L.   'Newfoundland in Colonial Policy, 1776–1825', unpublished thesis, B.Litt., Oxford, 1935.

Namier, Sir Lewis   'Monarchy and the Party System' (Romanes Lecture 1952), in *Personalities and Powers*, 1955, pp. 13–38.

Pares, Richard   *King George III and the Politicians*, Oxford, 1953.

Parkinson, Sir Cosmo   *The Colonial Office from Within 1909–1945*, 1947.

Parry, J. H.   'The Patent Offices in the British West Indies', *E.H.R.*, LXIX (1954), pp. 200–25.

Pearn, B. R.   'The Ionian Islands under the administration of Sir Thomas Maitland'. M.A. thesis summary *Bull. Inst. Hist. Res.*, II, pp. 62–3.

Penson, L. M.   'The London West Indies Interest in the 18th Century', *E.H.R.*, XXXVI (1921), pp. 373–92.
The Colonial Agents of the British West Indies, 1924.
'The Origin of the Crown Agency Office', *E.H.R.*, XL, (1925), pp. 196–206.

Prouty, Roger   *The Transformation of the Board of Trade, 1830–1855: a Study of Administrative Reorganization in the Heyday of Laissez Faire*, 1957.

Pugh, R. B.   'The Colonial Office', *Cambridge History of the British Empire*, vol. III., 1959, Chapter XIX, pp. 711–68.

Purcell, E. S.   *Life of Cardinal Manning*, 2 vols, 1895.

Ragatz, L. J.   *The Fall of the Planter Class in the British Caribbean 1763–1833*, New York, 1928.

Ridell, R. G.   'A Study of the Land Policy of the Colonial Office 1763–1855', *C.H.R.*, XVIII (1937), pp. 385–406.

Roberts, M.   'Lord Charles Somerset and the "Beaufort Influence"'. *Archives Year Book for South African History*, Capetown, 1951, II, pp. 1–34.

Schuyler, Robert   *The Fall of the Old Colonial System, a Study in British Free Trade, 1770–1870*, New York, 1945.
Parliament and the British Empire, New York, 1929.

Smith, W.   *The History of the Post Office in British North America, 1639–1870*, 1920.

Smith, William   'Canada and Constitutional Development in New South Wales', *C.H.R.*, VII (1926), pp. 95–114.

Smith, William   'Side-lights on the Attempted Union of 1822', *C.H.R.*, II (1921), pp. 38–45.

Spector, Margaret Marion   *The American Department of the British Government, 1768–1782*, New York, 1940.

Stephen, Caroline Emilia   *The Rt. Hon. Sir James Stephen . . . Letters with Biographical Notes*, Gloucester, 1906.

Stephen, Leslie   *Life of Sir James Fitzjames Stephen.* 1895.

Temperley, Harold   *The Foreign Policy of Canning 1822–1827. England, the Neo-Holy Alliance, and the New World*, 1925.

Theal, G. M. C.   *History of South Africa 1795–1872*, 5 vols., 1915.

Thomson, M.   *The Secretaries of State 1681–1782*, 1932.

Trevelyan, G. M.   ed. *The Seven Years of William IV, a Reign Cartooned by John Doyle*, 1952.

Tucker, H. F. G.   'The Press and the Colonies 1802–1833', unpublished M.A. thesis, Bristol, 1936.

Walpole, Kathleen A.   'Emigration to British North America under the early passenger acts, 1803–1842', Summary of M.A. thesis, *Bull. Inst. Hist. Res.*, VII, pp. 187–9.

Walpole, Spencer   *A History of England from the Conclusion of the Great War in 1815*, vols. I and II, 1815–30, 1878.

Webster, C. K.   *The Foreign Policy of Castlereagh, 1812–1815*, 1931.
The Foreign Policy of Castlereagh, 1815–1822, 1947.

Wheeler-Holohan, V.   *The History of the King's Messengers*, 1935.

Williams, E. Trevor   'The Colonial Office in the Thirties', *H.S.A.N.Z.*, May 1943, pp. 141–60.

Wood, Henry T.   *A History of the Royal Society of Arts*, 1913.

Woodward, E. L.   *The Age of Reform 1815–70.* Oxford, 1938.

Wrong, H.   *The Government of the West Indies*, 1923.

INDEX

Abbott, P. H., 196
Aberdeen, Earl, 120
Addington, Henry, 10–11
Admiralty, 22, 23, 86, 156, 171, 182–4, 249, 260, 284
Africa, 55, 88, 157–8, 247, 249, 283
Agents, Colonial, 24–5, 29–32, 35–6, 56, 63, 66–7, 89, 95, 171, 178, 195. *See also* Hibbert
Algiers, 75, 76, 158, 246
American Department (1768–1782), 13
Amyot, T., 31–2, 145, 264, 268, 276
Anspach, Margravine of, 17
Antigua, 236, 282
Arabic interpreter, 21, 74, 155. *See also* Salamé
Arbuthnot, Charles, 44, 67, 69
Arbuthnot, Mrs., 52
Audit, 184–91
Audit Office, 185, 195, 249. *See also* Colonial Audit Office

Bahamas, 54, 283
Baillie, George, 32, 56, 68, 94–5, 104, 107, 121, 180, 188, 269, 276, 279
Baillie, Thos., 65, 269
Banks, Sir Jos., 86
Barbados, 211, 236, 282
Barbary States, 248, 275, 283
Barnard, Edward, 63, 268, 276
Barrow, George, 86, 96, 271
Barrow, Sir John, Bart., 75, 86, 183
Bathurst, Henry, 3rd Earl: character, 17–19, 52–3, 84, 129, 201, 265;
business habits, 20, 89–92, 181, 183, 219–20, 221, 264;
attitude to Treasury, 162, 186–91, 215–6, 239;
in cabinet, 51, 176;
and House of Commons, 178;
and military departments, 22;
on slavery, 71–2;
on colonial acts, 197, 199–200;
on Customs salaries, 209, 210, 215–20, 221, 224, 225, 229, 230, 237;
sinecures, 150;
resignation, 102–3;
in Wellington government, 108, 110;
see also 24–5, 31, 36–8, 42, 50, 67, 74, 76, 78, 80, 85, 97, 107, 112, 125, 142, 144, 159–60, 173–4, 180, 263, 274, 280–1, 287
Bathurst, Georgina, 183–4
Bentham, Jeremy, 6
Bentinck, Lord William, 23
Berbice, 32, 186, 225, 247, 282
Bermuda, 282
Bigge, J. T., 36, 37, 83, 246

Bickley, Francis, 103
Blackwood, Arthur, 70, 99, 270
Blue Books, 34–5, 72
Blunt, Samuel Jasper, 70, 270
Board of Control, 3, 10
Board of Trade, 3, 4, 13–14, 45, 171–2, 259;
colonial laws, 196–200;
Custom House fees, 206–14;
also 2, 10, 19, 51, 81, 105, 148, 156, 159, 258. *See also* Huskisson *and* Stephen.
Brande, G. W., 189–91, 195
Brooke, W. H., 23, 160
Buller, Charles, 259
Bunbury, Major-General Sir Henry, 20–1, 41, 183, 263, 275
Burke, Edmund, 6, 173, 193, 237
Buxton, T. F., 180
Byron, Lord, 49–50, 258

Cabinet, 169–70, 174–6, 251, 259;
factions, 51, 101–3, 105, 219;
also 1, 10, 18–19, 70, 95, 116, 180, 262
Camden, Lord, 16, 263
Canada, 36, 55, 83, 108, 246
Canada, Lower, 30, 32, 106, 115–16, 178, 248, 282;
financial quarrel, 189, 203–4, 210–11, 224–5, 227, 234–5, 237;
and Jamaica, 233
Canada, Upper, 38, 110, 175–6, 203, 211, 246, 282
Canning, George, 50–1, 66–7, 70, 78–9, 81, 101, 105;
Prime Minister, 102, 107, 232
Cape Breton, 248, 282
Cape of Good Hope, 38, 55, 82, 83, 109, 141, 158, 178, 185, 189, 246, 247, 248, 250, 283
Carlyle, Thomas, 258
Carrington, G., 89
Castlereagh, Lord, 1, 13, 16, 44, 50, 84, 263
Ceylon, 55, 108, 158, 172, 185, 189, 247, 248, 283
Chantrey, Sir Francis, 68
Chamberlain, Joseph, 104
Chapman, James, 30, 65, 266, 274
Chapman, William G., 65, 270
Church of England, 179;
Chaplain General for Colonies, 76–7, 182, 259;
Ecclesiastical Commissioners, 4, 76, 250;
Archbishop of Canterbury, 76, 180
Civil Service, 5, 8, 130, 131, 147, 160, 163–4, 242–3, 261

305

Clerks, 2, 5, 12, 14, 21;
  position of, 23–33, 99, 119–20, 122,
    254, 258;
  selection, 33, 68, 96–9, 280–1;
  classification and promotion, 39, 43,
    118, 122, 256, 274–8;
  salaries, 30, 42, 44, 98, 160–1, 274–9;
  abilities, 256–8;
  chief clerk, 29–30, 129, 134, 148;
  senior clerks, 53–4, 56, 92–5, 255;
  extra and copying, 32–3, 39, 98, 121,
    155, 253;
  individuals, 30–3, 70, 95–8, 266–72;
  need for grades, 119–20, 253;
  resent pension fund, 45, 62, 164, 277;
  also 37, 80, 88, 135, 145
Colonial Audit Office, 56, 185–7, 191,
    194, 249
Colquhoun, Patrick, 139
Combermere, Lord, 71
Commissariat, 69, 249
Commissions of Enquiry, colonial, 36–7,
    72, 189;
  into colonial expenditure, 192–5;
  public service, 5, 242, 254;
  state of office, 138, 257;
  also 2, 74, 83, 158, 293–4
Commander-in-Chief, 22, 23, 171, 177,
    249
Consuls, 65, 157, 246
Contingencies, 14, 153, 155, 158, 161,
    255
Cooke, Edward, 16, 161, 263
Correspondence, arrangement, 141–2;
  docketing, 285–6;
  amount, 45, 244–51, 282–4;
  also 12, 27, 33
Cotton, Col. Willoughby, 103
Courtown, Earl of, 96
Cowley, A., 241, 244
Cox, Charles, 96, 98, 272
Craig, Sir James, 151
Croker, J. W., 111, 183
Crown, Whig attack on, 5, 6, 11, 243;
  revenues, 171, 203, 210;
  also 24, 25, 170, 207
Curaçao, 25, 32
Customs, 88, 144, 172–3, 181, 202–40,
    241, 250;
  officers, 205–7;
  abolition of fees, 209–12, 216–8
Cutler, Henry, 28–9, 268, 276

Dalhousie, Lord, 31, 151, 224–5
Davy, Sir Humphrey, 137
Declaratory Act 1778, 209, 210–1, 217
de la Garde, Charles, 21, 268, 275
Demerara, 25, 30, 186, 225, 247, 282,
    24 n.

Denham, Major, 140
Dickens, Charles, 258
Disraeli, Benjamin, 124, 254
Doyle, John, 111
Drummond, G. W. A., 85
Douglas, Sir Howard, 188, 226
Dominica, 282
Dundas, Henry, 9, 10, 12, 31, 105, 124,
    263

East India Company, see India Office
Eastern Department, 55, 88, 95, 109,
    111, 247
East Indies, 219, 247, 283
Edinburgh Review, 71
Ellenborough, Lord, 48, 108, 112, 179
Ellesmere, Earl of, see Leveson-Gower
Elliot, Hugh, 96
Elliot, Thomas Frederick, 95–6, 271
Elliott, Grey, 13
Emigration, 37, 38, 48, 72–3, 83, 88, 99,
    178, 248, 259
Essequibo, 247, 282
Exmouth, Lord, 74–5

Fay, C. R., 17, 192, 241
Fees, 148–52;
  Customs fees, 205, 207–9, 211–12,
    215–17, 232, 234
Forbes, John, 65–6, 268, 275
Foreign Office, 8–9, 26, 50, 62, 75, 81,
    84, 132, 156–7, 163, 166, 170, 251,
    260
Fortescue, Sir John, 16, 103
Franking, 26, 95, 144–5, 167
Franklin, Captain, 140, 148, 158, 183–4
Freeling, Francis, 144, 181

Gairdner, Gordon, 70, 270
Galt, John, 57, 181
Gambia, 249
George III. 5, 10
George IV, 97, 102, 106, 108, 173–4,
    198, 200
Gibraltar, 55, 60, 246, 248, 275, 283
Gladstone, John, 90
Gladstone, William Ewart, 69, 90
Goderich, Viscount, see Robinson,
    Frederick
Gold Coast, 186
Gordon, Adam, 30–1, 44, 68, 95, 121,
    123, 148, 266, 276, 279
Gordon, Sir Willoughby, 193
Goree, 249, 283
Goulburn, Henry, Colonial Under-
    Secretary, 17, 19–20, 27, 29, 33, 38,
    40, 42, 44–5, 47, 49, 58, 82, 179,
    263, 276, 287;
  Chancellor of the Exchequer, 89, 110,
    179, 182, 204, 232, 234

Gourlay, Robert, 140
Governors, 33, 56–7, 106, 170–1, 172, 187, 202–3; 207;
    selection, 108, 174, 177;
    fees, 149;
    terms, 107;
    instructions, 14, 34–5, 73, 141–2, 190, 285–6;
    customs question, 202–36
    also 82,104, 110, 112, 184, 188, 189, 191, 250
Gower, Lord, 105
Gower, Lord Francis Leveson, 109, 263
Grant, Charles, 198, 230
Granville, Lord, 99
Greville, Charles, 18, 45, 109, 111, 174, 258, 264–5, 274
Great Seal, 9, 149
Grenada, 282
Grenville, 50
Grillon's Club, 62, 86, 109

Hamilton, Rev. Anthony, 76–7, 182
Harrison, Edmund T., 70, 270
Harrison, George, 61, 188
Harrowby, Lord, 48
Hay, Robert William, 37, 75, 85–9, 94, 109, 112–13, 116–17, 118, 122, 127, 214, 223, 263, 270
Heligoland, 55, 109, 248, 275, 283
Herries, John Charles, 182, 192, 194, 209, 230, 232, 241
Hertslet, Lewis, 133
Hibbert, George, 89, 230–4
Hill, William, 189
Hobart, Lord, 11, 15, 31, 263
Hobhouse, Henry, 107
Hoblyn, Mr., 68
Holland, Dr. Henry, 69
Holland, Lord, 175
Home Office, 8–13, 50, 132, 156, 166, 170, 201, 248, 249
Honduras, 54–5, 247, 283
Horton, Robert John Wilmot, 48–50, 51–2, 77, 86, 99–100, 103, 178, 179, 230, 238, 239, 241;
    reorganizes office, 53–8, 61–8, 78–83, 84, 86, 88, 92, 95, 116, 119, 120, 123, 126, 135, 136–7, 141, 144;
    relations with Canningites, 48, 51, 66–7, 107;
    with Lord Bathurst, 53, 89–92, 107, 108;
    with Stephen, 58–61, 80, 101, 115;
    hopes for advancement, 107–8;
    retires, 108–9;
    on Customs question, 209–10, 214–23, 230, 232, 238–9;
    also 69, 160, 181–2, 190, 263, 280–1

House of Commons, 1, 36, 39, 50, 69, 85, 102, 105, 176, 177–80, 181, 219, 238, 240;
    retrenchment, 6, 7, 22, 41, 62, 66–7, 79, 238;
    and C.O. establishment, 22, 62, 79, 80, 82, 83, 85, 100, 119;
    1828 Committee on Finance, 7, 106, 130, 161–2, 164, 166, 191, 192;
    obtains information, 33–4, 37, 106, 138–9, 195, 284;
    also 9, 63, 100, 111, 112, 120, 149, 175, 209;
    see also Parliament
Housekeeper, 125, 128, 274
Hudson's Bay Company, 39
Hume, James Deacon, 214, 223, 231, 239
Hume, Joseph, 7, 50, 62, 75, 82, 85, 178, 287
Huskisson, William, 104–5, 178, 220, 239, 241;
    chief clerk, 29;
    Board of Trade, 51, 105, 209–10, 211, 212, 214, 215, 217, 220, 223–4, 239;
    agent for Ceylon, 66–7;
    Secretary of State, 73, 98, 101, 104–7, 108–9, 232–3;
    also 2, 4, 22, 35, 57, 84, 161, 219, 222, 230, 231, 252, 263, 265, 266

Ionian Islands, 55, 247, 249, 275, 283, 159
India, 3, 9, 10
India House, 3, 23, 57–8, 242, 253, 255, 257

Jadis, Vane, 96, 98, 272
Jamaica, 54, 177, 204, 207, 208, 248;
    defies Treasury order, 205, 228–31, 232–4;
    also 35, 104, 106, 108, 211, 236, 246, 283
Jenkinson, Charles, 1st Earl of Liverpool, 14
Jenkinson, Charles, 2nd Earl of Liverpool, 16–17, 48, 66–7, 78–9, 175–7, 238, 287;
    collapse, 101, 231;
    also 1, 13, 18, 32, 44, 50, 80, 82, 105, 174, 219, 230, 263.

Kelsey, Francis, 64, 97, 266, 276
Kelsey, Hugh Stuart, 97, 127, 271
Kemble, Fannie, 111
Kempt, Sir James, 106, 226, 235

Lancaster, Duchy of, 171
Land policy, 4, 38, 73, 83, 106–7, 112, 287

Laski, Harold, 69
Lawrence, W., 287
Leeves, Edward, 264–5
Leith, Sir James, 71
Le Sage, Arnauld, 130–1, 274
Librarian, 21, 31, 33, 88, 126, 138–40, 155, 157
Liverpool, Lord, *see* Jenkinson
Lord Privy Seal, 4, 112
Lyndhurst, Lord, 110
Lyon, Sir James, 158

Macquerie, Sir Lachlan, 177
Malta, 37, 55, 159, 172, 185, 189, 248–50, 275, 283
Manchester, Duke of, 230
Manning, Cardinal, 98, 120
Manning, Professor Helen Taft, 19, 33, 103
Mauritius, 31, 55, 59, 158, 172, 185, 189, 247, 248, 283
Martin, John, 98, 272
Marshall, J., 139
Matheson, W., 122, 271
Mayer, George, 33, 68, 138, 140–1, 244, 269, 274, 275
Mediterranean and Africa department, 54–5, 88, 94, 247, 249
Melville, Lord, 85, 89, 183
Merivale, Herman, 93, 256, 257
Messengers, 126, 131–4, 159, 166
Mint, 192, 250
Mill, J. S., 27, 58
Mitchell, Major T. L., 86–7
Montserrat, 282
Moody, Major Thomas, 63, 71–3, 122, 125, 140, 158, 190
Murdoch, W. H. C., 98, 272
Murray, Sir George, 97, 110–12, 113, 114, 115, 179, 234, 263, 265

Namier, Sir Lewis, 243
Napier, 20, 140
Navy Office, 156, 171, 184
Naval Officers, 211–12, 216, 220, 225, 232
Neilson, John, 234
Nelson, Horatio, 125
New Brunswick, 32, 55, 65, 190, 203, 206, 226–7, 236, 248, 282
Newfoundland, 55, 83, 186, 247, 282
New South Wales, 3, 36–7, 38, 55, 77, 83, 107, 172, 184, 186, 212, 244–5, 246, 247, 249, 250, 283, 287
Nevis, 282
North America, 37, 77, 83, 105, 107, 151, 202–3, 207, 211, 234, 248, 250
North American department, 54, 55, 88, 94, 109, 247

Northcote-Trevelyan Report, 5, 242, 253, 254
Nova Scotia, 55, 77, 203, 206, 211, 226, 235, 247, 282

Office keepers, 125, 126, 129, 130, 135, 157
Ordnance, 56, 137, 171, 172, 173, 249

Palmerston, Lord, 1, 40, 41, 108
Parliament, 25–6, 115, 204, 210, 245, 255, 262;
    abolishes customs fees, 212, 215, 217–18;
    superannuation acts, 162–5;
    also 5, 6, 8, 38, 83, 95, 119, 145, 152, 168, 184, 185, 193, 200, 201, 203, 209, 229;
    see also House of Commons
Park, Mungo, 158
Parkinson, C. Northcote, 70, 243–4
Patronage, 11, 15, 52–3, 96, 132, 144, 174, 190, 246
Peacock, Thomas Love, 58
Peel, Robert, 1, 2, 17, 19, 50, 51, 79, 101–2, 110, 241, 263
Pelham, Lord, 11
Penn, Granville, 15, 31, 264, 267
Pensions, 6, 8, 15, 23, 39, 42, 62, 65–6, 130, 133–4, 147, 151, 155, 161–6, 225, 266–9.
Pitt, William, 1, 2, 9, 10, 19, 105, 169, 202
Planta, Joseph, 62, 84, 264
Plasket, Richard, 33, 267
Porter, G. R., 35, 196
Porters, 128–30, 155
Portland, Duke of, 9, 10, 11, 13, 150
Post Office, 25, 56, 133, 143–6, 167, 170, 181, 182, 250
Précis writer, 15, 21, 80, 95, 100, 121
Prince Edward Island, 55, 228, 282
Privy Council, 13, 45, 60, 62, 80, 107, 115, 161, 162, 163, 170, 172, 174, 196–200, 259
Privy Seal, 9

Quarterly Review, 49, 69, 109

Red tape, 136
Reeves, John, 197
Registrar, 56, 81, 88, 180
Richmond, Duke of, 151
Robinson, Frederick, Viscount Goderich, 50, 51, 63, 64, 78, 102, 103–4, 105, 163, 182, 194, 230, 231, 232;
    also 27, 96, 98, 99, 108, 112, 127, 263
Royal Gazette, 42
Russell, Lord John, 30

Salamé, Abraham V., 74, 75, 269
Salaries, 6, 7–8, 15, 30, 98, 120, 147,
    160–1, 165; Colonial Office: (1815),
    274–6, (1821–2) 277, (1831) 278;
    expenditure on, 121, 151–2;
    uniformity in civil service, 39–45, 62;
    servants and messengers, 128–31;
    of Customs Officers, 205–6, 212, 217,
    227
Sarrazin, General, 54
Secret service, 23, 88, 117, 159–60, 268
Secretary at War, 28, 171, 249
Secretary of State, 8–12, 14, 22, 25–6,
    47, 145, 147, 201, 262, 263;
    fees 148–52
Shee, Sir George, 263, 268
Short, Henry Trevor, 68, 95, 268, 275,
    279
Schuyler, R. L., 237
Siddons, Mrs., 111
Sierra Leone, 55, 72, 172, 184, 186, 249,
    283
Sign Manual, 8, 26
Silberman, Leo, 69
Sinecures, 5, 23, 25, 39, 150, 212
Slavery, 37–8, 58, 63, 71–2, 74, 77, 82–
    3, 85, 91, 106, 112, 113, 179–80,
    204–5, 216
Slave Registry Office, 4, 32, 56, 148,
    167
Smith, Adam, 6
Smith, Peter, 33, 35, 67, 68, 75, 94, 95,
    189, 269, 274, 275, 279
Somerset, Lord Charles, 82, 178
Southey, Robert, 69
Southey, Thomas, 140
Sparks, Jared, 140
St. Kitts, 236, 282
St. Lucia, 172–3, 186, 248, 282
St. Vincent, 282
Stanley, Hon. E. G., 99, 108–9, 263
State Paper Offices, 8, 159
Stationery, 61, 77, 114, 135–6, 155–6,
    168
Stationery Office, 155–6
Stephen, James, Jr., 58–61, 73, 79–80,
    85, 91–2, 94, 100–1, 113–15, 237,
    239, 254–5, 259;
    remarks on clerks, 64–5, 99, 119–20,
    256–7;
    on Colonial Office, 87, 115–17, 118–
    20, 252–3;
    on Treasury, 182;
    on Colonial Acts, 196–200, 245;
    on agents, 36;
    on Customs fees, 207–8, 211–12, 216–
    18, 234;
    also, 4, 57, 63, 74, 104, 111, 122, 123,
    128, 153, 159, 190, 205, 214, 219,
    220, 223, 261, 279

Stephen, James, Sr., 179–80
Stewart, Hon. Charles, 16, 263
Stopford, Hon. Robert, 96, 270
Strachey, Edward, 58
Strachan, John, 28–9, 268, 276
Stuart, Hugh, 28–9, 264, 267, 276
Surinam, 248, 283
Swan River, 247

Talbot, Clere, 97, 272, 279
Taylor, Henry, 69–70, 270;
    comments on clerkship, 5, 64, 119,
    120, 253;
    on administration, 118, 137, 241, 242,
    264;
    on colleagues, 86, 94, 104, 111–2,
    118;
    also, 74, 80, 82, 86, 92, 234, 265
Taylor, Sir Herbert, 103
Tennyson, Alfred, Lord, 69
Thompson, G. A., 139
Thiacke, Dr., 158
Tierney, George, 11
The Times, 103
Tobago, 282
Tortola, 282
Translator, 21, 33, 74, 155
Treasury, 195, 241, 258;
    attempts to integrate civil service, 8,
    39–43, 92, 168;
    control of superannuation, 62, 134,
    162–6;
    Lord Bathurst's obstruction of, 186–
    91;
    consultation with C.O., 56, 171, 182,
    209–10, 213, 220–1, 239;
    control of colonial expenditure, 170,
    184–96;
    and C.O. expenditure, 129, 147–8,
    151–2, 154, 156, 159;
    T. officials in the colonies, 172, 206,
    221, 238–9;
    Custom House fees and salaries, 208–
    10, 216, 217, 220–37;
    attitude towards legislative colonies,
    203, 204–5, 213, 238–9;
    also, 2, 24, 26, 37, 61, 83, 88, 127,
    137, 138, 214, 215, 255, 260,
    261
Trevelyan, Sir Charles, 1, 138, 242
Trinidad, 29, 185, 189, 247, 248, 282
Tripoli, 246
Tucker, H. F. G., 259
Tunis, 246
Twiss, Horace, 111–12, 179, 263

Under-Secretary, 17, 44, 107, 127, 161,
    175, 262, 263;
    role of, 1, 19–21, 25, 47, 84, 87–91,
    94, 99, 116–18, 179;

Under-Secretary, appointment of 47–8, 84–5, 108, 109, 111–12;
need for two, 15–16, 78–9, 80;
division of duties, 20–1, 88, 109, 111, 116;
also, 14, 22, 29–30, 37, 41, 42, 57, 66, 75, 81, 92, 100, 110, 122, 123, 246, 255, 256, 257

Vansittart, Nicholas, 182
Van Diemen's Land, 34, 55, 74, 83, 172, 186, 247, 283
Villiers, Thomas Hyde, 63, 68, 81, 111, 269

Walker, James, 98, 121, 272
Walpole, J., 98, 272
War department of C.O., 12, 14, 20–2, 54, 246, 275, 284
Watt, James, 136
Webb, Sidney, 192, 242
Webster, Sir Charles, 103
Wedderburn, Lt. Col., 26, 264

Wellington, Duke of, 4, 18, 51, 68, 101, 102, 125, 177, 232;
Prime Minister, 97, 102, 103, 105, 108, 109, 110, 112, 232
Wentworth, W. C., 140
West Africa, 141, 249
West Indies, 9, 71, 77, 105, 108, 202–3, 244–5, 247, 250, 276;
Customs question, 37, 83, 205, 206, 207, 211, 237
West Indies department, 54, 55, 69, 88, 91, 109, 247
Westmorland, Lord, 102
Whigs, 5, 6, 9, 11, 103, 236
Wilberforce, William, 18, 58
Wilde, S. T., 280–1
Wilder, George, 33, 68, 81, 267, 276
Windham, William, 13, 15, 16, 32, 263
Windward and Leeward Islands, 69, 248, 283
Winslow, Edward, 100, 271
Wordsworth, William, 69
Wynn, C. E. W., 79

York, Duke of, 75